THE
PRINCIPLES OF LOGIC

Oxford University Press, Ely House, London W. 1

GLASGOW NEW YORK TORONTO MELBOURNE WELLINGTON
CAPE TOWN SALISBURY IBADAN NAIROBI LUSAKA ADDIS ABABA
BOMBAY CALCUTTA MADRAS KARACHI LAHORE DACCA
KUALA LUMPUR HONG KONG TOKYO

THE
PRINCIPLES OF LOGIC

BY

F. H. BRADLEY

O.M., LL.D., LATE FELLOW OF MERTON COLLEGE, OXFORD

SECOND EDITION
REVISED, WITH COMMENTARY AND
TERMINAL ESSAYS

VOL. I

OXFORD UNIVERSITY PRESS

FIRST EDITION 1883
SECOND EDITION 1922
CORRECTED IMPRESSION OF 1928
REPRINTED 1950, 1958, 1963, 1967

SET IN THE UNITED STATES OF AMERICA
REPRINTED FROM PLATES IN GREAT BRITAIN
AT THE UNIVERSITY PRESS, OXFORD
BY VIVIAN RIDLER, PRINTER TO THE UNIVERSITY

TO MY FRIEND

E— R—

THESE VOLUMES ARE
DEDICATED

PREFACE

It is with mixed feelings that this reissue of an old work is offered to the public. I am happy to find that a book of mine is still alive, and that after some forty years it has seemed worthy to reappear. On the other hand I regret that, while Logic during this interval has lived and moved, I myself have failed, except partially, to follow its advance. My available energy has been expended mainly in fields which more or less fall outside Logic proper. And it is too late for me now to make good my shortcoming, and to endeavour to master those more recent works which have succeeded in throwing, at the lowest estimate, much light on their subject.

Hence I could not rewrite my book so as to offer it as an adequate account of contemporary Logic. And on the other hand simply to reprint it, or again, so far as I am concerned, to let it die, seemed alike open to objection. I therefore decided, while reissuing the old volume, to add to it some notes and an appendix with a view to correct and supplement some part of its defects. At the same time I saw clearly that any such addition would still leave the book largely incomplete.

The course which I have followed may even perhaps result in some gain to the reader. He can, if he pleases, now verify any advance which in 1883 may have been made by my work. And its faults both of manner and matter—faults which recall to me those days when I was young—may possibly with some readers themselves be of service. They may be more than excused if anywhere they help in any way to excite a more living and personal interest in logical problems.

It is not that in this book or elsewhere I lay a claim to original discovery. In these pages there is perhaps no result which I do not owe, and where, if my memory served me better, I could not acknowledge my debt. But when a man has studied, however little, the great philosophers, and felt the distance between himself and them, I hardly understand how, except on compulsion, he can be ready to enter on claims and counterclaims between himself and his fellows. And all I care to say for myself is that, if I had succeeded in owing more, I might then perhaps have gained more of a claim to be original.

The present volumes contain a reprint of the book published in 1883. The text has not been altered except occasionally in the punctuation, and by the removal of mere misprints and of one or two obvious grammatical errors. The Commentary, which is new, has been placed after each chapter in the form of Additional Notes, and the Terminal Essays have none of them been published before. The Index, which I hope will be of service, is also new. But for this, however great its merits, I cannot claim to be responsible.

I regret that Dr. Bosanquet's *Implication and Linear Inference* came too late to be used. But I cannot end this Preface without some expression of my gratitude to Dr. Bosanquet for all that, since 1883, I have owed to him, and without some acknowledgment of how deeply this reissue is in debt to his invaluable works on Logic.

1922.

PREFACE TO FIRST EDITION

THE following work makes no claim to supply any systematic treatment of Logic. I could not pretend to have acquired the necessary knowledge; and in addition I confess that I am not sure where Logic begins or ends. I have adopted the title *Principles of Logic,* because I thought that my enquiries were mainly logical, and, for logic at least, must be fundamental.

I feel that probability is against me. Experience has shown that most books on Logic add little to their subject. There is however one reflection which may weigh in my favour. Both in England and in Germany that subject is in motion. Logic is not where it was, and can not remain where it is. And when one works with the stream a slight effort may bring progress.

I have in general not referred to those works to which I have been indebted. Amongst recent writers I owe most to Lotze, and after him to Sigwart. Wundt's book would have been more useful had it come to me earlier; and I may say the same of Bergmann's. I am under obligations to both Steinthal and Lazarus. And amongst English writers I have learned most from the late Professor Jevons. I may mention here that I should have owed certain observations to Mr. Balfour's able work, had I not seen it first when my book was completed. I should be glad to state my debts in detail, and in this way to express the gratitude I feel, but I doubt if it is now possible. I could not everywhere point out the original owners of my borrowed material, and I could not clearly state how much is not borrowed. I lay no claim to originality, except that, using the result of others' labour, I in some respects have made a sensible advance.

I wished at first to avoid polemics altogether. But, though I have not sought out occasions of difference, it is plain that

ix

too much of my book is polemical. My impression is that it will not suffice to teach what seems true. If the truth is not needed the reader will not work for it, nor painfully learn it. And he hardly will need it where he stands possessed of what seems an easy solution. Philosophy now, as always, is confronted with a mass of inherited prejudice. And, if my polemics bring uneasiness to one self-satisfied reader, I may have done some service.

I fear that, to avoid worse misunderstandings, I must say something as to what is called " Hegelianism." For Hegel himself, assuredly I think him a great philosopher; but I never could have called myself an Hegelian, partly because I can not say that I have mastered his system, and partly because I could not accept what seems his main principle, or at least part of that principle. I have no wish to conceal how much I owe to his writings; but I will leave it to those who can judge better than myself, to fix the limits within which I have followed him. As for the " Hegelian School " which exists in our reviews, I know no one who has met with it anywhere else.

What interests me is something very different. We want no system-making or systems home-grown or imported. This life-breath of persons who write about philosophy is not the atmosphere where philosophy lives. What we want at present is to clear the ground, so that English Philosophy, if it rises, may not be choked by prejudice. The ground can not be cleared without a critical, or, if you prefer it, a sceptical study of first principles. And this study must come short, if we neglect those views which, being foreign, seem most unlike our own, and which are the views of men who, differing from one another, are alike in having given an attention to the subject which we have not given. This, I think, is a rational object and principle, and I am persuaded that a movement which keeps to this line will not be turned back.

In conclusion I may be allowed to anticipate two criticisms which will be passed on my work. One reader will lament that he is overdone with metaphysics, while another will stand on his right to have far more. I would assure the first that I have stopped where I could, and as soon as I was able. And in answer to the second I can only plead that my metaphysics

are really very limited. This does not mean that, like more
gifted writers, I verify in my own shortcomings the necessary
defects of the human reason. It means that on all questions,
if you push me far enough, at present I end in doubts and
perplexities. And on this account at least no lover of metaphysics will judge of me hardly. Still in the end perhaps both
objectors are right. If I saw further I should be simpler.
But I doubt if either would then be less dissatisfied.

VOLUME I

BOOK I

JUDGMENT

CHAPTER I

THE GENERAL NATURE OF JUDGMENT

CHAPTER II

THE CATEGORICAL AND HYPOTHETICAL FORMS OF JUDGMENT

CHAPTER II (*Continued*)

CHAPTER III

THE NEGATIVE JUDGMENT

CHAPTER IV

THE DISJUNCTIVE JUDGMENT

CHAPTER V

PRINCIPLES OF IDENTITY, CONTRADICTION, EXCLUDED MIDDLE, AND DOUBLE NEGATION

CHAPTER VI

THE QUANTITY OF JUDGMENTS

CHAPTER VII

THE MODALITY OF JUDGMENTS

BOOK II.—PART I

THE GENERAL NATURE OF INFERENCE

CHAPTER I

SOME CHARACTERISTICS OF REASONING

CHAPTER II

SOME ERRONEOUS VIEWS

CHAPTER III

A GENERAL IDEA OF INFERENCE

CHAPTER IV

PRINCIPLES OF REASONING

CHAPTER V

NEGATIVE REASONING

Its general nature (1) and special principles (2). Can you argue from
two negative premises? Yes, but not from two bare denials (3–7).
When one premise is negative can the conclusion be affirmative? On
one special condition, yes (8–9) . . . . . Pages 274–283

CHAPTER VI

TWO CONDITIONS OF INFERENCE

Result reached (1). An identical point required in all reasoning (2).
Mere likeness not enough (3). Principle of Identity of Indiscerni-
bles stated and defended (4–9).
And one premise at least must be universal (10–13) . Pages 285–297

BOOK II.—PART II

INFERENCE—CONTINUED

CHAPTER I

THE THEORY OF ASSOCIATION OF IDEAS

The fact of psychical association is certain, but the theory which explains reproduction by the "Laws of Association" is false (1–7).
Main ground of objection (8). The true explanation of the fact
(9–12).
Errors refuted. No association by *Contiguity* (13–17), even if assisted
by *Similarity* (18). Similarity alone is left (19), and this too is a
fiction (20–22), which the facts do not require (23–25). The true
explanation (26–27). Misunderstandings removed (28–31). Wolff
and Maas adduced (32). An objection answered (33). Practical
conclusion (34–36).
Note. Indissoluble Association and the Chemistry of Ideas.
Pages 299–345

CHAPTER II

THE ARGUMENT FROM PARTICULARS TO PARTICULARS

CHAPTER III

THE INDUCTIVE METHODS OF PROOF

CHAPTER IV

JEVONS' EQUATIONAL LOGIC

VOLUME II

BOOK III.—PART I

INFERENCE—CONTINUED

CHAPTER I

THE ENQUIRY REOPENED

Our former account of inference was insufficient. There are inferences which will not come under our formula (1–9) Pages 389–392

CHAPTER II

FRESH SPECIMENS OF INFERENCE

Tests of the existence of inference (1–3). Claim of fresh specimens. A. Three-term Constructions (4–5). B. Arithmetic and Geometry (6–15). C. Comparison and Distinction (16–17). D. Recognition (18). E. Dialectic (19–22). F. Abstraction (23–24). G. Disjunctive Inference (25–29). H. Immediate Inferences (30–37).

CHAPTER III

GENERAL CHARACTERISTICS OF INFERENCE

Further character of inference as an ideal experiment (1–4). This type verified throughout our fresh instances (5–10).
Not every mental activity is reasoning (11). Judgment is not inference (12–18); nor is *all* Reproduction (19–22); nor is Imagination (23–24). Result obtained (25) .

CHAPTER IV

THE MAIN TYPES OF INFERENCE

Analysis and Synthesis are two main types (1). This not apparent (2), but shown throughout the whole of our instances (3–7). Tabular statement (8) .

CHAPTER V

ANOTHER FEATURE OF INFERENCE

CHAPTER VI

THE FINAL ESSENCE OF REASONING

CHAPTER VII

THE BEGINNINGS OF INFERENCE

BOOK III.—PART II

INFERENCE—CONTINUED

CHAPTER I

FORMAL AND MATERIAL REASONING

CHAPTER II

THE CAUSE AND THE BECAUSE

CHAPTER III

THE VALIDITY OF INFERENCE

CHAPTER IV

THE VALIDITY OF INFERENCE (*Continued*)

TERMINAL ESSAYS

ESSAY I

ON INFERENCE (pp. 597-621)

ESSAY II
ON JUDGMENT (pp. 622–641)

ESSAY III

ON THE EXTENSIONAL READING OF JUDGMENTS
(pp. 642–646)

Every judgment can be read in intension, but no judgment can be read *merely* so. And the same thing holds (*mutat. mutand.*) as to extensional reading (642–3).

Can, again, all judgment be taken as asserting or denying about some "individual" or "individuals"? Certainly not so, if "individual" is taken in its more ordinary sense (643). And the attempt to read thus all judgments involves torture (643–4).

The possibility of taking any idea as one particular psychical event makes applicable a mode of torture which still remains in principle irrational (644–6).

ESSAY IV

UNIQUENESS (pp. 647–658)

Uniqueness—two aspects of, one (a) positive and the other (b) negative. But the second, even if perhaps always present, rests in any case on the first. An objection answered (647–8).

Uniqueness is absolute or relative, and holds again either in principle or merely *de facto* (648–9). Positive uniqueness as absolute. Claims to its possession considered. (1) The Universe. (2) One single quality (650). (3) Qualities as many. A distinction is to be made here. The Many as mere particulars; but this is a false abstraction and not a given fact (650–2). Attempts to defend its claim (a) by external relations, and (b) by an appeal to Designation (652–3). (4) The "This." Certainly it offers itself as unique, but this claim holds only so long as we remain at the stage of Feeling (653–4). And even there the character of the "This" is inconsistent and not self-contained, and hence the claim of the "This" fails (654–5). (5) Finite Individuals. Their claim to uniqueness must be allowed if you take them as members in and of a perfect System (655–6). On the other hand this claim cannot be verified completely in detail (656–7). Recapitulation (657–8).

ESSAY V

THE "THIS" (pp. 659–661)

"This" is not specially a mark of external perception. Like "mine" and "now" it belongs to all Immediate Experience or Feeling generally (659).

Can it as an idea be predicated beyond its actual self? Certainly it

ESSAY IX

A NOTE ON ANALYSIS (pp. 691–694)

ESSAY X

A NOTE ON IMPLICATION (pp. 695–698)

Implication cannot be one-sided unless there is abstraction from or alteration of conditions (697). "A before B" is really reciprocal. Nor is there incompatibility between "before" and "after" except under *some* condition (698).

ESSAY XI
ON THE POSSIBLE AND THE ACTUAL (pp. 699–712)

The enquiry limited. The Possible may be opposed in three senses to the Actual, according as that is (I) not grounded, or (II) grounded fully, or (III) both at once. The second sense is the main one (699). The above illustrated. There is only one genuine Individual (699–701).

The Actual is not the same as what "exists," nor is it always based on Existence (701–2); nor is such a position saved by an appeal to the distinction between relative and absolute possibility (702–3). As against what is "imaginary," that which "exists" may be merely possible (703).

And within the world of Truth the possible is still opposed to the actual (703–5). Why Logic can not be consistent ultimately (705). Designation—what (706). Recapitulation (706–7). Possible and Actual within a grounded whole (707).

The above contrasted with an opposite view (707–10). The world as a mere "And" or "Together" of independent entities (708). But on any such view there is really no "world" at all, and possibility can have in the end no meaning (708–10).

Reality and Truth—their true relation stated (711–12).

ESSAY XII
ON THEORETICAL AND PRACTICAL ACTIVITY (pp. 713–728)

There is no such thing as a *mere* theoretical or *mere* practical activity (713–14). All theoretical activity is also practical (714–15). And all practical activity has a theoretical side and contains an idea and a judgment (715).

This position explained and defended against some errors (716–17). (i) In Practice the judgment has different levels (717). (ii) But its essence is not to anticipate a future fact—even if any reference at all to the future is essential (717–19). And any appeal here to a lower stage of experience is useless (719–20). Further, Judgment can not consist in a mere passage to the future (720–21). "Practice for practice' sake" as a gospel. Recapitulation (721–2).

How far and in what sense is the distinction of "theoretical" and "practical" legitimate and useful? The answer to this question explained and illustrated (722–4). Religion as the unity of one-sidednesses (724–5).

A summary statement of some views which I advocate on Truth, Activity, and Practice (725-8). Truth as Anticipation and Prediction, and as Experiment and Verification (726-7). Philosophy, its limits and genuine task (727-8).

THE PRINCIPLES OF LOGIC

BOOK I—JUDGMENT

CHAPTER I

THE GENERAL NATURE OF JUDGMENT

§ 1. It is impossible, before we have studied Logic, to know at what point our study should begin. And, after we have studied it, our uncertainty may remain. In the absence of any accepted order I shall offer no apology for beginning with Judgment. If we incur the reproach of starting in the middle, we may at least hope to touch the centre of the subject.[1]

The present chapter will deal with the question of judgment in general. It will (1) give some account of the sense in which the term is to be used; it will (11) criticize, in the second place, a considerable number of erroneous views; and will end (111) with some remarks on the development of the function.

I. In a book of this kind our arrangement must be arbitrary. The general doctrine we are at once to lay down, really rests on the evidence of the following chapters. If it holds throughout the main phenomena of the subject, while each other view is in conflict with some of them, it seems likely to be the true view. But it can not, for this reason, be put forward at first, except provisionally.

Judgment presents problems of a serious nature to both psychology and metaphysics. Its relation to other psychical phenomena, their entangled development from the primary basis of soul-life, and the implication of the volitional with the intellectual side of our nature on the one hand, and on the other hand the difference of subject and object, and the question as to the existence of any mental activity, may be indicated as we pass. But it will be our object, so far as is possible, to avoid these problems. We do not mainly want to ask, How does judgment stand to other psychical states, and in ultimate reality what must be said of it. Our desire is to take it, so far as we can, as a given mental function; to discover the general character which it bears, and further to fix the more special sense in which we are to use it.

§ 2. I shall pass to the latter task at once. Judgment, in the strict sense, does not exist where there exists no knowledge of truth and falsehood; and, since truth and falsehood depend on the relation of our ideas to reality, you can not have judgment proper without ideas. And perhaps thus much is obvious. But the point I am going on to, is not so obvious. Not only are we unable to judge before we use ideas, but, strictly speaking, we can not judge till we use them *as* ideas[2]. We must have become aware that they are not realities, that they are *mere* ideas, signs of an existence other than themselves. Ideas are not ideas until they are symbols, and, before we use symbols, we can not judge.

§ 3. We are used to the saying, "This is nothing real, it is a mere idea." And we reply that an idea, within my head, and as a state of my mind, is as stubborn a fact as any outward object. The answer is well-nigh as familiar as the saying, and my complaint is that in the end it grows much too familiar. In England at all events we have lived too long in the psychological attitude[3]. We take it for granted and as a matter of course that, like sensations and emotions, ideas are phenomena. And, considering these phenomena as psychical facts, we have tried (with what success I will not ask) to distinguish between ideas and sensations. But, intent on this, we have as good as forgotten the way in which logic uses ideas. We have not seen that in judgment no fact ever *is* just that which it *means,* or can mean what it is; and we have not learnt that, wherever we have truth or falsehood, it is the signification we use, and not the existence. We never assert the fact in our heads, but something else which that fact stands for. And if an idea *were* treated as a psychical reality, if it were taken by itself as an actual phenomenon, then it would not represent either truth or falsehood. When we use it in judgment, it must be referred away from itself. If it is not the idea *of* some existence, then, despite its own emphatic actuality, its content remains but "a mere idea." It is a something which, in relation to the reality we mean, is nothing at all.

§ 4. For logical purposes ideas are symbols, and they are

nothing but symbols.[4] And, at the risk of common-place, before I go on, I must try to say what a symbol is.

In all that is we can distinguish two sides, (i) existence and (ii) content. In other words we perceive both *that* it is and *what* it is. But in anything that is a symbol we have also a third side, its signification, or that which it *means*[5]. We need not dwell on the two first aspects, for we are not concerned with the metaphysical problems which they involve. For a fact to exist, we shall agree, it must be something. It is not real unless it has a character which is different or distinguishable from that of other facts. And this, which makes it what it is, we call its content. We may take as an instance any common perception. The complex of qualities and relations it contains, makes up its content, or that which it is; and, while recognizing this, we recognize also, and in addition, *that* it is. Every kind of fact must possess these two sides of existence and content, and we propose to say no more about them here.

But there is a class of facts which possess an other and additional third side. They have a meaning; and by a sign we understand any sort of fact which is used with a meaning. The meaning may be part of the original content,[6] or it may have been discovered and even added by a further extension. Still this makes no difference. Take anything which can stand for anything else, and you have a sign. Besides its own private existence and content, it has this third aspect. Thus every flower exists and has its own qualities, but not all have a meaning. Some signify nothing, while others stand generally for the kind which they represent, while others again go on to remind us of hope or love. But the flower can never itself *be* what it *means*.

A symbol is a fact which stands for something else, and by this, we may say, it both loses and gains, is degraded and exalted. In its use as a symbol it forgoes individuality, and self-existence. It is not the main point that *this* rose or forget-me-not, and none other, has been chosen. We give it, or we take it, for the sake of its meaning; and that may prove true or false long after the flower has perished. The word dies as it is spoken, but the particular sound of the mere pulsation was nothing to our minds. Its existence was

lost in the speech and the significance. The paper and the
ink are facts unique and with definite qualities. They are the
same in all points with none other in the world. But, in
reading, we apprehend not paper or ink, but what they
represent; and, so long as only they stand for this, their
private existence is a matter of indifference. A fact taken
as a symbol ceases so far to be fact. It no longer can be
said to exist for its own sake, its individuality is lost in its
universal meaning. It is no more a substantive, but becomes the adjective that holds of another. But, on the
other hand, the change is not all loss. By merging its own
quality in a wider meaning, it can pass beyond itself and
stand for others. It gains admission and influence in a world
which it otherwise could not enter. The paper and ink cut the
throats of men, and the sound of a breath may shake the world.

We may state the sum briefly. A sign is any fact that
has a meaning, and meaning consists of a part of the content
(original or acquired), cut off, fixed by the mind, and considered apart from the existence of the sign.*

§ 5. I must be permitted at this point to make a digression,
which the reader may omit, if he does not need it. Throughout this volume I do not intend to use the word "symbol"
as distinct from "sign," though there is a difference which
elsewhere might become of importance. A symbol is certainly
always a sign, but the term may be appropriated to signs of a
very special character. In contrast with a symbol a sign may
be arbitrary. It can not, of course, be devoid of meaning, for,
in that case, it would be unable to stand for anything. But
it may stand for that with which internally it is not connected, and with which it has been joined by arbitrary chance.
But even when signs have a natural meaning, when their
content carries us direct to the object of which they are
used, yet, if we take symbol in a narrow sense, a natural
sign need not be a symbol. We may restrict the term to

* It would not be correct to add, "and referred away to another
real subject"; for where we think without judging, and where we
deny, that description would not be applicable. Nor is it the same
thing to have an idea, and to judge it possible. To think of a
chimæra is to think of it as real, but not to judge it even possible.
And it is not until we have found that all meaning must be adjectival,
that with every idea we have even the suggestion of a real subject
other than itself.[7]

secondary signs. For example a lion is the symbol of courage, and a fox of cunning, but it would be impossible to say that the idea of a fox stands for cunning *directly*. We mean by it first the animal called a fox, and we then use this meaning to stand as the sign for one quality of the fox. Just as the image or presentation of a fox is taken by us in one part of its content, and referred away to another subject, so this meaning itself suffers further mutilation: one part of its content is fixed by the mind and referred further on to a second subject, viz. the quality in general, wherever found. It makes no difference whether we begin with an image or a sensible perception, for the perception itself, before it can be used, must be taken ideally, recognized, that is, in one part of its content. And the distinction again between the symbolism that is unconscious, and that which is reflective, does not touch the main principle.

In order to obviate possible objections, I have thought it best to make these remarks; but since I propose to use sign and symbol quite indifferently, the discussion has hardly any bearing on my argument.

§ 6. We might say that, in the end, there are no signs save ideas, but what I here wish to insist on, is that, for logic at least, all ideas are signs. Each we know exists as a psychical fact, and with particular qualities and relations. It has its speciality as an event in my mind. It is a hard individual, so unique that it not only differs from all others, but even from itself at subsequent moments. And this character it must bear when confined to the two aspects of existence and content. But just so long as, and because, it keeps to this character, it is for logic no idea at all. It becomes one first when it begins to exist for the sake of its meaning. And its meaning, we may repeat, is a part of the content, used without regard to the rest, or the existence. I have the " idea " of a horse, and that is a fact in my mind, existing in relation with the congeries of sensations and emotions and feelings, which make my momentary state. It has again particular traits of its own, which may be difficult to seize, but which, we are bound to suppose, are present. It is doubtless unique, the same with no other, nor yet with itself, but alone in the world of its fleeting moment. But, for logic, and in a matter of truth and falsehood, the case is quite changed. The "idea" has here become an universal, since everything else is subordinate to the meaning. That connection of attributes we recognize as horse, is one part of the content of the unique horse-image, and this fragmentary part of the psychical event is all that in logic we know of or care for. Using this we treat the rest as husk and dross, which matters nothing to us, and makes no difference to the rest. The "idea," if that is the psychical state, is in logic a symbol. But it is better to say, the idea *is* the meaning, for existence and unessential content are wholly discarded. The idea, in the sense of mental image, is a sign of the idea in the sense of meaning.[8]

§ 7. These two senses of idea, as the symbol and the symbolized, the image and its meaning, are of course known to all of us. But the reason why I dwell on this obvious distinction, is that in much of our thinking it is systematically disregarded. "How can any one," we are asked, "be so foolish as to think that ideas are universal, when every single idea can be seen to be particular, or talk of an idea which remains the same, when the actual idea at each moment varies, and we have in fact not one identical but many similars?" But how can any one, we feel tempted to reply, suppose that these obvious objections are unknown to us? When I talk of an idea which is the same amid change, I do not speak of that psychical event which is in ceaseless flux, but of one portion of the content which the mind has fixed, and which is not in any sense an event in time. I am talking of the meaning, not the series of symbols, the gold, so to speak, not the fleeting series of transitory notes. The belief in universal ideas does not involve the conviction that abstractions exist, even as facts in my head. The mental event is unique and particular, but the meaning in its use is cut off from the existence, and from the rest of the fluctuating content. It loses its relation to the particular symbol; it stands as an adjective, to be referred to some subject, but indifferent in itself to every special subject.

The ambiguity of "idea" may be exhibited thus. *Thesis,* On the one hand no possible idea can be that which it means. *Antithesis,* On the other hand no idea is anything but just what it means. In the thesis the idea is the psychical image; in the antithesis the idea is the logical signification. In the first it is the whole sign, but in the second it is nothing but the symbolized. In the sequel I intend to use idea mainly in the sense of *meaning*.*

§ 8. For logical purposes the psychological distinction of idea and sensation may be said to be irrelevant, while the distinction of idea and fact is vital. The image, or psychological idea, is for logic nothing but a sensible reality. It is on a level with the mere sensations of the senses. For both are facts and neither is a meaning. Neither is cut from a mutilated presentation, and fixed as a connection. Neither is indifferent to its place in the stream of psychical events, its time and relations to the presented congeries. Neither is an adjective to be referred from its existence, to live on strange soils, under other skies and through changing seasons. The lives of both are so entangled with their environment, so one with their setting of sensuous particulars, that their character is destroyed if but one thread is broken. Fleeting and self-destructive as is their very endurance, wholly delusive their supposed individuality, misleading and deceptive their claim to reality, yet in some sense and somehow they *are*. They have existence; they are not thought but given.† But an idea, if we use idea of the meaning, is neither given nor presented but is taken. It can not as such exist. It can not ever be an event, with a place in the series of time or space. It can be a fact no more inside our heads than it can outside them. And, if you take this mere

---

* There are psychological difficulties as to universal ideas, and we feel them more, the more abstract the ideas become. The existence and the amount, of the particular imagery or sensuous environment, give rise to questions. But these questions need not be considered here, for they have no logical importance whatever. I assume, after Berkeley, that the mental fact contains always an irrelevant sensuous setting, however hard it may be to bring this always to consciousness. But I must repeat that this is not a vital question. It is a mistake in principle to try to defend the reality of universals by an attempt to show them as psychical events existing in one moment. For if the universal we use in logic had actual existence as a fact in my mind, at all events I could not *use* it as that fact. You must at any rate abstract from the existence and external relations, and how much further the abstraction is to go seems hardly an important or vital issue.

† This statement is subject to correction by Chapter II.[9]

idea by itself, it is an adjective divorced, a parasite cut loose, a
spirit without a body seeking rest in another, an abstraction
from the concrete, a mere possibility which by itself *is* nothing.

§ 9. These paradoxical shadows and ghosts of fact are
the ideas we spoke of, when we said, Without ideas no judgment; and, before we proceed, we may try to show briefly
that in predication we do not *use* the mental fact, but only
the meaning. The full evidence for this truth must however
be sought in the whole of what follows.

(i) In the first place it is clear that the idea, which we use
as the predicate of a judgment, is not my mental state as
such. " The whale is a mammal " does not qualify real whales
by my mammal-image. For that belongs to me, and is an
event in my history; and, unless I am Jonah, it can not enter
into an actual whale. We need not dwell on this point, for
the absurdity is patent. If I am asked, Have you got the
idea of a sea-serpent? I answer, Yes. And again, if I am
asked, But do you believe in it, Is there a sea-serpent? I
understand the difference. The enquiry is not made about
my psychical fact. No one wishes to know if *that* exists
outside of my head; and still less to know if it really exists
inside. For the latter is assumed, and we can not doubt it.
In short the contention that in judgment the idea is my own
state as such, would be simply preposterous.

(ii) But is it possible, secondly, that the idea should be
the image, not indeed as my private psychical event, but still
as regards the whole content of that image? We have a
mental fact, the idea of mammal. Admit first that, as it
exists and inhabits my world, we do not predicate it. Is there
another possibility? The idea perhaps might be used apart
from its own existence, and in abstraction from its relations
to my psychical phenomena, and yet it might keep, without any
deduction, its own internal content. The " mammal " in my
head is, we know, not bare mammal, but is clothed with particulars and qualified by characters other than mammality ; and
these may vary with the various appearances of the image.*

* I may point out that, even in this sense, the idea is a product of
abstraction. Its individuality (if it has such) is conferred on it by
an act of thought. It is *given* in a congeries of related phenomena,
and, as an individual image, results from a mutilation of this fact
(Vid. inf. Chap. II.).

And we may ask, Is this *whole* image used in judgment? Is *this* the meaning? But the answer must be negative.

We have ideas of redness, of a foul smell, of a horse, and of death; and, as we call them up more or less distinctly, there is a kind of redness, a sort of offensiveness, some image of a horse, and some appearance of mortality, which rises before us. And should we be asked, Are roses red? Has coal gas a foul smell? Is that white beast a horse? Is it true that he is dead? we should answer, Yes, our ideas are all true, and are attributed to the reality. But the idea of redness may have been that of a lobster, of a smell that of castor-oil, the imaged horse may have been a black horse, and death perhaps a withered flower. And *these* ideas are *not* true, nor did we apply them. What we really applied was that part of their content which our minds had fixed as the general meaning.

It may be desirable (as in various senses various writers have told us) that the predicate should be determinate, but in practice this need can not always be satisfied. I may surely judge that a berry is poisonous, though in what way I know not, and though "poisonous" implies some traits which I do not attribute to *this* poison. I surely may believe that AB is bad, though I do not know his vices, and have images which are probably quite inapplicable. I may be sure that a book is bound in leather or in cloth, thought the sort of leather or cloth I must imagine I can not say exists. The details I have never known, or at any rate, have forgotten them. But of the universal meaning I am absolutely sure, and it is this which I predicate.

The extreme importance of these obvious distinctions must excuse the inordinate space I allot to them. Our whole theory of judgment will support and exemplify them; but I will add yet a few more trivial illustrations. In denying that iron is yellow, do I say that it is not yellow like gold, or topaze, or do I say that it is not any kind of yellow? When I assert, " It is a man or a woman or a child," am I reasonably answered by, " There are other possibilities. It may be an Indian or a girl "? When I ask, Is he ill? do I naturally look for " Oh no, he has cholera "? Is the effect of, " If he has left me then I am undone," removed by " Be happy, it was by the coach that he deserted you "?

The idea in judgment is the universal meaning; it is not ever the occasional imagery, and still less can it be the whole psychical event.

§ 10. We now know what to understand by a logical idea, and may briefly, and in anticipation of the sequel, dogmatically state what judgment does with it. We must avoid, so far as may be, the psychological and metaphysical difficulties that rise on us.

Judgment proper is the act which refers an ideal content (recognized as such) to a reality beyond the act.[10] This sounds perhaps much harder than it is.

The ideal content is the logical idea, the meaning as just defined. It is recognized as such, when we know that, by itself, it is not a fact but a wandering adjective[11]. In the act of assertion we transfer this adjective to, and unite it with, a real substantive. And we perceive at the same time, that the relation thus set up is neither made by the act, nor merely holds within it or by right of it, but is real both independent of and beyond it.*

If as an example we take once more the sea-serpent, we have an idea of this but so far no judgment. And let us begin by asking, Does it exist? Let us enquire if " it exists " is really true, or only an idea. From this let us go on, and proceed to judge " The sea-serpent exists." In accomplishing this what further have we done? And the answer is, we have qualified the real world by the adjective of the sea-serpent, and have recognized in the act that, apart from our act, it is so qualified. By the truth of a judgment we mean that its suggestion is more than an idea, that it is fact or in fact. We do not mean, of course, that as an adjective of the real the idea remains an indefinite universal. The sea-serpent, if it exists, is a determinate individual; and, if we knew the whole truth, we should be able to state exactly how it exists. Again when in the dusk I say, That is a quadruped, I qualify the reality, now appearing in perception, by this universal, while the actual quadruped is, of course, much besides four legs and a head. But, while asserting the universal, I do

---

*I may remark that I am dealing at present only with affirmation; the negative judgment presents such difficulties that it can hardly be treated by way of anticipation.

not mean to exclude its unknown speciality. Partial ignorance need not make my knowledge fallacious, unless by a mistake I assert that knowledge as unconditional and absolute[12].

" Are the angles of a triangle equal to two right angles? "[13] " I doubt if this is so," " I affirm that this is so." In these examples we have got the same ideal content; the suggested idea is the relation of equality between the angles of a triangle and two right angles. And the affirmation, or judgment, consists in saying, This idea is no mere idea, but is a quality of the real. The act attaches the floating adjective to the nature of the world, and, at the same time, tells me it was there already. The sequel, I hope, may elucidate the foregoing, but there are metaphysical problems, to which it gives rise, that we must leave undiscussed.

§ 11. In this description of judgment there are two points we may at once proceed to notice. The reader will have observed that we speak of a judgment asserting *one* idea, or ideal content, and that we make no mention of the subject and copula. The doctrine most prevalent, on the other hand, lays down that we have always *two* ideas, and that one is the subject. But on both these heads I am forced to dissent. Our second chapter will deal further with the question, but there are some remarks which may find a place here.

(i) It is not true that every judgment has two ideas. We may say on the contrary that all have but one.[14] We take an ideal content, a complex totality of qualities and relations, and we then introduce divisions and distinctions, and we call these products separate ideas with relations between them. And this is quite unobjectionable. But what is objectionable, is our then proceeding to deny that the whole before our mind is a single idea; and it involves a serious error in principle. The relations between the ideas are themselves ideal. They are not the psychical relations of mental facts. They do not exist between the symbols, but hold in the symbolized. They are part of the meaning and not of the existence. And the whole in which they subsist is ideal, and so one idea.

Take a simple instance. We have the idea of a wolf and we call that one idea. We imagine the wolf eating a lamb, and we say, There are two ideas, or three, or perhaps even more. But is this because the scene is not given as a whole?

Most certainly not so. It is because in the whole there exist distinctions, and those groupings of attributes we are accustomed to make. But, if we once start on this line and deny the singleness of every idea which embraces others, we shall find the wolf himself is anything but one. He is the synthesis of a number of attributes, and, in the end, we shall find that no idea will be one which admits any sort of distinction in itself. Choose then which you will say, There are no single ideas, save the ideas of those qualities which are too simple to have *any* distinguishable aspects, and that means there are no ideas at all—or, Any content whatever which the mind takes as a whole, however large or however small, however simple or however complex, is one idea, and its manifold relations are embraced in an unity.*

We shall always go wrong unless we remember that the relations within the content of any meaning, however complex, are still not relations between mental existences. There is a wolf and a lamb. Does the wolf eat the lamb? The wolf eats the lamb. We have a relation here suggested or asserted between wolf and lamb, but that relation is (if I may use the word) not a *factual* connection between events in my head. What is meant is no psychical conjunction of images. Just as the idea of the wolf is not the whole wolf-image, nor the idea of the lamb the imagined lamb, so the idea of their synthesis is not the relation as it exists in my imagination. In the particular scene, which symbolizes my meaning, there are details that disappear in the universal idea, and are neither thought of nor enquired after, much less asserted.

To repeat the same thing—the imagery is a sign, and the meaning is but one part of the whole, which is divorced from the rest and from its existence. In this ideal content there are groups and joinings of qualities and relations, such as answer to nouns and verbs and prepositions. But these various elements, though you are right to distinguish them, have no validity outside the whole content. That is one idea, which contains

* The psychological controversy as to the number of ideas we can entertain at once, can hardly be settled till we know beforehand what is one idea. If this is to exclude all internal complexity, what residuum will be left? But, if it admits plurality, why is it one idea? If, however, what otherwise we should call plurality, we now call single just because we have attended to it as one, the question must clearly alter its form.[15]

all ideas which you are led to make in it; for, whatever is fixed by the mind as one, however simple or complex, is but one idea. But, if this is so, the old superstition that judgment is the coupling a pair of ideas must be relinquished.

§ 12. I pass now (ii) to the other side of this error, the doctrine that in judgment one idea is the subject, and that the judgment refers another to this. In the next chapter this view will be finally disposed of, but, by way of anticipation, we may notice here two points. (a) In " wolf eating lamb " the relation is the same, whether I affirm, or deny, or doubt, or ask[16]. It is therefore not likely that the *differentia* of judgment will be found in what exists apart from all judgment. The *differentia* will be found in what differences the content, as asserted, from the content as merely suggested. So that, if in all judgment it were true that one idea is the subject of the assertion, the doctrine would be wide of the essence of the matter, and perhaps quite irrelevant. But (b) the doctrine (as we shall see hereafter) is erroneous. " B follows A," " A and B coexist," " A and B are equal," " A is south of B "—in these instances it is mere disregard of facts which can hold to the doctrine. It is unnatural to take A or B as the subject and the residue as predicate. And, where existence is directly asserted or denied, as in, " The soul exists," or, " There is a sea-serpent," or, " There is nothing here," the difficulties of the theory will be found to culminate.

I will anticipate no further except to remark, that in every judgment there is a subject of which the ideal content is asserted. But this subject of course can not belong to the content or fall within it,[17] for, in that case, it would be the idea attributed to itself. We shall see that the subject is, in the end, no idea but always reality; and, with this anticipation, we must now go forward, since we have finished the first division of this chapter. We must pass from the general notion of judgment to the criticism of certain erroneous views, a criticism, however, which is far from exhaustive, and in some points must depend for its fuller evidence upon the discussions of the following chapters.

II. § 13. Wrong theories of judgment naturally fall into two classes, those vitiated by the superstition of subject, predicate and copula, and those which labour under other defects. We will take the last first.

(i) Judgment is neither the association of an idea with a sensation, nor the liveliness or strength of an idea or ideas. At the stage we have reached, we need subject these views to no detailed examination. The ideas which they speak of are psychical events, whereas judgment, we have seen, has to do with meaning, an ideal content which is universal, and which assuredly is not the mental fact. While all that we have is a relation of phenomena, a mental image, as such, in juxta-position with or soldered to a sensation, we can not as yet have assertion or denial, a truth or a falsehood. We have mere reality, which *is*, but does not stand for anything, and which exists, but by no possibility could be *true*.

We will not anticipate the general discussion of "Asso-ciation" (vid. Book II. Part II. Chap. I.), and will pass by those extraordinary views the school holds as to universals. We will come at once to the result. There is an idea, in the sense of a particular image, in some way conjoined with or fastened to a sensation. I have, for instance, sensations of coloured points; and images of movement and hardness and weight are "called up" by these sensations, are attracted to, and cohere with them. And this sounds very well till we raise certain difficulties. An orange presents us with visual sen-sations, and we are to add to these the images just mentioned. But each of these images is a hard particular, and qualified by relations which exclude it from all others. If you simply *associate* this bundle of facts, who would take them as one fact? But if you blend their content, if, neglecting the exist-ence, you take a part of the quality of each, and transfer *that* to the object, then you may call your process by what name you please, but it certainly *is* not association (Vid. infr. Book II.).

But let us suppose that the ideas are united somehow with the sensation, yet where is the judgment, where is truth or falsehood? The orange is now before my sense or imagi-nation. For my mind it exists, and there is an end of it. Or say, "Cæsar will be angry." Cæsar here is the percep-tion, which, when further qualified, becomes "Cæsar angry." But this image again is simply what it is, it does not stand for anything, and it can mean nothing.

Let us suppose in the first place that the "idea" maintains itself, then no doubt, as one fact, it stands in mental relation with the fact of the sensation. The two phenomena coexist as a headache may coexist with a syllogism; but such psychical coherence is far from assertion. There is no affirmation; and what is there to affirm? Are we to assert the relation between the two facts? But that is given, and either to assert it or deny it would be senseless.* Is one fact to be made the predicate of another fact? That seems quite unintelligible. If in short both sensation and idea are facts, then not only do we fail to find any assertion, but we fail to see what there is left to assert.

But in the second place (giving up association proper) let us suppose that the "idea," as such, disappears, and that its mutilated content is merged in the sensation. In this case the whole, produced by blending, comes to my mind as a single presentation. But where is the assertion, the truth or falsehood? We can hardly say that it lies in the bare presentation itself. We must find it, if anywhere, in the relation of this presentation to something else. And that relation would be the reference of judgment. But on the present view both the something else and the reference are absent. We have first an unmodified and then a modified sensation.

The only way to advance would be to suppose, in the first place, that, while the "idea" maintains itself, it is distinguished from its content; and to suppose, in the second place, that both of these are distinguished from the sensation. We have then two facts, a sensation and an image, and beside these a content held apart from the image. We have now reached a condition which would make judgment possible, but the advance to this condition is not explicable by Association. Nor could the further steps be accounted for. You have the transference of the content from the image to the sensation, and the qualification of the latter as a subject; but both would be inexplicable. We may add that it is impossible for a sensation or sensations to serve as the subject in every judgment (vid. Chap. II.). And finally the consciousness that, what my act joins, is joined apart from it, is a fact not

---

* We might say that, on this view, the denial of a falsehood must *ipso facto* be false.

compatible with the psychology we are considering[18]. To sum up the whole—to merge the content of an image in a modified presentation, is but one step towards judgment, and it is a very long step beyond association: while conjunction or coherence of psychical phenomena is not only *not* judgment, but would not serve as its earliest basis and beginning.*

§ 14. But the definition, I shall be told, is a " *lively* idea associated with a present impression," and I shall be asked if *lively* makes no difference. And I answer, Not one particle; it makes no difference even if you suppose it true, and in addition it is false. The liveliness removes none of the objections we have been developing. Let it be as lively as you please, it is a mere presentation, and there is no judgment. The liveliness of the idea not only *is* not judgment, but it is not always even a condition. The doctrine that an idea judged true *must* be stronger than one not so judged, will not bear confrontation with the actual phenomena. You may go on to increase an idea in strength till it passes into a sensation, and there yet may be no judgment. I will not dwell on this point, since the unadulterated facts speak loudly for themselves, but will give one illustration. We most of us have at times the images of the dead, co-inhabitants of the rooms we once shared with the living. These images, mostly faint, at times become distressing, from their strength and particularity and actual localization in those parts of the room which we do not see. In an abnormal state such images, it is well known, may become hallucinations, and take their place in the room before our eyes as actual perceptions. But with an educated man they would be recognized as illusions, and would not be judged to be outwardly real, any more than the fainter and normal images are judged to be anywhere but in our own minds. Yet lively ideas associated with present

---

* It has been often remarked that, on Hume's theory of belief, there can *be* no difference between imagination and reality, truth and falsehood, and that why we *make* this difference is incomprehensible. J. S. Mill with great openness professed on this head the total bankruptcy of the traditional doctrine. He seems somehow to have thought that a complete break-down on a cardinal point was nothing against the main doctrine of his school, nor anything more than a somewhat strange fact. It was impossible that he should see the real cause of failure. We shall deal with Professor Bain's views lower down.

impressions—if we have not got them here, where are they?

§ 15. We turn with relief from the refutation of a doctrine, long dead and yet stubbornly cumbering the ground, to consider a fresh error, the confusion of judgment with practical belief. I cannot enquire how far *any* psychical activity is consistent with the theory of Professor Bain, nor can I discuss the nature of a psychical activity which seems physiologically to consist in muscular innervation; though I am bound to add that (doubtless owing to my ignorance) Professor Bain's physiology strikes me here as being astonishingly misty. And I must pass by the doubt whether, if we accept his view, we shall find the confusion between image and meaning in any way lessened[19].

We must remember that the question, Is judgment always practical, does not mean, Is the will in any way concerned in it. In that case it might be argued that *all* generation of psychical phenomena comes under the head Will. The question means, Does the essence of judgment lie, not in the production of truth and falsehood—states which alter nothing in the things they represent—but rather in the actual production of a change in real existence. Or, more simply, when an idea is judged to be true, does this mean that it *moves* some other phenomenon, and that its assertion or denial is nothing but this motion? The doctrine admits that an idea or ideas, when held true, differ vitally from the same when suggested; and it proceeds to assert that the *differentia* is the effect of the idea on our conduct, and that there is no other *differentia* at all.

There is a logical mistake we may point out before proceeding, for it is the error which has led Professor Bain astray. Assume that an asserted idea causes action, and that an idea, not believed in, does not influence conduct. From these premises can we conclude, Therefore judgment *is* influence? If, in other words, when A changes to B, we have an unfailing difference *q,* and *q* is not found except after A, does this warrant the assertion, that the alteration consists in *q*? Is it not quite possible that *q* follows from *p,* and that *p* is what really turns A into B? We shall do well to keep our eye on this logical fallacy. The assertion we are to examine is *not* that practical influence induces us to judge, or results from a judgment: What is asserted is that judgment *is* nothing else whatever.

Against this false *differentia* I shall briefly maintain, (*a*) that the *differentia* may be absent from the fact, (*b*) that it may be present with other facts, (*c*) that the fact contains other characteristics, which are the true *differentia,* and are absent from the false one, (*d*) that the latter has a positive quality which excludes the fact.

(*a*) If we test the theory by abstract instances such as, The angles of a triangle are equal to two right angles, it collapses at once. It is impossible to find always a practical influence exerted by the ideas. We may be answered " But they *might* exert it, you surely *would* act on them." And such an answer may pass in the school of " Experience "; but a poor " transcendentalist " will perhaps be blamed if he usurps such a privilege. He at least is not allowed to take tendency and possibility and mere idea for fact. And he can hardly be prevented from pressing the question, Is the influence there or not? If it is not there, then either Professor Bain's theory disappears, or he should alter his definition, and say that an idea passes into a judgment when enriched by potentialities and eventual tendencies[20]. If these are *not* ideas we should be told *what* they are; but if they are only ideas that go with the first ideas, then our answer is plain. In the first place it is not true that they are always there; in the second place it is not true that, when added, they must exert a practical influence.

(*b*) In the second place ideas may influence me, though I never do hold them for true. The feelings and emotions associated with an idea can often prevent or produce volitions, although the idea is not affirmed as true, and even while it is recognized as false. Though I do not believe that a slow-worm can bite, or a drone can sting, I may shrink from touching them. I may avoid a churchyard though I believe in no ghosts. An illusion no doubt, if recognized as such, does not influence volition either so much, or always in the same way; but still it may operate in spite of disbelief.* And it can hardly be a true view which forces us to say, If you judged it an illusion you would wholly disregard it, for such disregard *is* judgment.

---

* It may be said that *when* it operates the denial is suspended. But I confess I can find no ground for such a statement. At any rate it is certain that the idea can operate though a positive judgment is not there.

I will not dwell on a point it would be easy to illustrate. In passing, however, I may remind the reader of that class of ideas which influences our actions without seeming to be true. I refer to practical ideas, the representation of a satisfied desire which is now felt to be unsatisfied. It is certain that these move us to active pursuit, and it is equally certain they are not judged to be real[21]; for, if they were, then for that reason they would fail to move us.*

(c) But suppose that all judgment did really move to action. Would this show that judgment was nothing but such motion? Most certainly not so. We can observe what takes place in us, when a suggested idea is judged to be true; and clearly an activity (however hard to describe) does show itself there, and yet is not directed (except *per accidens*) towards making a change in the world and in ourselves. And if this true *differentia* can be verified, that should settle the question[22]. And again, apart from direct observation, we can argue indirectly. Assertion and denial, together with the difference of truth and falsehood, are real phenomena, and there is something in them which falls outside the influence of ideas on the will. It is comic if the judgment, It will rain to-morrow, is the same as buying an umbrella to-day; or, Put on your thick boots, is a truer form of, It rained hard yesterday. And when a child sees a berry and, as we say, judges, It made me sick before, it seems strange that the act of affirmation should consist in practical abstention to-day and should be nothing else.

(d) And not only are the genuine characteristics absent from a mere practical attitude, but we find present there a quality which is absent from real judgment. The truth of a suggestion is not a matter of degree, and the act which attributes an idea to reality either refers it, or does not refer it. It can hardly do either a little more or less and to a certain degree (cf. Chap. VII.). In strictness of speech all half-truths are no truths, and, " It is more or less true," really means, " It is true with a qualification," or " More or less of it is true, though as a whole it is not true." But the practical influence of ideas must have degree, and so possess a quality which judgment has not.

For these reasons, each of which can stand almost alone, it seems clear that the doctrine before us has failed. And

*I may refer on this point to my *Ethical Studies*, Essay VII.

one cause of the error seems to lie in the neglect of some important distinctions we may proceed to notice. Judgment is primarily logical, and as such has no degrees; the relation of the ideal content to reality must be there or not there. Belief, on the other hand, is primarily psychological, and, whether theoretic or practical, exists in a degree. (a) Intellectual belief or conviction is the general state which corresponds to the particular acts of judgment. To believe that A is B may mean that, whenever the idea A — B is suggested, I go on to affirm it; or, further, that the idea fills much space in my mind, is a persistent habit and ruling principle, which dominates my thoughts and fills my imagination, so that the assertion A — B is frequently made and has wide intellectual ramifications and connections. I should believe A — B less, if it more seldom arose, by itself or by implication, and had inferior influence. I should believe less still if, when A — B was suggested, I sometimes doubted it; and even less, if I affirmed it more seldom, and then with hesitation, against doubts, and with inability to maintain the attitude. On the other hand I should not believe at all, if I only were more or less convinced, perceiving more or less reason on both sides, inclined in one direction, but unable to cross the line and to affirm. (b) But in practical belief, beside these degrees of intellectual conviction, there is another element of more and less. Not only is the truth of the intellectual content more or less present, but in addition it can influence my will more or less. A desire stronger or more persistent, or more dominant generally, may answer to it on the one side, or on the other a weaker and more fleeting impulse. Beside existing more or less, it can move more or less. It is, I think, not easy to keep clear of confusion unless these ambiguities are noticed and avoided. But the main logical mistake which Professor Bain has committed is to argue from the (false) premise, " Belief must induce action," to the inconsequent result " Belief *is* that inducement." *

* In the third edition of his *Emotions* (1875) Prof. Bain apparently reconsiders the question, but I can neither tell if he abandons his theory, nor what it is that, if so, he puts in its place. As I am entirely unable to understand this last theory, my remarks must be taken to apply to the earlier one. Since this volume was written I have made acquaintance with Mr. Sully's criticism on Prof. Bain's doctrine (*Sensa-*

§ 16. (ii) Leaving now the first group of erroneous views we may proceed to consider another collection. These may be classed as labouring under a common defect, the false notion that in judgment we have a pair of ideas. We were engaged with this fallacy in § 11, and it will meet us again in the following chapter, so that here some brief remarks may suffice. In their ordinary acceptation the traditional subject, predicate, and copula are mere superstitions[24]. The ideal matter which is affirmed in the judgment, no doubt possesses internal relations, and in *most* cases (not all) the matter may be arranged as subject and attribute[25]. But this content, we have seen, is the same both in the assertion and out of it[26]. If you ask instead of judging, what is asked is precisely the same as what is judged. So that it is impossible that this internal relation can itself *be* the judgment; it can at best be no more than a condition of judging. We may say then, if the copula is a connection which couples a pair of ideas, it falls outside judgment; and, if on the other hand it is the sign of judgment, it does not couple. Or, if it *both* joined *and* judged, then judgment at any rate would not be *mere* joining. I will dwell here no more on the general error. We shall see its effects in some mistaken views we may proceed to notice.

(*a*) Judgment is not inclusion in, or exclusion from, a class. The doctrine that in saying, " A is equal to B," or " B is to the right of C," or " To-day precedes Monday," I have in my mind a class, either a *collection* or a *description,* of " things equal to B," or " to the right of C," or " preceding Monday," is quite opposed to fact. It is as absurd as the assertion that, in " It is our son John," or " It is my best coat," or " 9 = 7 + 2," I think of a class of " our sons John," or " my best coats," or " that which is equal to 7 + 2." If the view stood apart from implied preconceptions, and by itself as an interpretation of fact, it would scarcely, I think, be so much as discussed. And, as we shall be forced to recur to it hereafter (Chap. VI.), we may so leave it here.

tion and Intuition, 2nd ed. 1880). But *he,* I find, treats Prof. Bain's third edition (1875), in which an earlier edition of his own criticism is treated with the greatest respect, as if it either had no existence, or at all events was somehow irrelevant to the issue. For myself I must say that for the reason given above I confine myself to the earlier theory.[23]

(*b*) Judgment is not inclusion in, or exclusion from, the subject. By the subject I mean here not the ultimate subject, to which the whole ideal content is referred, but the subject which lies within that content, in other words the *grammatical* subject. In " A is simultaneous with B," " C is to east of D," " E is equal to F," it is unnatural to consider A, C, and E as sole subjects, and the rest as attributive. It is equally natural to reverse the position, and perhaps more natural still to do neither, but to say instead, " A and B are synchronous," " C and D lie east and west," " E and F are equal." The ideal complex, asserted or denied, no doubt in most cases will fall into the arrangement of a subject with adjectival qualities, but in certain instances, and those not a few, the content takes the form of two or more subjects with adjectival relations existing between them. I admit you may torture the matter from the second form into the first, but, if torture is admitted, the enquiry will become a mere struggle between torturers. It requires no great skill to exhibit every subject together with its attributes as the relation between independent qualities (subjects), or again even to make that relation the subject, and to predicate all the remainder as an attribute. Thus, in " A is simultaneous with B," it is as easy to call " exists in the case of AB " an attribute of simultaneity, as it is to call " simultaneous with B " an attribute of A. We may finally observe that existential judgments do not lend themselves easily to the mistake we are considering. And such negative judgments as " Nothing is here," will be found hard to persuade. But on both these points I must refer to the sequel (Chaps. II. and III.).

(*c*) Judgment is not the assertion that subject and predicate are identical or equal. This erroneous doctrine is the natural result of former errors. You first assume that in judgment we have a relation between two ideas, and then go on to assume that these ideas must be taken in extension. But both assumptions are vicious; and, if we consider the result, asking not if it is useful but whether it is true, we can hardly, I think, remain long in hesitation. That in " You are standing before me," or " A is north of C," or " B follows D," what we really *mean* is a relation either of equality or identity is simply incredible; and torture of the witness goes to such lengths that the general public is not trusted to behold it.*

However useful within limits the equation of the terms may be found, if you treat it as a working hypothesis (vid. Book II. Part II. Chap. IV.), yet as a truth it will not bear any serious examination. Let us look at it more closely.

(i) If what is asserted be *equality,* then that of course is identity in *quantity,* and is nothing else whatever[27]. And I must venture to complain of the reckless employment of this term. To use the sign = for *qualitative* sameness, or for individual identity (I do not ask here if these are different), is surely barbarous. No harm perhaps may come, but there should be some limit to the abuse and confusion we allow ourselves in practice. Let us then first take equality in its proper sense, to stand for an identity in respect of quantity. But, if so, if the subject and predicate are equated, if " Negroes are men," when written " All negroes = some men," is on a level with $2 = 12 - 10$—if what is said and signified is that between the terms, if you compare them numerically, there is no difference whatever, we can at once pass on. It is certain that *some* judgments, at least, can not express this relation of quantity, and it is certain again that, of those which can, it is only a very small class which do. Illustration is hardly wanted. "Hope is dead" would mean that, "In hope and a fraction of dead things there is exactly the same sum of units." And, in asserting that " Judgment is not an equation," I should express my belief that to divide both by 2 would not give the same quantity.

But the sign = does not seem to mean equality. It does not mean that the units of the subject and predicate are identical in *quantity.* It would appear to mean that they are the same altogether. The identity it asserts is not quantitative, but seems absolute. In " All Negroes = some men," the " = " represents exclusion of difference both quantitative and qualitative.

(ii) The identity is (*a*) not likeness; it is not a relation consisting in a partial qualitative identity, definite or indefinite. " Iron = some metal " can hardly mean " Some metal is similar to iron." Not only do the facts exclude this interpretation, but the theory would not work with it. If " similars " and "like-

* Vid. Jevons, *Principles of Science,* Chap. I. § 12.

ness" are phrases that occur, this is a proof that here, as in the case of =, the theory does not mean what it says, or quite know what it is doing. That when A is *like* B you may write one for the other, is of course quite untrue (cf. Book II.).

(*b*) The identity again is not definitely partial, consisting in sameness in some particular point or points of quality. For, on this interpretation, you could make no advance, until the point of sameness had been specified. And even then the equational theory would not work.

(*c*) Unless we suppose that both sides differ only in name, and that this difference of names is the import of the judgment—a view we shall glance at in a future chapter (Chap. VI.)—we must take the sign = to mean total sameness to the exclusion of *all* difference. But, if so, the theory must reform itself at once, if it desires to be consistent. It will not be true that " Negroes = some men," for certainly " some men " are not " = negroes." Nor again will it be true that negroes are equal to a certain stated fraction of mankind. That stated fraction is an universal adjective which might be applicable to other men as well as to negroes. If " is " or " = " stands for " is the same as," then it is as false to say " A *is* ⅙ B," as it was before to say " A *is* some B." " Some B " covers not only the B which is A; it may hold just as much of the other B, which we take as not-A. And it is so with " ⅙ B "; that applies just as much to the ⅚ which are not-A, as it does to the third which is identical with A. The quantification of the predicate is a half-hearted doctrine, which runs against facts, if " = " does mean *equal,* is ridiculous if " = " comes to no more than plain " *is,*" and is downright false if " = " stands for " *is the same as.*"

To be consistent we must not merely quantify the predicate, we must actually specify it. The men that are negroes are not any and every set of men, who have a certain number. They are those men who *are* negroes, and *this* is the predicate. Negroes = negro-men, and iron = iron-metal. The predicate now really and indeed seems the subject, and can be substituted for it. The idea is a bold one, and its results have been considerable; but if we look not at working power but at truth, the idea is not bold enough, and wants courage to remove the last contradiction.

That A should be truly the same as AB, and AB entirely identical with A, is surely a somewhat startling result. If A = A, can it also be true that to add B on *one* side leaves the equation where it was? If B does not mean o, one would be inclined to think it must make some difference. But, if it does make a difference, we can no longer believe that A = AB, and AB = A. If " iron-metal " is the same as " iron," how misleading it is to set down the two sides as different terms. If there really is a difference between the two, then your statement is false when by your " = " you deny it. But if there is no difference, you are wrong in affirming it, and in opposing " iron " to " iron-metal."

There is only one issue. If A is AB, then the A that *is* AB is not A but —AB. Both sides of the assertion are just the same, and must be so stated. Negro-men are negro-men, and iron-metal is iron-metal.* For consider the dilemma. B either is or is not an addition to A. If it is not an addition, its insertion is gratuitous; it means nothing on either side, may fall upon whichever side we choose, is absurd on both alike, and should be got rid of—then A = A. But if B is an addition, then A = AB cannot be true. We must add B on both sides, and AB = AB. In short B must disappear or have a place on each side.

We have now reached consistency, and the reader may ask, Is the result still false? I do not like to seem obstinate, and I prefer to reply, Do you think it is true? I will accept your answer. If you say that identical propositions are all false, I shall not contradict you (cf. Chap. V. § 1), for I also believe that a judgment which asserts no difference is nothing. But if you pronounce on the side of truth, I should like to ask a question. For an assertion to be true must it not assert something, and what is it that you take to be asserted above? That where there is no difference, there is no difference, that AB will be AB as long as it is AB? You can hardly mean that. Is the *existence* of AB what is secretly asserted? But, if so, we should say openly " AB exists," and our reduplication of AB is surely senseless. We know that it exists, not because we double it, but, I suppose, because we know of its existence.

* Cf. Lotze, *Logik,* 80-2.

But what then do we assert by $AB = AB$? It seems we must own that we do not assert anything. The judgment has been gutted and finally vanishes. We have followed our premises steadily to the end, and in the end they have left us with simply nothing. In removing the difference of subject and predicate we have removed the whole judgment.*

§ 17. We have seen the main mistakes of the foregoing doctrines. It is a more pleasing task to consider the main truth which each one of them has seized. (i) The views we began to criticize in § 13, have avoided the error of subject predicate and copula. They have seen that in judgment the number of ideas is not the main question, and that the essence of the matter does not lie in the ideas, but in something beyond them. Nor, to be more particular, is the implication of will in all judgment a complete mistake. It is true that, in an early stage of development, the intelligence is so practical that it hardly can be said to operate independently. It is true again that, in the evolution of self-consciousness, the opposition of idea and reality depends, to a degree I will not here discuss, upon volitional experience. And in these points there is truth in the theory, which, however much he may abandon it, we shall place to the credit of Professor Bain. And the view that in judgment we have an association of idea with sensation, and a coalescence of both elements, is far from being wholly destitute of truth. For (as we shall see in the following Chapter) the subject in all judgment is ultimately the real which appears in perception; and again it holds good that the lowest stage, in the development of judgment and inference alike, is the redintegration of ideal elements with sensuous presentation, in

---

* It is not worth while to criticize in detail a doctrine we can show is fallacious in principle. Cf. Chap. V. But among minor objections to the quantification of the predicate is its claim to silence you, and prevent you from saying what indubitably you know. It tells you you must not say "A is B," unless you also certify *how much* of B is A. But, even supposing that "so much of B" is the truth that you would affirm if you could, in numerous cases you can not affirm it. You know that A possesses a quality B, and, as to how the B, that is A, stands in extent to the B which is not A, you have no information. You must either then decline to quantify, or must abstain from speaking the truth you know. But it is not worth while to criticize in detail.

such a manner that the two are not distinguished, but run into one whole.

(ii) And from the second class of errors we may also collect important results. In the first place it is true that the content asserted is always complex. It can never be quite simple, but must always involve relations of elements or distinguishable aspects. And hence, after all, in judgment there must be a plurality of ideas. And, in particular, (*a*) though it is false that the predicate is a class in which the subject is inserted, and a fundamental error to take the universal in the form of a collection, yet it is entirely true that the predicate must be always an universal. For every idea, without exception, is universal. And again (*b*) though assertion is not attribution to a subject in the judgment, though it is false that the grammatical subject is the reality of which the predicate is held true, yet in every judgment there must be a subject. The ideal content, the adjective divorced, is made real once again by union with a substantive. And (*c*) the doctrine of equation, or identity of the terms, has itself grasped a truth, a truth turned upside down and not brought to the light, but for all that a deep fundamental principle.

Turned upside down, and made false, it runs thus. The object of judgment is, despite their difference in meaning, to assert the identity of subject and predicate when taken in extension. But turned the right way up it runs thus. The object of judgment is, under and within the identity of a subject, to assert the synthesis of different attributes. Whenever we write " $=$ " there must be a difference, or we should be unable to distinguish the terms we deal with (cf. Chap. V.). And when a judgment is turned into an equation, it is just this difference that we mean to state. In " $S = P$ " we do *not* mean to say that S and P are identical. We mean to say that they are *different,* that the diverse attributes S and P are united in one subject; that $S - P$ is a fact, or that the subject S is not bare S, but also $S - P$. And the reason why the theory of equation works, and is not mere nonsense, is that in fact it is an indirect way of stating difference. " The subject is the same " implies, and may be meant to convey, the truth that the attributes differ. We must refer to the sequel for further explanation, but at present our concern is briefly to point out that an identity must underlie every judgment.

But how is this possible? A is "prior to B," or "to the left of C," or "equal to D." The judgment asserts the equality, or sequence, or position of two subjects, and it surely does not say that both are the same. We must try to explain. We saw that all judgment is the attribution of an ideal content to reality, and so this reality is the subject of which the content is predicated. Thus in "A precedes B," this whole relation A — B is the predicate, and, in saying this is true, we treat it as an adjective of the real world. It is a quality of something beyond mere A — B. But, if this is so, the reality to which the adjective A — B is referred is the subject of A — B, and is the identity which underlies this synthesis of differences.

It is identical, not because it is simply the same, but because it is the same amid diversity. In the judgment, beside the mere distinction of the terms, we have an opposition in time of A to B. And the subject of which A — B is asserted, being subject to these differences, is thus different in itself, while remaining the same. In this sense every judgment affirms either the identity which persists under difference, or the diversity which is true of one single subject. It would be the business of metaphysics to pursue this discussion into further subtleties. We should there have to ask if, in the end, every possible relation does not involve a something *in* which it exists, as well as somethings *between* which it exists, and it might be difficult to reconcile the claims of these prepositions. But we have already reached the limit of our enquiries. The real subject which is implied in judgment,[28] will meet us again in the following Chapter; and that, we hope, may make clearer some points which at present remain obscure.

III. § 18. We have given some preliminary account of judgment, and have tried to dispose of some erroneous views. We pass now to our third task, and must make some remarks on the development of the function. As we have defined it above, judgment does not show itself at all the stages of psychical evolution. It is a comparatively late acquisition of the mind, and marks a period in its upward growth. We

should probably be wrong if we took it as a boundary which
divides the human from the animal intelligence; and in any
case we should be ill-advised to descend here into the arena
of theological and anti-theological prejudice (vid. Book III.
Part I. Chap. VII.). It is better to treat the mind as a single
phenomenon, progressing through stages, and to avoid all
discussion as to whether the lines, by which we mark out this
progress, fall across or between the divisions of actual classes
of animals. Thus with judgment we are sure that, at a certain stage, it does not exist, and that at a later stage it is
found in operation; and, without asking where the transition
takes place, we may content ourselves with pointing out the
contrast of these stages. The digression, if it be such, will
throw out into relief the account we have already given of
judgment. For judgment is impossible where truth and falsehood, with their difference, are not known; and this difference
cannot be known where ideas are not recognized and where
nothing exists for the mind but fact.[29]

§ 19. I do not mean that the lower forms, or that any
form, of soul-life is confined to the apprehension of simple
sensations. If the soul is ever the passive recipient of a given
product, to which it does not contribute and which it does not
idealize, yet in all actual mind a further step is made, and
we always possess more than what is given through sense.[30]
The impression, so to speak, is supplemented and modified
by an ideal construction, which represents the results of past
experience. And thus, in a sense, the lowest animals both
judge and reason, and, unless they did so, they must cease
to adjust their actions to the environment. But, in the strict
sense, they can neither reason nor judge; for they do not
distinguish between ideas and perceived reality.

That the thing as it is, and as it appears in perception, are
not the same thing, is, we all are aware, a very late afterthought. But it is equally an afterthought, though not equally
late, that there is any kind of difference between ideas and
impressions. For a more primitive mind a thing is or it
is not, is a fact or is nothing. That a fact should be, and
should yet be an appearance, should be true of, and belong
to, something not itself; or again should be illusion, should
exist and yet be false, because its content is an adjective

neither of itself nor of any other substantive—these distinctions are impossible for an early intelligence. A nonentity is not anything it can apprehend, and to it an error is never an illusion. And hence for this mind ideas never could be symbols. They are facts because they *are*.

§ 20. The presentations of the moment, the given sensations, are received into a world of past experience, and this past experience now appears in the form of ideal suggestion. In the lowest stages of mind there is as clear a difference between the *datum* that is given and the construction that is made, as there can be in the highest. But it is one thing to have a difference in the mind and another to perceive it; and for an early intelligence this contrast between sensation and idea, is quite non-existent. A presentation AB, by a feeling d, produces an action $\delta\varepsilon$, or, by an ideal transition b–d, is transformed into ABD; or may become AC, by the action of a–g, if g banishes B, and c is supplied. But, in all these cases, and in any other possible case, the process remains entirely latent. The product is received as a mere given fact, on a level with any other fact of sense.

If the object, as first perceived, could be compared with the object as finally constructed, there might be room for a doubt if the fact has become, or has been made by the mind. And still more if the ideas which perception excludes were ever attended to; if rejected suggestion, conflicting supplement, wrong interpretation, and disappointed action, were held before the mind, then a reflection might take place, which would antedate the slow result of development; and the sense of illusion would awaken the contrast of idea and reality, truth and falsehood. But all this is impossible. For the leading feature of the early mind is its entire and absolute practicality.[31] The fact occupies the soul no longer and no further than it tends to produce immediate action. The past and the future are not known except as modifications of the present. There is no practical interest in anything but the given, and what does not interest is not anything at all. Hence nothing is retained in its original character. The object, in its relation to present desire, changes ceaselessly in conformity with past adventures of failure or success. It contracts or extends itself, as the case may be, but it still remains the mere given object.

And while the ideas it assimilates become part of presentation, the ideas it excludes are simply nothing at all.

At a late stage of mind, among intelligent savages, the doctrine of a dream-world brings home to us the fact, that a mere idea, which exists and is unreal, is a thought not easy to lay hold of thoroughly. And, if we descend in the scale no further than to dogs, we are struck by the absence of theoretical curiosity. Let them see an appearance to be not what is seemed, and it instantly becomes a mere nonentity. An idea, we may say, is the shadow of an object; and that to a savage is another kind of object, but to a dog it is the thing or just nothing at all. The dog has not entered on that process of reflection which perhaps has not led to any very sure result. When his heart, like ours, is baffled and oppressed, and gives matter to his brain it has no strength to cope with, he can neither send his hopes into another world than this, nor repeat like a charm, and dream that he believes, that appearances may be nothing to a soul which feels them. I do not know the formula which would prove to his mind a satisfactory solution of his practical troubles; but his system of logic, if he had one, would be simple; for it would begin, I am sure, and would end with this axiom, "What is smells, and what does not smell is nothing."

§ 21. It would be difficult to detail the steps of the process by which ideas, as such, become objects of knowledge, and with truth and falsehood judgment comes in. And, apart from this difficulty, there is a question of fact which would constantly arise. Given a certain stage of development, does judgment already exist there or not? It might perhaps be right to connect the distinctions of truth and falsehood in general with the acquisition of language, but it is hard to say where language begins. And, in the stage before language, there are mental phenomena which certainly suggest the effective distinction of sensation and idea.

The provision made beforehand for changes to come can not always be taken as valid evidence. It seems clear that, in many cases, we should be wrong in supposing any knowledge of the future, as opposed to the present. It is certain at least that a presentation, accompanied by or transformed by feelings, is as effective practically as the clearest idea. But in certain animals there are much stronger indications. When artful contrivances, suitable to unseen events, are used in the pursuit of prey,[32] we are led to conclude that the difference of the situation, as it actually is and as it is anticipated, must come before the mind. And, where desire is unsatisfied, it is not always mere feeling, as against the object, which pervades the soul. The image of the desired, as against present perception, floats or is held before the attention, and the feeling of pain, we may suppose, must sharpen the contrast until at length the difference is seen. And we can mention here what perhaps may be an outward symptom of the change. No one can have been much with domestic animals, and failed to observe their constant and increasing use of the imperative. They *seem* at least to know what they desire, to expect assistance, and to be surprised at non-compliance. And though mere urgency of feeling, in the absence of ideas, might account for their tone, this interpretation would at times somewhat strain the phenomena.

But, if this is so, then judgment must come before language, and certainly cannot be distinctively human. And, just as after language has been developed, we do often dispense with it; just as the lowest, and perhaps the highest of our thinking, goes on without any words in the mind, so, we may suppose, before speech was developed, the *differentia* of judgment already existed.

We are not concerned in the controversy to which this might give rise. If we only know what we mean by judgment, it is little to our purpose where first it appears, and what animal first reaches it. The question is not at all easy to settle, and in passing I will merely suggest a reflection. It is not enough to show that in the mind of an animal an image exists together with a presentation of sense, and that this image, partly the same as the presented, is in collision with it, and again leads to action in relation to the presented. All this may exist, and yet the *differentia* still be absent; the image may not be seen to be mere appearance, to be either not real at all, or less real than the sensation. For, if the image is taken in relation to the perception, they may both be apprehended as one continuous changing fact; the prey may be *seen* as pursued and captured, and the actual object may appear to pass into the desired. And, where failure makes this impossible, what may after all be wanting is the intellectual identification of the image with the object. Apart from this logical process, we have a mere collision in the mind of two realities, whose struggle is felt. We have contest, and perhaps a following ejection; but we have no subjection, no degradation of one fact to the level of an appearance, that exists but in our heads. And in this case judgment would not have taken place.

§ 22. It might be interesting elsewhere to discuss at length these puzzles in psychology, but it will repay us better to pass to what is more certain. It is, in the first place, the *retention* of the false idea which tends to provoke comparison with reality, and which leads the way to the knowledge of appearance and truth and falsehood. And, in the second place, it is language which, if it does not originate, at least ensures and sharpens the contrast. When gregarious animals utter their ideas, the word is in a manner more permanent than the thought, and maintains itself against the fact it tries to express. And the spoken thoughts of the different individuals are sometimes in collision. They are not the same with one another, and therefore not the same with the single fact. And speech in its perversion to lies and deceit makes the dullest comprehend that words and ideas can be and be real, and can yet be illusion and wholly unreal in relation to facts. At this point it is seen that the word and the thought are not like other things. They not only exist but also mean something, and it is their meaning alone which is false or true. They are seen to be symbols, and this insight it is which in the strict sense constitutes judgment.

For in the early stage, to repeat it once more, the image is not a symbol or idea. It is itself a fact, or else the facts eject it. The real, as it appears to us in perception, connects the ideal suggestion with itself, or simply expels it from the world of reality. But judgment is the act which, while it recognizes the idea as appearance, nevertheless goes on to predicate it. It either attributes the idea to reality, and so affirms that it is true, or pronounces it to be merely a bare idea, and that the facts exclude the meaning it suggests. The ideal content which is also fact, and the ideal content which is nothing beyond itself, are truth and falsehood as they appear in judgment.

§ 23. Our object in the foregoing has been, not to chronicle a psychological transition, but to mark out distinctive stages and functions. We must endeavour, in conclusion, to obviate a very fatal mistake. The gulf between the stage of mind that judges and the mind that has not become aware of truth, may seem hard to bridge, and the account we have given may seem to rend facts apart. We may be thought in our extremity, when with natural conditions no progress is possible, to have forced upon the stage a heaven-sent faculty. On one side of your line, we may be told, you possess explicit symbols all of which are universal, and on the other side you have a mind which consists of mere individual impressions and images, grouped by the laws of a mechanical attraction. The distinction you have made amounts to a divorce. The higher stage can not exist as you describe it, or can not at least be developed from the lower.

In the sequel I shall criticize the whole doctrine of the " Association of ideas," but at present I will say thus much by anticipation.[33] I agree that, if the lower stages of the mind were really what they are in most English psychologies, it never would in any way be possible to pass to the stage where ideas are used in judgment. And this consequence I desire to accentuate and to emphasize. But the fashionable doctrine of " association," in which particular images are recalled by and unite with particular images, is, I think, not true of *any* stage of mind (vid. Book II. Part II. Chap. I). It does not exist outside our psychology. From the very first beginnings of soul-life universals are used. It is because the results of experience are fixed in an ideal and universal form, that animals are able, I do not say to progress, but to maintain themselves in bare existence.

§ 24. In England, I am afraid, the faithful tradition of accumulated prejudice, in which are set the truths of the " Philosophy of Experience," well-nigh makes idle an appeal to the fact. But I will try to state the fact, however idly. It is not true that particular images are ever associated. It is not true that among lower animals universal ideas are never used. What *is* never used is a particular idea, and, as for association, nothing ever is associated without in the process being shorn of particularity. I shall hereafter have to enlarge on the latter statement, and at present will deal with the false assertion, that merely individual ideas are the early furniture of the primitive mind.

In the first place it seems patent that the lower animals have not any idea *about* the individual. To know a thing as the one thing in the world, and as different from all others, is not a simple achievement. If we reflect on the distinctions it implies, we must see that it comes late to the mind. And, on turning to facts, we find that animals of superior intelligence are clearly without it, or give us at least no reason at all to think that they possess it. The indefinite universal, the vague felt type, which results from past perceptions and modifies present ones, is palpably the process of their intellectual experience. And when young children call all men father, it is the merest distortion of fact to suppose that they perceive their father as individual, and then, perceiving other individuals, confuse a distinction they previously have made.

But this is hardly the real point at issue. To know the individual as such will be admitted to be a late achievement. It can hardly be maintained that a rude intelligence, when it holds a type and rejects what disagrees with it, can be aware of that type as an unique individual. The question is really as to the *use* made of images in early knowledge. Are they *used* as universals, or *used* as particulars?

§ 25. It is agreed on both sides that, as psychical existences, ideas are particular like all other phenomena. The controversy is confined to the use we make of them. I should maintain that, so far as they remain particular, they are simple facts, and not ideas at all; and that, where they are employed to extend or to modify experience, they are never used in their particular form. When A-B is presented in perception, we are told that the result of a past perception B-C appears as particular images *b-c,* and that these images, called up, unite with the presentation. But nothing could be more false. It is not true that all the marks, and relations, and differences, which constitute the particularity of *b* and *c,* appear in the resultant A-B-C, or were in any way used in order to produce it. The image *c,* besides its content as *c,* had the indefinite detail of all psychical phenomena; but it was not this but the universal *c* which was used in A-B-C, and it is the perception A-B that re-particularizes *c* in accordance with itself. And, if this is so, we must say that what really operates is a connection between universal ideas. We have already, in an unconscious form, what, when made explicit, is the meaning of symbols.

I must trust to the sequel for elucidation (vid. Book II. II. Chap. I.), but the subject is so important that I will venture to insert some illustrations. When to-day I reach the place where yesterday my dog has either chased a cat or fought with an antagonist, the perception as we say " calls up " the ideas, and he runs eagerly forward. His experience, we will suppose, was of a white cat or a black retriever with a large brass collar. To-day images are " called up," not so definite perhaps, but still certainly with some detail, and we will suppose that the detail reproduces the experience. To-day it is a black cat that is found in the place, but with an ordinary dog that will make no difference. The whiteness of the image is quite irrelevant.[34] Or again, if to-day another dog be perceived, if only that dog be not glaringly different, an ordinary dog will certainly attack him, and the less intelligent he is the more catholic is his action. For it is not the whole image but a portion of the content which operates in his mind. He may turn from a small dog or a white dog or a smooth-coated dog, but size, blackness, and roughness, are the typical ideas which will certainly operate. It may be said, no doubt, that the ideas are particular, that they differ from the perception, and that it is the fault of the animal which fails to distinguish them. But why, I reply, does it fail to distinguish? Is a creature, intelligent as is a terrier, unable to see the difference between a white and black cat, or a Newfoundland and a sheep dog? " Yes," I shall be told, " he can if he attends to them, but here, although they both are present,* he does not

---

* This is a false assumption as will be shown hereafter. In the first place it is not true that, when the mind goes from A B to C, it has to pass through a particular image *b*. In the next place, if the particular *b* be present, we have no reason to suppose that it will have the qualities of the original perception B. If a white cat has been seen to-day, we saw that next day, if its image is white, the whiteness of that image need not be used; and again if its whiteness was not an

attend to them." But if so, I must rejoin, if the differences are not used, but remain inoperative, is not this a clear proof that what operates, and what is used, is a portion of the content, which is permanent amid differences, and which later becomes the universal meaning?

Again, if an animal has been burnt one day at the kitchen fire, the next day it may shrink from a lighted match. But how different are the two. How much more unlike than like. Will you say then that the match can not operate unless it first summons up, and then is confused with the image of a kitchen fire; or will you not rather say that a connection between elements, which are none of them particular, is produced in the mind by the first experience? But, if so, from the outset universals are used, and the difference between the fact and the idea, the existence and the meaning, is unconsciously active in the undeveloped intelligence.

§ 26. We must anticipate no further. In another place we shall show the fictitious nature of the "Laws of Association," as they have been handed down by our prevalent tradition. Our object here has been, in passing, to show that the symbolic use of ideas in judgment, although no early process of the mind, is a natural result of mental development. From the very first beginnings of intelligence it is the type that operates and not the image. The instance as such is never, and can never be, retained in the soul. The connection of certain elements in its content is all it leaves behind. You may call it, if you please, mere impotence of our imagination, or you may call it that idealizing function of the mind which is the essence of intelligence, still the fact remains that never at any stage can any fact be retained without some mutilation, some removal of that detail which makes it particular. The lower we descend in the growth of our own functions, or in the scale of animate nature, the more typical, the less individual, the less distinct, the more vaguely universal and widely symbolic is the deposit of experience. It is not symbolic in the sense that the meaning is at first perceived to be other than the fact. It is not universal in the

object of interest, there is no reason whatever why the image should be white, and not of some other hue. The generalized result left by past experience is always mutilated.

sense that analysis has distinguished the relevant from the irrelevant detail, and found elements more simple, and syntheses wider than are suggested by mere sense. But in the sense of not using the particular as particular, and of taking the meaning while leaving the existence, in the sense of invariably transcending the given, and of holding true always and valid everywhere what has ever and anywhere once been experienced, the earliest and the latest intelligence are the same from one end to the other of the scale of life.

ADDITIONAL NOTES

[1] On the question of Order in Logic cf. T. E. I.

[2] "We can not judge till we use them *as* ideas." This requires correction. See *Appearance*, Index, and *Essays,* pp. 32-3 and Index. And cf. the Index of this book s. v. Idea.

[3] "In England." This was published in 1883.

[4] "Symbols." This is wrong or at least inaccurate. A "sign" or "symbol" implies the recognition of its individual existence, and this recognition is not implied in an "idea." See *Essays,* p. 29, and the Index, s. v. Idea.

[5] "That," "what," "means" and "stands for" (cf. Chap. VI. § 2). All of these distinctions imply judgment, though that may not be explicit. And wherever you have any such distinction you have transcendence and an idea—though not always an explicit idea (see Note 2). Each of these distinctions, again, if you could perfect it, would imply and pass into all the rest.

[6] "Original content." This distinction (cf. the words "content (original or acquired)" at the end of § 4) refers to the difference pointed out in § 5. The point is, however, irrelevant, and § 5 should have been omitted.

[7] This footnote is wrong throughout, for there are no ideas not so "referred." See *Essays,* Chap. III and Index. The words in the text, "cut off, etc." are also incorrect. There are no ideas before or apart from their use, and that at first is unconscious. See Note 2.

[8] Here again we must remember that we are not to say (i) that an idea is there apart from its being used, or (ii) that, in using it, we must be aware of it as a mental thing. Further (iii) I was wrong to speak, here and elsewhere, as if with every idea you have what may be called an "image." How far and in what sense the psychical existence is always capable of being verified in observation is a difficult point to which I have perhaps not sufficiently attended. Still every idea, I must assume, has an aspect of psychical event, and so is qualified as a particular existence. In the footnote to p. 7 "sensuous" should have been "psychical." The amount of imagery required is

much exaggerated in p. 9. Cf. on the other side Chap. II, §§ 36, 37.

⁹ What I meant here was probably to remind the reader that the "categorical" may turn out to be really "conditional."

¹⁰ "Judgment (proper) is etc." (i) In this definition the word "act" raises a question, important in psychology and in metaphysics (see *Appearance* and *Essays*, the Indexes), but (so far as I see) not necessary in logic. (ii) "Recognized as such" is wrong (see Note 2). What I *should* recognize on reflection I may in fact ignore. Cf. §§ 10 and 13. (iii) "Beyond the act," and (below) "independent of it," are right for logic. For metaphysics, on the other hand, the problem raised here can not be ignored (see *Essays*, Index, s. v. *Act*). But as to recognition of the act (to return to that) the text is wrong. A perceived object changed by an idea, and the change ignored except as the development of the object—though not of the mere perceived object—here is the beginning of judgment in the proper sense. But, again, to take judgment as present wherever we have an object at all before the mind—is a view which is tenable.

¹¹ "Wandering adjective" should be "*loosened* adjective." And (three lines lower down) "relation" should be "*union.*"

¹² "Partial ignorance—absolute." The meaning and the great importance of these words have, I hope, been to some extent brought out in this book and in my later writings.

¹³ (i) "Are the angles &c.?". The false doctrine of "floating ideas" is involved here. See *Essays*, Index. (ii) "The same ideal content." Not so. See ibid. And cf. Bosanquet, *K & R*, pp. 114-15, 119, and *Logic*, I. 33.

¹⁴ This statement (cf. pp. 49, 56) requires correction. It is true that the ideal meaning is one; but it is also true that the subject is a special subject, and that it, in its special sense, must be there within the meaning (cf. Bosanquet, loc. cit.). The twofold nature of Reality as the subject of judgment was not sufficiently recognized by me. See below on p. 13. And cf. pp. 114, 477, and Index.

¹⁵ Cf. *Mind*, *N. S.* No. 41, pp. 20 foll.

¹⁶ "The relation is the same." But see Note 13.

¹⁷ "The subject can not belong to the content." This statement again requires correction. We have not a case here of mere Yes or mere No. See T. E. II. and Index. And cf. *Essays*, and again *Appearance*, the Indexes.

¹⁸ "And finally, &c." See Note 10.

¹⁹ On Bain's theory of Will cf. *Mind O. S.* No. 49, pp. 27 foll. The unjust neglect of Bain by Pragmatists, or their inability to learn from his adventurous errors, has, I think, cost them dear. See *Essays*, pp. 70-1. The reader will notice that, already in 1883, I was dealing with the question, What is *practical?* See for this the Note on p. 506, and T. E. No. XII.

²⁰ Cf. here *Essays* (ibid.).

²¹ "Not judged to be real." We should here add "in our existing

world," as otherwise the statement is not true.   See *Essays,* Chap. III, and specially p. 35, and cf. T. E. XII of this work.

²² On the nature of the feeling of *Consent* see *Essays,* p. 377, note, and *Mind, N. S.* No. 46, pp. 13 foll.

²³ Whether (see Prof. Sully, p. 79, note) Bain really modified his view, it is needless here to enquire.   My own difficulty with Bain was to get any rational idea as to what he meant by "intellect" and "knowledge" which apparently can remain itself in the absence of belief.   He (like J. S. Mill) is faced here by a problem, which, on their inherited premises, is quite insoluble, because radically perverted. See *Essays,* pp. 376-7.   Bain's view of intellect is again noticed in pp. 324, 491 of the present work.

²⁴ "Copula."   Dr. Bosanquet (*K & R,* pp. 167 foll.) rightly remarks here that the copula is essential, so far as it points to the analysis and synthesis, and the conditioned assertion of reality, which are present in all judgment.

²⁵ "(Not all)" should be "(though not in all cases *except in the end*)."   Cf. below, §§ 16, 17.   And see Note 28.

²⁶ "The same both in the assertion and out of it."   But see Note 13.

²⁷ "Equality."   The reader may consult here Dr. Bosanquet's remarks (*K & R,* pp. 104 foll.) though I do not wholly assent to them.

²⁸ All judgment falls in the end under the head of subject and attribute, in the sense that every judgment in the end asserts of a subject both diversity in unity and identity in difference—this subject being at once the ultimate and also a special reality.   For this fundamental and all-important doctrine see the Index of this work.

²⁹ The reader must not forget here that our definition of judgment was more or less arbitrary.   See Note 10.

³⁰ The reader will notice that, in §§ 19 and 20, much too little is made of movement and action following direct on sensation.   But for the purpose here in hand this point is perhaps not material.

³¹ "Absolute practicality."   But see Bk. III. Pt. I. Chap. VII.   For the character of "the early mind" cf. *Essays,* pp. 356-7, 376.   The further statement about "the dog" is of course exaggerated.

³² "In the pursuit of prey," and of course also otherwise.   With regard to the Imperative, though I still think that this remark was certainly worth making, I would emphasize the need of caution here as to correct interpretation of the facts.

³³ On "Association &c."   See later, Bk. II. Pt. II. Chap. I.   The remark on "most English psychologies" belongs, of course, to the date 1883.

³⁴ There is some exaggeration here as to the amount of particular detail, but what is said holds good, I think, in principle.

CHAPTER II

§ 1. In the foregoing chapter we have attempted roughly to settle the main characteristics of judgment. The present chapter will both support and deepen our conclusion. It will deal with problems, in part familiar to those who have encountered the well-known discussion aroused by Herbart. The length and the difficulty of this second chapter may perhaps be little warranted by success, but I must be allowed to state beforehand that both are well warranted by the importance of the subject in modern logic.

A judgment, we assume naturally, says something about some fact or reality. If we asserted or denied about anything else, our judgment would seem to be a frivolous pretence. We not only must say something, but it must also be about something actual that we say it. For consider; a judgment must be true or false, and its truth or falsehood can not lie in itself. They involve a reference to a something beyond. And this, about which or of which we judge, if it is not fact, what else can it be?

The consciousness of objectivity or necessary connection, in which the essence of judgment is sometimes taken to lie, will be found in the end to derive its meaning from a reference to the real. A truth is not necessary unless in some way it is compelled to be true (vid. Chap. VII.). And compulsion is not possible without something that compels. It will hence be the real, which exerts this force, of which the judgment is asserted. We may indeed not affirm that the suggestion S — P itself is categorically true of the fact, and *that* is not our judgment.[1] The actual judgment asserts that S — P is forced on our minds by a reality *x*. And this reality, whatever it may be, is the subject of the judgment. It is the same with objectivity.[2] If the connection S — P holds outside my judgment, it can hardly hold nowhere or in nothingness. It must surely be valid in relation to something, and that something must be real. No doubt, as before, S — P may not be true directly of this fact; but then that again was not what we asserted. The actual judgment affirms that S — P is in connection with *x*. And this once again is an assertion about fact.

There is a natural presumption that truth, to be true, must be true of reality. And this result, that comes as soon as we reflect, will be the goal we shall attain in this chapter. But we shall reach it with a struggle, distressed by subtleties, and perhaps in some points disillusioned and shaken.

§ 2. Less serious difficulties we may deal with at once. " A four-cornered circle is an impossibility," we are told, does not assert the actual existence of a four-cornered circle (Herbart, I. 93). But the objection is irrelevant, unless it is maintained that in every case we affirm the reality of the *grammatical* subject.* And this clearly is not always what we mean to assert. And such further examples as " There are no ghosts," or " This thought is an illusion," may be likewise disposed of. It is not the first form and haphazard conjunction of every proposition which represents reality. But, in every proposition, an analysis of the meaning will find a reality of which something else is affirmed or denied. " The nature of space excludes the connection of square and round," " The world is no place where ghosts exist," " I have an idea, but the reality it refers to is other than its meaning,"—we may offer these translations as preliminary answers to a first form of attack. And when Herbart assails us with " The wrath of the Homeric gods is fearful " (I. 99), we need give no ground before such a weapon. In Homer it *is* so; and surely a poem, surely any imagination, surely dreams and delusions, and surely much more our words and our names are all of them facts of a certain kind. Such plain distinctions as those between existences of different orders[3] should never have been confused, and the paradox lies on the side of those who urge such an objection.†

* Ueberweg seems to make this mistake, *Logik,* § 68.

† I admit that there are difficulties which for the moment we ignore. When no one reads Homer, of what subject can we predicate the wrath of his deities? Though the meaning of a term is a fact, most certain and quite undeniable, yet where is that fixed connection

And if, further, the discussion take the misleading form of an enquiry into the copula, we find merely the same misunderstandings unknowingly reproduced. Wherever we predicate, we predicate about something which exists beyond the judgment, and which (of whatever kind it may be) is real, either inside our heads or outside them. And in this way we must say that " is " never can stand for anything but " exists." *

§ 3. But Herbart, we shall find, is not so easily disposed of. He was not the man first uncritically to swallow the common-sense doctrine that judgment is of things, and then to stagger at the discovery that things are not words, or fall prostrate before a supposed linguistic revelation of the nature of the copula. In denying that judgment asserts a fact, he knew well what he stood on. It was no puzzle about the grammatical subject, but a difficulty as to the whole nature of truth and of ideas. We reflect about judgment, and, at first of course, we think we understand it. Our conviction is that it is concerned with fact; but we also see that it is concerned with ideas. And the matter seems at this stage quite simple. We have a junction or synthesis of ideas in the mind, and this junction expresses a similar junction of facts outside. Truth and fact are thus given to us together, the same thing, so to speak, in different hemispheres or diverse elements.

But a further reflection tends to dissipate our confidence. Judgments, we find, are the union of ideas, and truth is not found except in judgments. How then are ideas related to realities? They seemed the same, but they clearly are not so, and their difference threatens to become a discrepancy. A fact is individual, an idea is universal; a fact is substantial,

---

to be found? Does it lie in the dictionaries when no one opens them, or in the usage when no one is employing the word? But these questions bear as hardly on fact as on legend, and on things as on names. Mathematical truths at the least hold good inside mathematics. But where are mathematics? And we all believe that arsenic poisons, but if at the moment no dose is operating, nor any one in the world is thinking of arsenic, it poisons nothing. We shall hereafter return to the discussion of this problem.

* The reader may consult Jordan. *Die Zweideutigkeit des Copula bei Stuart Mill*, Gymn. Prog. Stuttgart, 1870; Brentano, *Psychologie*, Buch ii. Cap. 7. On the other side see Drobisch. *Logik*, §§ 55-6, Sigwart, *Logik*, I. 94.

an idea is adjectival; a fact is self-existent, an idea is symbolical. Is it not then manifest that ideas are *not* joined in the way in which facts are? Nay the essence of an idea, the more it is considered, is seen more and more to diverge from reality. And we are confronted by the conclusion that, so far as anything is true, it is *not* fact, and, so far as it is fact, it can never be true. Or the same result may have a different form. A categorical judgment makes a real assertion in which some fact is affirmed or denied. But, since no judgment can do this, they all in the end are hypothetical. They are true only of and upon a supposition. In asserting S — P I do not mean that S, or P, or their synthesis, is real. I say nothing about any union in fact. The truth of S — P means that, *if I suppose* S, I am bound *in that case* to assert S — P. In this way *all* judgments are hypothetical.*

The conclusion, thus urged upon us by Herbart, follows, I think, irresistibly from the premises. But the premises are not valid. Judgment, we saw in the foregoing chapter, can not consist in the synthesis of ideas. And yet it will repay us to pause awhile, and to enlarge on the consequences of this erroneous doctrine. To see clearly that, if judgment is the union of ideas, there then can be no categorical judgment, is a very great step in the understanding of Logic. And, through the next few sections, we shall endeavour to make this conclusion plain.

§ 4. The contrast and comparison of reality and truth no doubt involve very ultimate principles. To enquire what is fact, is to enter at once on a journey into metaphysics, the end of which might not soon be attained. For our present purpose we must answer the question from a level not much above that of common sense.[4] And the account which represents the ordinary view, and in which perhaps we may most of us agree, is something of this sort.

The real is that which is known in presentation or intuitive knowledge. It is what we encounter in feeling or perception. Again it is that which appears in the series of events that occur in space and time. It is that once more which resists our wills; a thing is real if it exercises any kind of force or

---

* Herbart, *Werke,* I. 92. He refers here to Wolff, by whom, in this point, he had been partially anticipated. Cf. Fichte, *Werke,* I. 69, 93.

compulsion, or exhibits necessity. It is briefly what acts and maintains itself in existence. And this last feature seems connected with former ones. We know of no action, unless it shows itself by altering the series of either space or time, or both together;[5] and again perhaps there is nothing which appears unless it acts. But the simplest account, in which the others possibly are all summed up, is given in the words, The real is self-existent. And we may put this otherwise by saying, The real is what is individual.

It is the business of metaphysics to subject these ideas to a systematic examination. We must content ourselves here with taking them on trust, and will pause merely to point out a common misunderstanding. It is a mistake to suppose that " The real is individual" means either that the real is abstractly simple, or is merely particular. Internal diversity does not exclude individuality, and still less is a thing made self-existent by standing in a relation of exclusion to others. Metaphysics can prove that, in this sense, the particular is furthest removed from self-existence. The individual is so far from being merely particular that, in contrast with its own internal diversity, it is a true universal (cf. Chap. VI.). Nor is this a paradox. We are accustomed to speak of, and believe in, realities which exist in more than one moment of time or portion of space. Any such reality would be an identity which appears and remains the same under differences; and it therefore would be a real universal.*

§ 5. Such, we may say, are some of the points which constitute reality. And truth has not one of them. It exists, as such, in the world of ideas. And ideas, we have seen, are merely symbols. They are general and adjectival, not substantive and individual. Their essence lies within their meaning and beyond their existence. The idea is the fact with its existence disregarded, and its content mutilated. It is but a portion of the actual content cut off from its reality, and

---

* The following reflection may interest the reader. If space and time are continuous, and if all appearance must occupy some time or space—and it is not hard to support both these *theses*—we can at once proceed to the conclusion, no mere particular exists. Every phenomenon will exist in more times or spaces than one; and against that diversity will be itself an universal.

used with a reference to something else. No idea can be real.

If judgment is the synthesis of two ideas, then truth consists in the junction of unreals. When I say, Gold is yellow, then certainly some fact is present to my mind. But universal gold and universal yellowness are not realities, and, on the other hand, what *images*[6] of yellow and gold I actually possess, though as psychical facts they have real existence, are unfortunately not the facts about which I desired to say anything. We have seen (Chap. I.) that I do *not* mean, This image of gold is in my mind joined psychically with this other image of yellow. I mean that, quite apart from my mental facts, gold in general has a certain kind of colour. I strip away certain parts from the mental facts, and, combining these adjectival remnants, I call the synthesis truth.

But reality is not a connection of adjectives, nor can it so be represented. Its essence is to be substantial and individual. But can we reach self-existence and individual character by manipulating adjectives and putting universals together? If not, the fact is not given *directly* in any truth whatsoever. It can never be stated categorically. And yet, because adjectives depend upon substantives, the substantive is implied. Truth will then refer to fact *indirectly*. The adjectives of truth presuppose a reality, and in this sense all judgment will rest on a supposal. It is all hypothetical; itself will confess that what directly it deals with, is unreal.

§ 6. More ordinary considerations might perhaps have led us to anticipate this result. The common-sense view of facts outside us passing over into the form of truth within us, or copying themselves in a faithful mirror, is shaken and perplexed by the simplest enquiries. What fact is asserted in negative judgments? Has every negation I choose to invent a real counterpart in the world of things? Does *any* logical negation, as such, correspond to fact? Consider again hypothetical judgments. *If* something is, *then* something else follows, but should neither exist, would the statement be false? It seems just as true without facts as with them, and, if so, what fact can it possibly assert? The disjunctive judgment will again perplex us. "A is *b* or *c*" must be true or false, but how in the world can a *fact* exist as that strange ambiguity

" *b* or *c?* " We shall hardly find the flesh and blood alternative which answers to our " or."

If we think these puzzles too technical or sought out, let us take more obvious ones. Have the past and the future we talk of so freely any real existence? Or let us try a mere ordinary categorical affirmative judgment, " Animals are mortal." This seems at first to keep close to reality; the junction of facts seems quite the same as the junction of ideas. But the experience we have gained may warn us that, if ideas are adjectives, this can not be the case. If we are unconvinced, let us go on to examine. " Animals " seems perhaps to answer to a fact, since all the animals who exist are real. But, in " Animals are mortal," is it only the animals now existing that we speak of? Do we not mean to say that the animal born hereafter will certainly die? The complete collection of real things is of course the same fact as the real things themselves, but a difficulty arises as to future individuals. And, apart from that, we scarcely in general have in our minds a complete collection. We *mean,* " Whatever is an animal will die,"² but that is the same as *If* anything is an animal *then* it is mortal. The assertion really is about mere hypothesis; it is not about fact.

In universal judgments we may sometimes understand that the synthesis of adjectives, which the judgment expresses, is really found in actual existence. But the judgment does not say this. It is merely a private supposition of our own. It arises partly from the nature of the case, and partly again from our bad logical tradition. The fact that most adjectives we conjoin in judgment can be taken as the adjectives of existing things, leads us naturally to expect that this will always be the case. And, in the second place, a constant ambiguity arises from the use of " all " in the subject. We write the universal in the form " All animals," and then take it to mean each actual animal, or the real sum of existing animals. But this would be no more an universal judgment than " A B and C are severally mortal." And we *mean* nothing like this. In saying " All animals," if we think of a collection, we never for a moment imagine it complete; we mean also " Whatever besides may be animal must be mortal too." In universal judgments we never mean " all." What we mean is " any," and " whatever," and " whenever." But these involve " if."

We may see this most easily by a simple observation. If actual existence were really asserted, the judgment would be false if the existence failed. And this is not the case. It would be a hazardous assertion that, supposing all animal life had ceased, mortality would at once be predicated falsely, and, with the re-appearance of animal existence, would again become true. But cases exist where no doubt is possible. " All persons found trespassing on this ground will be prosecuted," is too often a prophecy, as well as a promise. But it is not meant to foretell, and, though no one trespasses, the statement may be true. " All triangles have their angles equal to two right angles " would hardly be false if there were no triangles. And, if this seems strange, take the case of a chiliagon. Would statements about chiliagons cease to be true, if no one at the moment were thinking of a chiliagon? We can hardly say that, and yet where would any chiliagons exist? There surely must be scientific propositions, which unite ideas not demonstrable at the moment in actual existence. But can we maintain that, if the sciences which produce these became non-existent, these judgments would have *ipso facto* become false, as well as unreal?

The universal judgment is thus always hypothetical. It says " *Given* one thing you will *then* have another," and it says no more. No truth can state fact.

§ 7. This result is however not easy to put up with. For, if the truth is such, then all truths, it would seem, are no better than false. We can not so give up the categorical judgment, for, if that is lost, then everything fails. Let us make a search and keep to this question, Is there nowhere to be found a categorical judgment? And it seems we can find one. Universal judgments were merely hypothetical, because they stated, not individual substantives, but connections of adjectives. But in singular judgments the case is otherwise. Where the subject, of which you affirm categorically, is one individual, or a set of individuals, your truth expresses fact. There is here no mere adjective and no hypothesis.

These judgments are divisible into three great classes.[7] And the distinction will hereafter be of great importance. (i)

We have first those judgments which make an assertion about that which I now perceive, or feel, or about some portion of it. " I have a toothache," " There is a wolf," " That bough is broken." In these we simply analyze the given, and may therefore call them by the name of *Analytic judgments of sense.** Then (ii) we have *Synthetic judgments of sense,* which state either some fact of time or space, or again some quality of the matter given, which I do not here and now directly perceive. " This road leads to London," " Yesterday it rained," " To-morrow there will be full moon." They are synthetic because they extend the given through an ideal construction, and they all, as we shall see, involve an inference. The third class (iii), on the other hand, have to do with a reality which is never a sensible event in time. " God is a spirit," " The soul is a substance." We may think what we like of the validity of these judgments, and may or may not decline to recognize them in metaphysics. But in logic they certainly must have a place.

§ 8. But, if judgment is the union of two ideas, we have not so escaped. And this is a point we should clearly recognize. Ideas are universal, and, no matter what it is that we try to say and dimly mean, what we really express and succeed in asserting, is nothing individual. For take the analytic judgment of sense. The fact given us is singular, it is quite unique; but our terms are all general, and state a truth which may apply as well to many other cases. In " I have a toothache " both the I and the toothache are mere generalities. The *actual* toothache is not any other toothache, and the *actual* I is myself as having this very toothache. But the truth I assert has been and will be true of all other toothaches of my altering self. Nay " I have a toothache," is as true of another's toothache as of my own, and may be met by the assertion, " Not so, but *I* have one." It is in vain that we add to the original assertion " this," " here," and " now," for they are all universals. They are symbols whose meaning extends to and covers innumerable instances.

Thus the judgment will be true of any case whatsoever

---

* These analytic and synthetic judgments must not for one moment be confounded with Kant's. Every possible judgment, we shall see hereafter, is both analytic and synthetic. Most, if not all, judgments of sense are synthetic in the sense of transcending the given.

of a certain sort; but, if so, it can not be true of the reality;
for that is unique, and is a fact, not a sort. "That bough is
broken," but so are many others, and we do not say which.
"This road leads to London" may be said just as well of a
hundred other roads. "To-morrow it will be full moon," does
not tell us what to-morrow. Hereafter it will constantly be
true that, on the day after this day, there will be a full moon.
And so, failing in all cases to state the actual fact, we state
something else instead. What is true of all does not express
this one. The assertion sticks for ever in the adjectives; it
does not reach the substantive. And adjectives unsupported
float in the air; their junction with reality is supposed and
not asserted. So long as judgments are confined to ideas,
their reference to fact is a mere implication. It is presupposed
outside the assertion, which is not strictly true until we qualify
it by a suppressed condition. As it stands, it both fails as a
singular proposition, and is false if you take it as a strict
universal (cf. § 62 foll.).[8]

§ 9. But judgment, as we saw in the foregoing Chapter, is
not confined to ideas, and can not by any means consist in
their synthesis. The necessity for two ideas is a mere delusion,
and, if before we judged we had had to wait for them, we
certainly should never have judged at all. And the necessity
for the copula is a sheer superstition. Judgments can exist
without any copula and with but one idea.

In the simplest judgment an idea is referred to what is
given in perception, and it is identified therewith as one of its
adjectives. There is no need for an idea to appear as the
subject, and, even when it so appears, we must distinguish the
fact from grammatical show.[9] It is present reality which is
the actual subject, and the genuine substantive of the ideal
content. We shall see hereafter that, when "this" "here"
and "now" seem to stand as subjects, the actual fact which
appears in perception is the real subject, to which these
phrases serve to direct our attention. But of this in the
sequel; we have seen already, and have further to see, that
all judgments predicate their ideal content as an attribute of
the real which appears in presentation.

It is from this point of view that we must resume the
discussion. Standing on this basis, we must examine afresh

the various judgments which have passed before us, and must
ask for their meaning and further validity. Some difficulties
in our search for categorical judgments may have already
disappeared; but others as formidable must perhaps be
awaited. And, if we come to the result that all truth in the
end is true of reality, we must not expect to maintain that
doctrine in its crude acceptation.

§ 10. Our first movement however must be towards a
definition. A phrase we have used was designedly ambiguous. Are we to hold that the real, which is the ultimate
subject, and which, as we said, appears in perception, is
identical with the merely momentary appearance? We shall
see that this can not be, and that such a view could not
possibly account for the facts. At present we may offer
a preliminary argument against this mistake.

The subject which appears in the series of time, and to
which we attribute our ideas as predicates, must itself be real.
And, if real, it must not be purely adjectival. On the
contrary it must be self-existent and individual. But the
particular phenomenon, the momentary appearance, is not
individual, and is so not the subject which we use in judgment.

§ 11. We naturally think that the real, at least as we
know it, must be present. Unless I come into contact with it
directly, I can never be sure of it. Nothing in the end but
what I feel can be real, and I can not feel anything unless it
touches me. But nothing again can immediately encounter
me save that which is present.[10]   If I have it not here and now,
I do not have it at all.

"The present is real"; this seems indubitable. And are
we to say that the momentary appearance is *therefore* real?
This indeed would be mistaken. If we take the real as that
which is confined to a single "here" or a single "now" (in
this sense making it particular), we shall have questions on
our hands we shall fail to dispose of. For, beside the difficulties as to the truth of all universal judgments, we are
threatened with the loss of every proposition which extends
beyond the single instant. *Synthetic* judgments must at once
be banished if the real is only the phenomenon of a moment.
Nothing either past or future in time, nor any space I do not

directly perceive, can be predicated as adjectives of our one "now" and "here." All such judgments would be false, for they would attribute to the existent qualities which confessedly are non-existent, or would place the real as one member in a series of utter unrealities.

But perhaps we feel we may escape this consequence; or at all events feel so sure of our premise that we can not give it up. "The real is confined to one here or one now." But supposing this true, are we sure we know what it is we understand by our "now" and "here"? For time and extension seem continuous elements; the here is one space with the other heres round it; and the now flows ceaselessly and passes for ever from the present to the past.

We may avoid this difficulty, we may isolate the time we call the present, and fix our now as the moment which *is,* and has neither past, nor future, nor transition in itself. But here we fall into a hopeless dilemma. This moment which we take either has no duration, and in that case it turns out no time at all; or, if it has duration, it is a part of time, and is found to have transition in itself.

If the now in which the real appears is purely discrete, then first we may say that, as characterized by exclusion, the phenomenon, if apparent, is not self-subsistent, and so not real. But apart from that objection, and to return to our dilemma, the now and the here must have some extension. For no part of space or time is a final element. We find that every here is made up of heres, and every now is resolvable into nows. And thus the appearance of an atomic now could not show itself as any one part of time. But, if so, it could never show itself at all. Or, on the other hand, if we say the appearance has duration, then, like all real time, it has succession in itself, and it would not be the appearance of our single now.* From all which it is clear that a momentary appearance will not give us the subject of which we are in search.

---

* It is the business of metaphysics to prove these points at length. If time consists of discrete parts, it is hard to see how the fact of succession can possibly be explained, unless time be taken between these parts of time. And that would lead to untenable conclusions. But it is the fact of change which shows that time is continuous. The rate of change, the number of events in every part of time, may,

§ 12. It is a mistake to suppose that the present is a part of time, indivisible and stationary, and that here and now can be solid and atomic. In one sense of the word the present is no time. Itself no part of the process, it is a point we take within the flow of change. It is the line that we draw across the stream, to fix in our minds the relations of one successive event to another event. " Now," in this sense, stands for " simultaneous with "; it signifies not existence but bare position in the series of time. The reality is not present in the sense of given in one atomic moment.

What we mean, when we identify presence with reality, is something different. The real is that with which I come into immediate contact, and the content of any part of time, any section of the continuous flow of change, is present to me if I directly encounter it. What is given in a perception, though it change in my hands, is now and here if only I perceive it. And within that perception any aspect or part, which I specially attend to, is specially present, is now and here in another sense than the rest of that content. The present is the filling of that duration in which the reality appears to me directly; and there can be no part of the succession of events so small or so great, that conceivably it might not appear as present.

In passing we may repeat and may trace the connection of those shades of meaning we have found in " presence." (i) Two events in time are now to one another, if both are given simultaneously in *my* series. (ii) Since the real appears in the series of time, the effort to find it both *present* and *existing* within that series, creates the fiction of the atomic now. (iii) If the real can never exist *in* time, but only appear there, then that part of the series in which it touches me is my present. (iv) And this suggests the reflection that presence is really the negation of time, and never can properly be given in the

so far as we know, be increased indefinitely; and this means that in every part of time more than one event may take place. If the parts be discrete, then not only will motion imply that a thing is in several places in one time (and this is a fact), but also (which is absurd) that throughout all these places no time elapses, that they are strictly contemporaneous. I should be glad to enter into the discussion at length, but the subject cannot properly be treated by logic.

series. It is not the time that can ever be present, but only the content.

§ 13. But we must leave these intricacies. We must be satisfied with knowing that the real, which (we say) appears in perception, does not appear in one single moment. And if we will pause and reflect for a little, we shall see how hardened we are in superstitions. When we ask for reality, we at once encounter it in space and time. We find opposed to us a continuous element of perpetual change. We begin to observe and to make distinctions, and this element becomes a series of events. And here we are tempted to deceive ourselves grossly. We allow ourselves to talk as if there existed an actual chain of real events, and as if this chain were somehow moved past us, or we moved along it, and as if, whenever we came to a link, the machinery stopped and we welcomed each new link with our " here " and our " now." Still we do not believe that the rest of the links, which are *not* here and now, do all equally exist, and, if so, we can hardly be quite sure of our chain. And the link, if we must call it so, which is now and here, is no solid substance. If we would but observe it, we should see it itself to be a fluid sequence whose parts offer no resistance to division, and which is both now, and itself without end made up of nows.

Or we seem to think that we sit in a boat, and are carried down the stream of time, and that on the banks there is a row of houses with numbers on the doors. And we get out of the boat, and knock at the door of number 19, and, re-entering the boat, then suddenly find ourselves opposite 20, and, having there done the same, we go on to 21. And, all this while, the firm fixed row of the past and future stretches in a block behind us and before us.

If it really is necessary to have some image, perhaps the following may save us from worse. Let us fancy ourselves in total darkness hung over a stream and looking down on it. The stream has no banks, and its current is covered and filled continuously with floating things. Right under our faces is a bright illuminated spot on the water, which ceaselessly widens and narrows its area, and shows us what passes away on the current. And this spot that is light is our now, our present.

We may go still further and anticipate a little. We have

not only an illuminated place, and the rest of the stream in total darkness. There is a paler light which, both up and down stream, is shed on what comes before and after our now. And this paler light is the offspring of the present. Behind our heads there is something perhaps which reflects the rays from the lit-up now, and throws them more dimly upon past and future. Outside this reflection is utter darkness; within it is gradual increase of brightness, until we reach the illumination immediately below us.

In this image we shall mark two things, if we are wise. It is possible, in the first place, that the light of the present may come from behind us, and what reflects the light may also bestow it. We can not tell that, but what we know is, that our now is the source of the light that falls on the past and future. Through it alone do we know there exists a stream of floating things, and without its reflection past and future would vanish. And there is another point we must not lose sight of. There is a difference between the brightness of the now, and the paler revelation of past and future. But, despite this difference, we see the stream and what floats in it as one. We overcome the difference. And we do so by see-ing the continuity of the element in past, present and future. It is because, through the different illuminations, there are points of connection offered by what floats, in other words, a sameness of content, that the stream and its freightage be-come all one thing to us, and we even forget that most of what we see is not self-subsistent but borrowed and adjecti-val. We shall perceive hereafter that time and space beyond here and now are not strictly existent in the sense in which the present is. They are not given directly but are inferred from the present. And they are so inferred because the now and here, on which the light falls, are the appearance of a reality which for ever transcends them, and upon which resting we go beyond them.

§ 14. But this is to anticipate. The result, which at pres-ent we have wished to make clear, is that the now and here, in which the real appears, are not confined within simply discrete and resting moments. They are any portion of that continuous content with which we come into direct relation. Examination shows that not only at their edges they dissolve themselves over into there and then, but that, even within their limits as first given, they know no repose. Within the here is both here and there; and in the ceaseless process of change in time you may narrow your scrutiny to the smallest focus, but you will find no rest. The appearance is always a process of disappearing, and the duration of the process which we call our present has no fixed length.

It will be seen hereafter that in the above reflections we have not been wandering. Nor will it be long before we return to them, but we must now rediscuss from a better point of view those forms of judgment we before laid down (§ 7).

§ 15. Judgment is not the synthesis of ideas, but the reference of ideal content to reality. From this basis we must now endeavour to interpret the various kinds of judgment we have met with. And, beginning with the singular judgments of § 7, let us take the first division of these, which were called Analytic judgments of sense.

I. The essence of these is to hold only of the now, and not to transcend the given presentation. They may have neither grammatical subject nor copula, or again, on the other hand, may possess one or both.

A. In the judgments that have neither copula nor subject, an idea is referred (a) to the whole sensible reality, or (β) to some part of it.[11]

(a) When we hear the cry of "Wolf," or "Fire," or "Rain," it is impossible to say that we hear no assertion. He who raises the cry is always taken to affirm, to have uttered a sign and to have used it of the real. The practical man would laugh at your distinction that, in exclaiming "Wolf," I can not be a liar, because I use no subject or copula, but that, if I go so far as "This is a wolf," I am thereby committed. Such a plea, we must allow, would be instantly dismissed. In the "Wolf" or "Rain" the subject is the unspecified present environment, and that is qualified by the attribution of the ideal content "Wolf" or "Rain." It is the *external* present that is here the subject. But in some moment of both outward squalor and inward wretchedness, where we turn to one another with the one word "miserable," the subject is here the whole given reality.

Such single words, it may perhaps be said, are really interjections and never predicates. If they were really interjections, we must stubbornly maintain, they could not be the vehicle of truth and falsehood. And a real interjection that is nothing besides, is not so common as some persons suppose. An *habitual* interjection soon gets a meaning, and becomes the sign of a received idea, which, in reference to the content, may be an assertion of truth or falsehood.

But the fact is really beyond all question. You may utter a word which conveys to you, and which you know conveys to others also, a statement about fact. Unless then you are deceiving, you must be judging. And you certainly are judging without any other subject than the whole sensible present.

(β) But this is an extreme case; in nearly all instances but one piece of the present is the real subject. We qualify by our idea some one given aspect. But no subject or copula appears even here. A common understanding, or the pointing of a finger, is all that serves to limit the reference. Of a visible wolf I may predicate the words " asleep " or " running," or in watching a sunset, it is enough for me to say the word " down " or " gone," and every one knows I am judging and affirming. It might be said, no doubt, that the subject is elided, but this would be a mere linguistic prejudice. The genuine subject is not an idea, elided or expressed, but it is the immediate sensible presentation.*

And again it might be said that what we call the predicate is really the subject of an unexpressed existential judgment. But this cardinal mistake will be soon disposed of, when hereafter we deal with that class of judgments (§ 42).

§ 15. B. We pass next to those analytic judgments where a subject is expressed. The ideal content of the predicate is here referred to another idea, which stands as a subject. But in this case, as above, the ultimate subject is no idea, but is the real in presentation. It is this to which the content of both ideas, with their relation, is attributed. The synthesis of the ideal elements is predicated either (a) of the whole, or (β) of a part, of that which appears.

(a) In such judgments as " Now is the time," " It's all so dreary," or " The present is dark," an idea takes the place of

* For a further explanation, vid. Chap. III. § 2.

the unspoken reference of the preceding section. But the subject remains in both cases the same. An idea, it is true, intervenes between the reality and the predicate, and holds the place of immediate subject. But a moment's consideration will assure us that the subject of our assertion is still the presented. The immediate subject is the sign of a reference, either simple or embodying implications, to the whole given reality.

(β) We have a further advance when the presented fact is not the whole sensible environment, but only a part of it. In " There is a wolf," " This is a bird," or " Here is a fire," " there " " this " and " here " are certainly ideas, and stand no doubt for the subject of the judgment: * but, the moment we examine them, we find once more a reference to the reality, not now indefinite and embracing the whole, but still no more than a sign of distinction and indication. If these ideas are the true subject of a judgment, then so is a silent pointing with the finger.

§ 16. There is really no change when we go a step further, and take such judgments as " This bird is yellow," " That stone is falling," " This leaf is dead." The idea, which stands as the grammatical subject, is certainly more than an indefinite refer- ence, more even than a sign of indication. It not only distin- guishes a part from the environment, but it also characterizes and qualifies it. But if, before, the subject we *meant* was not an idea, but was presented fact, so also now does this remain the truth. It is not the bare idea, symbolized by " this bird," of which we go on to affirm the predicate. It is the fact dis- tinguished and qualified by " this bird," to which the adjective " yellow " is really attributed. The genuine subject is the thing as perceived, the content of which our analysis has divided into " this bird " and " yellow," and of which we predi- cate indirectly those ideal elements in their union.

The same account holds throughout all the variety of these analytic judgments. Let us complicate our assertion. " The cow, which is now being milked by the milk-maid, is standing

---

* It sounds, perhaps, rather shocking to call "there" or "here" subjects, but, if the text is understood, I need make no defence. On the nature of the ideas of "this," "now," and "here," we shall find later on a good deal to say.

to the right of the hawthorn tree yonder." In this judgment we have not one thing but several, and more than one statement about their relations. But it is still a part of the presented environment which is actually the subject and the real substantive of which this whole complex is indirectly asserted. If you deny this, then show me where you draw your line, and what point it is in the scale of judgments at which the idea takes the place of the sensible fact, and becomes the true subject. And confine the assertion to mere ideas. Take the ideal elements of a cow and a hawthorn tree and a milk-maid, and combine them ideally in any way you please. Then after they are combined, stand in presence of the fact, and ask yourself if *that* does not enter into your judgment. If, with the fact before you, you begin to reflect, you will find that, if you keep to mere ideas, you remove from the assertion just the thing you mean. In § 20 we shall return to this point, but at present we may deal with a popular error.

§ 17. There is a curious illusion, now widely spread, on the subject of proper names.[12] We find it laid down that a proper name has not got *connotation,* or, to use the more common technical term, it has no *intension.* In ordinary language, it *stands* for something but does not *mean* anything.

If this were true, it would be hard to understand what is signified by such judgments as " John is asleep." There are thinkers indeed, who fear no consequence, and who will tell us that here the *name* John is the subject of the proposition. And against these adversaries I confess I have no heart to enter the lists. They may say what they please without hindrance from me. But, if we are inclined to accept a less heroic solution, and to suppose the *man* John to be the subject of the judgment, then I do not quite see the purpose of the name, if we are not to mean by it anything at all. Why not simply omit it, and, pointing to the man, say the word " asleep "?

" But it stands for the man," I shall hear the reply, " and, even when he is present, it is a *mark* which serves to distinguish him much more clearly than pointing." But that is just what puzzles me. If there *is* an idea conveyed by the name, whenever it is used, then it surely means something, or, in the language which pleases you, it must be " connotative." But if, on the other hand, it conveys *no* idea, it would appear to be some kind of interjection. If you say that, like "this" and "here," it is merely the ideal equivalent of pointing, then at once it assuredly *has* a meaning, but unfortunately that meaning is a vague universal. For anything and everything is "this" and "here." But if you asseverate that it is the ideal counterpart of pointing in particular to John, then you must allow me to doubt if you comprehend what you are saying.

The word "mark" has two senses which perhaps we may confuse. It is something which *may be* made a means of distinction, or something which *has been* made such a means. I suppose, for I can do no more than suppose, that mark is not taken in the former sense, and that our man was not seen to be distinct from other men, because he was found to have the marking John. But, if it is the latter of these senses we adopt, then a name is a mark because it is a sign, and mark and sign are here identical.

Now a sign can not possibly be destitute of meaning. Originally imposed as an *arbitrary* mark, that very process, which makes it a sign and associates it firmly with the thing it signifies, must associate with it also some qualities and characters of that which it stands for. If it did not to some extent get to *mean* the thing, it never could get to *stand* for it at all. And can any one say that a proper name, if you are aware of its designation, brings *no* ideas with it, or that these ideas are mere chance conjunction? What connection, I would ask, would be left between the bare name and the thing it stands for, if every one of these ideas were removed? All would vanish together.

The matter is so plain I do not know how to explain it. The meaning of a sign need of course not be fixed. But is the thing it stands for quite invariable? If the "connotation" is unsteady, does the "denotation" never change? But where the latter is fixed there the former on its side (within limits) is stationary. You may have no idea what "William" connotes, but if so you can hardly know what it stands for. The whole question arises from a simple mistake and misunderstanding.

§ 18. "But after all the name is the sign of an individual, and meanings are generic and universal. Therefore the name can not have any content of which it is the sign." I have purposely put an objection in that form which suggests the conclusion I wish to arrive at. The name of a man is the name of an individual, which remains amid changing particulars, and therefore no judgment about such an individual is wholly analytic. It transcends the given, it becomes synthetic, and with it we pass into the second great division of singular judgments.

Proper names have a meaning which always goes beyond the presentation of the moment. It is not indeed true that such names must stand for objects, which endure through a train of altering perceptions. The unique thing they designate may appear but once, as an event shut up within one presentation. But that object would not be unique, nor proper to its own especial self, if it did not involve a reference to a series from which it was excluded. And mere analysis of sense could never suggest that limiting relation which gives it uniqueness.

And, when we take the proper names of objects which last and which reappear, then the given is transcended in a still higher sense. The meaning of such a name is universal, and its use implies a real universality, an identity which transcends particular moments. For, unless the person were recognized as distinct, he would hardly get a name of his own, and his recognition depends on his remaining the same throughout change of context. We could not recognize anything unless it possessed an attribute, or attributes, which from time to time we are able to identify. The individual remains the same amid that change of appearance which we predicate as its quality. And this implies that it has real identity. Its proper name is the sign of a universal, of an ideal content which actually *is* in the real world.

This assumption, and the practice of giving proper names, may no doubt be indefensible. What concerns us here is that the practice transcends presented reality. In " John is asleep," the ultimate subject can not be the real as it is now given; for " John " implies a continuous existence, not got by mere analysis. We have reached the class of synthetic judgments.

§ 19. II. In this second class of singular judgments (§ 7), we make generally some assertion about that which appears in a space or time that we do not perceive, and we predicate of a presentation something not got by analysis of its content. If I say "There is a garden on the other side of that wall," the judgment is synthetic, for it goes beyond perception. And in "Yesterday was Sunday," "William conquered England," "Next month is June," I certainly do not analyze what is merely given. In synthetic judgments there is always an inference,[13] for an ideal content is connected with the sensible qualities that are given us. In other words we have always a construction, which depends on ideas, and which only indirectly is based on perception (vid. Book II.).

And, this being so, it seems as if now we were unable to proceed. If the subject is the real that appears in perception, how can events in the past and future, or a world in space outside the presentation, and how even can qualities not given to sense be referred to the object and considered as its adjectives? We have already glanced at the solution of this problem, and what we now wish to show is the following. In synthetic judgments the ultimate subject is still the reality. That is not the same as the momentary appearance, and yet synthetic judgments are possible only by being connected with what is given at this very instant. The ideas of past and future events are projected from the base of present perception. It is only in that point that they encounter the reality of which they wish to be true.

"But past and future," the reader may object, "are surely realities." Perhaps they are, but our question is, Given a synthesis of ideas within my mind, how and where am I able to get at a reality to which to attribute them?[14] How am I to judge unless I go to presentation? Let the past and future be as real as you please, but by what device shall I come in contact with them, and refer to them my ideas, unless I advance directly to the given, and to them indirectly? It is possible, I am aware, to assert that past realities are directly presented, and possible also (for all I know) to say the same of the future, and of all the space I am not in contact with, and of all the qualities that I do not perceive. In this way, no doubt, we dispose of the difficulty, and indeed may make a very simple matter of any kind of problem, if indeed any problems any longer will exist.

§ 20. But the persons I write for, and who are not so blessed with easy intuitions, will feel this difficulty, and there may come a temptation to fall back once more on the abandoned heresy and to say, In these synthetic judgments the subject can not possibly be the reality. It must be an idea, and in the junction of ideas must lie the truth. And I think, perhaps, at the cost of repetition, we had better see where this temptation leads us.

When we say " It rained last Tuesday," we mean *this* last Tuesday, and not any other; but, if we keep to ideas, we do not utter our meaning. Nothing in the world that you can do to ideas, no possible torture will get out of them an assertion that is not universal. We can not escape by employing ideas of events in time, particulars as we call them. The event you describe is a single occurrence, but what you say of it will do just as well for any number of events, imaginary or real. If you keep to ideas it is useless to make a reference to the present, and say, " The Tuesday that came before *this* day." For we have seen before (§ 8), that in analytic judgments we are equally helpless. The real is inaccessible by way of ideas. In attempting to become concrete and special, you only succeed in becoming more abstract and wholly indefinite. " This " " now " and " mine " are all universals. And your helpless iteration, " not this but this," will not get your expression any nearer to your meaning. If judgment is only the union of ideas, no judgment is ever about the individual.

§ 21. We must get rid of the erroneous notion (if we have it) that space and time are " principles of individuation," in the sense that a temporal or spatial exclusion will confer uniqueness upon any content. It is an illusion to suppose that, by speaking of " events," we get down to real and solid particulars, and leave the airy region of universal adjectives. For the question arises, What space and time do we really mean, and how can we express it so as not to express what is as much something else? It is true that, in the idea of a series of time or complex of space, uniqueness is in one sense involved; for the parts exclude one another reciprocally. But they do not exclude, unless the series is taken as one continuous whole, and the relations between its members are thus fixed by the unity of the series. Apart from this unity, a point on its recurrence could not be distinguished from the point as first given. And elsewhere we might ask, how far such an unity is itself the negation of mere exclusivity.

But, to pass by this question, it is clear that exclusion within a given series does not carry with it an absolute uniqueness. There is nothing whatever in the idea of a series to hint that there may not be any number of series, internally all indistinguishable from the first. How can you, so long as you are not willing to transcend ideas, determine or in any way characterize your series, so as to get its difference from every possible series within your description? It is idle to say "this," for "this" does not exclude except in *this* sphere, and it is idle to say "my," for it is only in *my* element that yours and mine collide. Outside it they are indifferent, and the expression "my" will not distinguish one world from the other. If we simply attend to the series itself,[15] and, declining to look outside, confine ourselves to the consideration of its character, then all that it contains might be the common property of innumerable subjects, existing and enjoyed in the world of each, a general possession appropriated by none. The mere quality of appearance in space or time can not give singularity.

§ 22. The seeking for judgment in the synthesis of ideas once more has led us where there is no exit. With however little hope we must return to the doctrine, that judgment is the reference of an ideal content to the real which appears in time and space, which is to be encountered directly in presentation, but which can not be limited to a momentary instance. It is not by its quality as a temporal event or phenomenon of space, that the given is unique. It is unique, not because it has a certain character, but because it *is given*. It is by the reference of our series to the real, as it appears directly within this point of contact, or indirectly in the element continuous with this point, that these series become exclusive. We perhaps may be allowed to express this otherwise by saying, it is only the "this" which is real, and ideas will suffice so far as "thisness," but can never give "this." It is perhaps a hard saying, and announces difficulties we shall need both courage and patience to contend with.

§ 23. Everything that is given us, all psychical events, be

they sensations, or images, or reflections, or feelings, or ideas, or emotions—every possible phenomenon that can be present—both is " this " and has " thisness." But its stamp of unique-ness and singularity comes to it from the former and not from the latter. If we distinguish the aspects of existence and content [16] (Chap. I. § 4), and put on the one side *that* anything is, and on the other side *what* it is, then the thisness falls within the content, but the this does not fall there. It is the mere sign of my immediate relation, my direct encounter in sensible presentation with the real world. I will not here ask how " this " is related to existence, how far it holds of the actual fact, and how far only of the mere appearance; whether it *is* or is only *for me*. Apart from that, at least so much is certain, that we find uniqueness in our contact with the real, and that we do not find it anywhere else. The singularity which comes with presentation and is what we call " this," is not a *quality* of that which is given.

But thisness on the other hand does belong to the content, and is the general character of every appearance in space or time. Thisness, if we like, we may call particularity. Every-thing that is given us is given, in the first place, surrounded and immersed in a complex detail of innumerable relations to other phenomena in space or time. In its internal quality we find again a distinction of aspects, which we always can carry to a certain length, and can never be sure we have quite exhausted. And the internal relations of its component ele-ments in space or time are again indefinite. We are never at the end of them. This detail appears to come to us on compulsion; we seem throughout to perceive it as it is, and in no sense to make or even to alter it. And this detail it is which constitutes thisness.*

* The apprehension of this character, it may be objected, takes time, and, if any time for observation is given, the product, for all we know, has been altered. But this difficulty occurs in all observation. We everywhere assume, first, that things are not different unless we can discriminate them. And we assume, in the second place, our ability to distinguish a change in ourselves from a change in the object. We assume that more of the same object is observed, unless we have reason either to suppose that our fancy has wandered away from that object, or that the object itself has undergone a change. I do not here ask if these assumptions are valid. But I may remark in passing,

But such particularity in space or time, such an exclusive nature, after all, is only a *general* character. It falls in the content and does not give the existence. It marks the sort but it misses the thing. In abstraction from the this it is merely ideal, and, apart from the this, ideas as we know can not reach to uniqueness. No amount of thisness which an event possesses will exclude the existence of self-same events in other like series. Such exclusiveness falls all within the description, and that which is only of this description is simply such and can not be this.

In every judgment, where we analyze the given, and where as the subject we place the term "this," it is not an idea which is really the subject. In using "this" we do *use* an idea, and that idea is and must be universal; but what we *mean*, and fail to express, is our reference to the object which is given as unique.

§ 24. And here we encounter an awkward question. The reader possibly may be willing to accept our account of thisness. He may agree that, so far as in our use of the term we mean mere relativity in space or time, in other words particularity, we do not at all go beyond the content. And he may allow the consequence that we have so an idea which is only universal. But in using "this," he may go on to object that we have in addition *another* idea. We have the idea of immediate contact with the presented reality; and it is that idea which is signified by "this," and which qualifies the idea which stands as the subject of our analytic judgment.

We answer, Assuredly, if such were the case, the reference to fact would inevitably and always fall outside the judgment. Once again we should be floating in the air, and never be more than hypothetical. But the question raised need not so be dismissed, for it leads to an interesting if subtle reflection.

that the doubt if in introspection we examine a present, or only a past state of mind, should change its form. It should not take the two as exclusive here, unless it faces the same problem elsewhere. For the observation of external phenomena labours under the identical difficulty. If an internal fact can not possibly be *both* present *and* past, then an external fact must be likewise restricted. The two kinds of observation are not essentially different. External facts are not absolutely fixed, nor are internal facts in absolute flux.[17]

The idea of "this," unlike most ideas, can not be used as a symbol in judgment.

It is certain, in the first place, that we have the idea.[18] Indeed we could scarcely deny that we had it, unless in so doing we actually used it. Beside the idea of exclusion in a series, which is mere thisness, we have also the idea of my immediate sensible relation to reality, and, if so, we have "this." We are able to abstract an idea of presence from that direct presentation which is never absent; and presence, though it does not fall within the content, though we can hardly call it a quality of the appearance, yet is recognized as the same amid a change of content, is separable from it, and makes a difference to it. Thus ideally fixed "this" becomes an universal among other universals.

§ 25. But, despite the likeness, it is very different from an ordinary idea. Ideas, we shall remember, are used as symbols (Chap. I.). In my idea of a " horse " we have (i) the existence of an image in my head, (ii) its whole content, and (iii) its meaning. In other words we may always distinguish (i) that it is, and (ii) what it is, and (iii) what it signifies. The two first of these aspects belong to it as a fact. The third is the universal which does not belong to it, but is thought of without a relation to its existence, and in actual judgment is referred away to some other subject.

The idea of "this" has a striking difference. Distinguished as an aspect of presented reality, when we call it up we take any perception or feeling that is given, and, attending to the aspect of presence within it, recognize that as the meaning of our term. We contemplate it ideally, without any reference to the content of that which is actually before us.

But how shall we fare when, attempting a judgment, we attribute the adjective we have so cut loose to *another* substantive? It is here we are stopped. For any judgment so made we discover must be false. The other fact can not be presented without *ipso facto* altering the given. It degrades our given to one element within a larger presentation, or else it wholly removes it from existence. The given disappears and with itself carries our idea away. We are now unable to predicate the idea, since we no longer possess it, or if we still have it, then what supports it excludes that other fact to which we wish to refer it.

§ 26. To repeat the above, the presented instance of reality is unique. By discrimination we are able to fix that uniqueness in the shape of an idea. We thereupon try to make it the idea of something else. But, for the idea to be true of something else, that something else must be present and unique. We have then either two unique presentations, or one must disappear. If the first one goes, the idea goes with it. If the last one goes, there is now no fact for the idea to be referred to. In either case there can be no judgment. The idea, we see, is not the *true* idea of anything other than its own reality. It is a sign which, *if we judge,* can signify nothing except itself. To be least alone then when most alone, and to enjoy the delights of solitude together, are phrases which have a very good sense; but, taken in their bare and literal meaning, they would exemplify the contradiction we have here before us.

Between the fact and the idea of the " this " in judgment, there can be no practical difference. The idea of this would be falsely used, unless what it marks were actually presented. But in that case we should be trying to use a sign, when we have before us the fact which is signified. We can use the idea so far as to recognize the fact before us as a fact which is " this ; " but such a use does not go beyond the given. It affirms of the subject a predicate without which the subject disappears. It implies discrimination within the fact in which, since the aspect discriminated is not separable from the given, that given with its aspect still remains as the subject. So that the addition of the idea adds nothing to the subject. And if again it were possible to import the idea from the content of *another* fact, the operation would be uncalled for and quite inoperative.

And it is not possible. It would be, as we have seen, the attempt to have before us two unique facts at once. What we mean by " this " is the exclusive focus of presentation which lights up its content, and it is of that singular content that we use the idea. And to treat that idea as a meaning which could be true elsewhere, would be to bring into our focus another content. But since both must be unique, as well as the same, a dilemma arises which we need not draw out.

§ 27. And if "this" be used in a different sense, if it does not mark the presence of the whole sensible detail that falls within the focus; if it is used for that which I specially attend to, the result will be the same. If I make A my object to the exclusion of all others, then this special relation to myself must be false, if used of any other. If applied to A it can not possibly also be applied to B.

"But," it may be said, "I exclusively attend to both. A and B are both elements within the given 'this,' and hence I can predicate 'this' of either. I can transfer the idea, which I find is true of one, and use it as a predicate which is true of the other. And so, after all, the idea of 'this' will be used symbolically." I am afraid of losing the main question in subtleties, but I must reply by pointing out a confusion. Since A and B are both taken together, you can not exclusively deal with each separately. So much is now clear. But, on the other hand, if you take each by itself as a mere element in the "this," then you can not predicate "this" of *either*. Both will *belong to* the "this," but neither will *be* that to which they belong. They will be presented, but neither by itself will *be* the unique presentation. They will not have the "this" in common, but the "this" will have them. It will be their common substantive which will share its own exclusive nature with nothing.

I hardly think that by further intricacies we shall make more clear what can not be made obvious. If anything in the above has been grasped by the reader, I trust to have shown that the use of "this," as a symbol in judgment, is not only impossible, but that, if it existed, it would be wholly nugatory.*

§ 28. We escape from ideas, and from mere universals, by a reference to the real which appears in perception. It is thus

---

* "This" is not the only idea which can never be true as a symbol. I will not ask to what extent "this" means "for me," but what has been said of "this" will hold in the main of "I", "me" and "mine." But there are difficulties here which we can not discuss. We may remark in passing that, for the purposes of metaphysics, it would be necessary to find all those ideas whose content appears not able to be used as the adjective of something else. This would bear on the so-called "ontological proof." For the ideas of uniqueness &c., vid. infr. §§ 38, 39.[19]

our assertion attains the uniqueness without which it would not correspond to the fact. And analytic judgments, it may seem, are thus secured to us. But now, when we return to the question we asked in § 19, and when we pass to judgments that are synthetic, and extend to spaces and times not falling within the radius of direct presentation, we seem at first sight to be no better off. What we have gained, it may now appear, has been at the expense of everything beyond. The series of all our spaces and times will now have to be referred to the one unique point of contact with reality. It is only so that their content can be stamped with the mark of fact. But it seems impossible to establish this relation.

The content of these synthetic assertions we know is universal. It may be true of innumerable other series. This unsubstantial chain, if left to itself, does not touch the ground in any one point. On the other hand, the given source of reality refuses, it seems, to have anything to do with these floating threads. Their symbolic content can not be directly attributed to the presentation, because it is irreconcileable with the content of that. And, if we can not have another presentation, where is the fact in connection with which our universals can attain reality?

§ 29. We must turn in our difficulty to a result we got from a former discussion.[20] We saw that the real, which appears in perception, is not identical with the real just *as* it appears there. If the real must be " this," must encounter us directly, we cannot conclude that the " this " we take is all the real, or that nothing is real beyond the " this." It is impossible, perhaps, to get directly at reality, except in the content of one presentation: we may never see it, so to speak, but through a hole. But what we see of it may make us certain that, beyond this hole, it exists indefinitely. If by " this " we understand unique appearance, then, as " this " was not any part of the content, so neither is it any quality of the real, in such a sense as to shut up the real within that quality. It would belong to metaphysics to discuss this further, and we must here be content with a crude result. The real is what appears to me. The appearance is not generic but unique.

But the real itself is *not* unique, in the sense in which its appearance is so.[21]

The reality we divined to be self-existent, substantial, and individual; but, as it appears within a presentation, it is none of these. The content throughout is infected with relativity, and, adjectival itself, the whole of its elements are also adjectival. Though given as fact every part is given as existing by reference to something else. The mere perpetual disappearance in time of the given appearance is itself the negation of its claim to self-existence. And again, if we take it while it appears, its limits, so to speak, are never secured from the inroads of unreality. In space or in time its outside is made fact solely by relation to what is beyond. Living by relation to what it excludes, it transcends its limits to join another element, and invites that element within its own boundaries. But with edges ragged and wavering, that flow outward and inward unstably, it already is lost. It is adjectival on what is beyond itself. Nor within itself has it any stability. There is no solid point of either time or space. Each atom is merely a collection of atoms, and those atoms again are not things but relations of elements that vanish. And when asked what is ultimate, and can stand as an individual, you can answer nothing.

The real can not be identical with the content that appears in presentation. It for ever transcends it, and gives us a title to make search elsewhere.

§ 30. The endeavour to find the completeness of the real, which we feel can not exist except as an individual, will lead us first to Synthetic judgments of time and space. But, before we proceed, we may pause for a moment, to reflect on the general nature of the attempt. If the reality is self-existent, self-contained, and complete, it needs, one would think, no great effort of reason to perceive that this character is not to be found in a mere series of phenomena. It is one thing to seek the reality *in* that series; it is quite another thing to try to find it *as* the series. A completed series in time or space can not possibly exist.[22] It is the well-known phantasm of the spurious infinite, a useful fiction, it may be, for certain purposes and at certain levels of thought, but none the less a phantasm which, until it is recognized, stops the way of all true philosophic thought. It emerges often in the school of " experience," in its Logic and again in its Hedonistic Ethics, where it begets and will continue to beget chimæras. We shall meet it again in the present chapter, but must return to our search for reality within a series of phenomena, a search not yet degraded to a pursuit of phantasms, but carrying in itself the root of illusion.

§ 31. The real then itself transcends the presentation, and invites us to follow it beyond that which is given. On the other hand, we seem to find contact with reality and to touch ground nowhere, so to speak, outside the presented. How then is a content to be referred to the real, if it can not be referred to the real as perceived? We must answer that the content is referred *indirectly*. It is not attributed to the given as such; but, by establishing its connection with what is presented, it is attributed to the real which appears in that given. Though it is not and can not be found in presentation, it is true because it is predicated of the reality, and unique because it is fixed in relation with immediate perception. The ideal world of spaces beyond the sensible space, and of times not present but past and future, fastens itself on to the actual world by fastening itself to the quality of the immediate this. In a single word continuity of content is taken to show identity of element.

§ 32. But such continuity, and the consequent extension of the "this" as given, depend, like every other ideal construction, on identity.[23] An inference always, we shall see hereafter, stands on the identity of indiscernibles. Sameness of quality proves real sameness (vid. Book II. Part I. Chap. VI.). And the identity here has a double form. (i) In the first place the symbolical content must have "thisness." (ii) In the second place it must share some point with the "this."

To explain, (i) the idea we are to connect with perception must be the idea of something in space or some event in time. It must have the character of particularity, the general idea of indefinite detail and endless relation. We know by this that it is of the same sort as the content of the given. The description of both is one and the same. They both have "thisness," and therefore their element *may be* identical.

(ii) But, so far as we have gone, we still are left in the
world of universals, which *may* or *might* touch the ground in
some place and meet the fact which appears in perception,
but which do not certainly *do* thus. We wish, on the one side,
to pass beyond presented content, and, on the other side, to
connect with this content an ideal series; and we seek for a
link by which to fasten them together.

That link is found by establishing a point which is the
same in both, and is the same because its quality is the same.
The "this" contains a complex of detail, either times or
spaces (or both) in series, which we may call *c. d. e. f.* The
idea, on its side, contains a series of particulars *a. b. c. d.*
The identity of *c. d.* in each extends the perception *c. d. e. f.*
by the ideal spaces or times *a. b.,* and the whole is given
by synthetical construction as a single fact *a. b. c. d. e. f.*
The whole series now is referred to the real, and by the connection with unique presentation, has become a series of events
or spaces, itself unique and the same as no other series in the
world. It is thus by inference that we transcend the given
through synthetic judgments, and our following Books must
explain more clearly the nature of inference, and the enormous
assumption on which it reposes.

§ 33. Mental pathology will afford an illustration. There
are cases where the subject or, if we please, the Ego seems
divided in two. When one self is present the other is absent,
and the memories of either self are distinct. Their pasts and
futures do not ever touch. The explanation that is offered,
and which seems sufficient, will illustrate our theme. It is
because the *present* selves are different, that the past and
future selves are foreign. It is because one system of ideas
has not got a point of connection with the other system, or
has rather some point which excludes the connection,[24] that
the one can never be used to extend ideally a present which
belongs to the other. Some mode of morbid feeling or dis-
eased perception, given now in presentation, links on to itself
the ideas that are grouped by the same characteristic. The
whole ideal region where that colouring fails, may perhaps be
suggested, but can never be fixed in continuous relation with
the present perception.*

* Cf. Lotze, *Mikrokosmus*, I. 371.

§ 34. If we mean by phenomena the things we perceive, or the facts or appearances that are given to us, then the whole of England below our horizon (to say nothing at all of America and Asia), and every event that is past or future are *not* phenomena. They are not perceived facts. They exist in our minds as mere ideas, as the meaning of symbols. A phenomenon, I repeat, that is past or future is a sheer self-contradiction. It is time we thought of giving up our habit of talking about the " series of phenomena," or " thread of perceptions," or Heaven knows what else, as though we held these facts in our hands. One thing or the other. Either a phenomenon may be ideal, the content of a symbol and not even predicated directly of the present perception, or there is no phenomenon but what I here and now perceive. It is idle perhaps to appeal to facts in protest against the philosophy of " analysis " and the school of " experience." It is impossible, I know, to persuade the man who is wedded to these names, that he has failed to earn a legitimate title to neglect the first and to be false to the second. Profuse protestations, and jealousy of the untitled, are services found not too exacting, and which satisfy those who have long ago and cheaply become cool. But, for the sake of others, I will repeat once more. If a fact or event is what is felt or perceived, then a fact that is past is simple nonsense (cf. Book II. Part II. Chap. I.).

Of course, I know, it is easy to say that past events are all really there, and, being there, are remembered; as I presume the future, being all there, is anticipated. But suppose that there *is* a series of facts, both past and future, outside our minds, the question remains, How can they get in? You may say, if you like, They are fond of a change, and walk in and out bodily and meet and converse there. Or an omnipotent Creator has endowed the mind with an extraordinary organ, which perpetually can do what no one understands, and, defying the insidious arts of the analyst, proves by the way the immortality of the soul. Or perhaps you may find it a " final inexplicability." Ultimate facts always are inexplicable, and we must not be put out if they contradict those doctrines they must know to be true. For it is natural for the inexplicable to behave inexplicably.

But perhaps there are readers content to remain on a level with ourselves. If so they will continue to believe the conclusion that facts have brought to us. And that conclusion is that events past and future, and all things not perceived, exist *for us* only as ideal constructions connected, by an inference through identity of quality, with the real that appears in present perception. In what character (if any) these things may really exist *for themselves,* is a question for metaphysics.[25]

§ 35. Synthetic judgments thus cease to be merely adjectival, and they express a series of unique events by indirect reference to the real which appears in unique presentation. They are connected by an inference with the content of this appearance, and so far are directly related to perception. But their ideas are never referred as adjectives to the presentation itself. They are attributed to the reality, which both shows itself there, and extends itself beyond. The content of our perceptions, and the content of our ideal constructions, are both the adjectives of one reality. They are both appearances, which come to us in different ways, but which both (unless our assumptions are false) are valid and true of the real world.

§ 36. Memory of the past, and prediction of the future, are separated clearly from mere imagination.[26] In the former we have the reference to that reality which appears in perception. We have a judgment which is either true or false, because it implies a relation to fact. But imagination is without this reference. The merely imagined, we have seen before (Chap. I. § 14), may be stronger than that which we judge to be true. What we only fancy may have more thisness; it may have more compulsory and particular detail than that which we remember. But what it wants is a point of identity by which to fasten it on to the "this." And without such a link it must fall outside the series.

We generally, it is true, take forcible detail and strong particularity as a sign of fact, and look for its place in the series of events. But, if the place is not found, the imagined fact is never secured to us. The visions of dreams may be very definite, but the content of those visions refuses to link itself to the series of events connected with perception, and so, if we cannot get rid of the ideas, at least we stamp them as mere illusions.

If this were the place for an excursion into psychology, we should find some difficulties and many interesting questions. When once we have referred a content to the real, we generally tend to refer it again. We say that we know it happened at *some* time, though when we can not say. And we might be tempted perhaps to think that such ideas have greater strength or fuller detail than mere imaginations. This would be erroneous. It is not strength or detail which marks these ideas, but something so dim that we can not grasp it. It may be the general idea of reference to the " this," which, repelled by the content of the given " this," transcends it vaguely. It may be, on the other hand, some unconscious element of idea or feeling, which serves to identify in an indefinite way the imagined with fact. For it is a mistake to suppose that these links with reality need be anything explicit. A feeling so obscure that we are not aware of it, and which perhaps no effort of attention would be able to distinguish from its vague totality of consciousness, may serve as the basis by which we separate a truth from a fiction (§ 33). We must remember again that the point of connection may be, so to speak, in our inward selves, and not at all in the outward series. If a falsehood imagined is in the end believed, it is not always because it gains some kind of direct connection with outward fact. In the end it may actually identify itself with the habitual feeling which we have of ourselves. And this common meeting-ground of illusion and truth serves often to confuse them together in our minds. But we can not here further pursue these discussions.

§ 37. To resume, It is not the mere symbolic use of ideas which distinguishes truth from bare imagination. For imagination is not confined to particular images. Just as in perception it is hard to say where inference first appears, and where the analytic judgment becomes synthetic, so in much imagination we shall find the presence of a discursive element. The idea of a circle, we might say and say falsely, was nothing but an image; but the idea of a chiliagon would show us at once that there is a point where our imagery fails. And it is obvious that ideas of abstract relations may be held before the

mind without any judgment. This, however, is a content
which is wholly symbolic, and yet (where no hypothetical
judgment comes in) it is purely imaginary. It is detached
from the existence of the image in our minds, but it is not
attached to another reality.[27]

§ 38. We now perhaps are able to say what it is we mean
by the idea of an individual (or, we had better say, of a particular) fact. We saw the futility of seeking to find this in
the proper names of persons, for what they stand for is never
confined to a single event. The idea of particularity implies
two elements. We must first have a content qualified by
" thisness," and we must add to that content the general idea
of reference to the reality. In other words a particular must
first be represented in a series; this gives us the first element.
But so far we do not get beyond mere " thisness; " the
members are exclusive, within the series, but the whole collection is not unique. To get the complete idea of a particular fact we must make our series, so to speak, *externally*
exclusive as well and thus particular. And we do not do this
till we qualify it by the idea of reference to our unique
reality.

If we *actually* attributed the series to reality, we not only
should have got the idea that we wanted, but also more.[28] We
should have judged that our idea was true in fact. And in
this case we do not wish to go so far. We desire to have the
idea of uniqueness, but not to assert the reality of the idea.

We possess, as we have seen (§ 24) in the idea of " this,"
the idea of immediate contact with the real, and it is this idea
we must add to our series. When we think of the series both
as a whole, and as touching the real in a point of presentation,
we have thought of it then as truly particular. But there we
must stop. For if we went on to judge our idea to be true,
we should have to find it a special place in the unique series
which extends perception. And we saw that to use the idea
of " this " as the symbol of another content in judgment, was
quite impossible. So long, however, as we abstain from judgment, we can attach the aspect of " this " to a content other
than that which is really presented.

This is what we mean by the idea of a particular. There
is a difference when we come to an individual person. Our

idea is there particular, since it has limits within a particular series. But it also involves a real identity persisting throughout a change of events. And so it falls outside the class of mere synthetic judgments.

§ 39. Uniqueness is merely the negative side of the idea of "this." A content is unique when, although of a sort (and that means regarded from the aspect of content) it nevertheless is the same as no other, is the only one there is of its sort. Uniqueness implies the idea of a series,[29] and is then relative or absolute. It is relative when the series, which contains the element which excludes the others, is itself *not* unique. In any universe our fancy constructs, a thing may be unique but only unique within that universe. We have, on the other hand, absolute uniqueness when the series is connected with direct presentation. In that case the relations within the series fix against each other the elements it holds, and nothing can be fact without its appearing in that one series. But the real subject, which, in predicating uniqueness, excludes any other event of the kind, we must remember, is not the particular event as such and taken by itself. It is rather the real which appears in that particular and so excludes others. We have here a negative existential judgment, for the nature of which we must consult our Third Chapter.

§ 40. After meeting many difficulties, some of which, I trust, may have been overcome, we have finished our account of the second division of singular judgments. We must pass to the third, the assertions not confined to an event or a number of events in time (§ 7). But, before we proceed, let us pause for a moment, and, however dangerous the experiment may be, let us try to put before our very eyes a synthetic judgment. Let us call before our mind some series of pictures, like Hogarth's Progress of the harlot or rake; but let us also imagine something beside. One picture in the series must *be* the reality, the actual person in a real room, and on the walls of this real room must be hung the series of earlier and later pictures. By virtue of the sameness in the quality of the man, as he is in the room and is in the pictures, we, neglecting the appearance in particular frames, arrange the whole series as *his* past and future. We transcend in this way the visible room and the presented scene, and view the real life of the person extending itself as a series in time.

But the man in the real room that we see, is body and bones and breath and blood, while his past and future, if we mean by reality a sensible fact, are nothing in the world but glass and wood and paint and canvas. It is the same with all our future and past. The events of memory and of anticipation are facts now in our minds, but they no more *are* the reality they represent than paint and canvas are a throbbing heart. No doubt they stand for reality, and we flatter ourselves that, if they can not be fact, at least they are true. True indeed they may be if truth means a natural and inevitable way of representing the real. But if by their truth we understand more than this; if we say that the reality *is* as it appears in our ideal construction, and that actually there *exists* a series of facts past present and future—I am afraid that truth, if we came to examine it, would change into false-hood. It would be false if measured by the test of perception, and it may be, if tried by another standard, it would be falser still.

§ 41. The life of a man can not be presented in any one scene, and our very illustration has gone farther than we thought. That life is not even a mere succession of serial events, but contains (so we think of it) a something the same, a real identity which appears in all, but which is not any, nor even every, event. We find ourselves brought to the third main class of singular judgments,[30] and are speaking of a sub-ject which is not an event. These judgments are separated into two divisions, according as the individual with which they deal is related to some given period of time, or not to any time in particular.

III. (i) In the history of a man or nation we have a content referred to the real, but to the real as it appears throughout one certain part of that series which is deter-mined by relation to given perception. (ii) In the second division we must place any judgments we make about the Universe or God or the soul, if we take the soul to be eternal.[31] Our ideas are here identified with the real that we find in per-ception, but they do not not attach themselves to any one part of the phenomenal series. It may be said, of course, that such

judgments are illusory. But, as we saw, that conclusion, if
true, could only be established by a metaphysical enquiry we
have no place for. The judgments exist, and logic can do
nothing else but recognize them.

This third and last class of singular judgments is distinct
from the others. Its essence is that its ultimate subject is
not the real, as it appears in the " this " or in any one event
in the series. But the distinction is to a certain extent un-
stable. Just as analytic judgments are always tending to become synthetic, so here it is impossible to separate sharply the
first division of this class from synthetic judgments. On the
one hand the continuity of the element of time strictly excludes a mere serial character.[32] In every judgment about
events we unknowingly are asserting the existence of an identity. On the other hand an individual living in a series seems
naturally to belong to that class of judgment which constructs
a series. Since, however, when an individual is concerned,
we explicitly recognize something real, enduring throughout
the changes of events, it is better perhaps to keep up a distinction which in principle must be admitted to fluctuate. The
example of an individual person took us from analytic to
synthetic judgments. And it has served again to carry us on
further.

§ 42.[33] We have now considered all the three classes of
singular judgments, and have seen in what way they attribute
an idea to the real which appears. We have already anticipated the account to be given of Existential judgments, and
may deal with them rapidly. Confining ourselves here to those
which are affirmative, we can say at once that the subject in
all of them is the ultimate reality, either (a) as it appears in
some part of the series determined by the " this," or (b) as it
underlies the whole series of phenomena. When I say " A
exists," or " A is real," the content A is in truth the predicate.
We use it to qualify existence or reality, in one of the two
senses we have now mentioned.

The enquiry into existential propositions reduces to absurdity the notion that judgment consists in ideas. If we
add to the adjectival idea of A another adjectival idea of
reality, then, failing wholly in reference to fact, we fall

entirely short of judgment. But this is not all. The idea of
reality, like the idea of "this," is not an ordinary symbolic
content, to be used without any regard to its existence.[34] The
idea of what is real, or of that which exists, is found as an
element in that actual reality and actual existence which we
encounter directly. It can not in judgment be removed from
this, and be transplanted away to *another* reality. We have
here the same obstacle which met us before (§§ 25–27). The
idea cannot be predicated of anything except its own reality.
For, to get the idea, you must take it by a distinction from
what is given. If you then make it a predicate of anything
not given, you have a collision, and your judgment disappears.
But if, on the other hand, you predicate it of that which
actually is given, your procedure is idle. Why employ an idea
to assert reality when you have the fact, and when your ideal
synthesis is a mere analysis of this given reality, and attributed in the end to that as subject? "Real" is clearly the
adjective of "reality," and we know no reality but what appears in presentation. The idea then, to be true, must be
true of that reality. But, if so, we must have the subject
before us in the shape of fact, and, if we did not, the idea
would at once become false. For a more detailed discussion
we may refer to §§ 25–27.

Nor would it repay us here to examine the somewhat
surprising view which Herbart has advocated (vid. § 75).
Our enquiries in this chapter should have prepared us for the
result that the ultimate subject is never an idea, and that the
idea of existence is never a true predicate. The subject, in
the end, is always reality, which is qualified by adjectives of
ideal content.

§ 43. We cannot say there is a class of existential judgments, for all singular judgments have by this time been shown
to be existential. And, with this conclusion, we may pass beyond them to another branch of affirmative judgments. In
these we no longer have to do with any particular facts or
in any sense with separate individuals. They are universal in
the sense of transcending what is singular. They are not
"concrete" but "abstract," since, leaving things, they assert
about qualities, alone or in synthesis. In this respect, we may
remark in passing, there is no real difference between the

"general" and the "abstract;" for, taken in comparison with
the particular thing,[35] the general idea is a mere abstraction.

§ 44. We have reached the common type of universal
judgment; and the point in this which we notice at once, is
that every such judgment is concerned with adjectivals.[36]
They assert a connection between elements of content, and
say nothing about the place of those elements in the series of
events. In "Equilaterial triangles are equiangular" all I affirm
is that with one set of qualities you will have the other set,
but I make no assertion about where and when. And "Mammals are warm-blooded" does not tell me anything about this
or that mammal. It merely assures me that, finding one attribute, I shall find the other.

The fact that is asserted in an abstract judgment is not
the existence of the subject or predicate (§ 6), but simply the
connection between the two. And this connection rests on a
supposal. The abstract universal, "A is B," means no more
than "given A, in that case B," or "if A, then B." In short,
such judgments are always hypothetical and can never be
categorical. And the proper terms by which to introduce them
are "given," or "if," or "whenever," or "where," or "any,"
or "whatever." We should beware of "all."

§ 45. For the use of "all," we have seen above (§ 6), is
most misleading and dangerous. It encourages that tendency
to understand the universal in the sense of a collection,[37] which
has led to so many mistaken consequences. We shall glance
elsewhere at that extraordinary teaching on the subject of
quantity, in which the traditional logic delights. And we shall
see hereafter, when we come to inference, the absurd incom-
petence of the *dictum de omni*. For our present purpose we
need criticize no further the attempt to understand the "all"
collectively. Even if that use were justifiable in itself, it
would be irrelevant; for a judgment where "all" means a
real collection of actual cases,[38] belongs to a class we have already disposed of. If "all" signifies a number of individual
facts, the judgment is concerned with actual particulars. And
so it obviously is but one form of the singular judgment.
"All A is B," will be an abbreviated method of setting forth
that this A is B, and that A is B, and the other A is B, and

so on until the lot is exhausted. Such judgments fall clearly under the head of singular.

But, when this class is banished to the preceding category, have we any universal judgments left us? We can not doubt that; for there are judgments which do not assert the existence of particular cases. We come at once upon the judgments that connect adjectival elements, and that say nothing about the series of phenomena. These abstract universals are always hypothetical and never categorical.*

§ 46. At this point we must pause to encounter an objection. " The distinction," we may be told, " between categorical and hypothetical is really illusory. Hypothetical judgments can all be reduced to, and in the end *are* nothing but, a kind of categorical." If this were well founded, it would certainly occasion us serious difficulty. But I do not think we need much disturb ourselves.

" If A is B it is C," we may be told, " is equivalent to The instances or cases of A that are B are also C, and this is surely a categorical judgment." I answer, if " the cases of A that are B " means the existing cases of A B, and no others, then the judgment no doubt is categorical, but it is not an abstract universal. It is merely collective, and it most certainly does *not* mean what we meant by our hypothetical judgment. " If butter is held to the fire it melts " is no assertion about mere existing pats of butter. And when it is reduced to the form, " All cases of the holding of butter, &c.," it does not become any more categorical. " All cases " means here " *Suppose* any case."

Indeed, if we steadily keep in view the difference between a simple assertion about fact and an assertion on the strength of and about a supposition, we may perhaps be puzzled, but we are not likely to be led far astray by these elementary mistakes.

§ 47. And with this remark I could leave the matter. But

---

* The extensional theory of judgment and reasoning is dealt with elsewhere (Chap. VI. and Book II. Part II. Chap. IV.). We may here remark that, taking " A is B " to mean " the things that are A are the things that are B," the judgment must be singular, if an existing set of things be denoted, and will be universal and abstract if possible things are included as well.[39]

it is perhaps worth while, by another instance, to illustrate
the futility of this attempt to turn hypothetical into categorical
judgments.   J. S. Mill in his *Logic* (I. 4, § 3) approaches the
subject with an air of easy superiority.   " A conditional
proposition is a proposition concerning a proposition."

" What is asserted is not the truth of either of the propositions but the inferribility of the one from the other."   " If A is
B, C is D, is found to be an abbreviation of the following :
' The proposition C is D, is a legitimate inference from the
proposition A is B.' "

How this doctrine is connected with Mill's other views as to
the import of propositions, an expert in Mill-philology no
doubt could inform us.   But, left to ourselves, we can only
conjecture the doctrine he here intended to teach.   (i) If he
really meant " *inferribility,*" then *cadit quæstio.*   For at once
the statement is not about what is, but what may be or might
be.   It is not simply about existing propositions, but clearly
involves a supposal of some kind, and is therefore *not* reduced
to categorical form.   It is still *Suppose* you have got AB, *then*
you may go legitimately to CD.   (ii) But no doubt there is
more than this verbal quibble.   He tells us that one *is* an
inference from the other.   Does this mean (*a*) that both are
actually asserted, and that I further assert that I really have
argued to the second from the first?   Surely not that ; but then
what else?   (*b*) Can it mean that, without asserting either
proposition, I hold them in my mind, and affirm their connection?   It *may* mean this.   But then this process of taking
up a statement without believing it, and of developing its consequences, is in fact nothing else than a supposition.   The
connection asserted is not between realities, and the proposition is still hypothetical.   (iii) But the extraordinary illustrations towards the end of the section point to another
interpretation ; " The subject and predicate are names of propositions."   Without, however, attempting the hopeless task of
understanding, we may perhaps state the issue in the form
of a dilemma.   Either (*a*) one proposition, in the sense of
a little heap of words, does, as a particular event in my head,
now follow another such heap ; or (*b*) it *would* follow, *if*
the other were there.   The second alternative is of course still
hypothetical.   In the former at last we have got to something

categorical, but nothing to which a hypothetical judgment (or indeed any judgment) could possibly be reduced. It would be an error too gross to merit refutation.

Whatever else may be the meaning of the writer, we after all may remain sure of this. Either the categorical judgment, to which he professes to reduce the hypothetical, is *not* its equivalent; or else it contains, under some flimsy veil of verbal ambiguity, a supposition which is the condition of the judgment.

§ 48. Such universal judgments are all hypothetical, and with this conclusion we are landed once more in our former difficulties (§ 6). Judgment, we saw, always meant to be true, and truth must mean to be true of fact. But here we encounter judgments which seem not to be about fact. For a hypothetical judgment must deal with a supposal. It appears to assert a necessary connection, which holds between ideas within my head but not outside it. But, if so, it can not be a judgment at all; while on the other hand it plainly does assert and can be true or false.

We are not able to rest in this conclusion, and yet we can not take back our premises. Let us then try to look more closely at the problem, and ask more narrowly what is involved in these judgments. And, in the first place, we can not expect to succeed until we know what a supposal is.

A supposition, in the first place, is known to be ideal, and known perhaps to diverge from fact. At a low stage of mind, where everything is fact (cf. Chap. I.), it could not exist. For the supposed must be known as an ideal content, and, in addition, it has to be retained before the mind without a judgment. It is not referred as an adjective, either positively or negatively, to the real. In other words reality is not qualified either by the attribution or the exclusion of it. But though it does not judge, a supposition is intellectual, for (as such) it excludes desire and emotion. And again it is more than mere imagination, for it is fixed by attention and preserves, or should preserve, its identity of content (vid. Book III. Chap, III. §§ 23, 24). It certainly is all this, and yet this is not all. For to think of a chimæra is not quite the same thing as to *suppose* a chimæra.

A supposition means thinking for a particular end, and in

a special way. It is not a mere attending to a certain meaning,
or an analysis of its elements. It has a reference to the real
world, and it involves a desire to see what happens. We may
illustrate perhaps from other usages. " Say it is so for argument's sake," " Treat it as this and then you will see," are
much the same as, " Suppose it to be so." A supposal is, in
short, an ideal experiment.[40] It is the application of a content to the real, with a view to see what the consequence is,
and with a tacit reservation that no actual judgment has taken
place. The supposed is treated as if it were real, in order to see
how the real behaves when qualified thus in a certain
manner.

You might say it is the adding the idea of existence to a
given thought, while you abstain from judgment. But that I
do not think would be satisfactory. For it is not the mere
idea of existence that is used. What we use is the real that is
always in immediate contact with our minds, and which in a
variety of judgments we already have qualified by a certain
content. And it is to this that we bring up another idea, in
order to see what result will come of it.

§. 49. So far there is neither truth nor falsehood, for we
have not judged. The operation, we may say, is so far
" subjective." It is all our own doing, and all of it holds
inside our heads, and not at all outside. The real is not
qualified by the attribute we apply to it. But, so soon as we
judge, we have truth or falsehood, and the real is at once
concerned in the matter. The connection of the consequence,
of the " then " with the " if," of the result of our experiment
with its conditions, is the fact that is asserted, and that is true
or false of the reality itself.

But the question is *how*. You do not assert the existence
of the ideal content you suppose, and you do not assert the
existence of the consequence. And you can not assert the
existence of the connection, for how can a connection remain
as a fact when no facts are connected? " If you only had
been silent you would have passed for a philosopher." But
you were not silent, you were not thought a philosopher, and
one was not, and could not possibly *be,* a result of the other.
If the real must be qualified by the connection of the two, it
seems that it will not be qualified at all. Neither condition,

nor result, nor relation can be ascribed to it; and yet we *must* ascribe something, for we judge. But what can it be?

§ 50. When I go to a man with a fictitious case, and lay before him a question of conduct, and when he replies to me, " I should act in this way, and not in the other way," I may come from him with some knowledge of fact. But the fact is not the invented position, nor yet the hypothetical course of action, nor the imaginary relation between the two. The fact is the quality in the man's disposition.[41] It has answered to a trial in a certain way. But the test was a fiction, and the answer is no fact, and the man is not qualified by one or the other. It is *his* latent character that is disclosed by the experiment.

It is so with all hypothetical judgment. The fact that is affirmed as an adjective of the real, and on which depends the truth or falsehood, does not explicitly appear in the judgment. Neither conditions nor result of the ideal experiment are taken to be true. What is affirmed is the mere ground of the connection; not the actual existing behaviour of the real, but a latent quality of its disposition, a quality which has appeared in the experiment,[42] but the existence of which does not depend on that experiment. " If you had not destroyed our barometer, it would now forewarn us." In this judgment we assert the existence in reality of such circumstances, and such a general law of nature, as would, *if we suppose* some conditions present, produce a certain result. But assuredly those conditions and their result are not predicated, nor do we even hint that they are real. They themselves and their connection are both impossible. It is the diminution of pressure and the law of its effect, which we affirm of the actual world before us. And of course that law is resolvable further (§ 52).

§ 51. In all judgment the truth seems none of our making.[43] We perhaps need not judge, but, if we judge, we lose all our liberty. In our relation to the real we feel under compulsion (§ 4). In a categoric judgment the elements themselves are not dependent on our choice. Whatever we may think or say, they exist. But, in a hypothetic judgment, there is no compulsion as regards the elements. The second, indeed, depends on the first, but the first is arbitrary. It depends on my choice. I may apply it to the real, or not, as I please; and I am free to withdraw the application I have made. And, when the condition goes, the result goes too. The compulsion extends no further than the connection, and yet it does not extend to the connection as such. The relation of the elements in a hypothetical judgment is not an actual attribute of the real, for that relation itself is arbitrary. It need not be true outside the experiment. The fact which existed before the experiment, and remains true after it, and in no way depends on it, is neither the elements, nor the relation between them, but it is a quality. It is the ground of the sequence that *is* true of the real, and it is this ground which exerts compulsion.

§ 52. This quality of the real is not explicit in the judgment, and, in respect of that judgment, is occult or latent. We know it is there because of its effects, but we are not able to say what it is. We can not even tell, without further enquiry, that it is not the same as what we have asserted in another judgment, the elements of which, and also their relation, were very [44] different (cf. Chap. III. § 19). And, when we push the investigation further, and ask, Are these qualities, that thus seem to lie at the base of our judgments, *altogether* latent, or only latent each in respect of its peculiar judgment, then we get at once into difficult questions. It is certain on the one hand that we can find the grounds of many such judgments, which thus have *relatively* become explicit. But this only serves to bring us nearer to the doubt, whether in the end they have ceased to be latent. Do we ever get to a ground of judgment which we can truly ascribe to the real as its quality? Or are we left with ultimate judgments, which are certainly true, but neither the elements nor relations of which are true of reality? Must we say, in the end, that the quality, which we know is the base of our synthesis, remains in other ways altogether unknown and is finally occult? We seem here to be asking, in another form, for the limits of explanation, and it would be the task of metaphysics to pursue an enquiry which must here be broken off.[45]

§ 53. We have seen that, what hypothetical judgments assert, is simply the quality which is the ground of the consequence. And all abstract universals, we have seen, are hypothetical. It may here be asked, Are the two things one? Are all hypothetical judgments thus universal?

This might for a moment appear to be doubtful, since the real, to which application is made, is at times an individual. And for the purposes of this, and the following section, I will give some examples; "If God is just the wicked will be punished," "Had I a toothache I should be wretched," "If there were a candle in this room it would be light," "If it is now six o'clock we shall have dinner in an hour," "If this man has taken that dose, he will be dead in twenty minutes." It may surprise some readers to hear that these judgments are as universal as "All men are mortal:" but I think we shall find that such is the case.[46]

In the first place it is certain that in none of these judgments is the subject taken to be actually real. We do not say above that a just God exists, or that I have a toothache; we only suppose it. The subject is supposed, and, if we consider further, we shall find that subject is nothing more than an ideal content, and that what is asserted is not anything beside a connection of adjectives. The "that," the "this," the "I," the "now," do not really pass into the supposition. They are the point of reality to which we apply our ideal experiment, but they themselves are in no case *supposed*. More or less of their content is used in the hypothesis, and passes into the subject. But, apart from themselves, their content can not possibly be called individual.

§ 54. This would hardly be doubtful, were it not for the ambiguity of all these assertions, a point to which we should carefully attend. "If he had murdered he would have been hanged," may perhaps assert nothing but the *general* connection of hanging with murder, and the "he" is irrelevant. But "if God is just the wicked will be punished," may perhaps not say that punishment would follow from *any* justice, but only from justice that is qualified by omnipotence. On the other hand, when you say "If this man has taken that dose, &c.," you do not tell me if his speedy death would happen because the dose would poison any one, or would only poison such a man as he is, or would not even poison such a kind of man, unless under present special conditions. And the other examples would all entangle us in similar ambiguities. The supposition is not made evident, and reflection convinces us that, supposing we know the subject of the judgment, at all events we do not display our knowledge.

§ 55. And since this is so, since the adjectival content is not made explicit, since all we have is an indefinite reference to this or that case, we fall into the mistake of thinking it is the particular we have to deal with. But our real assertion, when we come to analyze it, never takes in the " that," or the " now," or the " this." It is always the content about which we assert. But, because we are not clear what that content is, and because we know it is to be found *in* the individual as supposed, we fire, so to speak, a charge of shot instead of a bullet, and take the individual as the point of reality to which our supposition is to be confined. In this way we give rise to the erroneous idea that the reality itself passes into the supposal. The fact, as we have seen, is that some of the content either is or makes part of the adjectival condition about which we assert. But, because that content has not been analyzed, we go to the individual to get it in the lump. The real judgment is concerned with nothing but the individual's *qualities,* and asserts no more than a connection of adjectives. In every case it is strictly universal as well as hypothetical.

§ 56. We have found, thus far, that all abstract judgments are hypothetical, and in this connection we have endeavoured to show what a supposition is, and to lay bare that occult affirmation as to the real, which is made in every hypothetical judgment. Singular judgments we have already discussed, and we found that, be they analytic or synthetic, they all at first sight seem categorical. They do not merely attribute to the real a latent quality, which manifests itself in an unreal relation, but they qualify the real by the actual content which appears in the judgment. It is not the mere connection, but the very elements which they declare to exist.

We have still remaining another kind of judgment (§ 7), but, before we proceed, it is better to consider the result we have arrived at. That result perhaps may call for revision, and it is possible that the claim of the singular judgment to a categoric position may not maintain itself.

CHAPTER II (*Continued*)

§ 57. What is the position in which we now find ourselves? We began with the presumption that a judgment,
if true, must be true of reality. On the other hand we found
that every abstract universal judgment was but hypothetical.
We have endeavoured to reconcile these conflicting views by
showing in what way, and to what extent, a conditional judgment asserts of the fact. But singular judgments stand apart,
and have claimed to be wholly categorical, and true of the
reality; and hence they demand a position above that given
to universal judgments. We must now scrutinize this pre-
tension. We must still defer all notice of those individual
judgments which transcend the series of events in time. Confining ourselves to judgments about the phenomenal series, let
us proceed to ask, Are they categorical? Do they truly and
indeed rank higher, and closer to the real world, than those
universal judgments which we found were hypothetical? We
shall perhaps do well to prepare our minds for an unwelcome
conclusion.

In passing from the singular to the universal judgment, we
seem to have been passing away from reality. Instead of a
series of actual phenomena connected with the point of present
perception, we have but a junction of mere adjectivals, the
existence of which we do not venture to affirm. In the one
case we have what seem solid facts; in the other we have nothing but a latent quality, the mere name of which makes us
feel uneasy. We have not quite lost our hold of the real, but
we seem to have left it a long way off. We keep our connection by an impalpable thread with a veiled and somewhat
ambiguous object.

But our thoughts may perhaps take a different colour, if
we look around us in the region we have come to. However
strange it may seem to us at first, yet our journey towards
shadows and away from the facts has brought us at last to

the world of science. The end of science, we all have been taught, is the discovery of *laws;* and a law is nothing but a hypothetical judgment. It is a proposition which asserts a synthesis of adjectivals. It is universal and abstract. And it does not assert the existence of either of the elements it connects.[47] It may *imply* this (§ 6), but such an implication is not essential. In mathematics, for instance, the truth of our statement is absolutely independent of the existence of either subject or predicate. In physics or chemistry the truth does not depend on the actual existence at the present moment of the elements and their relation. If it did so, the law might be true at one instant and false at the next. When the physiologist, again, tells us that strychnine has a certain effect on nerve-centres, he does not wait to enunciate his law until he is sure that some dose of strychnine is operating in the world; nor does he hasten to recall it as soon as he has lost that assurance. It would be no advantage to dwell upon this point. It may be regarded now as a certain result, that the strict expression for all universal laws must begin with an " if," and go on with a " then."

§ 58. And from this we may draw a certain presumption. If the singular judgment is nearer the fact, and if, in leaving it, we have actually receded from reality, yet at least in science that is not felt to be the case. And there is another presumption which may help to strengthen us. In common life we all experience the tendency to pass from one single case to some other instance. We take what is true at one time and place to be always true at all times and places. We generalize from a single example. We may deplore this tendency as an ineradicable vice of the unphilosophic mind, or we may recognize it as the inevitable condition of all experience, and the *sine qua non* of every possible inference (vid. Book II.). But in either case, let us recognize it or deplore it, we still do not feel the passage we have made as an *attempt* to go from the stronger to the weaker, from that which is more true to that which is less. And yet, without doubt, it is a transition away from the individual to the universal and hypothetical.

§ 59. But a matter of this sort is not settled by presumptions. There are prejudices, it may be, that operate both ways. And we may be told, on behalf of the singular judg-

ment, that it is *the fact* that these judgments are categorical.
For they do assert the actual existence of their adjectival content, and, attributing to the real an explicit quality, they are
truer than any hypothetical judgment, if indeed they are not
the *only* true judgments. Such, we take it, is the claim of the
singular judgment, and it can not be denied that its claim in
one respect is very well founded. It does *assert* the existence
of its content, and does affirm directly of the real. But the
answer we must make is that, although it does so assert and
affirm, yet, when we leave the popular view and look more
closely at the truth of things, the assertion and affirmation
which it makes are *false,* and the claim it puts forward rests
on a mistake. We must subject the pretensions of the singular judgment to an examination which we think may prove
fatal.[48]

§ 60. We need spend no time on the synthetic judgment.
In transcending what is given by actual perception, we without
any doubt make use of an inference. A synthesis of adjectives is connected with the present by virtue of the identity
of a point of content. By itself this synthesis is merely universal, and is therefore hypothetical. It becomes categoric
solely by relation to that which is given, and hence the whole
weight of the assertion rests on the analytic judgment. If that
is saved, it will then be time to discuss its extension; but if,
on the other hand, the analytic be lost, it carries with it the
synthetic judgment.

§ 61. Let us turn at once to the judgments which assert
within what is given in present perception. These seem
categorical because they content themselves with the analysis of
the given, and predicate of the real nothing but a content
that is directly presented. And hence it appears that the elements of these judgments must actually exist. An ideal content is attributed to the real, which that very real does now
present to me. I am sure that nothing else is attributed. I
am sure that I do not make any inference, and that I do not
generalize. And how then can my assertion fail to be true?
How, if true, can it fail to be categorical?

We maintain, on the other hand, that analytic judgments
of sense are all false. There are more ways than one of
saying the thing that is not true. It is not always necessary to

go beyond the facts. It is often more than enough to come short of them. And it is precisely this coming short of the fact, and stating a part as if it were the whole, which makes the falseness of the analytic judgment.

§ 62. The fact, which is given us, is the total complex of qualities and relations which appear to sense. But what we assert of this given fact is, and can be, nothing but an ideal content. And it is evident at once that the idea we use can not possibly exhaust the full particulars of what we have before us. A description, we all know, can not ever reach to a complete account of the manifold shades, and the sensuous wealth of one entire moment of direct presentation. As soon as we judge, we are forced to analyze, and forced to distinguish. We must separate some elements of the given from others. We sunder and divide what appears to us as a sensible whole. It is never more than an arbitrary selection which goes into the judgment. We say " There is a wolf," or " This tree is green ; " but such poor abstractions, such mere bare meanings, are much less than the wolf and the tree which we see; and they fall even more short of the full particulars, the mass of inward and outward setting, from which we separate the wolf and the tree. If the real as it appears is $X = a\,b\,c\,d\,e\,f\,g\,h,$ then our judgment is nothing but $X = a,$ or $X = a\text{–}b.$ But $a\text{–}b$ by itself has never been given, and is not what appears. It was *in* the fact and we have taken it out. It was *of* the fact and we have given it independence. We have separated, divided, abridged, dissected, we have mutilated the given.* And we have done this arbitrarily: we have selected what we chose. But, if this is so, and if every analytic judgment must inevitably so alter the fact, how can it any longer lay claim to truth?

§ 63. No doubt we shall be told, " This is idle subtlety. The judgment does not copy the whole perception, but why should it do so? What it does say, and does reproduce, at all events is there. Fact is fact, and given is given. They do not cease to be such because something beside themselves exists. To maintain that ' There is a wolf ' is false, because an abstract wolf is not given entirely by itself, is preposterous and ridiculous."

* Cf. here Lotze's admirable chapter, *Logik,* II. VIII.

And I am afraid that with some readers this will end the
discussion. But to those who are willing to venture further,
I would suggest as encouragement that a thing may seem
ludicrous, not because it is at all absurd in itself, but because
it conflicts with hardened prejudice. And it is a prejudice of
this kind that we have now encountered.

§ 64. It is a very common and most ruinous superstition
to suppose that analysis is no alteration, and that, whenever
we distinguish, we have at once to do with divisible existence.
It is an immense assumption to conclude, when a fact comes
to us as a whole, that some parts of it may exist without any
sort of regard for the rest. Such naive assurance of the
outward reality of all mental distinctions, such touching confidence in the crudest identity of thought and existence, is
worthy of the school which so loudly appeals to the name of
Experience. Boldly stated by Hume (cf. Book II. II. Chap. I.
§ 5), this cardinal principle of error and delusion has passed
into the traditional practice of the school, and is believed too
deeply to be discussed or now recognized. The protestations of fidelity to fact have been somewhat obtrusive, but
self-righteous innocence and blatant virtue have served once
more here to cover the commission of the decried offence in
its deadliest form. If it is true in any sense (and I will not
deny it) that thought in the end is the measure of things, yet
at least this is false, that the divisions we make within a
whole all answer to elements whose existence does *not* depend
on the rest. It is wholly unjustifiable to take up a complex,
to do any work we please upon it by analysis, and then simply
predicate as an adjective of the given these results of our abstraction. These products were never there as such, and in
saying, as we do, that as such they are there, we falsify the
fact. You can not always apply in actual experience that
coarse notion of the whole as the sum of its parts into which
the school of " experience " so delights to torture phenomena.
If it is wrong in physiology to predicate the results, that are
reached by dissection, simply and as such of the living
body, it is here infinitely more wrong. The whole that is
given us is a continuous mass of perception and feeling; and
to say of this whole, that any one element would be what it is
there, when apart from the rest, is a very grave assertion. We

might have supposed it not quite self-evident, and that it was possible to deny it without open absurdity.*

§ 65. I should like to digress so far as to adduce two examples of error, which follow from the mistake we are now considering. When we ask " What is the *composition* of Mind," we break up that state, which comes to us as a whole, into units of feeling. But since it is clear that these units by themselves are not all the " composition," we are forced to recognize the existence of relations. But this does not stagger us. We push on with the conceptions we have brought to the work, and which of course can not be false, and we say, Oh yes, we have here some more units, naturally not quite the same as the others, and—*voilà tout*. But when a sceptical reader, whose mind has been warped by a different education, attempts to form an idea of what is meant, he is somewhat at a loss. If units have to exist together, they must stand in relation to one another; and, if these relations are also units, it would seem that the second class must also stand in relation to the first. If A and B are feelings, and if C their relation is another feeling, you must either suppose that component parts can exist without standing in relation with one another, or else that there is a *fresh* relation between C and AB. Let this be D, and once more we are launched on the infinite process of finding a relation between D and C–AB; and so on for ever. If relations are facts that exist *between* facts, then what comes *between* the relations and the other facts? The real truth is that the units on one side, and on the other side the relation existing between them, are nothing actual.[50] They are fictions of the mind, mere distinctions within a single reality, which a common delusion erroneonsly takes for independent facts. If we believe the assurance of a distinguished Professor,† this burning faith in the absurd and the impossible, which was once the privilege and the boast of theology, can now not be acquired anywhere outside the sacred precincts of the laboratory. I am afraid it is difficult to adopt such an optimistic conclusion.

§ 66. And perhaps I may be pardoned if, by another illus-

---

* For the general validity of Analysis and Abstraction see Book III.[49]

† Vid. Huxley, *Hume,* pp. 52, 69.

tration, I venture to show how entirely the mind which is
purified by science can think in accordance with orthodox
Christianity.[51] In the religious consciousness God and Man
are elements that are given to us in connection. But, reflect-
ing on experience, we make distinctions, and proceed as above
to harden these results of analysis into units. We thus have
God as an unit on one side, and Man as an unit on the other:
and then we are puzzled about their relation. The relation
of course must be *another* unit, and we go on to find that we
should like something *else,* to mediate once more, and go between this product and what we had at first. We fall at
once into the infinite process, and, having taken up with poly-
theism, the length we go is not a matter of principle.

§ 67. To return to the analytic judgment. When I say
" There is a wolf," the real fact is a particular wolf, not like
any other, in relation to this particular environment and to
my internal self, which is present in a particular condition of
feeling emotion and thought. Again, when I say " I have a
toothache," the fact once more is a particular ache in a certain
tooth, together with all my perceptions and feelings at that
given moment. The question is, when I take in my judgment one fragment of the whole, have I got the right to
predicate this of the real, and to assert " It, *as it is,* is a fact of
sense "? Now I am not urging that the analytic judgment is
in *no* sense true. I am saying that, if you take it as asserting
the existence of its content as given fact, your procedure is
unwarranted. And I ask, on what principle do you claim the
right of selecting what you please from the presented whole
and treating that fragment as an actual quality? It certainly
does not exist by itself, and how do you know that, when put
by itself, it *could* be a quality of *this* reality? The sensible
phenomenon is what it is, and is all that it is; and anything
less than itself must surely be something *else.* A fraction of
the truth, here as often elsewhere, becomes entire falsehood,
because it is used to qualify the whole.

§ 68. The analytic judgment is not true *per se*. It can not
stand by itself. Asserting, as it does, of the particular
presentation, it must always suppose a further content, which
falls outside that fraction it affirms. What it says is true, if

true at all, because of something else. The fact it states is really fact only in relation to the rest of the context, and only because of the rest of that context. It is not true except under that condition. So we have a judgment which is really conditioned, and which is false if you take it as categorical. To make it both categorical and true, you must get the condition inside the judgment. You must take up the given as it really appears, without omission, unaltered, and unmutilated. And this is impossible.

§ 69. For ideas are not adequate to sensible perception, and, beyond this obstacle, there are further difficulties.[52] The real, which appears within the given, can not possibly be confined to it. Within the limit of its outer edges its character gives rise to the infinite process in space and time. Seeking there for the simple, at the end of our search we still are confronted by the composite and relative. And the outer edges themselves are fluent. They pass for ever in time and space into that which is outside them. It is true that the actual light we see falls only upon a limited area; but the continuity of the element, the integrity of the context, forbids us to say that this illuminated section by itself is real. The reference of the content to something other than itself lies deep within its internal nature. It proclaims itself to be adjectival, to be relative to the outside; and we violate its essence if we try to assert it as having existence entirely in its own right. Space and time have been said to be "principles of individuation." It would be truer to say they are principles of relativity. They extend the real just as much as they confine it.

I do not mean that past and future *are* actually given, and that they come within the circle of presentation. I mean that, *although* they can not be given, the given would be destroyed by their absence. If real with them, it would not be given; and, given without them, it is for ever incomplete and therefore unreal. The presented content is, in short, not compatible with its own presentation. It involves a contradiction, and might at once on that ground be declared to be unreal. But it is better here to allow it free course, and to suffer it to develope by an impossible consequence its inherent unsoundness.

§ 70. We saw that you can not ascribe to the real one part of what is given in present perception. And now we must go further. Even if you could predicate the whole present content, yet still you would fail unless you asserted also both the past and the future. You can not assume (or I, at least, do not know your right to assume) that the present exists independent of the past, and that, taking up one fragment of the whole extension, you may treat this part as self-subsistent, as something that owes nothing to its connection with the rest. If your judgment is to be true as well as categorical, you must get the conditions entirely within it. And here the conditions are the whole extent of spaces and times which are required to make the given complete. The difficulty is insuperable. It is not merely that ideas can not copy facts of sense. It is not merely that our understandings are limited, that we do not know the whole of the series, and that our powers are inadequate to apprehend so large an object. No possible mind could represent to itself the completed series of space and time; since, for that to happen, the infinite process must have come to an end, and be realized in a finite result. And this can not be. It is not merely inconceivable psychologically; it is metaphysically impossible.

§ 71. Our analytical judgments are hence all either false or conditioned. "But *conditioned,*" I may be told, " is a doubtful phrase. After all it is not the same as hypothetical. A thing is conditio*nal* on account of a supposal, but on the other hand it is conditio*ned* by a fact. We have here the difference between ' if ' and ' because.' [53] When a statement is true in consequence of the truth of another statement, they both are categorical." I quite admit the importance of the distinction, and must recur to it hereafter (Chap. VII. § 10). But I deny its relevancy for our present purpose.

The objection rests on the following contention. " Admitted that in the series of phenomena every element is relative to the rest and is because of something else, yet for all that the judgment may be categorical. The something else, though we are unable to bring it within the judgment, though we can not in the end ever know it at all and realize it in thought, is, for all that, fact. And, this being so, the statement is true; since it rests in the end, not at all on an ' if ' but upon a 'because,' which, although unknown, is none the less real. Let the analytic judgment admit its relativity, let it own its adjectival and dependent character, and it surely saves itself and remains categorical."

But even this claim it is impossible to admit. I will not raise a difficulty about the "because" which is never realized, and the fact which can never be brought before the mind. My objection is more fatal. In the present case there *is* no because,[54] and there *is* no fact.

We are fastened to a chain, and we wish to know if we are really secure. What ought we to do? Is it of much use to say, "This link we are tied to is certainly solid, and it is fast to the next, which seems very strong and holds firmly to the next; beyond this we can not see more than a certain moderate distance, but, so far as we know, it all holds together"? The practical man would first of all ask, "Where can I find the last link of my chain? When I know that is fast, and not hung in the air, it is time enough to inspect the connection." But the chain is such that every link begets, as soon as we come to it, a new one; and, ascending in our search, at each remove we are still no nearer the last link of all, on which everything depends. The series of phenomena is so infected with relativity, that, while it is itself, it can never be made absolute. Its existence refers itself to what is beyond, and, did it not do so, it would cease to exist. A last fact, a final link, is not merely a thing which we can not know, but a thing which could not possibly be real. Our chain by its nature can not have a support. Its essence excludes a fastening at the end. We do not merely fear that it hangs in the air, but we know it must do so. And when the end is unsupported, all the rest is unsupported. Hence our conditio*ned* truth is only conditio*nal.* It avowedly depends on what is not fact, and it is not categorically true. Not standing by itself, it hangs from a supposition; or perhaps a still worse destiny awaits it, it hangs from nothing and falls altogether.

§ 72. It will be said, of course, that this is mere metaphysics. Given is given, and fact is fact. Nay we ourselves distinguished above the individual from the hypothetic judgment, on the ground that the former went to perception, and that we found there existing the elements it asserted. Such a plain distinction should not be ignored, because it disappears in an over-subtle atmosphere. But I do not wish to take back this distinction. It is valid at a certain level of thought; and, for the ordinary purposes of logical enquiry, individual judgments, both synthetic and analytic, may conveniently be taken as categorical, and in this sense opposed to universal judgments.

But, when we go further into the principles of logic, and are forced to consider how these classes of judgment stand to one another, we are certain to go wrong, if we have not raised such questions as the above. It is not enough to know that we have a ground of distinction. We must ask if it is a *true* ground. Is it anything more than a point to reckon from? Is it also fact? Does the light of presence, which falls on a content, guarantee its truthfulness even if we copy? Are the presented phenomenon, and series of phenomena, actual realities? And, we have seen, they are not so. The given in sense, if we could seize it in judgment, would still disappoint us. It is not self-existent and is therefore unreal, and the reality transcends it, first in the infinite process of phenomena, and then altogether. The real,[55] which (as we say) appears in perception, is neither a phenomenon nor a series of phenomena.

§ 73. It may be said " This is only the product of reflection. If we are content to take the facts as they come to us, if we will only leave them just as we feel them, they never disappoint us. They neither hang by these airy threads from the past, nor perish internally in a vanishing network of never-ending relations between illusory units. The real, as it simply comes to us in sense, has nothing of all this. It is one with itself, individual and complete, absolute and categorical." We are not here concerned to controvert this statement. We are not called on to ask if anything that is given is given apart from intellectual modification, if there is any product we can observe and watch, with which we have not already interfered. We have no motive here to raise such an issue; nor again do we rejoice in that infatuation for intellect, and contempt for feeling, which is supposed to qualify the competent metaphysician. Nor will we pause to argue that frustrated feeling itself heads the revolt against the truth of sense. It was a baffled heart that first raised the suspicion of a cheated head.

You may say, if you like, that the real just as we feel it is true.[56] But, if so, then *all* judgments are surely false, and your singular judgment goes with the rest. For our present purpose we may admit your assertion, but, if it is meant as an objection, we answer it by asking the question, What then? Who is it who says this? Who counts himself so free from the sin of reflection as to throw this stone? Some man no doubt who has not an idea of the consequences of his saying; some writer whose pages are filled with bad analysis and dogmatic metaphysics; some thinker whose passion for " experience " is mere prejudice in favour of his own one-sided theory, and whose loyal regard for the sensible fact means inability to distinguish it from that first result of a crude reflection in which he sticks.

For the present we may assume, what metaphysics would discuss, that phenomena are what we can not help thinking them *in the end,* and that the *last* result of our thought is true, or all the truth we have. It is not the beginning but the end of reflection which is valid of the real; or we are such at least that our minds are unable to decide for aught else. And we have seen that our thinking about the real, if we remain at the level of the analytic judgment, will not stand criticism. The result of our later and, we are forced to believe, our better reflection is conviction that at least this judgment is not true. To assert as a quality of the real either the whole or part of the series of phenomena,[57] is to make a false assertion.

§ 74. The reality is given and is present to sense; but you can not, as we saw (§ 11), convert this proposition, and say Whatever is present and given is, as such, real. The present [58] is not merely that section of the phenomena in space and time which it manifests to us. It is not simply the same as its appearance. Presence is our contact with actual reality; and the reception of the elements of sensuous perception as existing facts is one kind of contact, but it is not the only kind.

In hypothetical judgments there is a sense in which the real is given; for we feel its presence in the connection of the elements, and we ascribe the ground to the real as its quality. Hypothetical judgments in the end must rest on direct presentation, though from that presentation we do not take the elements and receive them as fact. It is merely their synthesis which holds good of the real (§ 50), and it is in our perception of the ground of that synthesis that we come into present contact with reality. I will not ask if this contact is more direct than that which supports the analytical judgment. But at all events we may say it is truer; since truth is what is true of the ultimate real. A supersensible ultimate quality is not much to assert, but at all events the assertion seems not false.[59] On the other hand the categoric affirmation of the analytic judgment of sense we know is not true. The content it asserts we know is not real. And, taken in this sense, there remains no hope for the individual judgment.

§ 75. There is no hope for it at all, till it abates its pretensions, till it gives up its claims to superiority over the hypothetic judgment, and is willing to allow that it itself is no more than conditional. But it does not yet know the degradation that awaits it. It may say, " It is true that I am not categorical. My content is conditioned, and the ' because ' has turned round in my hands into ' if.' But at least I am superior to the abstract hypothetical. For in that the elements are not even asserted to have reality, whereas, subject to the condition of the rest of the series, I at least assert my content to be fact. So far at least I affirm existence and maintain my position."

But this claim is illusory, for if the individual judgment becomes in this way hypothetical, it does not assert that its content has *any* existence. If it did it would contradict itself, and I will endeavour to explain this.

The content $a–b$ in the categoric judgment was directly ascribed to real existence. The abstract universal judgment $a–b$ does not ascribe either a or b or their connection to the real;[60] it merely ascribes a quality x. The question now is Can you save the categoric $a–b$ by turning it into a hypothetical in which $a–b$ is still asserted of existence, though under a condition,—or must it become the universal $a–b$ which ignores existence? In the latter case it would simply mean, " Given a, then b." But in the former it would run,

" Given something *else,* then *a–b* exists." This illusory claim
is not very pretentious, but I wish to show that it is suicidal.

Drobisch (*Logik,* § 56), following Herbart (I. 106), trans-
lates the judgment, " P exists," into " If anything exists anywhere, then P exists." I consider this translation to be
incorrect; for it covertly assumes that something does exist,
and hence is in substance still categorical. And if we apply
this translation to the facts of sense, then what is really
supposed is the completed series of other phenomena, and
the translation must run thus, " If *everything else* exists, then
P exists." But the assertion is now suicidal, for " everything
else," we have seen above (§ 70), can never be a real fact.
The hypothetical assertion of existence [61] is therefore made
dependent on a condition which can not exist. Now it is
not true that the consequence of a false hypothesis must
be false; but it certainly is true, when an impossible ground
is laid down as the sole condition of existence, that in a
roundabout way existence is denied. The individual judgment, we saw, was false when taken categorically. And now,
we see, when taken hypothetically, instead of asserting it
rather denies, or at least suggests that denial may be true.

§ 76. The only hope for the singular judgment lies in
complete renunciation. It must admit that the abstract, although hypothetical, is more true than itself is. It must ask
for a place in the same class of judgment and be content
to take the lowest room there. It must cease to predicate
its elements of the real,[62] and must confine itself to asserting
their connection as adjectives generally, and apart from particular existence. Instead of meaning by " Here is a wolf,"
or " This tree is green," that " wolf " and " green tree " are
real facts, it must affirm the general connection of wolf with
elements of the environment, and of " green " with " tree."
And it must do this in an abstract sense, without any reference
to the particular fact. In a low and rudimentary form it thus
tends to become a scientific law, and, entirely giving up its
original claims, it now sets its foot on the ladder of truth.

§ 77. But it remains upon the very lowest round. Every
judgment of perception is in a sense universal, and, if it were
not so, it could never be used as the basis of inference. The
statement goes beyond the particular case, and involves a

connection of adjectives which is true without respect to
" this " " here " and " now." If you take it as ascribing its
ideal content to *this* reality, it no doubt is singular, but, if you
take it as asserting a synthesis *inside* that ideal content, it
transcends perception; for anywhere else with the same
conditions the same result would hold. The synthesis is true,
not here and now, but universally.

And yet its truth remains most rudimentary, for the connection of adjectives is immersed in matter.[63] The content is
full of indefinite relations, and, in the first vague form which
our statements assume, we are sure on the one hand to take
into the assertion elements which have nothing to do with
the synthesis, and, on the other hand, to leave out something
which really helps to constitute its necessity. We say for
example, " This body putrefies; " but it does not putrefy
because it is this body. The real connection is far more
abstract. And again on the other hand it would not putrefy
simply because of anything that *it* is, and without foreign
influence. In the one case we add irrelevant details, and in
the other we leave out an essential factor. In the one case
we say, " The real is such that, given *abc*, then *d* will follow,"
when the connection is really nothing but *a–d*. In the other
case we say, " The connection is *a–b*," when *a* is not enough to
necessitate *b*, and the true form of synthesis is *a* (*c*)–*b*.
Measured by a standard of scientific accuracy, the first forms
of our truths must always be false. They say too little, or
too much, or both; and our upward progress must consist in
correcting them by removing irrelevancies and filling up the
essential.*

§ 78. The practice of science confirms the result to which
our long analysis has brought us; for what is once true for
science is true for ever. Its object is not to record that complex of sensible phenomena, which from moment to moment
perception presents to us. It desires to get a connection of
content, to be able to say, Given this or that element, and
something else universally holds good. It endeavours to discover those abstract elements in their full completeness, and
to arrange the lower under the higher. Recurring to a term

* For explanation and illustration I must refer to Lotze's admirable
chapter cited above.

we used before, we may say its aim is to purge out "thisness," to reconstruct the given as ideal syntheses of abstract adjectives. Science from the first is a process of idealization; and experiment, Hegel has long ago told us, is an idealizing instrument, for it sublimates fact into general truths.

Both in common life and in science alike, a judgment is at once applied to fresh cases. It is from the first an universal truth. If it really were particular and wholly confined to the case it appears in, it might just as well have never existed, for it could not be used. A mere particular judgment does not really exist, and, if it did exist, would be utterly worthless (cf. Chap. VI. and Book II.).

§ 79. It is time that we collected what result has come from these painful enquiries. If we consider the ultimate truth of assertions, then, so far as we have gone, the categorical judgment in its first crude form has entirely disappeared. The distinction between individual and universal, categorical and hypothetical, has been quite broken through. All judgments are categorical, for they all do affirm about the reality, and assert the existence of a quality in that.[64] Again, all are hypothetical, for not one of them can ascribe to real existence its elements as such. All are individual, since the real which supports that quality which forms the ground of synthesis, is itself substantial. Again all are universal, since the synthesis they affirm holds out of and beyond the particular appearance. They are every one abstract, for they disregard context, they leave out the environment of the sensible complex, and they substantiate adjectives. And yet all are concrete, for they none of them are true of anything else than that individual reality which appears in the sensuous wealth of presentation.

§ 80. But, if we remain at a lower point of view, if we agree not to scrutinize the truth of judgments, and if we allow assertions as to particular fact to remain in the character which they claim for themselves, in that case our result will be somewhat different.[65] Abstract judgments will all be hypothetical, but the judgments that analyze what is given in perception will all be categorical. Synthetic judgments about times or spaces beyond perception will come in the middle. They involve an inference on the strength of an universal.

and so far they must have a hypothetical character. They again involve an awkward assumption, for you can go to them only through the identity of an element in the several contents of a perception and an idea. As however, on the strength of this assumption, the universal is brought into connection with the given, the " if " is so turned into a " because," and the synthetic judgment may be called categorical. The two classes, so far, will on one side be assertions about particular fact and on the other side abstract or adjectival assertions. The latter are hypothetical, and the first categorical.

§ 81. We have all this time omitted to consider that class of judgment which makes an assertion about an individual which is not a phenomenon in space or time (§ 41). Is it possible that here we have at last a judgment which is not in any sense hypothetical? Can one of these directly predicate of the individual real an attribute which really and truly belongs to it? May we find here a statement which asserts the actual existence of its elements, and which is not false? Can truth categorical be finally discovered in some such judgment as " The self is real," or " Phenomena are nothing beyond the appearance of soul to soul "? [66] It would seem to us strange indeed if this were so, and yet after all perhaps it is our minds that are really estranged.

But we can not here attempt to answer these questions. We can only reply when asked where truth categorical dwells, " Either here or nowhere."

ADDITIONAL NOTES

[1] " S — P." This form I found of course in use, and I employed it in this volume where that seemed convenient. I neither did nor do attach importance to its use. In § I, par. 3, " *is* not our judgment" should have been perhaps " *need not be,*" and, lower down, after " was not " might better have come " perhaps."

[2] " Objectivity." What this means is that it is *the object itself* which is this or that. The " subjective " = the irrelevant. See the Index of this work. And cf. *Appearance*, p. 237, and *Essays*, the Index.

[3] " Existences of different orders." See here the Index, s. v. *Ex-*

istence. And cf. *Essays,* Chap. III, and Index, s. v. *real world.* "Existence" and "exist" (like "fact") are used in the present work often in a wide sense. On the narrower sense, which limits "existence" to the temporal series of my "real world," cf. *Appearance,* p. 317, and *Essays,* Chap. XVI.

⁴ Unfortunately in this work, with regard to "reality," neither the view of Common Sense (whatever that is) nor any other view has been kept to consistently. Cf. Chap. II. § 72 and Bk. III. Pt. II. Chap. IV.

⁵ "Altering the series of either space or time." But in what world? In our own so-called "real world" only? Cf. Note 7.

⁶ "Images." But see Chap. I, Note 8. And (a few lines lower down) "quite apart from" should certainly have been "without regard to."

⁷ "Three great classes." These distinctions are all in the end untenable. See Bosanquet, *K & R,* Chap. I. All judgments without exception are conditional. See T. E. II, and cf. *Appearance* and *Essays,* the Indexes. On class (ii), the words "some facts of time or space" are of course qualified by the following words "which . . . perceive." For the third class cf. § 41. And, for a correction of the footnote with regard to Kant, see the Note to Chap. VI, § 28.

⁸ "Is false &c." It is false in the sense that its opposite also is true. See the Index, s. v. *Conditional.* And cf. *Essays,* p. 232.

⁹ For references as to the "real" and "grammatical" subject see Index, s. v. *Subject.* We must remember that there is no presumption anywhere that these two are identical. See Bosanquet, *K & R,* 163-4, 181 foll.

¹⁰ On the "present" &c. cf. § 74, and see *Appearance* and *Essays,* the Indexes s. v. *Time.* A view, such as that advocated, e.g., by Mr. Russell, I take (i) to deny the reality of apparent change, and (ii) to be incompatible with the fact of the appearance.

¹¹ "The whole sensible reality." But at the same time there *always* is selection. See the Index, s. v. *Judgment.* Cf. here Bosanquet, *K & R,* 164 foll.

¹² On proper names see Bosanquet, *K & R,* 73 foll., *Logic,* I, 47 foll.

¹³ "There is always an inference." How far the judgment itself is here an inference is, however, a further question. See *Essays,* p. 369, and Index, s. v. *Memory.*

¹⁴ "To attribute them" should have been "to attribute it or them."

¹⁵ "The series itself," that is, as we have it before us.

¹⁶ "Content" or "quality" means here anything distinguishable so as to be for us a content or quality. In saying that the "this" does not fall within the "what," we must add that it does not fall in the "that" either. For each of these is an abstraction. Again, where a quality is unique, it ceases to be so if you take it as distinct from its "that"—for, if so, there may be another instance. On Uniqueness &c. see further T. E. IV and V.

17 On these important points see *Essays,* Chap. VI.

18 On the question raised here as to the idea of "this" see the reference given in Note 16.

19 The one idea, so far as positive, is that of reality, or experience, as immediate. Under this one main head of immediacy fall the "now," "here," and "mine." It is under the last of these that we are concerned with Attention.

"Immediate contact with the presented reality" (§ 24), if taken as a definition, is, I think, wrong. "Contact" and "presentation" are further aspects not, in my judgment, belonging essentially or universally to immediate experience. See the references given in Note 16. But in the present volume I certainly did not always mean by "presentation" the outward or even the inward perception of an object. The reader, I fear, must be on his guard throughout against what is perhaps a careless use of this term.

20 "Former discussion." See §§ 10 foll.

21 Reality is unique (a) negatively and (b) positively. The given "this" also offers itself as unique. But an examination shows that we here have but appearance. The "this," through its content, negates itself as unique, and is seen to involve transcendence and ideality. On these points see T. E. IV and V.

22 "A completed series &c."—except (that is) when viewed in relation to a limited purpose and idea which it realizes.

23 "Identity." Cf. § 80, and see Bk. III. I. Chap. III. § 2.

24 "Or has rather some point &c." But we must remember that the "point" may be some quality of the whole. To the reference given to Lotze should be added "and *Med. Psych.,* p. 487 (published in 1852)".

25 I had at this time, I think, no acquaintance, as yet, with Herbartian psychology, or I should have noticed the doctrine that perceptions all survive below the conscious level, ready to emerge if and when the conditions serve. But I should have added—"However, this problem of 'dispositions' is solved ultimately (if it can be solved), what stands in the text holds good. For it is in the end only as an ideal construction that I can have before me the series of events past and future &c." Cf. *Mind, O. S.,* 47, p. 363. For Memory, see *Essays,* the Index.

26 On Imagination see Bk. III. I. Chap. III. § 23, and *Essays,* the Index.

27 The false doctrine of "mere ideas" recurs in this section. See Chap. I, Note 13. And, for "the image," see ibid., Note 8.

28 "If we *actually* &c." We do and must "attribute the series to reality," though not to reality as present. If the reader will consult the account of Uniqueness and of the idea of "This," in T. E. IV and V, he will, I hope, see his way to correct the mistakes of the text.

29 "Implies the idea of a series." This is very doubtful.

30 See above, Note 7.

31 "If we take the soul to be eternal." I did not mean "everlasting." I was alluding to the view that the whole essence of the

soul can not be identified with its appearance in one or more periods of time.

[32] "A mere serial character." The use of these words (I can now recall nothing) seems careless. Probably I meant "a mere discreteness in the events so that they do not exist in and by connection into one whole."

[33] §§ 42, 43. The division into (a) and (b), in § 42, is clearly wrong, if only because it omits all the worlds of events which fall outside my "real" world. See Note 3.

We may perhaps distinguish "Singular" judgments (1) about my "real" world, or (2) about some "imaginary" world of events. (3) "General" judgments might perhaps be those referring to some, if not all, of the above worlds. (4) Judgments become "abstract" when this reference is struck out. Whether we have (5) to recognize abstract worlds or regions, taken somehow to "exist," though sensible existence in time and space is struck out, I will not offer to discuss. There will remain (6) judgments taken otherwise than as falling under the above heads. But, for myself, I attach little importance to such distinctions, even if tenable. What is important is to keep in mind that every judgment is, in various ways and degrees, conditioned and conditional.

Instead of using "existence" as one with "reality," it is far better, I think, to limit it to the sphere of events. But, if so, though all judgments will be "real," certainly not all will be "existential." See the Index.

[34] The difficulty as to the "symbolic" use of such ideas as "this" and "real" is dealt with in T. E. V.

[35] "The particular thing" should be "the particular or individual thing."

[36] "Adjectivals." The words "even where these are not taken so ostensibly" should have been added.

[37] On the Collective Judgment (cf. Bk. II. II. Chap. III. § 3) my treatment is one-sided. It ignores the fact that this judgment asserts a connection of content within an aggregate of individuals taken as exhaustive. On the Collective and Generic Judgments the reader is referred to Dr. Bosanquet's *Logic*, I, 152 foll., and 209 foll.

[38] "Collection of actual cases." "Actual" does not mean "given as present."

[39] "Will be universal and abstract." This, I think, is wrong. See Chap. VI, § 1.

[40] "Ideal experiment." But (a) we must remember that there are no *mere* ideas. Every idea is referred to its own world as there real and true, and as, so far, not merely "in my head." And (b) the "reality," to which my idea is opposed, is not necessarily "fact" in the sense of belonging to my "real world." It itself may be "imaginary," though here, as against my idea, it is taken as real.

Having then an idea, or rather a truth, holding in one region, we may be said to apply this to another region of reality with a view to observe the result. This other reality, as we have it, repels our idea, or admits its opposite, and hence, taken on one side, the result is doubt. But on the other side it is a judgment made subject to an x. We assert, that is, not S — M — P, but S(x)— M — P. M — P, we say, is true, but, as to S — M, we have not got that actually, and, further, we do not know what qualification of S is involved in the reality of S — M.

For the logical meaning of "If" the reader is referred to T. E. II, and to Dr. Bosanquet's *Logic*, the Index, s. v. *Hypothetical*. We can, I think, easily see its psychological nature and origin, if we take the case of means (M) to an end desired, a certain alteration, that is, of a given fact (S). I may have one or more ideas of these means, but there is something in S, *as I have it,* which repels them all. I, however, retain them because they are (a) relevant and interesting, and also (b) possible. They contain, that is, some of the conditions of S, as that is to be altered, and I do not know that there really are counter-conditions in S itself. On the other side I do not know, and I will not assume, that S does *not* contain these. Hence I refrain from action, and assert S — M — P subject to a doubt as to S — M. I hold, in other words, S(x)— M — P as true. And here x means (a) that further conditions are involved, and that (b) as to the nature and effect of these I am more or less ignorant.

The supposed (to pass to another point) is in one aspect (M — P) quite certain and actual. It is in connection with S (as known) that M — P is but possible. And I may add that, where S itself is taken as possible only, the supposed is here *doubly* possible. But, essentially and always, what is supposed is taken as possible.

This statement may seem at first to be in conflict with plain facts, such as the example given on p. 87 (cf. *Essays,* pp. 37-40). I may be told that possibility is here certainly excluded. I would on the other side, however, ask the reader to reflect whether certainty is not contrary to the very meaning of "If." And, since to my mind that point is clear, I conclude that any appearance to the contrary rests on what may be called linguistic or rhetorical artifice. I actually, that is, assert or deny some real connection, and so far there is no "If." But, for some unstated reason, I desire at the same time to suggest that things throughout might have been otherwise. And I convey at once my undoubting judgment and my doubtful suggestion by licentiously applying "if" to the undiscriminated compound. "The destruction of the barometer (§ 50) caused the absence of warning— *and* it need not have been so." And "since you are well (which you might not have been)" is the double meaning conveyed in "si vales bene est." We may notice further in this connection that it is common to refute an asserted S — P by showing it as true *only* if the impossible is supposed.

41 "The fact is the quality in the man's disposition." (i) It is so *here,* but even here a "disposition" apart from any circumstances is an impossible abstraction. Further (ii), if "disposition" is used to explain "conditional," then obviously, since the very meaning of

"disposition" involves a standing "if," the explanation is circular (see *Appearance*, Index, s. v. *Dispositions*). (iii) The objection to "quality" is that it seems merely to repeat (what we knew before) that things are so; and to admit (if we add "latent") that we do not know *how* (Cf. *Appearance*, p. 362.).

[42] "A quality which has appeared . . . experiment." This statement (see above) may involve a vicious abstraction.

[43] There is much here that requires correction. (i) I surely, in the case of every categorical judgment, am not forced to make it. The "arbitrary" character of all judgment and inference is discussed in T. E. I and II. (ii) Logical compulsion means merely that the object is so, whatever else I am pleased to fancy. And if a hypothetical judgment did *not* say that much, it would be no judgment at all. (iii) And further, to make the result of the "experiment" disappear from the reality is in principle vicious.

[44] "Were very different." The "very" here is objectionable. See Chap. III, § 13.

[45] With regard to the limits of explanation I will merely state here that—except in a relative sphere where assumptions are made— all judgments and all truth on my view involves what is inexplicable. There is in every case a certain amount of unknown condition (x). The question in any particular case will be as to the nature and amount in the end of this x. See *Appearance*, p. 581 and its Index, and that of *Essays*, s. v. *Inexplicable*.

[46] The conclusion drawn in §§ 53-56 is, I think, sound on the whole, though in part perhaps inaccurate. Even in the case of a designated particular we can hardly say broadly that this falls outside the supposal. On the other hand certainly we fail to get this, as merely designated, within the supposal and the judgment. The judgment therefore will, more or less against our wish, turn out to be abstract merely and only conditional—though neither in form. See *Essays*, pp. 38-40, and the Index of that work, and of this, s. v. *Designation*.

[47] "It does not assert the existence." Yes, it does assert this and must do so. But what existence and where is in every case the question. See on § 2 and Chap. I, § 10.

[48] For the doctrine that all judgments are conditional see *Essays*, Index, s. v. *Judgment*.

[49] Cf. T. E. I and IX, and *Essays*, pp. 299 foll.

[50] The real truth . . . actual." This is the doctrine for which I have now for so many years contended. See *Appearance* and *Essays*, the Indexes. Relations exist only in and through a whole which can not in the end be resolved into relations and terms. "And," "together" and "between," are all in the end senseless apart from such a whole. The opposite view is maintained (as I understand) by Mr. Russell, and was perhaps at last tacitly adopted by Prof. Royce. But, for myself, I am unable to find that Mr. Russell has ever really faced this question. See *Essays*, Index, s. v. *Unity*.

[51] In "orthodox Christianity," the "orthodox" was meant to be emphatic.

52 On the actual content of the "this" see T. E. IV and V, and the Index.

53 On conditioned and conditional, see T. E. II, and *Essays*, the Index.

54 "There is no because," i.e. of the character which you assume and require. The argument here is, in my opinion, sound, but it is perhaps better put as follows. The condition, on which the judgment holds, is unknown, and it admits also the opposite of what is asserted. The judgment therefore, in its present form, is at once both true and false. See *Essays*, Index, s. v. *Conditional*.

55 The "real." See on § 4.

56 "You may say &c." It is of course the English empiricist of 1883 who is being addressed here. As to how far the criticism is now out of date, the reader must judge for himself.

57 "The whole or part of the series of phenomena," i.e. as such.

58 "The present." Cf. §§ 11 foll.

59 "The assertion seems not false." On the other side, since it depends on an unknown condition, and since therefore its opposite also is possible, it has not absolute truth. In this point, and so far, it is like the "analytical judgment of sense." On the other hand it is higher and truer because, and so far as, its condition is less unknown and less dependent on mere "matter of fact."

60 "Does not ascribe . . . real." This, we have seen (Note 3) is wrong. But, if "existence" meant my "real world" of events, it could stand. On the "quality" see Note 41.

61 If "existence" (Notes 3 and 33) means my "real world," then to say of anything that its existence is implied in there being such a world, is, so far, unconditional assertion. But on the other hand, so far as this world itself is not absolutely real and true, the assertion becomes, so far, merely relative, and dependent on an unknown condition. If you could say that P, as such, is implied in the real, that would make P true absolutely.

To "the consequence of a false hypothesis &c.," we should, I think, add "unless by an abstraction the hypothesis is taken as *merely* false."

62 'It must cease to predicate—real" should be "It must cease to predicate its elements, as such, of the perceived real."

63 "Immersed in matter." For "matter of fact" see *Essays*, pp. 377-80.

64 "Assert the existence . . . that" should be "assert their content of that." And "can ascribe . . . as such" should be changed to "can ascribe to reality its content unconditionally."

65 The division made in § 80 is (we have seen) indefensible, if only because the "imaginary" is left out. See Note 33. And for the "awkward assumption" cf. § 32.

66 "Soul to soul." Cf. Note 31. And (lower down), to the question raised by "Either here or nowhere," the answer, I think, must be "in the end nowhere." But for the sense of this reply I must refer to my *Appearance* and *Essays*.

THE NEGATIVE JUDGMENT

§ 1. After the long discussion of the preceding chapter, we are so familiar with the general character of judgment that we can afford to deal rapidly with particular applications. Like every other variety, the negative judgment depends on the real which appears in perception. In the end it consists in the declared refusal of that subject [2] to accept an ideal content. The suggestion of the real as qualified and determined in a certain way, and the exclusion of that suggestion by its application to actual reality, is the proper essence of the negative judgment.

§ 2. Though denial, as we shall see, can not be reduced to or derived from affirmation, yet it would probably be wrong to consider the two as co-ordinate species. It is not merely as we shall see lower down (§ 7), that negation presupposes a positive ground. It stands at a different level of reflection. For in affirmative judgment we are able to attribute the content directly to the real itself. To have an idea, or a synthesis of ideas, and to refer this as a quality to the fact that appears in presentation, was all that we wanted. But, in negative judgment, [3] this very reference of content to reality must itself be an idea. Given X the fact, and an idea $a - b$, you may at once attribute $a - b$ to X; but you can not deny $a - b$ of X, so long as you have merely X and $a - b$. For, in order to deny, you must have the suggestion of an affirmative relation. The idea of X, as qualified by $a - b$, which we may write $x (a - b)$, is the ideal content which X repels, and is what we deny in our negative judgment.

It may be said, no doubt, that in affirmative judgment the real subject is always idealized. We select from the whole that appears in presentation, and mean an element that we do not mention (Book III. I. Chap. VI. § 12). When we point to a tree and apply the word " green," it may be urged that the subject is just as ideal as when the same object rejects the offered suggestion "yellow." But this would ignore an important difference. The tree, in its presented unity with reality, can accept at once the suggested quality. I am not always forced to suspend my decision, to wait and consider the whole as ideal, to ask in the first place, Is the tree green? and then decide that the tree is a green tree. But in the negative judgment where "yellow" is denied, the positive relation of "yellow" to the tree must precede the exclusion of that relation. The judgment can never anticipate the question. I must always be placed at that stage of reflection which sometimes I avoid in affirmative judgment.

§ 3. And this distinction becomes obvious, if we go back to origins and consider the early development of each kind. The primitive basis of affirmation is the coalescence of idea with perception. But mere non-coalescence of an idea with perception is a good deal further removed from negation. It is not the mere presence of an unreferred idea, nor its unobserved difference, but it is the failure to refer it, or identify it, which is the foundation of our first denial. The exclusion by presented fact of an idea, which attempted to qualify it, is what denial starts from. What negation must begin with is the attempt on reality, the baffled approach of a qualification. And in the consciousness of this attempt is implied not only the suggestion that is made, but the subject to which that suggestion is offered. Thus in the scale of reflection negation stands higher than mere affirmation. It is in one sense more ideal, and it comes into existence at a later stage of the development of the soul.*

§ 4. But the perception of this truth must not lead us into error. We must never say that negation is the denial of an existing judgment. For judgment, as we know, implies belief; and it is not the case that what we deny we must once have believed. And again, since belief and disbelief are incompatible, the negative judgment would in this way be made to depend on an element which, alike by its existence or its disappearance, would remove the negation itself. What we deny is not the reference of the idea to actual fact. It is the mere idea of the fact, as so qualified, which negation ex-

* Compare on this whole subject Sigwart, *Logik,* I. 119 and foll. I do not, however, wholly accept his views.

cludes; it repels the suggested synthesis,[4] not the real judgment.

§ 5. From this we may pass to a counterpart error. If it is a mistake to say that an affirmative judgment is presupposed in denial, it is no less a mistake to hold that the predicate alone is affected, and that negation itself is a kind of affirmation. We shall hereafter recognize the truth which this doctrine embodies, but, in the form it here assumes, we can not accept it. The exclusion by fact of an approaching quality is a process which calls for its own special expression. And when we are asked to simplify matters by substituting " A is Not-B " for " A is not B," we find an obvious difficulty. In order to know that A accepts Not-B, must we not already have somehow learnt that A excludes B? And, if so, we reduce negation to affirmation by first of all denying, and then asserting that we have denied,—a process which no doubt is quite legitimate, but is scarcely reduction or simplification.

§ 6. There is a further objection we shall state hereafter (§ 16) to the use of Not-B as an independent predicate. But at present we must turn to clear the ground of another error. We may be told that negation " affects only the copula ; " and it is necessary first to ask what this means. If it means what it says, we may dismiss it at once, since the copula may be wanting. If the copula is not there when I positively say " Wolf," so also it is absent when I negatively say " No wolf." But, if what is meant is that denial and assertion are two sorts of judgment, which stand on a level, then the statement once again needs correction. It is perfectly true that these two different sorts of judgment exist. The affirmative judgment qualifies a subject by the attribution of a quality, and the negative judgment qualifies a subject by the explicit rejection of that same quality. We have thus two kinds of asserted relation. But the mistake arises when we place them on a level. It is not only true that, as a condition of denial, we must have already a suggested synthesis, but there is in addition another objection. The truth of the negative may be seen in the end to lie in the affirmation of a positive quality; and hence assertion and denial cannot stand on one level.[5] In " A is not B " the real fact is a character x belonging to A, and which is incompatible with B. The basis of negation is really the assertion of *a quality that excludes* (*x*). It is not, as we saw, the mere assertion of the quality of exclusion (Not-B).

§ 7. Every negation must have a ground, and this ground is positive. It is that quality *x* in the subject which is incompatible with the suggested idea. A is not B because A is such that, if it were B, it would cease to be itself. Its quality would be altered if it accepted B; and it is by virtue of this quality, which B would destroy, that A maintains itself and rejects the suggestion. In other words its quality *x* and B are discrepant. And we can not deny B without affirming in A the pre-existence of this discrepant quality.[6]

But in negative judgment *x* is not made explicit. We do not say what there is in A which makes B incompatible. We often, if asked, should be unable to point out and to distinguish this latent hindrance; and in certain cases no effort we could make would enable us to do this. If B is accepted, A loses its character; and in these cases we know no more. The ground is not merely unstated but is unknown.

§ 8. The distinctions of " privation " and " opposition " (Sigwart, 128 foll.) do not alter the essence of what we have laid down. In a privative judgment the predicate " red " would be denied of the subject simply on the ground that red was not there. The subject might be wholly colourless and dark.[7] But if " red " were denied on the ground that the subject was coloured green, it would be the presence of an opposite quality that would exclude, and the judgment would then be based on positive opposition. This distinction we shall find in another context to be most material (cf. Chap. VI. and Book III. II. Chap. III. § 20); but, for our present purpose, it may be called irrelevant. In the one case as in the other, the subject is taken with a certain character; and by addition as well as by diminution that individual character may be destroyed. If a body is not red because it is uncoloured, then the adding-on of colour would destroy that body as at present we regard it. We may fairly say that, if the predicate were accepted, the subject would no longer be the subject it is. And, if so, in the end our denial in both cases will start from a discrepant quality and character.

§ 9. It may be answered, no doubt, that the subject, as it is now and as we now regard it, is not the same thing as the subject itself. In the one case, the subject rejects a suggestion through a quality of its own, in the other it may reject on the strength of *our* failure. But I must persist in denying that this objection is relevant. In both cases alike the subject is taken as somehow determined; and it is this determination which (whatever it comes from) does give the subject a positive character, which in both cases lies at the base of the denial. No subject could repel an offered suggestion simply on the strength of what it was *not*. It is because the "not-this" must mean "something *else*," that we are able to make absence a ground for denial. We shall all agree that the nothing which *is* nothing can not possibly do anything, or be a reason for aught.[8]

These distinctions do not touch the principle we stand upon, but I admit they give rise to most serious difficulties.[9] And, mainly for the sake of future chapters, it may be well if we attempt here to clear our ideas. And (i) first, when we have a case of " opposition," there the subject repels the offered predicate because it has in its content a positive quality, filling the space which the predicate would occupy, and so expelling it. If a man has blue eyes, then that quality of blueness is incompatible with the quality brown. But (ii), when we come to privation, two cases are possible. In the first of these (*a*) within the content of the subject there is empty space where a quality should be. Thus, a man being eyeless, in this actual content lies the place where his eyes would be if he had them. And this void can not possibly be a literal blank. You *must* represent the orbits as somehow occupied, by peaceful eyelids, or unnatural appearance. And so the content itself gets a quality, which, in contrast to the presence of eyes, may be nothing,* but which by itself has a positive character, which serves to repel the suggestion of sight.

§ 10. But privation can rest on another basis (*b*). The

* I may mention that, though contrast can not always be taken as holding true of the things contrasted, yet for all that it may rest on a positive quality. Thus, even in the case of a word like blindness, we should be wrong if we assumed that the blind man is qualified simply by the absence of sight from the part which should furnish vision. His mind, we can not doubt, has a positive character which it would lose if another sense were added.

content of the subject may contain no space which could possibly be qualified by the presence of the predicate. What rejects the predicate is no *other* determination of the content itself, but is, so far as that content itself is concerned, an absolute blank. It is difficult to find illustrations of this instance. If I say "A stone does not feel or see," it may rightly be urged "Yes, because it *is* a stone, and not simply because it is nothing else." But we can find an example of the privation we want in the abstract universal. The universal idea (cf. Sigwart, 130), if you keep it in abstraction, repels every possible extension of its character. Thus "triangle," if you mean by it the mere abstraction, can neither be isosceles nor scalene nor rectangular; for, if it were, it would cease to be undetermined. We may invent a stupid *reductio ad absurdum:* This isosceles figure is certainly a triangle, but a triangle is certainly not isosceles, therefore——.

If we release the universal from this unnatural abstraction, and use it as an attribute of real existence, then it can not support such a privative judgment. For, when referred to reality, we know it must be qualified, though we perhaps can not state its qualification. Once predicate triangle of any figure, and we no longer can deny every other quality. The triangle is determinate, though we are not able to say how. It is only the triangle as we happen *not* to know it, which repels the suggestion of offered predicates. It is our ignorance, in short, and not the idea, which supports our exclusion of every suggestion.

§ 11. In a judgment of this kind the base of denial is neither the content of the subject itself, nor is it that content *plus* a simple absence; for a simple absence is nothing at all. The genuine subject is the content of the idea *plus my* psychological state of mind. The universal abstraction, ostensibly unqualified, is determined by my mental repulsion of qualities. And the positive area which excludes the predicate really lies in that mental condition of mine. My ignorance, or again my wilful abstraction, is never a bare defect of knowledge. It is a positive psychological state. And it is by virtue of relation to this state, which is used as content to qualify the subject, that the abstraction, or the ignorance, is able to become a subject of privation. We shall see that, in this form, the universal may more truly be called particular (Chap. VI. § 35); for it *is* determined and qualified, not by any development of the content, but simply by extraneous psychological relation.[10]

§ 12. The various kinds of negative judgment follow closely the varieties of affirmation. The immediate subject may be part of the content of present perception (" This stone is not wet "); or it may be found in some part of the series of space, or again of time, which we do not perceive (" Marseilles is not the capital of France," " It did not freeze last night "). Again what is denied may be a general connection (" A metal need not be heavier than water "). In this last case it is of course the unexpressed quality at the base of the hypothesis (Chap. II. § 50) which the real excludes.[11] But, in all negative judgment, the ultimate subject is the reality that comes to us in presentation. We affirm in all alike that the quality of the real excludes an ideal content that is offered. And so every judgment, positive or negative, is in the end existential.

In existential judgment, as we saw before (Chap. II. § 42), the apparent is not the actual subject. Let us take such a denial as " Chimæras are non-existent." " Chimæras " is here ostensibly the subject, but is really the predicate. It is the quality of harbouring chimæras which is denied of the nature of things. And we deny this because, if chimæras existed, we should have to alter our view of the world. In some cases that view, no doubt, can be altered, but, so long as we hold it, we are bound to refuse all predicates it excludes. The positive quality of the ultimate reality may remain occult or be made explicit, but this, and nothing else, lies always at the base of a negative judgment.

§ 13. For logical negation can not be so directly related to fact as is logical assertion.[12] We might say that, as such and in its own strict character, it is simply " subjective: " it does not hold good outside my thinking. The reality repels the suggested alteration; but the suggestion is not any movement of the fact, nor in fact does the given subject maintain itself against the actual attack of a discrepant quality. The process takes place in the unsubstantial region of ideal experiment. And the steps of that experiment are not even asserted to exist in the world outside our heads. The result remains, and is true of the real, but its truth, as we have seen, is something other than its first appearance.

The reality is determined by negative judgments, but it can not be said to be directly determined. The exclusion, as such, can not be ascribed to it, and hence a variety of exclusions may be based on one single quality. The soul is not an elephant, nor a ship in full sail, nor a colour, nor a fire-shovel; and, in all these negations, we do make an assertion about the soul. But you can hardly say that the subject is determined by these exclusions as such, unless you will maintain that, after the first, the remainder must yield some fresh piece of knowledge. You may hold that " all negation is determination," if you are prepared to argue that, in the rejection of each new absurd suggestion, the soul exhibits a fresh side of its being, and in each case performs the special exclusion by means of a new quality. But it seems better to say that nothing is added by additional exclusions.[13] The development and application of these may proceed *ad infinitum,* but the process is arbitrary and, in the end, unreal. The same quality of the soul which repels one predicate, repels here all the rest, and the exclusion itself takes place only in our heads.

I do not mean to deny that a thing may be qualified by the exclusion of others, that the real character of a fact may depend on what may be called a negative relation. What I mean to say is that the negative judgment will not express this. It asserts that a predicate is incompatible, but it does not say that either the predicate, or the incompatibility, are real facts. If you wish to say this you must transcend the sphere of the negative judgment.

§ 14. We must not, if we can help it, introduce into logic the problems of the " dialectical " view.[14] It may be, after all, that everything is just so far as it is not, and again is not just so far as it is. Everything is determined by all negation; for it is what it is as a member of the whole, and its relation to all other members is negative. Each element in the whole, itself the whole ideally while actually finite, transcends itself by mere self-assertion, and by mere self-emphasis brings forth the other that characterizes and negates it. If everything thus has its discrepant in itself, then everything in a sense must be its own discrepancy. Negation is not only one side of reality, but in the end it is either side we please. On this view it would be doubtful if even the whole is positive; for it *is* just so far as by position it disperses itself in its own negation, and begets from its dispersion the opposite extreme. It is doubtful if we may not transform the saying that " Everything is nothing except by position," into " Everything by position is its proper contrary, and nothing by position is all and everything."

If this is so, there would remain no quality which is simply positive; and logical negation, in another sense than we have given it above, becomes the soul and, we sometimes are inclined to think, the body of the real world. But we are not called upon to discuss this view (cf. Chap. V.), for our result will stand in any case, I think, in its principal outline.

A mere logical negation,[15] it is fully admitted by the dialectical method, need not express a real relation. And, this being so, it seems the better course to consider it by itself as merely subjective, and to express the real implication of exclusives by an affirmative judgment, which sets forth that fact. What denial tells us is merely this, that, when *we* bring the discrepant up, it is rejected. Whether what repels it is entirely independent, or whether it has itself produced or solicited what it excludes, is quite irrelevant. And it is still more irrelevant to ask the question if the first rejection is merely coquettish, and will lead in the end to a deeper surrender. This all goes beyond what denial expresses, for that, merely by itself, is not asserted beyond our minds.

The dialectical method, in its unmodified form, may be untenable. It has, however, made a serious attempt to deal with the relation of thought to reality. We can hardly say that of those eminent writers who are sure that logic is the counterpart of things, and have never so much as asked themselves the question, if the difference and identity, with which logic operates, are existing relations between actual phenomena.

§ 15. To resume, logical negation always contradicts, but never asserts the existence of the contradictory. To say " A is not B " is merely the same as to deny that " A is B," or to assert that " A is B " is false. And, since it can not go beyond this result, a mere denial of B can never assert that the contradictory Not-B is real. The fact it does assert is the existence of an opposite incompatible quality,* either in the immediate or ultimate subject. This is the reason why the suggested A — B is contradicted; and it is only because this something else is true, that the statement A — B is rejected as false. But then this positive ground, which is the basis of negation, is not *contradictory*. It is merely discrepant, opposite, incompatible. It is only *contrary*. In logical negation the denial and the fact can never be the same.

§ 16. The contradictory idea, if we take it in a merely negative form, must be banished from logic. If Not-A were solely the negation of A, it would be an assertion without a quality, and would be a denial without anything positive to serve as its ground. A something that is only not something else, is a relation that terminates in an impalpable void, a reflection thrown upon empty space. It is a mere nonentity which can not be real. And, if such were the sense of the dialectical method (as it must be confessed its detractors have had much cause to suppose),[16] that sense would, strictly speaking, be nonsense. It is impossible for anything to be *only* Not-A. It is impossible to realize Not-A in thought. It is less than nothing, for nothing itself is not wholly negative. Nothing at least is empty thought, and that means at least my thinking emptily. Nothing means nothing else but failure. And failure is impossible unless something fails; but Not-A would be impersonal failure itself (§ 11).

Not-A must be more than a bare negation. It must also be positive. It is a general name for any quality which, when you make it a predicate of A, or joint predicate with A,[17] removes A from existence. The contradictory idea is the universal idea of the discrepant or contrary. In this form it must keep its place in logic. It is a general name for any hypothetical discrepant; but we must never for a moment allow ourselves to think of it as the collection of discrepants.

§ 17. Denial or contradiction is not the same thing as the assertion of the contrary; but in the end it can rest on nothing else.[18] The contrary however which denial asserts, is never explicit. In " A is not B " the discrepant ground is wholly unspecified. The basis of contradiction may be the assertion A–C or A–D, C and D being contraries of B. But

* On the nature of incompatibility see more, Chap. V.

again it may perhaps be nothing of the sort. We may reject
A–B, not in the least on the ground of A, but because A
itself is excluded from reality. The ultimate real may be
the subject which has some quality discrepant with A–B. For
contradiction rests on an undetermined contrary. It does not
tell us what quality of the subject excludes the predicate.
It leaves us in doubt if the subject itself is not excluded.
Something there is which repels the suggestion; and that is
all we know. Sokrates may be not sick because he is well, or
because there is now no such thing as Sokrates.

§ 18. Between acceptance and rejection there is no middle-
point, and so contradiction is always dual. There is but one
Not-B. But contrary opposition is indefinitely plural. The
number of qualities that are discrepant or incompatible with
A, can not be determined by a general rule. It is possible of
course to define a contrary in some sense which will limit the
use of the term; but for logical purposes this customary
restriction is nothing but lumber. In logic the contrary should
be simply the discrepant. Nothing is gained by trying to
keep up an effete tradition. If a technical distinction can
not be called necessary, it is better to have done with it.

§ 19. Contradiction is thus a "subjective" process, which
rests on an unnamed discrepant quality. It can not claim
"objective" reality; and since its base is undetermined, it is
hopelessly involved in ambiguity. In "A is not B" you know
indeed what it is you deny, but you do not say what it is you
affirm. It may be a quality in the nature of things which is
incompatible with A, or again with B. Or again it may be
either a general character of A itself which makes B impossible, or it may be some particular predicate C. That "a
round square is three-cornered," or that "happiness lies in
an infinite quantity," may at once be denied. We know a
round square, or an infinite number, are not in accordance
with the nature of things. But "virtue is quadrangular," or
"is mere self-seeking," we deny again because virtue has no
existence in space, and has another quality which is opposite
to selfishness.

"The King of Utopia died on Tuesday" may be safely
contradicted. And yet the denial must remain ambiguous.
The ground may be that there is no such place, or it never

had a king, or he still is living, or, though he is dead, yet he died on Monday. This doubtful character can never be removed from the contradiction. It is the rejection of an idea, on account of some side of real fact which is implied but occult.

§ 20. We may conclude this chapter by setting before ourselves a useful rule. I think most of us know that one can not affirm without also in effect denying something. In a complex universe the predicate you assert is certain to exclude some other quality, and this you may fairly be taken to deny. But another pitfall, if not so open, yet no less real, I think that some of us are quite unaware of. Our sober thinkers, our discreet Agnostics, our diffident admirers of the phenomenal region—I wonder if ever any of them see how they compromise themselves with that little word " *only.*" How is it that they dream there is something else underneath appearance, and first suspect that what meets the eye veils something hidden? But our survey of negation has taught us the secret, that nothing in the world can ever be denied except on the strength of positive knowledge. I hardly know if I am right in introducing suggestive ideas into simple minds; but yet I must end with the rule I spoke of. We can not deny without also affirming; and it is of the very last importance, whenever we deny, to get as clear an idea as we can of the positive ground our denial rests on.

ADDITIONAL NOTES

[1] This chapter contains some serious erors. I have since accepted in the main Dr. Bosanquet's account of negation. See his *K & R* and *Logic.* I have briefly discussed the whole matter in T. E. VI.

[2] " That subject," i.e., as in one with a selected determination. See Chap. I, §§ 11 and 12.

[3] The abstraction of the idea from all " reference " is not defensible. See on Chap. I, § 10. There is always some region in which an idea is real. It is only where the perceived world is taken as the one real object, that other worlds are merely " subjective " (§ 13).

As to whether affirmation and denial are co-ordinate, we may say that in the end they are so, because the conscious use of ideas as ideas implies both a positive and negative aspect. But denial can be called more " reflective," in the sense that we become aware of it later. We must retain an excluded idea before we can know it as excluded. The beginning of affirmation, we may say, is an object before me changed ideally so as to lead to action. The beginning of negation is the exclusion of an ideal change in the object—this exclusion not being retained by the mind, though action is thereby prevented. By "action" (I should add) is not meant necessarily action which is "practical." Thus it is not true that we have a separate suggestion and then consciously apply it. The attempt to identify may at first appear to us not as an attempt, but simply as the actual exclusion, where not the actual qualification. It is when we hold the suggestion, while excluding it from our perceived and selected object, that we first have denial in the proper sense of the word.

⁴ The "suggested synthesis" (here and lower down) needs correction in the sense of the foregoing Note.

⁵ It is true that a excludes b because it is a. It is true that there is a ground and a Why, and that *in the end* you can not make this Why explicit. But the same holds good also of b, as distinct from and so as negative of a. On the other hand this two-sided negation is at first implicit only and does not appear. You begin positively (as we saw above) with a designated object (Ro) qualified further ideally. It is only later and through reflection that, instead of such an object, Ro (ab), we arrive at a world qualified everywhere by distinctions, at once connected with and opposed to one another, and

so can write our object as

$$\begin{array}{c} R \\ \diagup\;\diagdown \\ a\;—\;b \end{array}$$

⁶ I have, here and everywhere, altered "disparate" where in the original text it was used wrongly for "discrepant." I am quite unable to account for this mistaken use, which, I am sorry to add, recurs frequently, and for the sake of the reader has been now throughout corrected.

⁷ "Colourless and dark." If "dark" meant "visibly dark"— which I do not think it did mean—there would be a mistake here. See Bosanquet *K & R*, p. 247.

⁸ On the subject of Incompatibility the reader is referred to *Appearance*, Appendix, Note A, and to Bosanquet's *Logic*.

⁹ These distinctions are (i) exclusion by a specified incompatible; (ii) exclusion of a quality from a space in a subject where that quality is looked for; (iii) exclusion from an assumed space taken as empty on the ground of absence, i.e. of my failure to find the quality there. If you were to drop the assumption made here, and were to reject the empty space, as being either meaningless or itself for some known reason excluded, the above exclusion would become sound. But at the same time it would cease to rest upon failure and mere privation. What on the other hand damns the privative judgment, as ultimate, is its assumption, based on mere ignorance, of an empty space in the character of the Universe. Where however you know positively that the Universe is in a certain respect determinable further, there your failure to find a particular qualification

(*a*) is a ground for denial, just so far as you have reason to think your knowledge complete. But see the Notes on Chap. VII, §§ 13 and 28, and see T. E. VII. And cf. *Appearance* and *Essays,* the Indexes, s. v. *Privation.*

¹⁰ " Extraneous psychological relation " should be perhaps " a distinction turned into a separation and made an exclusion on a mere extraneous psychological ground."

¹¹ " The unexpressed quality." See on Chap. II, § 50.

¹² " Fact " here should be " perceived fact." And negation is " subjective" in the sense that *mere* negation, *mere* exclusion, is an abstraction and is by itself really nothing at all. Cf. §§ 15-19. Otherwise negation is *not* "subjective," though it *is* more "reflective" than is affirmation (§ 2).

¹³ " Nothing is added by additional exclusions." It is true that the *abstract* negation takes no account of the " how," which therefore, so far, may be the same. But to go beyond this is wrong (Chap. I, § 52). See T. E. VI.

¹⁴ " Dialectical view." But, apart from this, in logic we may and must insist that Reality has to be regarded as a disjunctive totality, as the positive unity of diversities each of which is one and is *not* the others. In our intellectual world we *must* take every element as within a whole, and as qualified by its relations in that whole, and, further, as qualified by them internally. By " internally " is meant that the element itself, and not merely something else, is qualified. Hence everything will imply its relations both positive and negative. On the other hand we must not say of anything that it is nothing beyond its implications—even though *what else* it is we are unable in the end to state. The problem of identity and diversity is, I agree, not in the end soluble (see *Essays,* pp. 240, 264). And our whole world, as merely intellectual, is not ultimately real.

¹⁵ " A mere logical negation." The *mere* must be emphasized.

¹⁶ " Much cause " should perhaps be " some cause."

¹⁷ " Or joint predicate." In a sense it never is anything but a joint predicate. See *Appearance,* Appendix, Note A.

¹⁸ The main point is this, that denial means exclusion from and by the real. *Mere* denial, however, rests on *abstract* exclusion, which, as abstract, is really nothing. Actually the real excludes because the real is qualified incompatibly, and may be so in a variety of senses, the whole of which variety is ignored by the abstract denial. See on § 13.

CHAPTER IV

§ 1. The disjunctive judgment may fairly complain that by most logicians it is hardly dealt with. It is often taken as a simple application of the hypothetical, and receives the treatment of a mere appendage. It is wonderful in how many respectable treatises not the smallest attempt is made to understand the meanings of " if " and of " either—or."

The commonest way of regarding disjunction is to take it as a combination of hypotheses. This view in itself is somewhat superficial, and it is possible even to state it incorrectly.[2] " Either A is B or C is D " means, we are told, that if A is not B then C is D, and if C is not D then A is B. But a moment's reflection shows us that here two cases are omitted. Supposing, in the one case, that A *is* B, and supposing, in the other, that C *is* D, are we able in these cases to say nothing at all? Our " either—or " can certainly assure us that, if A is B, C–D must be false, and that, if C is D, then A–B is false. We have not exhausted the disjunctive statement, until we have provided for four possibilities, B and not-B, C and not-C.

§ 2. But however complete may be the cases supposed, disjunctive judgments can not really be reduced to hypotheticals. Their meaning, no doubt, can be given hypothetically; but we must not go on to argue from this that they *are* hypothetical. The man who illustrated everything else has touched this point too in the *Gentlemen of Verona:*

Speed. But tell me true, will't be a match?
Launce. Ask my dog: if he say, ay, it will; if he say, no, it will; if he shake his tail and say nothing, it will.
Speed. The conclusion is then that it will.
Launce. Thou shalt never get such a secret from me but by a parable (Act II. Scene v.).

It is indeed by an indirect process, and by making secret a categorical judgment, that hypotheticals can express disjunction.

I do not mean that the " either—or " is purely categorical.
I mean that to some extent at least it *is* categorical, and
declares a fact without any supposition. In " A *is b* or *c* "
some part of the statement is quite unconditional. It asserts
a fact without any " if " at all. And when pressed with the
objection, " But you can not deny that it *is* reduced to a combination of supposals," we need not take long to practise an
answer. A *combination* of hypotheticals surely does not lie
in the hypotheticals themselves. It lies in the mind which
combines them together, and surveys the field which together
they exhaust. It is nonsense to say you are able to " reduce "
a statement to elements of a certain character, when these
elements, if taken merely by themselves and without a
peculiar mode of union, are able to express nothing like the
statement.[3] The basis of disjunction, the ground and foundation of your hypotheticals, is categorical.[4]

§ 3. There is, no doubt, some difficulty about the categorical nature of disjunctive judgments. " A is *b* or *c ;* " but this
mode of speech can not possibly answer to real fact. No real
fact can be " either—or." It is both or one, and between the
two there is nothing actual. We can hardly mean to say that
in fact A *is b* or *c*. On the other hand, we are far from
expressing simple ignorance. If we merely said " I do not
know if A is *b,* and I do not know if A is *c*," that would not
be equivalent to the original statement. And that we make
an assertion can be shown in this way. If the subject of our
predicate " either—or " were proved not to exist, our statement would be false. It is clear not only that the subject
has existence, but that it also possesses some further
quality.[5]

The distinction of the apparent and the ultimate subject,
which we had to make in our former discussions, must not
here be forgotten. " A is either *b* or *c* " need not always imply
that A is a fact. For example, I may say that " either A
exists or does not exist." The subject here is the nature of
things, and this either repels the content A or is qualified by
it. But still the assertion remains categorical. Throughout
the rest of the chapter I shall take A to stand for the real
subject, and the reader must remember that in every case
the apparent subject may belong to the predicate, and that what

is asserted respecting A may only be true of the ultimate subject.

And the same remark applies to such examples as " Either A is B or C is D." The subject in this case is not A or B or again C or D. The subject is the real, which is qualified by the predicate A–B or the predicate C — D.

§ 4. The assertion in " A is *b* or *c* " is not that A *is b* or *c*. What then do we affirm? We say in the first place that A exists. In the next place we certainly give it some quality.[6] What quality do we give it? If it can not be either *b* or *c*, can it possibly be something that falls between them? No, for that would be neither. For instance, grey is not white or black, and it excludes both colours. The predicate of A, while neither *b* nor *c*, must not be a quality exclusive of either. It must then be a quality common to both, which is not yet either, but is further determinable as one or the other.

§ 5. If we like to call this basis *x,* then " A is *x* " is categorically true. We may in some cases have distinguished *x* and given it a name, but in other cases it is unnamed and implicit. " Man, woman, and child," have a common basis in " human being." In " white or black " the quality " coloured, and coloured so as to exclude other hues," is the attribute asserted. " In England or America," " alive or dead," commit us to the statements " somewhere not elsewhere " and " organized being." And so, if we call a man " bad or good," we say at least he is a moral agent. There is no exception to the truth of this rule. Even existence and non-existence have so much in common that, in any sense in which we can use them, they imply some kind of contact with my mind. We have seen (Chap. III.) that there is no pure negation. So, in every disjunction and as the ground of it, there must be the assertion of a common quality, the sphere within which the disjunction is affirmed.

§ 6. But *x* is not any universal whatever which happens to be common to *b* and *c*. It is particularized further. It excludes the opposite of each of these qualities, and can not be the negative of " *b* or *c*." It is affirmed as fully determined not outside the region which is covered by *bc*. But since *b* and *c,* as predicates of A, are incompatible, it can not be *both* of them. The conclusion remains that it must be *one*. " One single

element of the region enclosed by bc " is the predicate common
to b and c. And this predicate it is which, in disjunction, we
categorically assert of A.

So much is fact and no hypothesis; but this by itself would
not be the assertion "b or c." The disjunctive judgment is
not wholly categoric. Being sure of our basis, the quality x,
upon this universal we erect hypotheses. We know that b
and c are discrepant. We know that A is particularized
within b and c, and therefore as one of b and c. It can not be
both, and it must be some one.[7] So much is the fact. To
complete the disjunction we add the supposal, "If it is not
one it must be the other." If A is not b, it must be c; and it
must be b, if it is not c. This supposal completes the " either
—or." Disjunctive judgment is the union of hypotheticals on
a categoric basis.

§ 7. We shall return to consider this process further, but
at present we may pause to correct a mistake. It has been
doubted if alternatives are always exclusive.[8] "A is b or c,"
it is said, may be taken to admit that A is possibly both. It
may either be bc or b or c. And, no doubt, in our ordinary
disjunctive statements we either leave the meaning to be
gathered from the context, or really may not know what it is
that we mean. But our slovenly habits of expression and
thought are no real evidence against the exclusive character
of disjunction. "A is b or c" does strictly exclude "A is both
b and c." When a speaker asserts that a given person is a
fool or a rogue, he may not *mean* to deny that he is both. But,
having no interest in showing that he is both, being perfectly
satisfied provided he is one, either b or c, the speaker has not
the possibility bc in his mind. Ignoring it as irrelevant, he
argues as if it did not exist. And thus he may practically be
right in what he says, though formally his statement is downright false; for he has excluded the alternative bc.[9]

And it is not always safe to be slovenly. It may be a
matter of vital moment to make our disjunction accurate and
complete, and to know if we mean "A is b or c," or "A is
bc or b or c." About the commonest mistake in metaphysics
is the setting up of false alternatives. If we either admit bc
as a predicate when b and c are discrepant, or exclude bc
when b and c are compatible, we are liable to come to most

false conclusions. And the very instance we have quoted above should read us a lesson. It is false that the alternative "either rogue or fool" does never exclude the possibility of both. It is a common thing to make this mistake. When we try to guess a man's line of conduct, we first lay it down he is fool or rogue, and then afterwards, arguing that he is certainly a rogue, we conclude that his conduct will be deliberately selfish. But unfortunately the man has been a fool as well, and was not in any way to be relied on. It is often impossible to speak by the card, but still inaccuracy remains inaccuracy. And, if we do not mention the alternative "or both," when held to our words we certainly exclude it.

If we mean to say "A is *b* or *c* or again *bc*," the process of the judgment is very simple. A exists and is further determined. It is determined within the region *bc*. A excludes all qualities which are incompatible with *b* and *c* and again with *bc*. Within *bc* fall *b* and *c* and again *bc*, and nothing else falls there. And since these are discrepant, A is but one of them. So far the fact, and then come the hypotheses. If A as determined excludes *b* and *c* it must be *bc*; if it excludes *c* and *bc* it is *b*; if it excludes *b* and *bc* it is *c*. The number of discrepants is of course irrelevant to the nature of the process.

§ 8. But the inaccuracy we have noticed has a natural foundation. We are accustomed to use "or" with an implication, and at times we forget whether "or" stands alone or must be taken as so qualified. I will briefly illustrate. If, in drawing up a rule, I lay down that "the number of tickets being limited, each person shall be entitled to a red ticket or a white one," it is at once understood that the alternatives are incompatible. A ticket means here obviously one *at most*. But, if I say "No one shall be entitled to pass within this enclosure except the possessor of a white or red ticket," I should hardly be taken to exclude the man who was qualified by both. A ticket means here one *at least*. And it becomes very easy to misunderstand, and to suppose that "or" in each of these cases has a different force.

But in both cases "or" means precisely the same. In the second, as in the first, it is rigidly disjunctive. But in the second of our instances "or" does not stand alone. It is qualified by an unexpressed "if not" or "failing that." And this implication makes a vital difference.

§ 9. The alternatives which are offered are *not* red and white. I am not to be admitted, given white *or* red. The entitling conditions (so far as they are contemplated) are firstly "white," and then "red, white failing" or "red without white;" and it can hardly be maintained that *these* conditions are compatible. For, if white is there, then red can not make good the failure of white, and the red, that is specified as excluding white, can not by any means admit its presence. What you mean to say is, Suppose white is there, then *cadit quæstio;* but, if white is not there, red will answer the purpose. And you express your meaning by assigning two alternatives, "white present" on the one hand, and, on the other hand, "red coupled with the absence of white." And this *practically* provides for every possibility.

The logical objection which may be raised against it is not that its "or" is partly conjunctive, for this, as we have seen, is a pure mistake. The disjunction is faulty not because it is conjunctive, but because it is incomplete. It ignores the possibility of the co-existence of red and white, and in form it might be construed as excluding it. But the reason is obvious. You are never forced to consider separately this individual possibility, since you can always treat it as a simple case of the presence of white. If "white" really means "white with or without red," and "red" means "red on the failure of white," and if the absence of both is fully provided for, then the disjunction is absolutely complete and exhaustive. And these alternatives (i) white with or without red, (ii) red without white, and (iii) failure of both, are absolutely incompatible.

§ 10. And this I think is the answer to an argument brought forward by Professor Jevons (*Principles,* p. 73). Against the exclusive character of alternatives he urges an indirect argument. If that were so, he objects, the negative of such a term as "malleable-dense-metal" could not be "not-malleable or not-dense or not-metallic." There would be seven distinct alternatives, and this would be absurd.

I must remark, in the first place, that I wholly fail to see the absurdity. If you mean to exhaust the cases which ex-

clude the term " malleable-dense-metal," the absurdity would
lie in their number being less than what follows from the
number of possible combinations. But if you mean to say
that, if " or " is exclusive, you can not deny the term which is
offered unless you set out *all* the cases which exclude it, then
this is just the mistake we have been considering. In " not-
malleable or not-dense or not-metallic " the disjoined are incompatible, but the full possibilities are not set out. You
must understand with each " or " the implication of " failing
that." " Not malleable " does not mean the *isolated* presence
of non-malleability. It is not *one* possibility: it is a class
that covers several. It means the absence of malleability,
whether the subject is metallic or not-metallic, dense or not-
dense. You may fairly object that combinations are ignored,
or else that the term " not-malleable " is ambiguous, since it is
used to cover a number of cases. But these technical objections would have little importance, and they do nothing to
show that " or " does anything but rigidly disjoin.

§ 11. Despite my respect for Professor Jevons, I can not
admit any possible instance in which alternatives are not
exclusive. I confess I should despair of human language, if
such distinctions as separate " and " from " or " could be
broken down. And, when I examine the further evidence
produced, it either turns on the inaccurate modes of expression we have lately discussed, or consists in what I must be
allowed to call a most simple confusion. We are told that
the expressions " wreath or anadem," or again " unstain'd by
gold or fee " (Jevons, p. 70), show that " or " may sometimes
be non-exclusive. But this is quite erroneous. The alternatives are meant to be rigidly incompatible. The distinction is
however not applied to the thing, but simply to the names. If
we suppose that the terms are quite synonymous, then " wreath
or anadem " means " you may call it by either name you
please." The thing has two titles, one of which is at your
service. I hardly think Professor Jevons would assert that we
are asked to use *both names at once*. So, if " fee " is not
meant to be distinct from " gold," the assertion is that there is
no stain arising from the thing you may term indifferently
gold or fee. The idea of your wanting to say both at once is
quite ignored.

I will try to make the matter clearer by inventing a piece
of imaginary dialogue. A. Who is the greatest Roman poet?
B. His name is Virgil. A. What, not Vergilius? B. Yes,
Virgil or Vergilius. A. I understand: he has two names. I
will call him henceforth " Vergilius-Virgil," and then I shall be
safe. B. Excuse me: in that case you must be wrong. You
may call him by either of the names you please, but not by
both of them at once.

It is not worth while to multiply illustrations. In every
instance that can be produced, we have either a loose mode of
common speech, or else the " or " denotes incompatibility,
whether that lie in the simultaneous use of alternative names,
or in the facts themselves.

§ 12. The mere statement, of course, may fail to tell us
which of these incompatibilities is before us. And no one can
deny that alternatives are often presented in a very inaccurate way. It is an excellent thing in all these questions
to refer to the common usages of language, but we must
remember that in those usages, besides what one calls " unconscious logic," there also may lurk mere looseness and care-
lessness. It may not be amiss to illustrate the mistake we
have just been discussing, by a parallel ambiguity in the
hypothetical judgment. It is, of course, the established doctrine that, while you may argue from ground to consequence,
you can not demonstrate from consequence to ground.[10]   And,
although from a metaphysical point of view this doctrine is
certainly open to doubt, still for logical purposes it is sufficiently valid. But yet, by appealing to loose expressions,
we might show that the ground is the *only* ground, and can
therefore be inferred from the presence of the consequence.
Sigwart has called attention to these cases (*Logik*, I. 243; and
Beiträge, 59). " If you run hard you will catch him," is
often an indirect way of saying, " You will not catch him
unless you run hard." But such mere loose phrases are no
valid reason for impugning the doctrine that, unless this fact is
specially stated, the condition is not given as a *sine qua non*.
When the context shows that our expressions are not to be
strictly interpreted, we are at liberty to take " either—or " as
compatible, and " if " may be the same as " not unless." But

we should remember that what a thing can pass for may differ widely from what it really *is*.

§ 13. It is time we left these misleading errors to return to the discussion of the matter itself. The detail of the process in disjunctive judgments can not fully be dealt with till we come to inference. But here we may partly prepare the ground.

In the first place, as we shall see in the following chapter, disjunction does not rest on Excluded Middle. The latter is merely a case of disjunction.

" A is *b* or *c* " asserts, as we saw, that A exists and possesses a quality. That quality, further, falls within *bc*. It is affirmed to be what is common to both, and it is stated also to be further determinable within *bc*. In other words, it excludes all discrepant with both *b* and *c*.

We have seen this above, and the point I wish here to bring forward is the following. How do we know, and how can we know, that there is not something discrepant with *bc* and yet compatible with A? All rests upon this; and what does this rest on?

We must answer, for the present, that it rests on our impotence.[11] There is no great principle on which we can stand. We can not find any opposite of *b* or opposite of *c* which is not also an opposite of A; and we boldly assume that, because we find none, therefore there is none. The conclusion from impotence may itself seem impotent, but, as we shall hereafter see, there remains some doubt if it may not in the end be taken as the ground and the sole ground we have for believing anything (Book III. II. Chapter III.).

§ 14. We may state the whole matter once more thus. " A is *b* or *c* " may be expressed by (i) If A is *b* it is not *c,* and If A is *c* it is not *b,* (ii) If A is not *b* then it is *c,* and If A is not *c* then it must be *b*. The first two hypothetical statements are erected on the knowledge that *b* and *c* as predicates of A are incompatible, or that A*bc* can not possibly exist.

The second pair are based on the assumption that, because we do not find a predicate of A which excludes *b* or *c,* therefore there is none. Every opposite of *b* or of *c,* that we find, is an opposite of A. Hence there remains this result; within the limit of A there is no not-*b* but *c,* and no not-*c* but *b:* and

A must have some further quality. This is the ground for our second two hypotheticals.

So we see the essence of disjunctive judgment is not got by calling it a combination of supposals. It has a distinctive character of its own. It first takes a predicate known within limits, and defined by exclusion, and then further defines it by hypothetical exclusion. It rests on the assumption that we have the whole field, and by removing parts can determine the residue. It supposes in short a kind of omniscience. Its assertion again, if not quite categorical, is certainly not quite hypothetical. It involves both these elements. And it implies, in addition, a process of inference which will give us cause for reflection in the future.

ADDITIONAL NOTES

[1] On the subject of Disjunction the reader is referred to Dr. Bosanquet's *Logic*. I fully accept his main view; but, before proceeding in consequence to point out some errors made in this volume, I will add a few remarks which may perhaps assist the reader.

Disjunction means " or," and, viewed psychologically, " or " stands for Choice. Hence it may be useful to consider here how choice arises. Where something is desired, where there are various ways of realizing this end, and where I find that I can not have all of these as a whole and at once—and where, by this negation, action has been suspended—the result may be choice. And, in choosing, I accept one way while rejecting the rest. Or, again, I foresee, let us say, that an event affecting me must actually happen, and that, so far, there are no two ways, but that, as to *how* the event will happen and affect me, the ways are various. And let us add that I perceive that these diverse modifications, while impossible all at once, are otherwise, each of them, more or less in my power. Here, as above, after suspending action I identify myself in choice with one of these modes, while rejecting the rest. And obviously the " or " thus contained in choice is exclusive; and any other view as to " or " would, here at least, conflict with plain fact.

We may note further that in choice the alternative need not merely be dual. The incompatibles that are each possible may be clearly more than two. And this plurality in the " or " holds, I would add, not merely psychologically and in choice, but equally belongs to the " or " of logical disjunction. The necessary duality of disjunction —in the sense that the incompatibles, which are each possible, can not be taken as more than two—is to my mind a view which, so far, is contrary to fact.

What is true here is that when, and so far as, in choice or otherwise, you identify yourself with one possibility, the residue tends to be regarded or at least treated, so far, as not even possible. It is taken for our purpose, we may say, in the lump and as all one, and so, we may add, is taken but as one only. But in the above attitude (to speak strictly) there is really no question of number, since what is rejected is viewed merely from the side of its general quality.

Having now noticed the character of " or " as we find it in choice, I will go on to deal briefly with the origin and nature of logical disjunction. Before this arises we have found that Reality, as this or that recognizable object, has various qualities. We have passed, that is, beyond the stage of an immediate unity of one and many. We have reached a level where the distinguished many are recognized as diverse, and yet, as each and also the rest, belonging somehow to the one object. And the object possesses this diversity, so far, all together and at once. The qualities thus seem simply conjoined and are called compatible. But we go on to discover, in the same or in some other object, qualities not found thus together, and we call these, so far, incompatible. The object may have now one and now another, but never has at once both or all. On the other side (here is the point) the object *has* these qualities. It has them, now one and now another, according to the conditions. It has them, that is, not simply, but according as it itself is made diverse, so as itself to enter into and become this one qualification while rejecting the others. And, since we find that this holds good also with regard to these other incompatibles, the object is now qualified by them all, but qualified disjunctively. While on one hand the object is all, it is on the other hand each singly and each exclusively according to the diverse conditions.

Such in outline, we may say, is the origin of Disjunction, and its intellectual importance and necessity can not well be overestimated. But we are led none the less to look beyond it to a higher and more ultimate stage, where we return to Conjunction in a different sense and at a higher level. In a complete and perfect system, where all conditions were filled in, the real Universe would have all its determinations at once, all as connected and each as qualifying the others and the whole. And here negation would disappear except as one aspect of positive and complementary distinction. But for us this ultimate stage of the intellect remains an ideal, in the sense that it can not in detail and everywhere be attained completely.

This ideal, I must add, in no way justifies the doctrine that in logic " or " can anywhere have a sense which is not exclusive. In other words—so far as " or " ceases to exclude—both " or," and disjunction with it, have so far ceased as such to exist. See below, on § 7.

[2] " To state it incorrectly." I can not now recall the origin of this remark, which seems at best negligible. For the possibility of reduction to *two* hypotheticals see Bosanquet, *K & R*, p. 208.

3 "It is nonsense." Certainly (I must insist) it is so. We may illustrate by the attempt to reduce relational wholes, and even perhaps all facts, to relations and terms.

4 "The basis . . . is categorical." This, however, is subject to a qualification, for which see Bosanquet, *Logic* (Ed. II), I, 328.

5 It is of course not true that disjunction assumes the existence of its subject (cf. Chap. V, § 23), if that means "existence in my real world." The subject may be hypothetical or otherwise "imaginary." But there is in the end an Ultimate within which all disjunction falls and which has no negative.

6 The use of " quality " here is objectionable. See on Chap. II, § 50.

7 "It can not be both and it must be some one." If " some one " means "one only," this would anticipate the disjunction. It should mean " must be, so far, within the field of both while not both." The disjunction implied in " one only " requires hypotheticals to complete it and make it explicit. The same requirement, though not in the same sense, holds, I think, of our knowledge that b and c are incompatible.

8 I am more than ever convinced that the view which takes " or " as not always exclusive is utterly untenable, except perhaps by way of of a mere convenient artifice. On the whole question, and for a refutation of technical objections, see Bosanquet, *Logic* (Ed. II), Vol. I, pp. 355 foll. The subject is now perhaps exhausted, but I will allow myself to add one or two remarks.

(i) The evidence from psychology seems to me to be all on one side. " Or " answers to choice, and choice seems nonsense if it means that you can have all at once. And this consideration ought, I submit, to carry great weight.

(ii) The fallacy of " false alternative," I would further remind the reader, may be said perhaps to dominate our lives. But how could this be so, if " or " were not taken instinctively as everywhere exclusive? And the fallacy does not lie in our assuming this as true. It lies, on the other hand, in our forgetting constantly the actual nature of our subject. We may say that (apart from exceptional cases) in every judgment made in life the real subject is other than that which is formulated. It is really that which is " understood " for the purpose in hand, which limited purpose, not being made explicit, is easily ignored or forgotten. Thus, in " A is b or c," the A which we *mean* is A qualified and limited by our special object and interest. It is of and within this qualified A that our " b or c " holds. And it is when we ignore or forget this, and when we go on to take A simply and unrestrictedly in the sense of " A anyhow," that the fallacy everywhere tends to arise. But this tendency, with its false result, points, I submit, to our unfailing reliance on the exclusiveness of " or."

The arguments against its exclusiveness seem to me plausible only when this unexpressed qualification of A is ignored. In our actual use of " or," A means an A not only where the possibility of Abc is excluded, but also where it is tacitly set aside as irrelevant to our purpose. And, when we remember this, the case against exclusiveness, to my mind, disappears.

(iii) If we keep to *mere* " or," then " or " is both exhaustive and exclusive ; and, if we are to argue against the second of these characters, we must also argue against the first. After stating that A is *b* or *c*, we may receive the answer " yes or both " without any feeling that our statement has been denied. But, on just the same principle, we may accept a suggested addition of " or *d*," not as a correction but as a complement. And yet to argue from this that disjunction is not taken as exhaustive would, if plausible, be erroneous. The " or *d* " is accepted because, and so far as, A did *not* mean " A pure and simple." It in fact meant, for our purpose, something like " A, whatever else A elsewhere may be." Hence a correction and a replacement of A by a wider subject is (we feel) not called for here by the addition of " or *d*." And thus the actual disjunction is really exhaustive, just as on the same principle (we saw above) it was really exclusive—unless, that is, the disjunction in both cases has ceased, as such, to exist, and has really given way to some lower or higher mode of assertion.

[9] " His statement is . . . false." And it therefore, I presume, can lead formally to the equally false result " He is either wise or honest " (Keynes, *Formal Logic,* p. 280, note). This, if correct, I take to confirm the doctrine of my text, which doctrine, I venture to think, here and elsewhere, Dr. Keynes has failed to understand.

[10] " The established doctrine." The doctrine is, however, in the end untenable. See Bosanquet, *Logic* I, Chap. VI. I have fully accepted his view ; see *Appearance,* Index, s. v. *Cause,* and T. E. X. Apart from this, the instance in the text may serve to illustrate the ambiguity of ordinary language.

[11] For privation and impotence as a ground of knowledge see on Chap. III, § 9. So far as our knowledge is completely systematized, privation, of course, so far ceases to exist.

CHAPTER V

THE PRINCIPLES OF IDENTITY, CONTRADICTION, EXCLUDED
MIDDLE, AND DOUBLE NEGATION.

§ 1. After discussing negative and disjunctive judgments,
we may deal at once with the so-called " Principles " of Identity, Contradiction, and Excluded Middle; and we will add
some remarks on Double Negation.

The principle of Identity is often stated in the form of a
tautology, " A is A." If this really means that no difference
exists on the two sides of the judgment, we may dismiss it
at once. It is no judgment at all. As Hegel tells us, it sins
against the very form of judgment; for, while professing to
say something, it really says nothing. It does not even assert
identity. For identity without difference is nothing at all.
It takes two to make the same, and the least we can have is
some change of event in a self-same thing, or the return to
that thing from some suggested difference. For, otherwise, to
say " It is the same as itself " would be quite unmeaning. We
could not even have the appearance of judgment in " A is A,"
if we had not at least the difference of position in the different
A's; and we can not have the reality of judgment, unless some
difference actually enters into the content of what we assert.

§ 2. We never at any time wish to use tautologies. No
one is so foolish in ordinary life as to try to assert without
some difference. We say indeed " I am myself," and " Man is
man and master of his fate." But such sayings as these are
no tautologies.[1] They emphasize an attribute of the subject
which some consideration, or passing change, may have
threatened to obscure; and to understand them rightly we
must always supply " for all that," " notwithstanding," or
again, " once more." It is a mere mistake to confuse what
Kant calls " analytical judgments " * with tautologous statements. In the former the predicate is part of the content of
the conception A, which stands in the place of, and appears as,

* This is not the sense in which I have used " analytical." p. 48.

141

the subject. But in every judgment of every kind a synthesis is asserted. The synthesis in Kant's analytical judgment holds good within the sphere of the conception; and the real subject is not the whole of A, but is certain other attributes of A which are *not* the attribute asserted in the predicate. In " All bodies are extended " what we mean to assert is the connection, within the subject " bodies," of extension with some other property of bodies. And even if " extended " and " body " were synonymous, we still might be very far from tautology. As against some incompatible suggestion, we might mean to assert that, after all misapprehension and improper treatment, the extended is none the less the extended. And, again, we might be making a real assertion of a verbal nature. We might mean that, despite their difference as words, the mean- ing of " body " and " extended " was the same. But mere tautology with deliberate purpose we never commit. Every judgment is essentially synthetical.

§ 3. The axiom of Identity, if we take it in the sense of a principle of tautology, is no more than the explicit statement of an error. And the question is, would it not be better to banish irrevocably from the field of logic such a source of mistake? If the axiom of Identity is not just as much an axiom of Difference, then, whatever shape we like to give it, it is not a principle of analytical judgments or of any other judgments at all. On the other hand, perhaps something may be gained if a traditional form can get a meaning which con- veys vital truth. Let us try to interpret the principle of Iden- tity in such a way that it may really be an axiom.

§ 4. We might take it to mean that in every judgment we assert the identity of subject and predicate. Every connection of elements we affirm, in short all relations and every differ- ence, holds good only within a whole of fact.[2] All attributes imply the identity of a subject. And taken in this sense the principle of Identity would certainly be true. But this perhaps is not the meaning which, for logical purposes, it is best to mark specially.

§ 5. There remains a most important principle which, whether it be true or open to criticism, is at least the *sine qua non* of inference. And we can not do better than give this the name of principle of Identity, since its essence is to emphasize sameness in despite of difference. What is this principle? It runs thus: " Truth is at all times true," or, " Once true always true, once false always false. Truth is not only independent of me, but it does not depend upon change and chance. No alteration in space or time, no possible difference of any event or context, can make truth falsehood. If that which I say is really true, then it stands for ever."

So stated the principle is not very clear, but perhaps it will find acceptance with most readers. What it means, how-ever, is much more definite, and will be much less welcome. The real axiom of Identity is this: *What is true in one context is true in another.*[3] Or, If any truth is stated so that a change in events will make it false, then it is not a genuine truth at all.

§ 6. To most readers this axiom, I have little doubt, will seem a false statement. For the present it may stand to serve as a test if our previous discussions (Chap. II.) have been understood. If every judgment in the end is hypothetical, except those not directly concerned with phenomena—if each merely asserts a connection of adjectives, in this sense that *given* A then B must follow—we see at once that under any conditions it will always be true. And we shall see here-after that in every inference this result is assumed as a prin-ciple of reasoning, and that we can not argue one step with-out it.

§ 7. We saw that such judgments as " I have a toothache," in their sensuous form, are not really true. They fail and come short of categorical truth, and they hardly have attained to hypothetical. To make them true we should have to give the conditions of the toothache, in such a way that the con-nection would hold beyond the present case. When the judg-ment gave the toothache as the consequent coming according to law from the ground, when the judgment had thus become universal, and, becoming this, had become hypothetical, then at last it would be really true, and its truth would be uncondi-tional and eternal.

I know how absurd such a statement sounds. It is impos-sible, I admit, however much we believe it, not to find it in a certain respect ridiculous. That I do not complain of, for it is not our fault. But it is our fault if the common view does not seem *more* ridiculous. I say that " I have a toothache " to-day. It is gone to-morrow. Has my former judgment become therefore false? The popular view would loudly protest that it still is true, for I *had* a toothache, and the judgment now holds good of the past. But what that comes to is simply this. The judgment is true because answering to fact. The fact alters so that it does not answer; and yet the judgment is still called true, because of something that does not exist. Can anything be more inconsistent and absurd? If the change of circumstance and change of day is not a fresh context which falsifies *this* truth, why should any change of context falsify *any* truth? And if changed conditions make any truth false, why should not all truth be in perpetual flux, and be true or false with the fashion of the moment?

§ 8. We shall discuss this question more fully hereafter (Bk. II. Part I.), but may here anticipate a misunderstanding. To ask " Does space or time make no difference " is wholly to ignore the meaning of our principle. We ask in reply, " Does this difference enter into the content of A? If it does, then A becomes *perceptibly* diverse, and we confessedly have left the sphere of our principle. But, if it does not so enter, then the truth of A is considered in abstraction from spaces and times, and their differences are confessedly irrelevant to its truth. We thus meet the objection by offering a dilemma. You have abstracted from the differences of space and time, or you have not done so. In the latter case your subject itself is different; in the former case it is you yourself who have excluded the difference.

We may indeed on the other side be assailed with an objection. We may be asked, " What now has become of the identity? Has it not disappeared together with the differences? For if the different contexts are not allowed to enter into the subject, how then can we say what is true in one context is true in another? It will not be true in any context at all." But we answer, The identity is not contained *in* the judgment " S — P," since that takes no kind of account of the differences.[4] The identity lies in the judgment, " S — P is true everywhere and always." It is this " everywhere " and " always " that supply the difference against which S — P becomes an identity. The predicate attributed to the real belongs to it despite the difference of its diverse appearances. We do not say the appearances are always the same, but the quality keeps its nature throughout the appearances. And with this reply we must here content ourselves.

§ 9. When we come to discuss the nature of inference we shall see more fully the bearing of the principle. It stands here on the result of our former enquiries, that every judgment, if it really is true, asserts some quality of that ultimate real which is not altered by the flux of events. This is not the place for metaphysical discussion, or we might be tempted to ask if identity was not implied in our view of the real. For if anything is individual it is self-same throughout, and in all diversity must maintain its character.

THE PRINCIPLE OF CONTRADICTION.

§ 10. Like the principle of Identity, the principle of Contradiction has been often misunderstood. And in the end it must always touch on a field of metaphysical debate. But, for logical purposes, I think it is easy to formulate it in a satisfactory way.

It is necessary before all things to bear in mind that the axiom does not in any way explain, that it can not and must not attempt to account for the existence of opposites.[5] That discrepants or incompatibles or contraries exist, is the fact it is based on. It takes for granted the nature of things in which certain elements are exclusive of others, and it gives not the smallest reason for the world being such in nature and not quite otherwise. If we ever forget this, the Law of Contradiction will become a copious source of illusion.

§ 11. If the principle of Contradiction states a fact, it says no more than that the discrepant is discrepant, that the exclusive, despite all attempts to persuade it, remains incompatible. Again, if we take it as laying down a rule, all it says is, " Do not try to combine in thought what is really contrary. When you add any quality to any subject, do not treat the subject as if it were not altered. When you add a quality, which not only removes the subject as it was, but removes it altogether, then do not treat it as if it remained." This is all the meaning it is safe to give to the axiom of Contradiction; and this meaning, I think, will at once be clear, if we bear in mind our former discussions. The contrary is always the base of the contradictory, and the latter is the general idea of the contrary. Not-A for example is any and every possible contrary of A (Chap. III. § 16).

§ 12. We have to avoid, in dealing with Contradiction, the same mistake that we found had obscured the nature of Identity. We there were told to produce tautologies, and here we are by certain persons forbidden to produce anything else. " A is not not-A " may be taken to mean that A can be nothing but what is simply A. This is, once again, the erroneous assertion of mere abstract identity without any difference. It is ordering us to deny as a quality of A everything that is *different* from A, and in this sense not-A. But differents and discrepants should never be confused. The former do not exclude one another; they only exclude the denial of their difference. The discrepant with A can never be found together with A in any possible subject, or be joined to it in the relation of subject and attribute.[6] The different from A does not exclude, unless you attempt to identify it with A. It is not A generally, but one single relation to A, which it repels.

As we saw before, there is no logical principle which will tell us what qualities are really discrepant. Metaphysics, indeed, must ask itself the question if any further account can be given of incompatibility. It must recognize the problem, if it can not solve it. We might remark that no thing excludes any other so long as they are able to remain side by side, that incompatibility begins when you occupy the same area; and we might be tempted to conclude that in space would be found the key of our puzzle. But such other experiences as that assertion and denial, or pain and pleasure, are incompatible, would soon force us to see that our explanation is insufficient. But in logic we are not called upon to discuss the principle, but rest upon the fact. Certain elements we find *are* incompatible; and, where they are so, we must treat them as such.

§ 13. There is no real question of principle involved in such different ways of stating the axiom as " A is not not-A," " A is not both *b* and not-*b*," " A can not at once both be and not be." For if A were not-A, it would be so because it had some quality contrary to A. So also, if A has a quality *b*, it could only be not-*b* by virtue of a quality discrepant with *b*. And again, if A both were and were not, that would be because the ultimate reality had contrary qualities. The character in which it accepted A, would be opposite to the quality which excluded A from existence. Under varieties of detail we find the same basis, repulsion of discrepants.

A simple method of stating the principle is to say, " Denial and affirmation of the self-same judgment is wholly inadmissible." And this does not mean that if a miracle in psychology were brought about, and the mind did judge both affirmatively and negatively, both judgments might be true. It means that, if at once you affirm and deny, you must be speaking falsely. For denial asserts the positive contrary of affirmation.[7] In the nature of things (this is what it all comes to) there are certain elements which either can not be conjoined at all, or can not be conjoined in some special way; and the nature of things must be respected by logic.

§ 14. If we wish to show that our axiom is only the other side of the Law of Identity, we may state it thus, " Truth is unchangeable, and, as discrepant assertions alter one another, they can not be true." And again, if we desire to glance in passing at the metaphysical side of the matter, we may remind ourselves that the real is individual, and the individual is harmonious and self-consistent. It does not fly apart, as it would if its qualities were internally discrepant.

§ 15. Having now said all that I desire to say, I would gladly pass on. For, notwithstanding the metaphysics into which we have dipped, I am anxious to keep logic, so far as is possible, clear of first principles. But in the present instance the law of Contradiction has had the misfortune to be flatly denied from [8] a certain theory of the nature of things. So far is that law (it has been contended) from being the truth, that in the nature of things contradiction exists. It is the fact that opposites are conjoined, and they are to be found as discrepant moments of a single identity.

I need hardly say that it is not my intention compendiously to dispose in a single paragraph of a system which, with all its shortcomings, has been worked over as wide an area of experience as any system offered in its place. My one idea here is to disarm opposition to the axiom of contradiction, as it stands above.[9] But I clearly recognize that, if not-A were taken as a pure negation, no compromise would be possible. You would then have to choose between the axiom of contradiction and the dialectical method.

I will say, in the first place, that whatever is conjoined is therefore *ipso facto* shown not to be discrepant. If the elements co-exist, *cadit quæstio;* there is no contradiction, for there can be no contraries. And, saying so much, I feel tempted to retire. But yet with so much I shall hardly escape. " Have not we got," I hear the words called after me, " have we not got elements which any one can see negate one another, so that, while one is, the other can not be; and yet have we not got very many conceptions in which these discrepants somehow co-exist? It is all very well to say, ' then not contrary;' but try them, and see if they are not exclusive."

It is plain that I must stand and say something in reply. But I think I shall hardly be so foolish as to answer, " These conceptions of yours are merely phenomenal. Come to us and learn that knowledge is relative, and with us give up the Thing-in-itself." For without knowing all that would be poured on my head, I can guess some part of what I should provoke. " *You* say ' give up the Thing-in-itself '? Why that is all that you have *not* given up. You profess that your knowledge is only phenomenal, and then you make the law of Contradiction valid of the Absolute, so that what it excludes you are able to know is *not* the Absolute. That is surely inconsistent. And then, for the sake of saving from contradiction this wretched ghost of a Thing-in-itself, you are ready to plunge the whole world of phenomena, everything you know or can know, into utter confusion. You are willing to turn every fact into nonsense, so long as this Thing-in-itself is saved. It is plain, then, for which you really care most. And as for ' relativity,' it is you yourselves who violate that principle. Your turning of the relative into hard and fast contraries is just what has brought you to your miserable pass." I confess I should hardly care to subject myself to all these insults; and I had rather Mr. Spencer, or some other great authority—whoever may feel himself able to bear them, or unable to understand them—should take them on himself.

If I chose to turn and provoke a contest, I know of another weapon I might use. I might say, " Your conceptions are partial illusions. They are crude popular modes of representing a reality whose nature can not be so portrayed. And the business of philosophy is to purify these ideas, and never to leave them until, by removal of their contradictions, they are made quite adequate to the actual fact." But, after all, perhaps I could only say this for the sake of controversy, and controversy is what I am anxious to avoid. And for this end I think that some compromise may perhaps be come to. Without calling in question the reality of negation, and the identity of opposites, are we sure that we can not understand that doctrine in a sense which will bear with the axiom of Contradiction? This axiom is not like the principle of Identity. It is a very old and most harmless veteran; and for myself I should never have the heart to attack it, unless with a view to astonish common-sense and petrify my enemies. And in metaphysics we can always do that in many other ways.

What I mean is this.[10] Supposing that, in such a case as continuity, we seem to find contradictions united, and A to be b and not-b at once, this may yet be reconciled with the axiom of Contradiction. A we say is composed of b and not-b; for, dissecting A, we arrive at these elements, and, uniting these, we get A once more. But the question is, while these elements are *in* A, can they be said, while there, to exist in their fully discrepant character of b and not-b? I do not mean to suggest that the union of contraries may be that misunderstanding of the fact which is our only way to understand it. For, if I felt sure myself that this were true, I know it is a heresy too painful to be borne. But, in the object and within the whole, the truth may be that we never really do have these discrepants. We only have moments which *would be* incompatible if they really were separate, but, conjoined together, have been subdued into something within the character of the whole. If we so can understand the identity of opposites—and I am not sure that we may not do so—then the law of Contradiction flourishes untouched. If, in coming into one, the contraries as such no longer exist, then where is the contradiction?

But, I fear, I shall be told that the struggle of negatives is the soul of the world, and that it is precisely *because* of their identity that we have their contradiction. It is true that the opposition which for ever breaks out leads to higher unity in which it is resolved; but still the process of negation is there. It is one side of the world which can not be got rid of, and it is irreconcileable with the non-existence of discrepants in a single subject. Each element of the whole, without the other, is incompatible with itself; but it is none the less incompatible with the other, which for ever it produces or rather becomes.

I am after all not quite convinced. If the law of Contradiction is objected against because, in isolating and fixing the discrepant, it becomes one-sided, is it not quite possible that, in denying the law, we have become one-sided in another way? If the negation itself, while negative on one side, is on the other side the return from itself to a higher harmony—if, that is to say, the elements are not discrepant without each at once, by virtue of its discrepancy and so far as it is discrepant, thereby *ipso facto* ceasing to be discrepant, then surely, in denying the law of Contradiction, we ourselves have fixed one side of the process, and have treated the contrary as simply contrary. The contrary which the law has got in its head, is the contrary that entirely kills its opposite, and remains triumphant on the field of battle. It is not the contrary whose blows are suicidal, and whose defeat must always be the doom of its adversary. It is incompatibles fixed as such, it is discrepants which wholly exclude one another and have no other side, that the axiom speaks of. But dialectical contraries are only partially contrary and it is *our* mistake if we keep back the other side. And if an opponent of the law reminds me that the existence of these two sides within one element is just the contradiction, that in the *b* which is contrary to not-*b* the implication of not-*b* makes it self-contradictory, then I must be allowed to say in reply that I think my objector has not learnt his lesson. The not-*b* in *b* is itself self-discrepant, and is just as much *b:* and so on for ever. We never have a mere one-sided contrary.

But it is one-sided and stationary contraries that the axiom contemplates. It says that they are found,[11] and no sober man could contend that they are not found. No one ever did maintain that the dialectical implication of opposites could be set going in the case of every conjunction that we deny. It can hardly be maintained that there *are* no discrepants, except these contraries which at the same time imply each other. And the law of Contradiction does not say any more than that, when such sheer incompatibles are found, we must not conjoin them.

Its claims, if we consider them, are so absurdly feeble, it is itself so weak and perfectly inoffensive, that it can not quarrel, for it has not a tooth with which to bite any one. The controversy, first as to our actual ability to think in the way recommended by Hegel, and secondly as to the extent to which his dialectic is found in fact, can not only *not* be settled by an appeal to the axiom, but falls entirely outside its sphere. Starting from the fact of the absolute refusal of certain elements to come together, and wholly dependent upon that fact, so soon as these elements do come together the axiom ceases forthwith to be applicable. It is based upon the self-consistency of the real, but it has no right to represent that consistency except as against one kind of discrepancy. So that, if we conclude that the dialectic of the real would in the end destroy its unity, that has nothing to do with the axiom of Contradiction. Like every other question of the kind, the validity of dialectic is a question of fact, to be discussed and settled upon its own merits, and not by an appeal to so-called " principles." And I think I may venture to hazard the remark, that one must not first take up from uncritical views certain elements in the form of incompatible discrepants, and then, because we find they are conjoined, fling out against the laws of Contradiction and Excluded Middle. They, such as they are, can be no one's enemy; and since no one in the end can perhaps disbelieve in them, it is better on all accounts to let them alone.

PRINCIPLE OF EXCLUDED MIDDLE.[12]

§ 16. The axiom that every possible judgment must be true or false,[13] we shall see is based on what may be called a principle. It is however doubtful if the axiom itself should receive that title, since it comes under the head of disjunctive judgment. We must not imagine that our axiom supplies the principle of disjunction. It is merely one instance and application of that principle.

§ 17. If we recall the character of the disjunctive judgment, we shall remember that there we had a real, known to

be further determined. Its quality fell (i) within a certain
area; and (ii) since that area was a region of discrepants, the
real was determined as one single member. On this basis [14]
we erected our hypotheticals, and so the "either—or" was
completed.

Excluded Middle shows all these characteristics. In it we
affirm (i) that any subject A, when the relation to any
quality is suggested, is determined at once with respect to
that predicate within the area of position and negation, and
by no relation which is incompatible with both. And (ii) we
assert that, within this area, the subject is qualified as one
single member. And then we proceed to our "either—or."

§ 18. Excluded Middle is one case of disjunction: it can
not be considered co-extensive with it. Its dual and contradictory alternative rests on the existence of contrary
opposites. The existence of exclusives without reference to
their number is the ground of disjunction, and the special case
of assertion and denial is developed from that basis in the
way in which contradiction is developed from exclusion.
Common discrepant disjunction is the base, and the dual
alternative of *b* and not-*b* rests entirely upon this.

§ 19. Excluded Middle is one kind of disjunction: and we
must proceed to investigate the nature of that kind. (i) Disjunction asserts a common quality. In "*b* or not-*b*" the
common quality asserted of A is that of general relation to *b*.
(ii) Disjunction asserts an area of incompatibles. Affirmation
or denial of *b* is here the area within which A falls. The
evidence that it does not fall outside and that all the discrepants are completely given, may be called my impotence
to find any other.[15] (iii) Disjunction attributes to the subject
A one single element of the area. And this part of the process
does not call here for any special remark.

§ 20. We find however, when we investigate further, a
point in which the axiom of Excluded Middle goes beyond
the limits of disjunctive judgment. It contains a further
principle, since it asserts a common quality of all possible
existence. It says, Every real has got a character which
determines it in judgment with reference to every possible
predicate. That character furnishes the ground of some
judgment in respect of every suggested relation to every

object. Or, to put the same more generally still, Every element of the Cosmos possesses a quality, which can determine it logically in relation to every other element.

§ 21. This principle is prior to the actual disjunction. It says beforehand that there is a ground of relation, though it does not know what the relation is. The disjunction proceeds from the further result that the relation falls within a discrepant sphere. We thus see that, on the one hand, Excluded Middle transcends disjunction, since it possesses a self-determining principle which disjunction has not got. On the other hand, in its further development, it is nothing whatever but a case of disjunction, and must wait for the sphere of discrepant predicates to be *given it as a fact*.[16]

§ 22. The disjunction is completed by the fact that, when any predicate is suggested, the quality of every element is a ground of either the affirmation or the denial of the predicate. It compels us to one and to one alone; for no other alternative can possibly be found.

And here the opposition, directed before against the axiom of Contradiction, must again be confronted. It is false, we are told, that A must either be *c* or not-*c*. We have often to say " both," and sometimes " neither." But I think perhaps the discussion at the end of the foregoing chapter will have strengthened us to persist. I fully admit that often, when challenged to reply Yes or No, it is necessary to answer " Yes *and* No " or " Neither." But, I venture to think, that is always because the question is ambiguous, and is asked from the standpoint of a false alternative.[17] " Is motion continuous? Yes or no." I decline to answer until you tell me if, by saying Yes, I am taken to deny that it is *also* discrete. In that case perhaps, instead of saying Yes, I should go so far as to answer No. There may be a middle between continuity and discretion; there can be none between continuous and not-continuous.

The ground of the objection to the Excluded Middle is, I am bold enough to think, fallacious. Given not fixed discrepants but dialectical opposites, the existence of these together in one single subject does not give us the right to a negative judgment. One can not be made use of as the positive ground on which to build the denial of the other.

One does not wholly remove the other, and, failing to do so, it is not qualified as a logical contrary. For it is only the discrepant which destroys its opposite that can serve as the base of a negative judgment. And, failing the denial of one quality through the other, the answer must be that both are present, and the denial of either is wholly excluded. But I fear it is hard altogether on this point to effect a compromise. If the negative of *b* is ever simply not-*b,* and if this is the other which is implicated with *b* in one subject A, then I grant the Excluded Middle disappears. But, I think, in this case it will carry along with it enough to ruin what is left behind. And I must leave the matter so.

§ 23. The Excluded Middle, as we saw before, is a peculiar case of the disjunctive judgment; and I think this insight may serve us further to dispel some illusions which have gathered round it.

In the first place we must not think it is a formula, by applying which we can magically conjure elements of knowledge from the unknown deep. It is nonsense to say that it gives us a revelation that any subject must have one of two predicates. For, even if we do not make a logical mistake and really have got contradictory qualities, that is still not the right way to put the matter. Denial is not the predication of a contradictory; and all that Excluded Middle tells us is that, given any possible element of knowledge, you must be right in either affirming or denying any suggestion that is made about that.

We learnt, in our chapter on the Disjunctive Judgment, that this judgment must assume the existence of its subject,[18] though that subject may not be the grammatical subject. And when, in the case of Excluded Middle, we are told it will guarantee us the truth of either *b* or not-*b* as a predicate of A, we naturally ask, " But what guarantees to us the existence of A ? " And we get no answer. Things in themselves either are *b* or are not *b.* Undoubtedly so, but *what is the real subject of this statement?* It perhaps after all is not " Things-in-themselves," but is ultimate reality, which may totally reject the whole offered synthesis. In this case we shall at once be able to say that Things-in-themselves are not anything at all in the real world, though, considered as illusions, they no doubt have qualities. On the other hand, if Things-in-themselves *are* taken as such to have existence, then that is not proved by our Excluded Middle, but is a sheer assumption on which we base it and which it presupposes.

§ 24. But when we are told, " Between the true and the false there is a third possibility, the Unmeaning "[19] (Mill, *Logic,* II. vii. § 5), we must answer, " Yes, an unmeaning possibility, and therefore none at all." The doctrine that propositions need neither be true nor yet be false because they may be senseless, would introduce, I agree, " a large qualification " into the doctrine of the Excluded Middle. But I am inclined to think that this " qualification " might be larger than it seems to be, and might be operative perhaps beyond the limits so sparingly assigned to it. But surely, on the one hand, it is clear that a proposition which has no meaning is no proposition; and surely again, on the other hand, it is clear that, if it does mean anything, it is either true or else false. And when a predicate is really known *not* to be " one which can in any intelligible sense be attributed to the subject "—is not that itself ground enough for denial?[20] But logicians who actually (Mill, *loc. cit.*) are ready to take divisible finitely and divisible infinitely as *contradictories,* are justified in expecting extraordinary events. Suppose these terms to be absolutely incompatible, that would hardly bring them under Excluded Middle, unless we are prepared to formulate the axiom thus: Whenever predicates are incompatible, then, although there be *three or more* possibilities, it is certain that one of *these two* possibilities must always be true. But perhaps this " qualification " might tend to create more difficulties than it solves.

§ 25. If we turn from these somewhat elementary mistakes, and consider the amount of actual knowledge vouchsafed to us by the Excluded Middle, I hardly think we shall be much puffed up. We must remember that, even if we are able to assert about such a subject as Things-in-themselves, we must always be on our guard against an error. We may be affirming about the meaning of a word, or about a mere idea in our heads, and may confuse these facts with another kind of fact (p. 42). But, even supposing we keep quite clear of this mistake, yet when we come to negative judgments there is ambiguity, unavoidable and ceaseless, about the positive ground of the denial. We may penetrate so far into hidden mysteries as perhaps to be privileged solemnly to avouch that Things-in-themselves are not three-cornered, nor coloured rose-red, nor pock-marked nor dyspeptic. But what does this tell us? What more should we know, if we spent our breath and wasted our days in endless denials of senseless suggestions? If the ground of negation remains the same,[21] each particular denial asserts nothing in particular (Chap. III. pp. 121, 124).

§ 26.[22] Confined to its limits the Excluded Middle is rigidly true. But you may easily assert it in a shape which would exhibit a parallel falsehood to those we considered in examining the Principles of Identity and Contradiction. "Everything," we might say, "is either simply the same as any other, or else has nothing whatever to do with it."

Once again, in conclusion, I must call attention to the positive principle which underlies the Excluded Middle. We assume that every element of knowledge can stand in some relation with every other element. And we may give this, if we please, a metaphysical turn, though in doing so we go beyond the equivalent of the Excluded Middle. We may say, If the real is harmonious and individual, it must exist in its members and must inter-relate them.

§ 27. I may notice by way of appendix to this subject a somewhat subtle argument of Professor Jevons, which I regret to state I am unable to understand. He argues * that to say "A = B or b" must be incorrect. For the negative of "B or b" will be Bb, and by consequence a, the negative of A, must itself be Bb. And the objection to this is that Bb = o. But because "every term has its negative in thought," therefore the negative of A can not be = o, and the premise "A = B or b" is thus indirectly proved false. Professor Jevons proceeds to draw from this a general conclusion that any judgment, in the form "A = B or b," is necessarily erroneous, and that we must write instead of it "A = AB or Ab."

Though I fully agree with this last result, yet Professor Jevons' reasoning, as I understand it, appears to me unsound,

*Principles, p. 74. For the meaning of Professor Jevons' symbols I must refer to his work.

and I can not reconcile his conclusion with his process. I will take the latter point first. It appears to be right to judge " A = AB or Ab." But what is the negative? I suppose the negative is AbB, and we must conclude that a = AbB. But the term AbB most clearly = 0. So that, after all, we are left with a conclusion which proves the falsity of our premise.

The result is thus out of harmony with the argument, but for all that the result is perfectly true. It *is* true that we can not say " A = B or b," and I will proceed to show *why* this must be true. We must take it that A has a determinate quality; but what is *merely* B or b is anything whatever. Bb being nothing, what is simply not-Bb will therefore be anything. And, as A is something definite, " A = anything " will of course be false. The sphere " B or b " is wholly unlimited.

This confirms the doctrine we have above adopted (p. 123). If you take not-B as the bare and simple negation of B, it is nothing at all. And if you keep to this sense, then " A = not-B " could not be true. The true meaning of not-B is any indefinite general quality which does exclude B. And, so long as A is something definite, A can not be this. I am inclined to think from the presence of x (*Principles*, pp. 94, 95) that Professor Jevons would agree with this doctrine.

But the conclusion, which Professor Jevons uses as false, is not only quite true, but is the necessary result of the true doctrine he accepts. Taking A as the genuine subject [23] that lies at the base of the disjunction, then " a = nothing " must follow at once, since " A is B or not-B " does assume and postulate that A is real. If a were anything *but* non-existent, you could not use A as the base of a disjunction. What is wrong is not this conclusion or its premises, but the mistaken idea about the negative which Professor Jevons has embraced.

I confess I am not sure if I apprehend him rightly, but he seems to argue that the non-existent is not thinkable, and hence, because the negative of everything is thinkable, you must never have a negative which is non-existent. Now I admit that, if " existence " is used in the widest possible sense, this argument is tenable. The unreal, the impossible, and the non-existent will every one of them exist, provided they are thinkable. And, since even nothing itself [24] in this sense exists, it is obvious the whole argument thus disappears.

But, if it does not disappear, and if existence be taken in anything like the sense of reality, the argument becomes vicious. We have no right to assume that the contradictory of an idea which is true, must itself be real. Take for instance the idea of " reality " itself. I could not even admit that in thought all ideas are qualified by their negations. I should doubt if the highest term we arrive at can be said to have an opposite even in thought, although by an error we are given to think so. But to hold that what contradicts the real must be real, is a logical mistake which I cannot venture to attribute to Prof. Jevons.

I may end with the remark that it would be entertaining and an irony of fate, if the school of " Experience " fell into the cardinal mistake of Hegel. Prof. Bain's " Law of Relativity," approved by J. S. Mill, has at least shown a tendency to drift in that direction. " Our cognition, as it stands, is explained as a mutual negation of the two properties. Each has a positive existence because of the presence of the other as its negative " (*Emotions,* p. 571). I do not suggest that Prof. Bain in this ominous utterance really means what he says, but he means quite enough to be on the edge of a precipice. If the school of " Experience " had any knowledge of the facts, they would know that the sin of Hegel consists, not at all in the defect, but in the excess of " Relativity." Once say with Prof. Bain that " we know only relations "; once *mean* (what he says) that those relations hold between positives and negatives, and you have accepted the main principle of orthodox Hegelianism.

DOUBLE NEGATION. [25]

§ 28. It is obvious that *duplex negatio affirmat.* To say " It is false that A is *not* B " is equivalent to the positive assertion, " A is B." But this is not because the added negation barely negates the original judgment. For if that were all, we should be left with nothing. If mere not-A is simply zero, then not-not-A is, if possible, less. And we must not say that negation presupposes a positive judgment, which is left in possession when the negative is negated. For we saw before (Chap. III. § 4) that this positive judgment is not presupposed.

§ 29. The real reason why denial of denial is affirmation, is merely this. In all denial we must have the assertion of a positive ground; and the positive ground of the second denial can be nothing but the predicate denied by the first. I can not say " It is false that A is not b," unless I already possess the positive knowledge that A is b.[26] And the reason of my incapacity is that no *other* knowledge is a sufficient ground.

§ 30. I will briefly explain. We know well by this time that, in judging A not to be b, I presuppose a quality in A which is exclusive of b. Let us call this y. I now desire to deny my judgment, and need, as before, some quality as the ground of my new denial. Let us take some quality other than b. Let this quality z be exclusive of y, and let us see what we have. We have now Az with the exclusion of y which excluded b. But that leaves us nowhere. We can not tell now if A is b, or is not b, because z itself, for anything we know, may also exclude b, just as much as y did. What, in short, we have got is our own private impotence to deny " A is b"; but what we want is an objective ground for declaring such a denial to be false.

The same result holds good with any other quality we can take, excepting b itself. The only certainty that b is not absent is got by showing that b is present. For the possible grounds of the exclusion of b being quite indefinite, you cannot get rid of them by trying to exhaust the negations of b. You could only do that if the number of possibilities with respect to A had already been limited by a disjunctive judgment. And this is not here the case.

Suppose, for instance, we have the judgment that " Ultimate reality is not knowable," and we wish to assert that this judgment is false. We expose the ground on which it is based, and go on to show that this ground is not valid. Our proceeding, no doubt, may be perfectly admirable, but all that it gives us is the right to doubt the original judgment, and to deny the truth of the basis it stands on. If we wish to *deny* the original judgment, we can not do that by refuting our antagonists. We must show ourselves that reality *is* knowable. The ground for the denial of " A is *not b*," must lie in " A *is b*." [27]

§ 31. I will endeavour to remove a possible source of misapprehension. It might be urged that in practice the denial of a judgment can always be denied by something other than the judgment itself. Thus, for instance, " It did rain yesterday," may be false, because it snowed or because it was fine. But each of these can be denied on the ground of the other. The result of our double negation of " it rained," might be either " it snowed," or again " it was fine ": and we might return to " it rained," by virtue not of a double but of a triple denial.

But this objection would rest on a misunderstanding. It is perfectly true that, in denying " it rained," I must imply and make use of some discrepant quality. It is, once more, true that what I have in my mind, and should assign as my reason, may be either " it snowed " or again " it was fine." But it is a mistake to conclude that the denial really rests upon either the one of these or the other. Whatever you might have had in your mind, no logic could force you to allow that your denial had committed you to either " it snowed " or " it was fine." What we *use* in denial is not the *whole* discrepant: it is that part of the discrepant which answers our purpose. The denial asserts no more than the existence of so much quality as is enough to exclude the judgment " it rained." This universal " so much " is possessed by either " it snowed " or " it was fine," and *this* you can not banish by anything short of the judgment " it rained." In other words, if you say " it did not rain," you are at once committed to a positive " because," but you are committed to nothing but an unspecified quality. The evidence for this quality no doubt in the end must be found in the presence of a contrary assertion, but the mere contradiction does not affirm this or any particular contrary. It affirms merely *some* contrary, and you get rid of this only by the judgment " it did rain." We find here once more the constant ambiguity, which we have seen (Chap. III. § 19) makes the use of negation so precarious. It is so difficult to work with double denial that I hardly can expect in the present volume to have supplied no example of the error I condemn.*

* Mr. Venn, I think, has certainly done so.[28] When I had the pleasure of reading his *Symbolic Logic*, I congratulated myself on the fact that I had already written the present and all the preceding chapters. I have not found occasion in consequence to alter anything of what I had written, but I should like to use one of his principal doctrines to exemplify the fallacious use of the negative. I have added this discussion as a mere appendix, for it hardly carries the subject further. It is due to myself to defend my own views against a counter theory from a writer of established and merited reputation.

After calling attention to the ambiguity of affirmative universals, the doubt, that is, if they affirm the existence of their grammatical subject, Mr. Venn, if I understand him rightly, asserts that at all events the negative is *not* ambiguous (p. 141). I will not here enquire if in other places he is compelled to recognize that the opposite of this assumption is true. At all events the foundation he here seems to build on is the assertion that negatives have only one meaning. " It comes to this therefore that in respect of what such a proposition affirms it can only be regarded as conditional, but that in respect of what it denies it may be regarded as absolute " (142). The affirmation of xy is always ambiguous, since x may not be *actual;* but the denial of x not-y is perfectly clear. And upon this basis he seems to build his doctrine.

Now the reader of this volume will know that a negation is always ambiguous. We may consider this as settled, and I will not re-discuss the general question. I will first call attention to the seeming absurdity of Mr. Venn's doctrine. He teaches in effect that, although you do not know what a statement means, you can always tell what you mean by denying it. And he ought to hold that the ambiguity of a judgment at once disappears, if you deny it and then deny your denial. This course has not generally been found so successful.

But it is better to show the actual mistake. And we will preface our criticism by setting down some elementary truths. You can not argue from the assertion of possibility to the assertion of actuality, but you can always argue from the denial of possibility to the denial of actuality. To deny possible x (you must of course not take " possible " as " *merely* possible ") is by implication to deny actual x. Now the simple application of this commonplace doctrine is that, if you are given a connection xy and do not know whether it is possible or actual, at all events, if you deny its possibility, you may be very sure that you also, and as well, have denied its actuality. This is literally (unless I misunderstand him) the whole principle which Mr. Venn unconsciously proceeds upon, and the idea that it could lead to any great result, or to a better understanding of hypotheticals, seems somewhat strange.

I can not be quite sure of his exact procedure, but I think it is this.

The affirmative judgment both affirms and denies. Mr. Venn will not say that what it affirms is mere possibility, but he quietly assumes that what it denies is impossibility. (If he does not do this, he makes a simpler mistake to which I will return.) That is to say, he tacitly and without any justification assumes that x not-y asserts the *impossibility* of $xy;$ and it is solely by denying this arbitrary fixture that the positive xy becomes unambiguous. But if he wishes to restrict the affirmative judgment to the minimum sufficient to deny the denial of possibility, surely it would be better to say at once, "The affirmative judgment does not assert more than bare possibility." He would so have done openly and in an intelligible manner the very thing he has in effect done, indirectly and most objectionably, by going round through two denials. The procedure could in no case have become *more* arbitrary.

I will put the same thing otherwise. With affirmative judgments possibility is the minimum: with negative judgments impossibility is the maximum. Now it is *uncertain* (we may so interpret Mr. Venn) if the affirmative xy asserts the maximum (actuality) or the minimum (possibility), but it is certain that it unambiguously denies the negative. But, if the negative becomes unambiguous because it is arbitrarily fixed at its maximum degree (impossibility), then surely it is clear that we thereby, and *ipso facto,* are fixing the affirmative at its minimum degree. For so far at least as the affirmative denies and is *not* ambiguous, it is so because its minimum is enough. And the fallacy is simple. This minimum is not enough unless the negative is fixed at the maximum. Suppose not-xy to mean "xy *does* not exist," then "xy is possible" ceases to deny this: for, although xy may not exist, it still can be possible. Again if xy meant "xy is actual," then "xy is impossible" (or, again, "if x then no y") is not its contradictory, and goes a long way beyond its denial. In short, since not-xy means either *de facto* non-existence or else impossibility, it seems absurd to assert that the denial of this is not ambiguous. And if you mean to fix the meaning of the negative arbitrarily, it seems absurd to shrink from doing the same by the positive.

In conclusion, if we suppose that not-xy is really meant to assert non-existence, that is to deny the actuality of $xy,$ then the error is palpable. You first say you do not know whether xy asserts existence or possibility, and yet you say it denies the non-existence of xy. But possibility, not affirming existence, of course can not deny non-existence, and the whole process disappears unless you rapidly shuffle from one term to the other.

This hidden equivocation soon begins to bear fruit in the curious reasoning which immediately follows (p. 143). If I do not misapprehend Mr. Venn, he tries to make a passage from bare possibilities to a positive existential judgment. I confess his metaphysics take away my breath; and I am bound the more to admire his audacity as he somewhat poses as abjuring "transcendentalism," and likes to take things "in a perfectly matter of fact way." But let us see what this way is. We suppose four possibilities, (i) x with y, (ii) x not-y, (iii)

y not-x, and (iv) not-x not-y. We have first a *conditional* assertion of xy, and this destroys (ii). We have next a similar assertion of yx, and this destroys (iii). We have therefore, after this second assertion, but two possibilities, (i) and (iv).

"Before, the positive possibilities were three in number, now they are reduced to two; for it is implied that everything must be either both x and y or neither of the two. Carrying this process one step further, we see that three such" [i.e. conditional] "propositions would be requisite to establish unequivocally the existence of any one of the four classes. If we expunge $\overline{xy}$" [i.e. not-x not-y] "also, we are then reduced at last to an assertion of existence, for we have now declared that xy is *all*, viz. that within the sphere of our discussion everything is both x and y" (p. 143).

Now, so far as I can see, we may understand this process in two different ways, but on either understanding the argument is vicious. The first way is to take our possibilities as holding within an exhaustive disjunction. As Mr. Venn says, we know "that everything must be either xy, or x not-y, or y not-x, or not-x not-y" (142). The disjunction will rest here on a positive existential proposition, and the inference will be quite correct. But the objection is that, on Mr. Venn's theory, we can hardly assume that we have such a disjunction. At least I do not understand why the assertion, Everything is one of four possibilities, should be able to be taken in its *positive* meaning. We surely are bound, if we wish to be unambiguous, to take it as denying. And if you take it as denying, *it does not prove the conclusion.* It asserts that what is *not* one of four possibilities is nonexistent (or impossible), but it does not say that anything exists. The *possibility* of everything is all that is asserted, and from this the argument will not take you to more than the sole possibility of xy. If you start with nothing but possibilities, you can not cross from a bare possibility to actual existence simply on the ground that the *other* possibilities have sunk into nothingness. At least I am sure "transcendentalists" especially would be interested in learning Mr. Venn's "matter of fact way" of accomplishing this exploit.

We thus see that the reasoning can not be based on an affirmative existential disjunction. And without this foundation it is thoroughly unsound. Not-x not-y is to be suppressed by a conditional judgment, and in its dying struggles is to establish xy as "an assertion of existence." I will not ask what the conditional proposition could be. "If anything exists then xy exists" might answer the purpose; but it would not do so unless it were really unconditional, and covertly contained the very assertion that "xy is actual." And this I think is the alternative to which we are brought: we either completely abandon and throw over our doctrine of the superiority of the negative, and avowedly start with an affirmation of existence; or else we prove the existence of xy through a double denial which assumes the conclusion in order to extract it.

We may verify the presence of the same ambiguity in the ex-

traordinary assertion that contrary judgments, such as " All *x* is *y* "
and " No *x* is *y*," can be compatible (145). It is not worth while to
enter into a discussion of this matter. They are of course compatible
if you allow yourself to play on their ambiguity; but how in that case
they can be said to be contrary I have no conception. " The interesting and unexpected application " is to me, I confess, not anything
beyond a confused example of a well known doctrine concerning the
relations of possibility and existence. But I confess besides that, I
have never been much used " to discuss the question in a perfectly
matter of fact way."

I need not mention what seem to me other mistakes of much the
same kind. And, beside these, there are some statements in connection
with the hypothetical judgment with which I do not agree, but for
which, I think, my treatment of the subject has provided sufficiently.
I am sorry to be forced, both here and again (Chap. VII.), to emphasize my difference with Mr. Venn. And by way of compensation I
should like, if he will allow me, to offer a suggestion. If Mr. Venn
had not such a horror of " metaphysics " and " transcendentalism," if
he was a little less resolved to be " matter of fact," and " discuss the
question entirely on scientific or logical ground," I fancy he would
have come somewhat nearer a solution of the problems it is his merit
to have undertaken. At any rate I suspect his idea of science might
have been expanded, and some prejudices as to " matter of fact "
have been somewhat loosened. He would certainly have imbibed a dis-
like for artifices, and such a scruple against entertaining commodious
fictions, as in itself would have saved him from a succession of serious
logical mistakes.

ADDITIONAL NOTES

[1] On the idea of a term being related to itself see *Essays*, Index,
s. v. *Terms*.

[2] " Within a whole of fact." " Fact " is of course to be understood here in the widest sense.

[3] All truth must abstract, and, so far as it is truth, it can not
be made false from the outside. How far any truth which abstracts
can be wholly true, I have discussed elsewhere. See *Appearance* and
Essays, the Indexes.

[4] " In the judgment S — P." Add " of which we were speaking."
And, after " becomes an identity," add " and so enters as an element
into a fresh S — P." In the next sentence the " it " (in " belongs to
it ") is to be emphasized.

[5] What the reader should keep in mind is the following. Differences are *all* incompatible if you attempt *simply* to identify them.
They are again all compatible if and so far as they are *merely conjoined*. Wherever there is conjunction there is something more in
the conjoined whole than mere identity, so that here the whole, *as*

simply identical, does not attempt to enter into each diversity. The whole, however, if it is to be made intelligible, must become disjunctive. The aim of disjunction (see Chap. IV, § 1) is to replace the conjunctive unity by the discovery and statement of *conditions.* As to why certain conjunctions are possible in fact, while others are not so—logic does not enquire. The question of detail belongs here mainly, I think, to psychology. On the above see *Appearance,* Appendix, Note A, and Bosanquet's *Logic,* II, Chap. VII.

⁶ " The discrepant with A . . . attribute." This sentence should run, " The incompatible with A is what is not a mere joint predicate with A in any subject, nor is joined to it . . . attribute."

⁷ " For denial . . . affirmation." In this sentence "the " should be " a."

⁸ " From a certain theory." " From " is here, I think, rightly used in contradistinction to " by."

⁹ The main point here is as follows, Incompatibles exist, and no one denies this fact. And, so far as they exist, the Law of Contradiction holds. The real question is as to the limits within which, and the conditions under which, incompatibles are found and can be justified. How far in other words is the truth of contradiction, as such, only relative and more or less of an appearance? What, as I understand it, the Dialectical Method is concerned to deny is merely the absolute, utter and final, truth of fixed incompatibles. On the whole matter see my *Appearance,* Index, s. v. *Contradiction.*

¹⁰ " What I mean, &c." The point here is that, where you have differences in A, A is never mere and bare A. Cf. on § 10.

¹¹ " Stationary contraries " . . . " are found." Yes, but as an appearance only. See Note 9.

¹² On the principle of Excluded Middle, while once more referring the reader to Bosanquet's *Logic,* I will add a few words. This principle presupposes a disjoined world of incompatibles, and its truth is but relative and limited to Reality taken in the character of such a world. So far as the real is otherwise, as being either below or, again, above the level of disjunction, the principle does not hold. If we accept the view that no truth is quite true and no error merely false—a view advocated in my *Essays* and *Appearance*—we must admit that Excluded Middle, however necessary and important, is not true absolutely.

In rejecting it as the principle of disjunction, I meant to deny that disjunction stands upon it in the shape of a ready-made base. We may on the other hand take it as containing the abstract form of disjunction. It is disjunction made all-embracing and dual by grouping all the incompatibles, save only one, under their negative aspect, with the result that nothing is left beyond assertion or denial. The leaving the other members of the whole thus artificially blank, is of course a grave shortcoming. For, merely in the shape of such an abstraction, these other members are not real positively, and so are not real at all. Knowledge is not advanced by the exhaustiveness of disjunction effected formally through an artificial duality. Its real object is to discover in concrete detail the full connection of its elements.

Excluded Middle is, however, in a sense more fundamental, and goes, we may say, further than *mere* disjunction. For it asserts the actual being of the disjunctive world. We affirm in it that Reality is a region where "either or" holds, and that everything is so determined as to fall within this sphere—everything, that is, so far as it is not self-contradictory or otherwise senseless. (For the connection between these two ideas see T. E. VIII.) But, as was remarked above, we have here a relative truth which is taken wrongly if made absolute.

I may add that the principle that every idea is attributed to Reality, and is therefore in some sense real, has no special connection with Excluded Middle. And the same thing holds again of the corollary that, where all possibles but one are excluded, the one left is actually real.

[13] "True or false." See, however, the preceding Note.

[14] "On this basis." But see on Chap. IV, § 6.

[15] "My impotence." See on Chap. III, § 9.

[16] "Must wait" . . . fact." But it is better, I think, to take Excluded Middle as assuming, not only connection everywhere throughout the Universe, but also that special kind of connection which holds between incompatibles. See Note 12.

[17] "False alternative." But, if we say this, surely we must mean that Excluded Middle has been assumed to hold outside its own limited sphere, and that hence it does *not* hold everywhere. Again, in the next paragraph, "fallacious" can not, I think, stand. But I agree that it is certainly possible, and sometimes easy, to object wrongly to the legitimate and necessary use of Excluded Middle.

[18] "The existence of its subject." But see on Chap. IV, § 3.

[19] Mill's misuse of "contradictories" can be excused, I presume, as a mere slip; but his doctrine of a "third possibility" seems really something worse. He takes the possibility—with regard to an offered judgment—that it is senseless, and therefore no actual judgment; and he then places this itself as a possibility under the judgment as actual, and as itself falling between the two other possibilities of truth and falsehood. Cf. Bosanquet, *Logic,* I, 352 (Ed. II).

Conceivably all that Mill meant was to warn us that an unmeaning idea or judgment is none, and so must not be used. But, if so, his meaning, I submit, was expressed by a serious blunder. The writer whom he criticizes, we may also do well to remind ourselves, made use of the word "judgment" rather than "proposition."

[20] "Ground enough for denial." It would be better, for "denial," to substitute "rejection with a denial of possibility."

[21] "Ground of negation remains the same." We should add "or at least is not known." See on Chap. III, § 13.

[22] For this section, as also for § 20, see Note 12.

23 Taking A as the genuine subject." "Genuine" is to be emphasized. See on Chap. IV, § 3. And, again, for "reality" and "existence," see on Chap. II, § 2.

24 "Even nothing itself." For "nothing" see *Essays*, the Index, and T. E. VII.

25 "Double Negation." There is a serious mistake in these pages. The whole subject has, I think, been made clear in Bosanquet's *Logic*, I, pp. 302-7. Cf. his *K & R*, pp. 230 foll.

The main point here is this. Double negation holds where the alternatives are limited to two, and it does not hold otherwise. And in denial we have always this dual alternative.

The error in my treatment is as follows. I did not see that (as Dr. Bosanquet has shown) all denial sets up an exhaustive dual disjunction (Cf. T. E. VI). Judgment divides the world, we may say, into the selected and the residual Reality, and in denial what is excluded must qualify the latter. Having so an "either—or"—when we have denied our denial the affirmative only is left.

So much for my mistake; but, apart from this, my discussion did well, I think, to insist on an important truth. Since all denial rests on a positive ground, though this is not stated in and by the denial, we may hence be led into error. We may make the ground of negation, as we happen to have that in our minds, an essential part of the denial. We covertly, that is, in "A (x) is not b" explicate the x, and treat this, in the form e.g. of c, as being the sole ground of our denial. We thus turn "A (x) is not b" into "A (c) is not b," and so without right come back from the denied absence of b to the presence of c. For instance, having decided to wait because the ground will not be dry, and, having then the denial that there has been rain, I may rush to the conclusion that the ground will be dry— forgetting snow or dew. I have turned "not after rain," into "dry," by taking wrongly the simple denial as qualified.

26 "Positive knowledge." We must add "direct or indirect." "It is false that the ground will not be dry" rests on the exclusion, *however arrived at*, of every state incompatible with dryness.

27 "A is b." "Or" (we should add) "in the knowledge that what excludes b does not belong to A, but is (where it is anything) something merely accidental.

28 I now regret the asperity of this criticism. Dr. Venn probably had no idea of his challenge and of the provocation which he gave. And how far he ought to have been aware of this, I have now certainly no wish to discuss.

CHAPTER VI

§ 1. If in considering an idea you attend to its content,[1] you have its intension or comprehension. Its extension may be taken in two different senses. It is an instance or instances, ideal or actual.[2] It refers ultimately to the real, but it may directly signify (a) any other more concrete idea which contains the intension, or (b) any individual of which the intension can be predicated. Thus if " horse " signifies the attributes possessed by a horse, it is taken in intension. If it signifies any other idea which includes " horse," e.g. cart-horse or race-horse, it is taken in extension. And again, it is otherwise taken in extension if it is used for individual horses.*

§ 2. We have come again upon a distinction which is now familiar. An idea is symbolic, and in every symbol we separate what it *means* from that which it stands for. A sign indicates or points to something other than itself; and it does this by conveying, artificially or naturally, those attributes of the thing by which we recognize it. A word, we may say, never quite means what it stands for or stands for what it means. For the qualities of the fact, by which it is recognized and which correspond to the content of the sign, are not the fact itself. Even with abstracts the actual case of the quality is hardly nothing but the quality itself. The idea and the reality are presumed to be different.

It is perhaps an ideal we secretly cherish, that words should mean what they stand for and stand for what they mean. And in metaphysics we should be forced to consider seriously the claim of this ideal. But for logical purposes it is better to ignore it. It is better to assume that the meaning is other than the fact of which the meaning is true. The fact is an individual or individuals,[3] and the idea itself is an universal. The extension can not be reduced to intension.

* If it were used for *possible* horses, it would be taken in sense (a). Cf. pp. 171, 179, 186.

§ 3. The difference may be expressed by the terms " denotation " and " connotation." These phrases have found favour with the English public, and the indiscriminate use of " connotation " marks one kind of superior person.[4] But they serve no useful purpose in logic. They are unnecessary and objectionable.[5] They have no advantage over the terms in general use, and they have in addition a positive vice. To " connote " is to " imply "; and the meaning of a word is not its implication. With the names of individuals the meaning may perhaps be said to be " connoted," but with adjectives such as " red," and abstracts such as " redness," what is " connoted " is clearly not at all the attributes but the individual reality. Nothing but ambiguity can arise from such perversions. If you *will* use a word which signifies implication, to convey what more usually is the direct meaning, you must expect the confusion which your unfortunate choice has already to some extent occasioned.

§ 4. Hand in hand with this slovenly terminology there goes a superstition we have in part refuted (Chap. II. § 17). We are told that words may be " non-connotative." They may signify, we are told, a subject only or only an attribute. Both of these assertions must be rejected. No word such as " whiteness " stands simply and solely for the abstract quality.* It means this directly; but it indirectly points to an implied individual, an actual case of whiteness. And still less can be said for the doctrine we have already refuted. The name of an individual must carry with it and imply certain attributes, or else its attachment to that individual becomes a psychological impossibility. It is mere want of thought which allows us to suppose that a sign can mean nothing and yet stand for something.

§ 5. It would be as easy to prove that a word may mean nothing and may also stand for nothing. And it may be useful, perhaps, at this point to digress. We have seen that all propositions are " real " (p. 42). Verbal propositions become *manifestly* real, if you write them " The meaning of S is P." But there is a class of judgments where the subject has

---

* All ideas imply a reference of their content to the real (p. 3), and hence to the individual. We may notice besides that abstracts imply *within their content* a supporting subject. They are doubly adjectival.[6]

got no definite meaning, and is not a perfect sign. If we take such a statement as " *magistri* is the genitive case of *magister*," we might be tempted to assert that some words are devoid of both extension and intension.

"Theophilus is Greek," "Theophilus is dear to God," "Theophilus has the measles." The last of these informs us of the disease of a man. The second tells us the meaning of a name. The first assures us that a word is a member in a system of signs, but it seems to give us nothing which that word stands for and nothing that it means. If a sign were something with a *definite* signification, then we could not say that all words are signs. We may know of a sound no more than this, that it is a sign. It stands for something, but we do not know what; and it means something also, but what we do not know.

And we are not at the end. This last remnant of ordinary extension and intension is doomed to vanish. I may treat the word as a common noise. " Why did you make that noise *Theophilus* when you saw that man? *Theophilus* is not a pleasant sound." We have here no signification and no meaning, nor have we any longer a word. But even here in a rudimentary form we have the sides of extension and intension. We may distinguish two elements that are blended in *Theophilus*. Even here it is universal, and is the product of abstraction and generalization. The sound that I should know under all its differences, of varying tone, of the person uttering, and of places and times, is one side of the whole. The other is *this* particular utterance and other possible particular utterances. The elements still co-exist at this early stage of their evolution. We can never separate the one from the other except by a mistake.

§ 6. Let us dismiss for ever the term " connotation," and try to keep clear of the errors it beacons. We may pass to a doctrine of another kind, not so misleading but equally idle. Extension and intension, we are told, are related and must be related in a certain way. The less you happen to have of the one, the more you therefore must have of the other. This statement has often passed itself off as both true and important. I confess that to me it has always seemed either false or frivolous.[7]

(a) If we take extension to mean that number of real individuals of which the meaning is true, then it is ludicrously false that an increase of the extension is a decrease of the meaning. The logician who, impelled by the practical syllogism, begets a child, does not find his doctrine verified by the fact. The conclusion, which appears from the union of the premises, no doubt may surprise him and add to his experiences, but it may not diminish the " comprehension " with which he hears the word child. His new-born instance may destroy his definition of the genus *homo* as *animal risibile,* but the content it shears off will be largely made good by other attributes. He may say, what he never thought to have said, *All* children are scourges.

It is obvious that fresh instances may increase the intension by the discovery of attributes essential but overlooked. The doctrine understood in this sense is false. And if you write " possible " for " actual " individuals, still diminution of the meaning need not add to the number. If possible means that which is presumed to exist, we may remark that the complex may be possible in fact just as much as the simple; the simple indeed by itself may be impossible. But if possible means what can be produced by artificial and arbitrary thinking (p. 203), we have now obviously left the sense of extension we have been dealing with. The extension has ceased to lie in the individuals; [8] it has become those groups of attributes in which analysis can find the meaning.

§ 7. But (b) even if we give this sense to extension, the doctrine is not true. If you compare ideas, the narrower meaning does not always have the wider application. Take a simple instance. The idea of the visible has, we may all admit, a fuller meaning than the ideas of that which can be tasted or smelt. But the latter have not got any greater extension. Everywhere, if you take adjectives or combinations of adjectives, which are co-ordinate and which can not be subsumed the one under the other, the doctrine ceases to have any bearing. Since the greater emptiness has not been got by further abstraction, there is no reason why the adjective which has less content should be predicable of a greater number of kinds.

And if for marks and combinations of marks we substitute laws or modes of combination, the same thing holds good. If these laws do not stand the one under the other, but simply fall under a common head, then you have no right, on comparing these laws, to expect the emptier to be the more wide and the wider to be more empty.

§ 8. There undoubtedly is *some* truth in the doctrine, but that truth does not come to much more than this. If you take adjectival marks or laws, and choose to arrange them in the form of a pyramid; if you place at the bottom, and as the stones of your lowest layer, all those ideas which have nothing subordinate; if you form the second and superimposed layer by subtracting the differences from two of these stones, and by placing the residue left by the operation on the top of the pair; and if you so proceed to pile layer upon layer, so as to form a mass which grows narrower with each tier—if all this is done, then it is geometrically true that the higher you go up the fewer stones you will find, and the lower you go down the more stones you will have. And since you have gone up by leaving out differences, it is obvious that the narrower the pyramid becomes the more stones will each single stone have to stand upon, and the more there will be of which it can be predicated. This is undeniable, but what does it come to? It comes to this, that *if* you arrange your material in a certain geometrical figure, *then* it will have certain geometrical properties. That is true, but it seems to me quite frivolous.

§ 9. It is true, I admit, that if B must be C, then, supposing A should ever be B, it will also be C. But, if you offer me this as a truth about A, I can hardly affect to feel very grateful. It looks to me more like a truth about B. You begin to establish a claim to gratitude when you show me also that A *is* B, or is likely to become so. And this is the real question at issue. If you arrange ideas in a certain way they will have the qualities of that arrangement. Who doubts it? What first may be doubted is the possibility of so arranging *all* ideas; and what may next be doubted is the wisdom of the arrangement. If it is not the natural relation of the material, if it is forced and arbitrary, then the truth you offer me may after all be sterile. It may have little or nothing to do with the actual matter in hand.

If you confine yourself to the ideas of adjectivals, then

(though I will not undertake to maintain it) I think that with
more or less of regularity you may effect your pyramidal
arrangement; but I think you much over-estimate its value.
If reasoning were always the subsumption of a stone on a
lower tier under a stone belonging to a higher layer, then
your construction would begin to serve as a machine and
would even live; your ladder would grow green and blossom
as the tree, not of pedantry, but of knowledge. But reasoning
is really not always subsumption, and with the cutting off that
root of delusion your tree shows dead, and breaks before the
breath of actual existence. The importance ascribed to your
arrangement of ideas comes from a fundamental mistake
(See Book II. Part I. Chap. II.).

§ 10. And there remains an objection we can not discuss
but must not pass over. If you do not confine yourself to
the ideas of adjectives and their combinations, what then?
Take ideas of individuals. If you have ideas of smaller
wholes, enclosed in and subordinated to larger wholes, will
it there be true that the wider the synthesis the emptier it
becomes? Are universals always more abstract than particulars? Is it certain that the idea of a state has less content
than the idea of any one of its citizens? Are we sure that
the soul is more of an abstraction than any particular psychical
event? Is the idea of God assuredly less full than the idea
of a molecule? And if we consider the idea of synthetical
unity, it does not appear that the higher and wider function
of synthesis need have less attributes than a subordinate function. If we entertain the belief that syntheses are possible
which are not the abstraction from lower syntheses, but are
the individuations of these lower abstractions, then the doctrine which has showed itself to be idle once more becomes a
positive error.

This objection, I am aware, will not press very heavily.
There are few readers not so wise in their own esteem as to
convict this suggestion of folly or madness.[9] It would belong
to metaphysics to lay folly at the door of its true possessors. It
is sufficient here for our logical purpose to have pointed out an
objection, disregarded and despised, but in itself not despicable.

Apart from this possible ground of dissent, and confining
ourselves to the consideration of marks and the modes of

their union, we may sum the matter so. The law of the relation of extent to intent is not a law of ideas themselves; it is a law of pyramidal arrangement; and that arrangement in the case of ideas, where it is possible, is not of importance. It may fairly be relegated to our logical lumber-room.

§ 11. The question which is next to claim our notice is still concerned with Extension and Intension.[10] If we leave mere ideas and go on to judgments, it has been asked whether these make a statement in respect of the extension of their elements, or the intension, or both. And this is a topic we can not quite pass over, as it presents us with several dangerous illusions. I will begin by the assertion that every proposition can be read in whichever of these ways we prefer. I will then show, in the first place, how all can be interpreted in extension, and will prove the same, secondly, with respect to intension.

§ 12. Every judgment makes a double affirmation, or a single affirmation which has two sides. It asserts a connection of different attributes, with an indirect reference to an identical subject; or it directly asserts the identity of the subject, with an implication of the difference of its attributes. If you prefer to consider the identity of the subject (immediate or ultimate), you read the judgment in extension. If again you emphasize the connection of the differences, you take the judgment intensionally. It is not true that every judgment is *naturally* read in both of these ways. It is true that all judgments can be read correctly in either manner, and read legitimately.

If you take the proposition " Dogs are mammals," then this means either that, where anything is a dog, the same individual thing will be a mammal; or that, given in anything the attribute dog, you will certainly have with it the attribute mammal. And it is possible to interpret every judgment in this self-same way.

§ 13. Dismissing for the present the intensional reading, let us consider interpretation in *Extension*. We find here the presence of misleading errors. It is a common doctrine that when we read in extension we assert inclusion in a class or collection. We are told that in " Dogs are mammals " no attribute is really affirmed of dogs; the assertion is that the

things called dogs are included within the class of mammals.
I can discover little in this current theory but error and
confusion.

It sounds at least palpable, when we hear of enclosing
within a class. But try to handle it, and at once your grasp
is closed upon mist and unreality. The class, if it is to be
real at all, must be, I presume, an aggregate or collection of
individuals; and this must exist either in my head or else
outside it. The latter alternative can hardly be meant. There
is no actual physical aggregation which answers to every
general name. For every single mark would be the ground of
such an aggregate, and I can not suppose that any one believes
that these strange complications of groups or herds actually
exist *in rerum natura*.

§ 14. "The class is mental. It is no group of things. It
is our own private way of putting images together within our
own minds." But, at the risk of seeming to affect singularity,
I am bound to assert that within my own mind I can not find
these classes. By a class I suppose you mean a group of
images which actually exist; but when I come to the facts
and look into my mind, and survey what is there when I hear
the word "mammals" or "triangles" or "cats," I scarcely ever
am able to find an actual group. The idea that "mammals"
is the name of a flock of mammal-images, herded together in
my mental field, and that among these I can see the little
pack of dogs, and all the cats sitting together, and the rats,
and the rabbits, as well as the elephants, all marked with
curious references and cross-references to heads "quadruped"
and "carnivorous" and "placental" and Heaven knows what
else—I do not think that this looks like the fact.

§ 15. These flocks and herds are pure mythology, they are
nothing real. But let us suppose that they really exist. Entertaining fables, we may unawares embrace a truth. Let
"mammals" be a group of mammal-images; and let "dogs"
be a mental pack of dog-images; and let the judgment "Dogs
are mammals" be the inclusion of the former within the
latter. But what does this mean?

If I look at the mammals I either know which mammals
are dogs, or this is hid from me. (*a*) Suppose that I know it.
The *inclusion* then means that a certain definite number of

my present mammal-images are also dogs, and that these are surrounded or mixed up with the residue of mammal-images which are not dogs. The judgment asserts a spatial relation in my mind of the dog-mammals to the mammals which are rats and cats and rabbits and the rest. But such juxtaposition, let it be ever so actual in my imagination, is clearly not what we meant by our judgment. I wanted to say something real about dogs; but this local relation fabled in my head does not even pretend to represent external existence.

(b) And if I do *not* know which mammals are dogs, the case is not altered. I regard my mental conglomeration of mammals, and fail to distinguish the dogs from the cats. I can not say which image is a dog-image, but I know that the dogs are every one there. They are inside the mammal-fold and not outside. The mammals range over a mental park, and all the dogs are on this side of the paling. But that again is not what I meant to assert. The local position of my canine images with respect to the enclosure which bounds my mammals, is not the idea which I meant to convey by " Dogs are mammals."

§ 16. These interpretations are fictions—that is one objection. But it is followed by another—they are unprofitable fictions. They are not only baseless: they also are useless. They do *not* read the *whole* proposition in extension. If the extension means the *objects* called mammals, then in neither case is " mammals," in this sense, the predicate. In saying " Dogs are enclosed by mammals," I do not say that " Dogs *are* mammals." A group of objects is one thing; a spatial relation, indefinite or definite, to that group of objects is clearly another thing. And, what is more, that relation is an attribute of dogs. The local relation is not the things themselves, and it certainly is predicated as qualifying dogs.* If the ostensible predicate has been taken in extension, the proposition has in part been read intensionally; for it *has* asserted an attribute of the subject. The inclusion within the class has no meaning, if the class *is* the mere individuals themselves, and the copula simply asserts them of the subject. But if the judgment affirms a spatial relation to some of those individuals,

---

*I do not say the spatial relation of A to B is *nothing but* an attribute of A. Still it *is* such an attribute.

or the area they all occupy, or the fence that confines them, then what the judgment really affirms is an attribute.

§ 17. If we keep to extension we must keep to the objects, and it is these we must try to predicate of the subject. In " Dogs are mammals " we must try to assert " some mammals " of dogs. What is affirmed must be identity. The dogs and dog-mammals are all the same thing. (Cf. Chap. I. § 17.)

If they were *wholly* the same there would be no difference. They could not then be at all distinguished, and both sides of the judgment would fall together. The judgment would disappear. Hence a difference must exist; and what we mean to say must come to this, that, Though the dogs and dog-mammals are the same, yet for all that—what? Here we have to join issue.

For all that, we may say, they are sometimes inside the mammal-enclosure and sometimes outside, and that is the difference. The dog-mammals sometimes are packed by themselves, and go wandering off in the mental distance, and at other times their images, compelled by some secret influence, consort with all whose blood flows warmly. But this strange mythology would not answer to our meaning. We never intended to say that the dogs could exist indifferently on each side of a hedge which grows in our minds.

§ 18. " The dog-mammals and the dogs are all the same, and yet for all that their *names* are different. You have a set of individuals which obviously in themselves are simply themselves. The difference asserted is the difference of their two signs 'mammal' and 'dog.' That surely is a very palpable thing, and, in saying 'Dogs are mammals,' we mean to assert that certain definite indivisible objects have got two names. It happens that they have been christened twice, or christened with two names, and this is the real heart of your mystery."

The explanation possesses the merit of simplicity. It is perhaps too simple for sophisticated mortals. Belief in it will not " come with observation," but demands a new birth from the world of fact into the world of faith. Philosophy has not revealed it, and not many wise are likely to accept it. The creed of nominalism is no theme for argument. To those

who believe that assertions about things assert nothing but
names, the universe has long ago given up its secrets, and
given up everything.

§ 19. The first interpretation asserts that the individuals,
notwithstanding their sameness, cross and recross the mam-
mal-fence. The second asserts that, although they are the
same, their names are different. The first interpretation is a
fiction; the second ignores the fact to be interpreted. Neither
expresses the meaning of the judgment; and both in the end
do predicate attributes. The change of position with respect
to a herd or the pale that encloses it, is a spatial attribute.
The possession of one or two or three names is again an
attribute. The subject *is* not two different names; it *has*
them. One name *is* not the other; it *co-exists* with it. One
thing as distinguished *is* not the other thing; both have a
quality which is the same. On the nominalist interpretation
the actual predicate is *not* taken in extension. The interpretation is not only ludicrously false, but, if we take it as true, it
still asserts an attribute of the subject.

The natural and the true interpretation of "Dogs are
mammals" is that dog and mammal are different attributes,
and that these differences co-exist within the same things; or
again, that, though the things are certainly the same, for all
that they possess two different attributes, dog and mammal.
But this natural interpretation involves the abandonment of
the theory of inclusion within the predicate.

§ 20. And if you understand extension in a different sense,
the result is the same. The class of mammal may be taken
to contain, not only the collection of individuals which are
mammals, but also the kinds of thing which are mammal.
"Dog is one kind, and the judgment includes it among all the
other kinds." It is doubtful what this means, but, whatever
it means, the extension is not affirmed as a predicate. If I
have in my mind a known or unknown aggregate of kinds,
and say that dog is in the midst of this aggregate, then I
assert of dog a spatial relation to a set of elements or the area
they occupy. But this relation is surely an attribute. If
again I mean that dog is an unit which, taken in addition
with other units, amounts to the sum which I call "mammal,"
then I assert a relation to the other units, and a further

attribute that results from this relation. If I mean that dog possesses mammal, and that other kinds, known or unknown, do so, or that dog is like these other kinds in possessing mammal, then again I assert an attribute of dog, the having an attribute, and the identity in this respect with some other kinds.

These interpretations are all forced and unnatural. They none of them are really what I have in my mind when I say "Dogs are mammals." Inclusion is not what I mean to assert. But, if I assert it, then my predicate is an attribute. The whole or part of the extension of mammals is not the real predicate. The predicate is that which I either affirm or deny of the subject, and a thing is not the same as a relation between itself and something else.

§ 21. If you say, "The dogs, with other things, make up a certain amount we know as mammals," then this contribution to a certain number is an undeniable attribute. If you say, "The dogs share a quality mammal with a heap of other things," this again is an attribute. If you suppose dogs and mammals to be two different lots in two adjoining folds, and if you pull up the mental hurdles which separate them, then you can not say, "The dogs are in the mammals," unless you are prepared to embrace a marsupial or some other such hypothesis. They are related locally to the other mammals or to the area or fence within which all mammals are circumscribed. And this local relation is an attributive predicate.

The mythology you invoke is not strong enough to save you, and, if you throw yourself into the arms of Nominalism, then you have not only an account of the fact which is absurdly insufficient, but the difference of names is still an attribute.

And if, in the end, to escape from your difficulties, you say "The class is no *real* collection in my head or out of it. It is a name that stands for the *possible* objects that have a certain attribute," then the answer is simple. If the class is no longer an aggregate or collection, it has become little else than a mere *description*. "Dogs are included in a possible group of things which are mammals," "Dogs are of the description mammal," "Dogs possess the attribute mammal"—what is the difference between these three assertions? I ask you, is there any, and if so, what? To include real dogs among mere possibilities can hardly be the end you have in view.[11] You must mean, "The dogs possess this attribute, and by virtue of this attribute are related to other possible mammals." The last part of the sentence calls for interpretation. "Dogs," we must read it, "are not only mammals but, supposing anything else to be mammal, then we may argue a relation between this thing and dogs." What relation? Surely not juxtaposition; that is too preposterous. The relation meant must surely rest on nothing whatever but the joint possession of the attribute. The inclusion in the class of possible mammals means nothing but the having the attribute mammal, and in addition, a hypothetical relation of identity with anything else of the same description. We predicate two things, in the first place a quality, and then a relation to possible objects supposed to have the same quality. Both of these predicates are attributes, and the last is an addition which may be superfluous. It is a mistake to think that the phrase "possible" will help us anywhere into anything but bad metaphysics. And the favourite prey of this delusion is the men who think themselves above metaphysics.

We may briefly sum up this matter thus. The only way to read the *whole* judgment in extension [12] is to take it as asserting a relation of identity between different individuals. Two individuals are one though their attributes differ.[13] This is simply the other side of the judgment that different attributes are interrelated within the same individual. To take the subject as included in the predicate is in the first place to substitute fiction for fact, and in the next place *is* to predicate an attribute and is not to read the whole judgment in extension. But if the subject alone be taken in its extension, then what is asserted is obviously a connection of attributes within an individual or individuals.

§ 22.[14] Every judgment can be read in extension. Although some present two or more subjects in relation, yet all can be reduced to the affirmation of a connection of content within one subject. In "A is to the right of B," the whole presentation is the subject, and the spatial relation of A to B is an attribute of that. In "Cæsar is sick," the same person is said to be sick as well as Cæsar. And in "Dogs are mammals," there are certain things which are declared to be both. In this sense of extension every proposition can be read extensionally.

We have now to ask if every judgment can be taken in *intension*. Can not only the predicate, but also the subject be reduced to mere content? Do they all assert a connection of attributes? And this question at first sight may be answered in the negative. In "Cæsar is sick," we certainly have a junction of adjectives, but it will be said, "We have something else beside. There is the individual of whom these qualities are predicated; and this individual is finite and determined. Admitted that in every intensional judgment you have a reference to the ultimate reality, and that this reality is individual, yet the ultimate subject does not affect the judgment.[15] It is given undetermined except so far as it is determined by the judgment: and hence it does not interfere with the connection of the adjectives. But when you have a finite subject, then that subject interferes. In 'Cæsar is sick,' the judgment is not true unless you make it of this one Cæsar. You can not get rid of the individual person, and, while he remains, he prevents your reading the judgment in *intension*."

§ 23. We have already cut the ground from under this objection by proving that every such judgment is hypothetical and strictly universal (Chap. II.). If the subject is taken as an existing individual or set of individuals, then no doubt the judgment is categorical, and can not possibly be read intensionally. "All these six sheep have got the rot," "William invaded England," "I have a headache": if "these sheep," or "William," or "I," are taken as sensible individuals in the series of time, then that character enters into the assertion, and we can not reduce it to a hypothetical synthesis of adjectives. But then our analysis in Chapter II. has shown us that the reduction is demanded. When we press for the final truth of the judgment, the particular subject becomes an unspecified condition of the content. The assertion is thus hypothetical. It conjoins mere adjectives, though what it conjoins is vague and undetermined. The true subject of the judgment is, not this or that finite person or thing, but the ultimate reality. All the qualities of the ostensible sub-

ject pass into the condition of a universal connection of
attributes. It would be idle to repeat the painful enquiries
which have established this result. It stands or falls with our
second chapter, and while it stands it carries the conclusion
that every judgment can be read in intension.

§ 24. Thus, when the ostensible subject is a particular
phenomenon [16] or collection of phenomena, no ordinary means
will reduce the judgment. To take it in intension we must
apply the drastic treatment we discussed in Chapter II. But
in other instances the remedy is more obvious, and is easier
to administer. " Some trespassers must be prosecuted,"
" Some English citizens are to be hung," " In some impossible
cases right would be wrong." These assertions would, I presume, be called particular, but none of them need refer to
this or that phenomenon. The " some " may mean " under
some condition." It may describe the attribute, not point to
the individuals.

There are cases where " some " most clearly does not
indicate this or that particular or set of particulars. " Some
crimes are deserving of capital punishment," " In some dis-
eases the patient should be secluded ": we mean here that,
given a crime or disease of a certain sort which we do not
specify, then something else would in that case follow. The
judgment couples mere attributes with attributes. It does not
assert the existence of this or that crime or disease. It is
hypothetical, and is naturally read at once in intension.[17]

§ 25. " Some " again may mean an unknown number.
" Some English citizens will be hung next year," may mean,
not one sort, but one unspecified quantity of English citizens
will suffer this fate. A particular event is here asserted, and
the proposition must in the end be reduced by the method
laid down in Chapter II. But the event it foretells has already in part been stripped of particularity. The forming a
number, or contributing to an amount, is an universal attribute: it is a general adjective, and to this extent the subject
has been already purified. When read in intension the judgment runs thus, " Given certain conditions, part unspecified,
part specified as the attribute of English citizen and the attribute of amounting to a certain number, *then*," etc.

It is an elementary mistake to suppose that number [18]

confers particularity and destroys intension. And the error reveals a deep foundation of bad metaphysics. Number is surely nothing but an attribute. And how can the addition of an universal quality force us to take a judgment merely in extension? How can it even help towards such a result? You may say, perhaps, that nothing is numbered save actual phenomena, but such an assertion would be incompatible with fact. " In the single case of two men being three men, four men would be six men "—this is, I presume, an hypothetical judgment. Not only *can* you take it as connecting attributes, but I do not see how you can take it otherwise.[19] It is idle to object that the subject is really the imagined example, where two is three, and that this example is a particular event. For it is nothing of the sort. It is a supposed condition which, if it existed, would really be single, but does not exist and will never be anything real at all.

§ 26. The idea that a numerical subject is particular vanishes as soon as we confront it with facts. The numerical character is nothing but a character. It is nothing but an adjective, and no adjective or accumulation of adjectives will make anything else than an abstract universal. Suppose that a phenomenon is capable of division in fact or in idea. Its divisibility is a general quality, which other phenomena might also possess, and which would not difference one from the other. To be regarded as a collection of units summed by means of addition to a certain quantity, is an attribute not special to any single phenomenon: it can in no sense bestow uniqueness. And again, if the subject is taken as a quantity which stands in a certain fractional relation to another quantity, it is absurd to think that, on the strength of these mere qualities, you leave universals and get to existence.[20] " If a penny is thrown one thousand times, half the number of throws will most probably give head ": we have here a purely intensional judgment. There is nothing contained in it but bare universals: there is nothing but hypothetical junctions of adjectives. Of course, if you say, " *This* penny in half its throws will now give heads," the case is altered: but the numbers have not changed it. The subject is particular, not because it *is* numerical, but because it is *not* so, because over and above it has now been taken as a particular fact. It must be reduced by the method laid down in Chapter II. But so far as it is numerical it is *already* reduced, and is already nothing whatever but attributes.

§ 27. We may pass on to consider another superstition. If the intension signifies the meaning of a word, and the extension is the number of actual objects of which the meaning can be truly predicated, then both extension and intension are relative to our knowledge, and naturally fluctuate with altering experience. For instance, " mammal " is a term whose meaning has changed and will change. We can fix no limit to the possible information the word may convey, for we do not know how many attributes in the end may be found to be implied in the quality of giving suck. And the number of objects we denominate " mammal " is of course not stationary. Such considerations may seem too obvious to be ignored, but their neglect has given rise to a serious mistake.

In certain judgments, where the predicate is not of the " essence " of the subject, we are warned that an intensional reading is impossible. " All American citizens know the name of their President," is, we are told, to be taken in extension (Venn, *Symbolic Logic,* p. 395).[21] It can not connect one set of attributes with another set of attributes, because the connection it asserts is accidental. But the mistake here is obvious. If I know every single American citizen, so as on this knowledge to make my assertion, I surely must know by the selfsame process that the attribute I assert exists in each. *After* I have noticed each single citizen, it is one of his attributes and part of his meaning to know the name of his President, and, before I have done so, I can say nothing at all. If the extension is increased, so also is the meaning. And the objection that, if the mark were part of the intension of " American," we should assert it of American citizens in the future as well as at present, may at once be dismissed. If the subject stands also for " all Americans in the future," then the attribute becomes at once part of their meaning. But, if the subject is confined to the present time, then the mark is the meaning of " present Americans," and you have no right to apply it beyond.

The judgment is particular, not in the least because it is " accidental," but because American citizens are facts in time.

It would be just as particular if I changed it into " American
citizens are Americans." And of course if the citizens meant
by the subject are neither real men, nor real images, but mere
possibilities, the judgment is hypothetical at once, and we
need not have recourse to Chapter II. to effect its reduction.

§ 28. This same mistake lay at the foundation of the doctrine (§ 4) that proper names have no " connotation." [22] The
meaning is not fixed, and this leads to the idea that no meaning exists. The simple enquiry " Is the denotation fixed? "
leads at once to the result that, here as everywhere, intension
and extension fluctuate together.

Both are relative to our knowledge. And the perception
of this truth is fatal to a well-known Kantian distinction. A
judgment is not fixed as " synthetic " or " analytic ": its
character varies with the knowledge possessed by various
persons, and at different times. If the meaning of a word
were confined to that attribute or group of attributes with
which it set out, we could distinguish those judgments which
assert within the whole one part of its contents from those
which add an element from outside (p. 142) ; and the distinction thus made would remain valid for ever. But in actual practice the meaning itself is enlarged by synthesis. What is added
to-day is implied to-morrow. We may even say that a synthetic
judgment, so soon as it is made, is at once analytic. Kant
has really no need of this unfortunate division, which he
seems to have inherited. The real question which he means
to ask is, What kind of synthesis does each judgment contain,
and what in each synthesis is the principle of unity? [23]

§ 29. To sum up the result [24]—a proposition is read intensionally, when both subject and predicate are taken as
attributes hypothetically related. Whenever the ostensible
subject is no individual or collection of individuals the
judgment is *naturally* understood in intension. Where the
subject is one or more actual phenomena, the judgment can
not be interpreted *naturally* as a hypothetical connection of
attributes. But although not natural, this interpretation is
legitimate, and is also necessary. When we leave first appearances and ask for truth, we find that any phenomenal judgment, whose subject refuses to be taken as content, is a
judgment which is *false* (Chapter II.).

The error we must avoid is the idea that a class is a mere aggregate of individuals.[25] Such aggregates in my head or outside my head are barren mythology: they do not really exist. And if we mean by a class a possible aggregate of possible * individuals, we have no longer any collection. For possibilities occupy no place in the series of events connected with perception. They are not actual individuals, but merely ideal. A possible horse is anything which might conceivably possess the qualities, first of general uniqueness, and then of equine nature (Chap. VII.). Thus if the class means the attribute with reference to a hypothetical collection, to include in the class is to predicate an adjective. It is to assert an attribute, and through that attribute to assert a relation of identity and difference with any other instance.

§ 30. We have by this time had perhaps more than enough of the quantity of judgments, and yet there is a question we have not fully cleared up. The distinctions "universal," "particular," and "singular," fall under quantity, and it may be well that we should more definitely state here the meaning in which we take these terms. The common logic, we shall all remember, ranks singular and universal judgments together, and opposes the particular to both of these. A particular judgment is a judgment which fails to take the subject explicitly and avowedly in the whole of its extension; and other judgments are considered universal because in them you have all of the subject. This arrangement we shall not proceed to discuss. It is sufficient for the technical use of the syllogism, and it is perhaps in itself not so foolish as it seems to be. We need not however pause to examine it. We may be satisfied if we succeed in making clear our own interpretation.

§ 31. The subject is not only beset with ambiguities, but it tends at each moment to cross the border and to enter the field of metaphysics. I am afraid it is impossible for me here to defend the interpretation which I have adopted. I must content myself with trying to exhibit clearly the doctrine which seems metaphysically true, and which agrees with the logical results we have arrived at.

* I suppose we do not always mean "*judged* possible." Cf. p. 4 *note*.

We may realize some difficulties which obscure the subject, if we state them in the form of thesis and antithesis. (i) Nothing that is real is universal, (ii) All that is real is universal, (iii) Nothing that is real is particular, (iv) Most that is real is particular. I believe in the truth of *all* these propositions, and will endeavour to show that they are not in conflict. But first it is better to advocate each.

§ 32. (i) *Nothing that is real is universal.* Indeed, how should it be? What is real is substantial and exists by itself: it is individual. But the universal is nothing whatever but an adjective. It is an epithet divorced, a shadow which apart from its body is nothing, and can not exist.

(ii) *Everything that is real is universal.* How can it be otherwise? For what exists must be individual, and the individual is no atom. It has an internal diversity of content. It has a change of appearance in time, and this change brings with it a plurality of attributes. But amid its manyness it still remains one. It is the identity of differences, and therefore universal.

(iii) And so we see that *No real is particular.* For if particular, then not individual, and if not individual, then non-existent. The particular is atomic. It excludes all difference. It is itself and nothing beyond itself. And that self is simple: it is so far as it is nothing else. The true particular in respect of quality is shut up in one quality; relations it can not be said to *have;* in respect of time it has no continuance, and in space it can not occupy extension. Its existence in space is nothing but a point, in other words, is nothing spatial. Such a particular is of course not to be verified in experience. It is a metaphysical *ens rationis,* an abstract universal [26] which can not be real.

(iv) And it can not be real because, if not all, at least *Most reality must be particular.* [27] For in existence the individuals which are real are finite. To some extent at least they are defined by their limits. It is because they repel other things that they are what they are. Exclusion by others, and exclusion of others, enters into their substance; and where this is there is particularity.

§ 33. It is obvious here that in thesis and antithesis words have been used with different meanings. And this result we desired to establish. The *abstract* universal and the *abstract* particular are what does not exist. The *concrete* particular and the *concrete* universal both have reality, and they are different names for the individual.

What is real is the individual; and this individual, though one and the same, has internal differences. You may hence regard it in two opposite ways. So far as it is one against other individuals, it is particular. So far as it is the same throughout its diversity, it is universal. They are two distinctions we make within it. It has two characters, or aspects, or sides, or moments. And you consider it from whichever side you please, or from the side which happens for the purpose of the context to be the emphatic or essential side. Thus a man is particular by virtue of his limiting and exclusive relations to other phenomena. He is universal because he is one throughout all his different attributes. You may call him particular, or again universal, because, being individual, he actually is both, and you wish to emphasize one aspect or side of his individuality. The individual is both a concrete particular and a concrete universal; and, as names of the whole from different points of view, these both are names of real existence.

§ 34. The abstract universal and abstract particular are both unreal, because neither are names for the individual. They take the two aspects or characters of the whole, and, turning them into independent existences, then assert their reality. But one side of a whole can not stand by itself except in our heads. It is nothing but an adjective, an internal distinction which we try to take as substantial fact. We can all see that this holds good of abstract universals. The oneness or identity of a man, we know, is not found when we search the series of mental phenomena. But the same is true of the abstract particular. If you take atoms seriously, and deny their extension, you find at once you are dealing with something which can not be fact. Mere exclusion in space of other spaces is nothing real. A reality in space must have spatial diversity, internal to itself, and which it does not exclude. And this holds again with psychical atoms. For, as observed, they have internal multiplicity, duration in time, quality, and degree; and as anything else they could not be observed. An atom which really was particular, which was not divisible at least in idea, could not possibly be fact. It is one aspect of fact torn away from the rest, and is nothing in itself and apart from the act which tears it away.

§ 35. The abstract particular and the abstract universal are mental creations, which, if taken as fact outside our heads, are different examples of the same mistake. Both are distinctions within a whole, hardened into units that stand by themselves. And not only do they spring from the same mistake, but we may even say that they are the same error. The abstract triangle in and by itself is found to exclude all further predicates (cf. p. 119). Determined by that division and consequent exclusion which gave it its origin, it has become particular. And the particular itself, because produced by mental separation, is really no more than an adjective divorced, or abstract universal. The dialectical method has laboured to show that, here as everywhere, insistence upon a onesided view brings out by negation the opposite onesidedness. The universal, the more we emphasize its character, divides itself the more from the whole. We make its being depend on exclusion, and it turns in our hand into its logical contrary. The particular again, excluding others, and being so far as it merely excludes, is its own negative relation to other particulars. It falls beyond itself into a series of units pervaded by an universal identity, and itself has there become its own opposite. In this speculative movement, if we take it in the character it claims for itself,[28] I neither myself profess belief nor ask it from the reader. But I think we may go so far as this, that in the end the individual is real, and that abstract universal and abstract particular are distinctions taken within that reality, which a mistake has afterwards turned into divisions and hardened into units. If we do not admit that each is a moment which, by negation of itself, affirms the other and begets the whole, we may certainly say that each has sprung from the same mistake, and is an illusion of the self-same kind. And we may muster courage, perhaps, to profess that the individual is the identity of universal and particular.

§ 36. We must keep in view the following distinctions. We have first the abstract universal and particular, and

neither of these can exist in nature.[29]   On the other side we
have the individual, and the individual is the only thing which
is real.   But where this real is finite it may be taken from two
points of view: it is concrete particular or concrete universal.
In so far as it is a finite individual which excludes all others,
so far it is a *relative* particular.   But because it includes a
diversity of content, it is therefore also a relative universal.

There is here, I confess, a doubtful point I am forced to
leave doubtful.   It might be urged that, if you press the
enquiry, you will be left alone with but a single individual.
An individual which is finite or relative turns out in the end
to be no individual; individual and infinite are inseparable
characters.   Or again, it might be said, the individual is
finite, and there can not be an absolute individual.   Metaphysics, it is clear, would have to take up these questions, and
in any case to revise the account which is given in this chapter.
But that revision must be left to metaphysics; and for the purposes of logic we may keep the distinctions already laid down.
We have (i) the real, supposed to fall into (*a*) absolute individual or concrete universal, (*b*) relative individual or concrete universal or concrete particular; and (ii) the unreal, consisting (*a*) of the abstract universal, and (*b*) of the abstract
or absolute particular.

§ 37.   We may now attempt to lay down what we mean by
universal judgments.   Such a judgment is one whose subject
is universal.   And it is obvious that here we have more than
one meaning.   An universal judgment may be (i) absolute,
or (ii) relative.

(i) In the first case we have again two divisions.   Such a
judgment may (*a*) be abstract, or again (*b*) may be concrete.
If (*a*) the judgment is abstract, the ostensible subject will of
course be an attribute.   The statement will truly be hypothetical,[30] since the actual subject is non-phenomenal reality.
The ordinary kind of universal judgment such as " The angles
of a triangle are equal to two right angles " is, as we have seen
(Chap. II.), of this description.   And it is universal for two
reasons.   The grammatical subject is an abstract universal:
while the actual subject, the ultimate reality, is a concrete universal and is also absolute.   This is the first and more ordinary kind of judgment which we are able to call absolutely

universal. But (*b*) it is necessary to mention another sort. Any statement made concerning a reality which is not considered finite will also be an absolute universal judgment. Nothing will fall outside the subject, and the predication will be categorical. I do not say that such judgments are practicable; but they are logically possible,[31] and must be provided for.

§ 38. (ii) A judgment is relatively universal where the subject is a finite individual or collection of individuals. It is universal, because the subject is the identity of its own internal diversity. In " Cæsar is sick," Cæsar is not affirmed to be nothing but sick: he is a common bond of many attributes, and is therefore universal. But this judgment is relative, because Cæsar is one man among other men; and, if you take him so, he himself is particular.

§ 39.[32] A judgment which is absolutely *particular* can not exist. It would have a subject completely shut up and confined in the predicate. And such a judgment, if it came into being, would not be a judgment. For it obviously would say nothing else of the subject or predicate than themselves. " This is this " may be taken as the nearest example.

A *relative* particular judgment is one where the subject is this or that singular or collection. It is the same as the relative universal judgment, but is taken from another side of its nature. The subject excludes all other individuals, and so is particular; but within itself it has a diversity, and so is universal. It possesses attributes other than the predicate, and may be taken within another context. It thus serves as a middle term in reasoning, as is shown in the third of the syllogistic figures.

§ 40. We have seen before (Chap. II. § 45) that no logical difference separates the singular and collective judgments.[33] It is ridiculous to think that if one individual is not universal, you reach universality by adding on others. The number of units is quite irrelevant, since, however many they become, each remains a singular. And this or that collection of individuals is as hard a particular as any individual found in the collection. Nay, from this point of view, the single individual himself turns out to be a mere collection. Considered logically they are both alike. Excluding others, they are relative particulars. Common to all their internal diversity and identical throughout it, they both alike are relative universals.

§ 41. No judgment has or can have a subject shut up within the limits of one single predicate. If we remain at the popular point of view, and admit those judgments where the subject is nothing but a finite phenomenon or set of phenomena, yet even these judgments are universal relatively. The subject will serve as a middle in reasoning. It is hence the identity of differences, and it could not be that if it were only particular. Every judgment is thus universal, and in the end they all may be said to be universal absolutely. For, if we exclude the possibility of non-phenomenal finite individuals, we have shown (Chap. II.) that every judgment to be true must predicate of the absolute individual, either hypothetically or categorically. And the former of these cases must, in the end, be reduced to the latter. The finite subject changes in our hands into a heap of mere adjectival conditions, and, since these conditions can never be complete, the statement loses its categorical force. But becoming hypothetical it predicates indirectly a latent quality [34] of the ultimate reality, and so once more is categorical, true categorically of the absolute subject.

§ 42. All judgments are thus alike universal, but it can not be said they are universal equally. If the subject of one judgment is a whole which includes the subject of another, the first is certainly the more universal. And again, if we take two abstract judgments, they are both hypothetical, but the one may assert a more abstract connection than is affirmed in the other. The purer hypothesis, the one most set free from irrelevant conditions, will be also more true. It will predicate in a higher sense of the universal subject, and therefore may be called the more universal. But if the connection, although less concrete, is not more pure, we must then not call one judgment more universal than the other, unless we qualify universal by abstract.[35]

§ 43. I will repeat in conclusion the distinctions it is right we should keep in mind. The real is individual. The merely universal or merely particular are unreal abstractions. Concrete universal and concrete particular are the individual from different points of view. But we could not say that an absolute individual was really particular, since it would have no relation to anything outside.

Particular judgments, if taken categorically, are precisely the same as relative universal. The phenomenal individual, or collection of individuals, is the identity of diverse relations and qualities. Universal judgments are relative or absolute. If relative, they are the same as particular judgments. If absolute, they are either hypothetical or categorical. In the first the ostensible subject is an abstraction: in the second it must be the ultimate reality. Particular categorical judgments may all be reduced to abstract or hypothetical universals, and these again to categorical universals. In the end all truth, if really true, is true of the ultimate non-phenomenal fact.

ADDITIONAL NOTES

[1] "Its content," i.e. in abstraction from its reference.

[2] "Ideal or actual." By "actual" I evidently meant here "existing in our "real world." But the "ideal" instance, though not in this sense "real," must be taken as an individual or particular. The extension always means the particular object or objects to which the meaning is applicable. We may note that the word "any" implies always, if strictly used, a number of individuals (Cf. *Essays*, p. 286). The statement, in the footnote to this page, as to "possible horses" is wrong. It forgets that the "imaginary" also is "real" and can be individual. Cf. on Chap. II, § 45, note.

[3] "The fact is &c." The "fact," however, may be "imaginary."

[4] "The indiscriminate use—person." This detestable misuse—as well as that of "distinctly" for "clearly" or "undoubtedly"—seems now gone out of fashion.

[5] "Unnecessary and objectionable." Dr. Keynes (*Formal Logic*) has not induced me to alter my opinion. He is, I presume, right in saying that what Mill meant by "connotation" was merely "*conventional meaning*"; and I very possibly also in some other point may not have represented Mill's view fairly. But that his innovation was useless and objectionable I remain convinced, and why it should not be quietly buried, Dr. Keynes, I think, has failed to show. For the meaning of Proper Names I refer the reader to Bosanquet's Logic, I, pp. 50-1.

[6] Cf. here Bosanquet, *Logic*, I, 47.

[7] "False or frivolous." Cf. p. 486. The doctrine clearly, except within certain limits, is false. But to call it everywhere worthless is, on the other hand, to fall into error. Subsumption (§ 9) has its own value. See Bosanquet, *Logic* I. 55 foll.

8 " Has ceased to lie in the individuals." But see Note 2.

9 " There are few readers." This perhaps, even in 1883, was an exaggeration.

10 On the subject of §§ 11-29 see further T. E. III.

11 " To include real dogs &c." should be " to include dogs, perhaps real, &c."

12 " The only way . . . extension." I do not, by " in extension," mean " merely in extension "; for this on my view is not possible.

13 " Two individuals . . . differ." We should add, " And, where you have only one individual, you can still, by more or less of violence, bring it under the above head. For, dividing it by a distinction, you can so make the one individual into two."

14 Sections 22 foll. require correction. No judgment can on my view be read *merely* in intension (see Note 10). Any passage in the text therefore, which seems to imply that possibility, should be amended. In § 22, par. 2, the words " reduced to mere content " are ambiguous and misleading. Though nothing but " content " enters into a judgment, the question as to the reference and the extension remains (cf. Notes 1 and 2).

15 How far and in what sense " the ultimate subject " does, and does not, enter into the judgment is discussed elsewhere (see on Chap. I, § 12). It is true that, so far as the judgment depends on Designation, it remains conditional (see Index, s. v. *Designation*). But to pass from this to the assertion of a *mere* conjunction of adjectives is at least misleading. What in the text I really was attacking is the position of any one who takes the content of the judgment as depending on individuals or particulars, known merely by Designation so as to preclude an intensional reading of the judgment. Anything beyond this was to overshoot the mark, if not to fall into error. On Designation see the Index, s. v., and *Appearance* and *Essays,* the Indexes. On " the ultimate subject " see on Chap. I, § 12.

16 " A particular phenomenon " should have been " a *merely* particular &c."

17 " Naturally read at once in intension," but not *merely* intensionally, however much the emphasis falls on the intension. The words " It is hypothetical " are again misleading here, as is also the reference to " existence," if that means " existence in my real world."

18 " Number." The mark here is once again overshot. I was really concerned to deny that mere " numerical " sameness and difference is possible, and that particulars, diverse in this sense, and so unique, can enter into a judgment and so exclude an intensional reading.

19 " How you can take it otherwise." (Cf. the " impossible cases " of § 24.) These words should be corrected in accordance with what has been laid down in previous Notes. And so again with " nothing of the sort." There is aways an extensional side in judgment, however much this side may be wrongly emphasized or misinterpreted.

20 " And get to existence," i.e. in such a sense as to exclude an intensional reading.

21 It is, I think, unnecessary to ask if I here represent Dr. Venn's contention fairly. If "all American citizens" means "all that now exist," the extensional aspect, I can agree, is naturally emphasized, though the statement becomes, I presume, obviously false. But in any case the intensional aspect of the judgment is there. I would add that the use of "hypothetical" and "hypothetically" (in §§ 27 and 29) would better have been here avoided. Cf. Note 17.

22 "Proper Names." See Note 5.

23 Kant is not a writer whom I can suppose myself to understand, but my criticism seems, at least in part, to be unfair both in the footnote to Chap. I, § 7 and also here. However insufficient his answer, Kant did not, I presume, neglect "the real question" as to the nature of the synthesis within the idea, and as to how far, and by what right, this limited synthesis can be transcended.

On the real importance of the distinction between the essential and the accidental, see Bosanquet, *K & R,* pp. 59 foll.

24 The statement here is far less correct than that in § 12. After "actual phenomena" add "real or imaginary." And, after "judgment which is *false,*" add "In any case, even where we refer to one or more particulars and the emphasis is on the extension, the intensional aspect is still there."

25 On *Class* see *Essays,* pp. 283 foll. A class is an aggregate, but is also more. The *mere* aggregate is that which here and everywhere is mythical.

"Possible individuals." The statement here is, at the least, misleading. Possible horses, as actually imagined, are real individuals, though, except as psychical events, they do not enter into my "real" world. The footnote here repeats an error for which see Note 2. "Possible horses," again, are not the same as the possibility of horses, which latter is, itself as such, hardly a particular fact, except, once more, in the sense of a psychical event.

"A relation of identity, &c.," should have been "a relation of identity with, and difference from, every &c." For the Collective Judgment see Chap. II, § 45.

26 "An abstract universal." Though this statement is correct, it might have been better to have said merely "an abstraction."

27 "Most reality." All reality, that is, except the Universe itself. In the next sentence, and again lower down, "existence" is not to be confined merely to "my real world." See Chap. II, Note 3. And (in § 33, line 4) to "what does not exist" we should add "as such." For everything conceivable has existence in some sense.

28 "Character it claims for itself," should be, I think, "character so often claimed for it."

29 "Exist in nature" should be "as such be real." And, in the following paragraph, "as such" should again be added to "and (ii) the unreal."

30 "Hypothetical." Here (in § 37 (i), and again in § 41) "conditional" would be a better term to use, if either term is required.

³¹ "Logically possible." But even here the judgment will be subject to a condition. See *Essays*, pp. 228 foll., and T. E. II.

³² I have in §§ 39-41 assumed that merely external relations are impossible or at least would be useless.

³³ "No logical difference." This seems to be unnecessary, and is incorrect (see on Chap. I, § 45). And the sentence "Nay . . . collection," though true, seems to be here more or less parenthetical.

³⁴ "A latent quality." See on Chap. I, § 50.

³⁵ This § 42 seems wanting in clearness, and I can not recall what exactly was in my mind when I wrote it. It appears to contemplate first (1) the case of two concrete wholes, and to lay down that the one which includes the other, or (we should add) is, generally, the more inclusive, is the more universal. We have next (2) the case of two abstract judgments, one of which is higher than the other as being more general, and also "purer," in the sense of containing fewer unanalyzed, and perhaps irrelevant, conditions. The former judgment is therefore more universal as really covering and including more ground. Then we have (3) apparently two cases. In one of these (a) the judgment *should be* more universal in the sense of No. 2, but fails really to be so, because, though in a more general sphere— and, in this sense, more abstract—it contains as much or even more internal irrelevancy than is found in the other. Or (b) we have the case of a judgment which holds in a narrow, and so abstract, region, and therefore does not really cover more or even as much ground as is covered by a less "pure" and more concrete, but in effect wider, judgment.

We should here remember that, if our knowledge were completely systematic, these distinctions, at least in part, would cease to hold. But, as things are, our pure and abstract knowledge is really, though not ostensibly, conditioned by that enormous mass which it fails to explain and comprehend, and so really to include. Hence the knowledge (say) of a mathematician may in one sense be far narrower and less universal than the knowledge (say) of a biologist. The above remarks may perhaps serve to explain, and, where necessary, to correct the text of § 42 in detail. The subject is perhaps too difficult to admit of any brief statement.

CHAPTER VII

THE MODALITY OF JUDGMENTS *

§ 1. Modality is not an alluring theme. I should be glad to plead the fragmentary nature of the present work as an excuse for passing it by in silence. But for the sake of clearness it is necessary to make an excursion into the subject, neglecting those parts of it which do not seem to concern us here.

We must begin by stating an erroneous view. Modality may be supposed to affect the assertion in its formal character, and without regard to that which is asserted. We may take for instance a content S — P, not yet asserted, and may claim for modality the power of affirming this content S — P, unaltered and unqualified, in several ways. S — P, it is supposed, may be asserted, for instance, either simply or problematically or apodeiktically, and may yet remain throughout S — P: and thus, though the content is unmodified, the assertion is modal.

§ 2. This doctrine rests on a misunderstanding. There are no degrees of truth and falsehood.[1] If S — P is fact, it can not be more than fact: if it is less than fact, it is nothing at all. The dilemma is simple. S — P is affirmed or it is not affirmed. If it is not affirmed, it is not judged true at all. If it is affirmed, it is declared to be fact, and it can not be more or less of a fact. There clearly can be but one kind of judgment, the assertorical. Modality affects not the affirmation, but what is affirmed. It is not mere S — P that is asserted modally: it is another content, a modified S — P. In other words, you do not say that the mere idea S — P holds good in fact; you first say something else *about* S — P, and it is then this new and different idea which really is asserted.

§ 3. Modality in this sense, it has been rightly observed, has no natural limits. There are endless ways of modifying a judgment so as to make a fresh judgment. You may take

* Cf. Sigwart, *Logik*, pp. 189 and following.

the idea of a judgment S — P and express any attitude of your mind towards it. You may say "I make it," or "wish to make it," or "fear to make it," or "can not make it," or "am inclined to make it," or "am forced to make it." All these are simple assertorical statements about my condition of mind. They have a psychological not a logical bearing, and may at once be dismissed.

§ 4. The different ways in which *we* can stand to a judgment S — P are a matter for psychology rather than for logic. Logical modality must be limited to that which seems to affect the idea S — P, and to affect it in its relation to the world of reality. If we say, "I wish S — P were a fact," this once more is a psychological mode. The content S — P is not here first modified and then attributed to the ultimate subject. Neither itself nor anything we can call a modification of itself, pretends to be either true or false. The judgment in fact is concerned with nothing but my mental attitude.

Either logic has nothing to do with modality, or modality affects S — P from the side of truth and falsehood. The ideal content must be referred to or else denied of reality. But the reference or denial itself is simple, and can not be modified.[2] What therefore must in some way be modified is the content itself. Not S — P but a transformed and conditioned S — P is the assertion made by logical modality.

§ 5. The modes of S — P which logic has to consider are three in number. In each case we assert, we refer some idea to ultimate fact, we begin the judgment by saying, "It is true," —but we go on to fill up the blank in each case by a different idea. It is true that S — P is actual, or is possible, or again is necessary. The idea pronounced true is "actual S — P," or "possible S — P," or "necessary S — P." These modes we retain for consideration, dismissing all others. But our choice is not really so arbitrary as it seems. We have here in a veiled and hidden shape the distinction of categorical and hypothetical assertion. The possible and the necessary are special forms of the hypothetical; and between the assertorical and the categorical there is no difference whatever.[3]

I shall begin by asking (i) the general meaning which in logic we assign to the predicates possible, necessary, and real. I shall then point out (ii) that the possible and the necessary have no real existence. But on the other hand I shall show (iii) that these modal assertions, though as such and in themselves they are not true of fact, must always rest on a basis of assertion which is true or false of actual reality.

§ 6. (i) We need not ask what we mean by (*a*) assertorical judgment. It is judgment categorical or unconditioned. " S — P is real," attributes S — P, directly or indirectly, to the ultimate reality. And on this point we have nothing to add to the explanations already given in Chapter II. The assertorical judgment may be dismissed from our thoughts. To draw a difference between a categorical judgment on the one hand, and on the other a judgment which asserts reality, is plainly impossible. The assertorical is simply the categorical, taken in contrast with the possible and the necessary.

§ 7. And these are nothing but phases of the hypothetical. What may be and what must be involve a supposition. Neither is declared to be actual fact: they both are inferred on the strength of a condition, and subject to a condition.

(*b*) It is easy to give the general sense in which we use the term *necessity*. A thing is necessary if it is taken not simply in and by itself, but by virtue of something else and because of something else. Necessity carries with it the idea of mediation, of dependency, of inadequacy to maintain an isolated position and to stand and act alone and self-supported. A thing is not necessary when it simply *is;* it is necessary when it is, or is said to be, *because of* something else.

And where necessity is " internal," this meaning is retained.[4] For it is not the totality which in this case is necessitated. There is a diversity of elements contained in the whole, and these elements are divided into that which constrains and that which follows. In an unseparated world there could be no necessity.

§ 8. In a work on metaphysics the word " because "[5] would lead us straight to some fundamental difficulties, which will meet us again in our concluding Book. Is there any because outside of our heads? Is it true that one thing *is* by means of another, and because of another? Or are we forced to admit that every fact, while it *is* no doubt and is also perhaps *together with* others, is not an adjective depending on these others, has no real bond that fastens it to its environment, nor is subject to any alien influence? The objection would assail us: "'One fact is *and* another fact is,' so much is true; but 'One fact is and *so* another fact is,' must always be false. It is giving reality to mere ideal connections." And, if we escaped this objection, we should find another lying in wait for us. "You may say that one reality is the *cause* of another, and you may, if you please, add to this that the second is *because* of the first. But, if you venture to convert this assertion, and assume that whenever you have a *because* you have also a cause, you fall into error of the worst description. A cause is real, a because is ideal; you may have the one and do often have it, where the other is impossible. They do not always co-exist; and where they do co-exist, they do not always coincide; and where they coincide, they are not identical. They are not the same thing: they are not even two different faces of the same thing. They are nothing but counterparts, two parallel series which have no common points but possess some terms which have a constant relation" (Book III.).

§ 9. In a work of this kind we can not grapple with the problems offered us. We must here admit the objection and retire before it. We must admit that in logic "because" does not stand for a real connection in actual fact; [6] we must allow that necessity is not a bond between existing things. For logic what is necessary is nothing beyond a logical consequence. Necessity is here the force which compels us to go to a conclusion, if we start from premises. The "because" expresses an ideal process of mental experiment, which gives as its result a certain judgment. It does not guarantee the truth of this judgment, if you take it by itself. It does not guarantee the truth of the *data* which the process starts from, and on which it operates. A necessary truth may be, and commonly is, categorical, but, so far as its necessity goes, it is hypothetical. It ceases to be hypothetical only when it ceases to be *merely* necessary.[7]

§ 10. I admit it is not the same thing to affirm "*If* M is P *then* S is P," and "*Since* M is P *therefore* S is P."[8] And the difference is obvious. In the latter case the antecedent is a fact, and the consequent is a fact: they are both categorical (Chap. II. § 71). In the former case the antecedent may be false and the consequent impossible. But the necessity in each case is one and the same. S — P *must* be true, if you take M — P, and take S — M, and draw the conclusion. That is all the necessity it is possible to find. The knowledge that S — M M — P are both true, and that S — P is a statement which holds of fact, falls outside the necessity and does not increase it. The hypothetical result becomes categorical by an *implied* addition. And the hypothetical *connection* may not even then become categorical. The bond of necessity is a logical passage, and to say that this logical passage itself exists in fact demands an assumption which can not be hazarded in the face of objections. In logic we must be content to say that, if the premises are categorical, the result is categorical. We can not add that this result is *necessary,* unless for a moment we treat the *data* as hypotheses, and mean no more than *If* S — M M — P are given, then S — P must *follow.*

§ 11. We are able to urge a two-fold argument to show that necessity is hypothetical. We can reason from principle, and again from usage. The argument from principle [9] we may repeat as follows. Logical necessity is an ideal process, and you can not *assume* that either ideas or process are facts. Even if the ideas exist in fact, and exist in corresponding sequence, you can not *assume* that in this sequence your process exists. Your ideal operation works with ideas, and, so far as you know, it works only with ideas. The idea may be more than a mere idea, but it is *as* an idea that it goes into the experiment. And a mere idea is no more than a mere supposal. The result, so far as necessitated, is therefore so far *not* categorical. This we may call the argument *a priori.*

And we have in addition an argument from usage. A necessary judgment, a statement introduced with " It must be so," may assert what not only fails to be actual but is plainly impossible. " If two were three then four must be six " presents us with a truth which is compulsory. The result must follow; it is necessary truth; but it does not follow in actual existence, and could not follow there, since both antecedent and consequence, and their actual junction, are impossibilities. It is not true that apodeiktic modality strengthens our assertions. It serves rather to weaken them. If S *is* P, there is an end of doubt. If S *must be* P, we know indeed that, given something else, we can be sure of S — P, but we are certain of no more. The apodeiktic mode either leaves our doubts, or removes them only by the covert assertion of the condition of S — P. Where the necessary asserts strongly it borrows its strength from a concealed assertorical. I will conclude this section in Sigwart's words. " There is a common idea that the apodeiktic judgment stands for something higher than the assertorical. It is believed that, if we start from the problematic judgment and ascend to the apodeiktic, we steadily increase the certainty of our knowledge, and add to the worth and dignity of our assertions. This idea must be relinquished. All mediate certainty must stand in the end on immediate knowledge : the ultimate premises of every proof can not be proved. The usages of life stand in comic discrepancy with the emphasis we lay upon apodeiktic certainty. The sayings ' It must be so,' ' It must have so happened,' are judgments apodeiktic : but the confidence they express has most modest limits." (*Logik,* I. 195.)

§ 12. (*c*) A necessary truth is a truth which results from assumed conditions.[10] If we imply, as we very commonly do, that those conditions are actual, then the result is categorical. But, though the necessary may be real, its necessity is hypothetical. What have we now to say about *possibility?* When S — P is possible, does that mean that S — P would exist as fact, if something else were fact? Is possibility in short a form of hypothetical necessity?

It sounds strange when we hear that the possible falls under the head of the necessary. But it is at least as surprising to learn that the necessary may be impossible or nonexistent; and this we already know to be the case. On such subjects as these our first impressions may be worth very little.

The possible is that which is known or assumed to be the consequence of certain conditions. So far the possible is one with the necessary, where it is implied that the antecedent is real. But it differs in this point; for S — P to be possible all the conditions which make S — P necessary must be supposed, but only a part of them need be assumed to exist. It is implied that a part of the antecedent exists, but as to the other part we are left in ignorance. Thus the *partial* existence of the conditions of S — P is the *differentia* which separates

the species "possible" from the genus "necessary." Take
a judgment such as this, Given *abcd* then E must follow.
Add to it the judgment, or the supposition (§ 15), that *ab*
exists, while *cd* is not known to exist, and we get the possible.
E is now a possibility. We have an assumed fact *ab,* we also
have ideal conditions *c* and *d,* assumed to be compatible with
ab,[11] but not taken to exist. We have a hypothetical judgment,
Given *abcd,* we should have E. And from this, by the assumption that *ab* exists, we pass to "We may in fact have E."
In other words, *ab* is the "real possibility" of the possible E.
It is known to be real, or at least is treated as if it were so
known (§ 15).

§ 13. Everything possible must be *really* possible. It must
stand on a reality assumed to exist, and taken as part of that
sum of conditions which would make S — P an actual fact.
Possibility apart from or antecedent to the real world is utter
nonsense.

But the basis of fact may vary indefinitely. S — P is
possible in the highest sense when the detailed conditions
which make it necessary are fully known, and a part of these
detailed conditions is also taken to exist.[12] This highest sense
sinks by slow degrees to the lowest of all, where "possible"
stands for "not known to be impossible." Here we do not
know what special conditions give S — P. Our basis of fact
is nothing but the assumption that the nature of the world
admits S — P.[13] Because reality does not in our knowledge
exclude S — P, we take reality as one existing condition of
S — P, and we assume not only that the rest may be found,
but also that they are compatible with reality. In this lowest
and barest sense of possibility it is really wrong to call S — P
possible. It is better to say, We do not know that S — P is
impossible.*

Between these extremes come many degrees. In the hypothetical judgment about S — P we may not know the special
conditions of S — P, but we may know a smaller or greater
amount of them, and, where we are ignorant, we may have
more or less reason to make an assumption. And in respect to
the partial existence of these conditions, our knowledge admits

---

* We rest our assertion on a privative judgment. Cf. Chap. III.
§ 8, and p. 213.

of many stages, and we make assumptions with grounds that
may vary almost indefinitely. We should gain nothing here
by dwelling on these varieties, and prefer to give some simple
illustrations.

§ 14. Are disembodied spirits possible? Let us agree to
take the most unfavourable view for the sake of argument.
We have no direct experience of the existence of such spirits,
and the question is whether we can call them possible. We
know no conditions which would give the result. We have no
reason to think such imagined conditions compatible with the
real nature of things.[14] On the other hand we can not reject
the idea as impossible, since we have no right to affirm " It is
incompatible with the nature of things." We should content
ourselves with saying, " Your proposed assertion is not certainly false, but there is no ground for thinking it true. Our
ignorance is forced to admit a ' bare possibility,' but it gives
not the very smallest reason for entertaining that idea as real.
And such bare possibilities, we have seen, are none; they
are ' idle frivolities, that have no place in the minds of reasonable men.' "

The case we have given is, as we have given it, an example of the lowest sense of " possible." Let us go a step
higher. " It is possible that some of the planets are inhabited."
We have here the hypothetical judgment that under certain
conditions life would result; and to some extent we know these
conditions, while we supplement our ignorance by assumptions
for which we have reasonable ground. These special conditions again are in various planets known to exist in part and in
different amounts. Our judgment that this or that planet may
be tenanted thus varies through different degrees of possibility,
according to the amount of this partial existence.

But now take the assertion " That coin may have given
head." Here we know, on the one hand, special conditions
which must exhibit head, and we know on the other hand that
part of these conditions really exists. This is possibility in its
highest form.

§ 15. We have noticed that possibility may stand not on
fact but on supposition. If a coin had three sides, then it
would be possible that neither head nor tail should be uppermost. There is here no vital change in the meaning of

" possible." For the real basis is supposed to exist, and the possible is subject to the supposition. But we should not here say that S — P *is* possible; we can not strictly go beyond " It *would be* possible." It is possible, *if* by a fiction of thought you treat the unreal as if it were real, or the unknown as if it were known. We must distinguish such hypothetical from actual possibility. For, just as we more commonly imply that the necessary exists, so we imply and must *ordinarily* even be taken to assume that the ground of the possible is actual fact and not merely supposed.[15]

§ 16. We have now discussed the meanings of " possible " and " necessary," so far as to see that both are forms of the hypothetical. And with this conclusion we have anticipated the result of our second enquiry, Does logical modality exist in fact?[16]

(ii) We saw long ago that hypothetical judgments, as such, are not true *in rerum natura*. Neither the subject, nor the predicate, nor again the connection, need exist in fact. What is true of fact is the quality that forms the base of that connection. The junction itself may be non-existent and even impossible. We shall verify this result in the possible and the necessary.

§ 17. (*a*) We have seen that what must be is never necessary save on the hypothesis of some condition. We have seen that this antecedent, and the consequence which follows, may claim no existence and may have no possibility.[17] The necessity in these cases, if we mean the necessary connection of the elements, does not exist outside our ideas; it is not true of fact.

And again, when the antecedent and with it the consequence have actual existence, and appear in a relation which is clearly the counterpart of logical necessity, the same result holds. We saw that the difference between the cause of knowledge and the cause of existence staggers our assumptions. And even when the two seem to us to coincide, how can we assume that they are ever identical? It is a great thing to say that what is true in thought must hold in fact. But it is something more to maintain that thinking and existence appear as two sides of a single reality, and to insist that every logical process must be found in fact, and that all real con-

nection is, if we could see it, a logical process. We shall recur
to these questions in a later Book. For the present we may
repeat that, if such a doctrine is tenable in metaphysics, it
can not be supported in a logical treatise. The objections it
calls forth, if they could be disposed of, could be disposed of
only by a complete revolution of our current doctrine as to
mind and things.[18]

For logic the necessary must remain the hypothetical.
Facts for logic must be facts that *are* and that never *must be*.
The real connection which seems the counterpart of our logical
sequence, is in itself not necessary. It is necessary for us,
when in ideal experiment we retrace the process of actual fact.
But, at least in logic, we must not assume that our ideal relation is the bond of existence. The ideal compulsion of logical
necessity is as strong where the premises are known to be
false, and the antecedent can not be believed to exist, as where
we start from categorical truths and pass from them to a categorical conclusion. If in both these cases there is logical
necessity, how can we ever be safe in assuming that such
necessity is found in existence?

§ 18. (*b*) And when we pass from the necessary to the
possible, our conclusion remains. The possible, as such, exists
nowhere at all but in the heads of men.[19] The real is not
possible unless for a moment you think of it as unreal. When
the possible becomes real it ceases at once to be a mere possibility. For metaphysics I will not deny that the possible *might*
bear another meaning. But for logic, wherever a fact appears,
a possibility vanishes. It is not merely that the possible is
confined within the limits of human thinking. It can not
exist outside the domain of human doubt and human ignorance.

We have seen that to say "S — P is possible," means,
"S — P would follow under certain conditions, some at least
of which are not known to be present." And at this stage of
our enquiry, we may say at once that the sequel of such a
hypothetical judgment can not be taken to have actual existence. The antecedent is not fact, the connection is not fact,
and the consequence is not fact. Or, if they are fact, their
"factual" character must be either unknown or put out of
our minds, when we treat them as possible. If we knew the
reality we should make no supposals; or, if we made them,

we should know that they were *made* and, as such, did not
exist.

§ 19. Common usage enforces our conclusion. The accused
obviously is guilty or is not guilty (Sigwart, 228). But we
say " It is possible he may be either." That is grossly false,
if you take it as asserting about the fact. A fact is not and
can not be an alternative. The possible existence of both
guilt and innocence is relative to our knowledge; it exists only
in our heads, and outside them has no meaning. A ship has
sailed from Liverpool for America, and we say " It may have
arrived in New York, or again it may be at the bottom of the
sea." If you make this statement of the actual fact, it *can not*
be true. It is not possible that a ship should be in two places
at once. It must actually be somewhere; and, being actually
there, it is not possibly elsewhere, nor even possibly where it
is. The possibility is nothing beyond a supposition founded
on our real or hypothetical ignorance. Outside that ignorance
and that supposition it is not anything at all.

§ 20.[20] We have now shown in the first place that
" necessary " and " possible " are both hypothetical. We have
seen in the second place that, at least for logic, they do not
exist, as such, in the world of fact. It remains to show that,
although " subjective," they must rest on a basis of categorical
assertion about reality.

(iii) We have only to recall the doctrine we reached in
our Second Chapter, to perceive at once the truth of this conclusion. We saw there that all judgment in the end was
categorical. The basis of the hypothetical must be fact, and
without that basis the judgment would be false.

(*a*) We need give ourselves no pains to verify this result
in the case of necessity. We have seen that " S — P is a
necessary truth " means " S — P follows from something
else." This something else need not be fact, and, where it is
fact, that can not be assumed to make any difference to the
ideal connection. We can not say " In fact S — P really is a
necessary consequence as such." But, the connection being
hypothetical, it on the other hand demands a basis which is
categorical. All necessity affirms a real ground explicit or
implicit. It thus so far has actual existence, not in itself, but
indirectly and simply in its ground (Chap. II.).

§ 21. When we come (b) to the possible, we are tempted to think it has less actuality than belongs to the necessary,[21] since a part of its conditions remains unspecified. But, unless we imply that the antecedent of the necessary exists in fact, such a comparison would be illusory. In neither case can we assume that antecedent or consequent exists; and when we pass from what must be to what only may be, the ground of the judgment seems in either case to be equally real.

In the merest hypothetical possibility we have an assertion about actual fact. We affirm the necessity of S — P following from *abcd,* conditions a part of which is supposed. And in this we attribute the base of that connection to ultimate reality. But in an ordinary assertion of possibility we imply the existence of a part of *abcd,* and thus make another statement about fact. What we do in a case of so-called *bare* possibility again is this. We first, on the strength of a privative judgment [22] (§ 13), conclude that the conditions are compatible with reality. We then get the *existence* of a part of these unspecified conditions by taking the real (*because* it is compatible) as a joint condition. Thus reality, taken in some unknown character and passing into the conditions, gives partial existence unknown to the antecedent; while the same reality, in another character, then guarantees the hypothetical sequence of S — P. We thus in the end (whatever we may think of them) have two categorical assertions.

In " A disembodied spirit is possible " we start by denying that it is impossible. This judgment rests, first, on the assumption that the real has an actual unknown quality, which, in the second place, if you take it together with other unspecified conditions, makes a hypothetical antecedent from which " disembodied spirit " follows as a consequence. As the ground of this second judgment we have to attribute another unknown quality to the real to serve as the basis of the hypothetical connection. We have thus two assertions about the nature of things.

§ 22. Let us now take an instance of rational possibility. If we say " It is possible A holds the ace of trumps," we know there are conditions which would give this result. Such or such an arrangement of the pack, such or such adjustments of the muscles in the person who cuts and the person who deals, *must* give the ace to A. The ground of this judgment consists in mechanical and other laws, in accordance with which the result would follow. These laws we regard as qualities of the real, and this is one of our assertions. We next affirm that an event has happened, viz. the dealing of the pack, which presents in fact a certain part of our antecedent; in other words, which gives reality to our supposed conditions to a certain point and within a limit. The antecedent is not actual in that full and especial form which gives the ace to A, but it is there in that outlined and partial character which gives the ace to some one player.

Everywhere, where we say that S — P *is* possible, we assert a real possibility of S — P. We must assume a fact which actually is, though it is not S — P. And we assume that this fact would under some conditions give us S — P. That is, we categorically assert the ground of an hypothetical judgment; and again we categorically assert the existence of a fact which forms part of the antecedent. These two positive assertions can everywhere be found in the most guarded statement about an actual possibility; and the former is required for mere hypothetical possibility.

We have now accomplished the third task we set before us. We have shown that the necessary as well as the possible has a basis in fact and depends upon experience. A modal judgment has to make an assertion about reality. But the judgment itself expresses a truth which is not a fact. Modality is but hypothetical, and hypothetical connections exist only in our thoughts.

§ 23. There are various points in connection with the subject which claim our attention. We are accustomed to hear of " capacities " and " faculties," and to use such phrases as " potential energy," with but little regard for their actual meaning. The " potential " is regarded as something real, stored up outside existence, which hereafter may emerge in the world of fact. This deplorable piece of effete metaphysics takes a leading place in popular versions of the truths of physics. Potential energy of course as such has no real existence. It is merely the consequence in a hypothetical judgment where the conditions are not all taken as actual. It would be better to say, " Though there is no energy, there is something actual which exists as the real possibility of energy." But even this correction leaves a residue of error.

In strictness of speech a real possibility of S — P can not exist as such.[23] It should mean that reality which, *if you place it in an ideal construction,* develops S — P as a consequence. Itself is fact, and the attribute at the base of the hypothetical judgment again is fact: but that judgment with its elements can not be taken as fact. We are met by this dilemma. Apart from the judgment the real is mere fact and has no potentiality; but within the judgment the reality itself has ceased to be real. It has taken its place in a mental construction. Unless you are prepared to make ideal elements determining forces in the processes of nature, you can not properly believe in real possibilities. And I think, upon any metaphysical theory, it would be better to find some other expression.

§ 24. But I shall hear: " Conditions are surely real.[24] Before life began its conditions could be present. And the real possibility being a condition, as such you must allow it to exist." In the above I see nothing but the same mistake. A condition as such can not be said to exist. A condition is an element in a hypothetical judgment and, outside that judgment, it is no condition. If you say, " A exists and *is* an actual condition of B," you are speaking inaccurately. What real bond corresponds to your phrase? B *is* not in existence, and if the other conditions do not appear, it will not exist. And yet you say, " A *is* one of its conditions." If you wish to be accurate you should say, " A is something which, if taken from existence and placed within an ideal construction, mentally gives rise to B." All beyond is unwarranted.

A condition *ex vi termini* does not as such exist; and to define the cause as " the sum of the conditions " is to commit a serious metaphysical mistake. It is saying, " The reality which gives rise to reality is made up by adding mere ideas together." * But the cause must be fact, and its effect must

---

* Of course the word *sum* again is open to criticism. It implies a theory of the union of the elements, which certainly can not be taken for granted. But to clear up this point a long digression would be wanted. There are some remarks on causation in Book III. II. Chap. II.

be fact. We should do better to call the cause the meeting of
elements which, in the moment of their union, begin a process
which issues in the change we call the effect. An actual union
of actual elements is the cause. Each element by itself and
apart from this union *is* not even a condition. It becomes a
condition when you place it ideally in union with others. But,
in order to do that, you must make it an idea. In its character
of condition it must so far cease to be fact.

I am far from suggesting that the want of accuracy I have
just been noticing is always error. The phrases " potential "
and " condition " and " possibility " may be harmless and
useful. We ought all to be able to employ them safely. But
I fear that too often the case is otherwise. Too often they
prove mere engines of illusion, drowsy sops thrown down to
make reason slumber. If we believe in something that neither
is nor is not, but rules some strange middle-space between
existence and nothingness, let us at least have courage to
profess our opinion. Do not let us use words in using which
we take refuge from doubt in blind ambiguity.

§ 25. It was blind ambiguity and little beside that lay at
the root of a controversy we remember. Amongst those who
vexed themselves and others with disputes on the " Permanent Possibilities of Sensation," [25] how many adopted the
obvious course of asking what lay hid in this spell? We know
now that a *real* possibility means something which, in itself
and in fact, is no possibility, but must be something actual.
It is a veritable fact which actually exists; and to this we
must add here the idea of *permanence*. I suppose this means
that our actual fact has, against something else, at least a
relative duration and freedom from change. But now *what* is
this real or, I should say, these reals, which do not change, and
which an attribute of the reality guarantees to produce the
consequence of sensation, so soon, that is, as you have transformed them into ideas, and placed them within ideal constructions? Are they real things, as distinct from sensations,
or, if not, *what* are they? I do not say that the asking this
question is enough to explode the theory of J. S. Mill. I will
say that the answer to it, *however it is answered,* must alter
at least the statement of that theory, and change at least some
of the points in dispute.

I must be pardoned for seeing in another use of this delusive phrase an ambiguity which threatens the conclusion. If
there are difficulties in the way of making pleasure, in the
sense of atomic and momentary feelings, the end of life, can
we be said to escape them if we say Happiness is the end, and
if Happiness is defined as a permanent possibility of pleasant
feeling? We are met by the objection, If the end is pleasure
then it surely must lie in actual pleasure. But if it lies in
actual pleasure, it can hardly lie in mere possible pleasure.
Either the end is pleasure present and actual, such pleasure
again as has a quality (itself also pleasure) which guarantees
a hypothetical result of ideal pleasure, *and* this present pleasure
is also *permanent*—either this, I say, or Hedonism is given up,
for something *not* pleasure is made the end. Here again I
must venture to make the remark that the answer to the objection must modify at least the statement of the doctrine.[26]

§ 26. We may turn from these criticisms to a positive
result laid down by Sigwart (182, 227), and which our discussion of possibility should have served to make clear. The
particular judgment, in the end and really, we found to be
nothing but a hypothetical in which the conditions remained
imperfect (Chap. II.). In the problematic form of judgment
we once again encounter the particular. The one is the other
under a disguise which disappears before our scrutiny. The
particular judgment " Some S is P " is the same as the judgment " S may be P." The assertion that S does actually exist
is not contained in the particular judgment,[27] any more than
it is in the problematic. " Some S is P " asserts no more than
that, S being given in ideal connection with other conditions,
of which conditions some part is assumed or supposed to be
actual, then P will follow. And this is precisely the sense of
" S may be P." Both are imperfect hypothetical judgments,
and both are founded on a basis of fact believed in or supposed (§ 15).

§ 27. Reality in itself is neither necessary, nor possible,
nor again impossible. These predicates (we must suppose in
logic) are not found as such outside our reflection.[28] And to
a knowledge and reflection that had command of the facts
nothing ever would be possible. The real would seem necessary, the unreal would seem impossible.

The impossible is that which must be unreal.[29] We might call it, if we chose, one kind of the necessary. When we say of S — P that it can not exist, we do not merely mean that in ideal experiment the suggestion of S — P directly vanishes. We suppose for a moment that S — P is real. Then on that hypothesis we see that the conditions from which alone S — P would follow are directly or indirectly incompatible with the real. The real, if changed in ideal construction so as to afford the conditions of S — P, is changed in such a way as to cease to be itself. The alteration removes some attribute that we assign to the real; and this attribute, in our reflection, by means of its exclusion of other possibilities, thus generates the impossible and becomes the necessary.

Impossibility and necessity are correlative ideas. They emerge together. The real does not seem necessary until it has excluded what is incompatible, and reasserted the attribute which is the ground of the exclusion.[30] Because of this attribute nothing else can be, and the attribute must be because nothing else is. The unreal again is not impossible until we have seen, not merely that it fails, but that its supposed success would destroy what is, and what must be because its opposite is excluded.

§ 28. These ideas suggest a number of difficulties. In a later book we must return to one of them, and may content ourselves here with a brief indication. The impossible we see must always imply a positive quality, known or assumed to belong to the real. If X is impossible, this means and must mean that an actual X would remove by its presence some positive attribute we take to be real.

This bears on a point which already has engaged us (§§ 13, 21). The possible may be taken as anything whatever which is not real nor yet impossible.[31] We objected to this process, as frivolous in its result and insecure in its method. The method is insecure, since it passes from the absence of known incompatibility to the assumption of compatibility. We take X to be compatible, if the real, as we know it, will pass unabridged into a set of conditions which give X as a consequence. Again, so far as we know, X is *not incompatible,* when the suggestion of X as an attribute of the real calls forth no answer affirmative or negative. And the doctrine

we object to passes direct from want of incompatibility to
compatibility. In the one case X is possible, since it follows
from conditions a part of which is supplied by the real. But
in the other case we can say nothing about reality, unless we
make an enormous assumption.

§ 29. We offer our suggested X to the real, and the real
is passive: X is not excluded. This privative judgment, if
we wish to understand it, must be reduced to an ordinary
negative where a positive quality in the subject rejects. What
is the positive quality here? It is the mental presence of the
real with such and such attributes. Now even the smallest
addition to these present attributes is an alteration of the real,
as we have it in our minds, against which it asserts itself in
the character it bears at the actual moment. In other words,
the base of our assertion that X is *not* rejected by the real, is
the assumption that the real differs in no point from the real
as at this moment it is present.

Now it is one thing to say "Whatever I judge true holds
good of reality," and another thing to say "What I fail to
judge true is absent from reality." And there is this very
great difference between them. In the first case we assume
that, whatever *else* may be, at least so much is true. In the
second we go so far as to say that what we have in our minds
is co-extensive with reality. But, if we hold to this, we ought
to go further. What the real does *not* exclude is not possible,
it is actual and necessary (pp. 118-19). And if we shrink
from this assertion, ought we to maintain that X is even
possible?

§ 30. The mistake is apparent. A privative judgment (as
we saw in Chapter III.) is not true of a subject, if that subject
is confined to something without the sphere of the predicate.
It then becomes obviously frustrate and unmeaning. You can
not predicate absence unless you predicate the positive space
from which the absent is lacking (Chap. III.). We shall find
that this holds good of ultimate reality. To say of it, " It is
without the rejection of X," is to say of it something which
has no meaning unless, so to speak, the place left empty by
this mere privation is occupied by a positive attribute. We
ought to be able to say There is a quality the presence of
which guarantees, or goes to guarantee, the absence of the

exclusion of X. But this quality would obviously be either
the presence or compatibility of X. It is on the ground of this
presence or compatibility that we ought to assert the possibility
of X. For otherwise we fall into circular argument.

I will give an illustration. Suppose I were to say that an
isosceles triangle with three unequal angles is certainly possible, and possible because it is not impossible. The universal
triangle, so far as I am supposed to know it, tells me nothing
about the nature of the isosceles.[32] On the privative judgment
that the universal triangle does not reject my idea, I call it
possible. Is not this absurd? It is absurd, because a privative
judgment, where the subject is left entirely undetermined in
respect of the suggestion, has no kind of meaning. Privation
gets a meaning, where the subject is determined by a quality
or an environment which we have reason to think would give
either the acceptance or the rejection of X. But, if we keep
entirely to the bare universal, we can not predicate absence,
since the space we call empty has no existence.

§ 31. Or if our privative judgment has a meaning, then it
has a false meaning (Chap. III.). It rests on a confusion
between the universal and its psychological existence. We
take the idea, as we find it existing within our minds as a
psychical event, and then confound the determination it so gets
with its logical qualities. We say Here is a fact, and we can
not find that it does reject X. But the answer is simple. In
the first place we have the *reductio ad absurdum.* Since the
real has a quality on the ground of which it must accept or
decline every possible suggestion (Chap. V.) ; and since the
real here *ex hyp.* does not decline, it therefore must accept.
X is not possible, it is actual and necessary. In the next place
we directly deny the premise. In your experiment you have
not got the reality, and you ought to know that you have not
got it. If you wish to determine your empty universal so as
to get an answer in regard to X, you have nothing to do with
the psychological setting of this universal. The psychical
environment is not the space which, in respect to X, must be
full or empty. It is quite irrelevant and must be discarded.
You must fill out your idea by adding to its *content.* When
the content is supplied to such an extent that, in saying, " Rejection of X is still absent," you mean that some of the condi-

tions of X are already present—when you mean that there are
qualities which do affect the prospects of X, that a part of that
attribute, which when complete will accept or reject X, is
already there and that part is favourable—then I admit you
may found possibility on your privative judgment.[33] The complaint I make is that your proceeding is frivolous. You have
in your hands the positive ground on which your judgment is
based directly, and you choose to proceed in a way which is
indirect and in this case circular (Chap. V. § 28).

We should never trust a privative judgment until we have
seen its negative form. We should never trust a negative
judgment until we have seen its affirmative ground. We
should not take our impotence as a test of truth, until we at
least have tried to discover the positive counterpart of that
failure. The observance of these rules might preserve us from
errors which sometimes are dangerous.

The relation of necessity and impossibility to our mental
impotence is a subject which would carry us beyond the present
volume. We shall add some remarks in our concluding Book.
In the present chapter we have yet to see how modality is the
passage from judgment to reasoning. But, before we indicate
that transition, we must rapidly deal with a most important
application of modality, so far at least as to show its connection with our general view.

§ 32. If Logic professed to supply a method for the discovery of truth, the logician could not mention the theory of
Probability [34] without shame and confusion. The fruitful
results of the modern rival would offer themselves in damag-
ing contrast with the sterility of the old and privileged veteran.
And, where a true view of the claims of logic makes this contrast impossible, the logician, it may seem, has no right to
trespass within the limits of another science. The objection
is heightened when the writer on logic confesses himself un-
acquainted with mathematics. He may appear in this case to
be talking about things of which he knows nothing.

But the objection rests on a misunderstanding. The principles on which probabilities are reckoned, the actual basis and
foundation of the theory, are not themselves mathematical.
Before mathematics can deal with the subject some assump-

tions are necessary; and, though these assumptions can be justified by their results, it is desirable to examine them simply by themselves, to see what they are and whether they are true. An enquiry of this sort, by whomsoever it is made, is a logical enquiry.

§ 33. Probability, we know, has to do with possibilities. And starting from this, at the point we have reached, we can go at once to an important result. No statement we make about probabilities can, as such, be true of the actual facts. This is half the truth, and we must not forget it. But it is not *more* than half, nor is it even the half best worth remembering. It is just as true that an assertion about chances does make an affirmation about reality. Every hypothetical judgment, we have seen, must rest upon some categorical basis. The conclusions we have adopted enable us to say without further enquiry, Any theory which calls the doctrine of chances merely " objective," or merely " subjective," is certainly false. It is a vicious alternative which, if it were sound, would upset general results we have found to be true, and which is contrary to the special facts of the case.

§ 34. I shall return hereafter to the consideration of this root-mistake, but it is better to begin with a statement of the truth. We are to omit the subject of probability in general, and confine ourselves to the particular instance of that which is called mathematical probability. And the point which first presents itself to our notice, is the necessity of limiting the possibilities. Before we can advance a single step we must have the whole of the chances before us. This exhaustive survey may rest on knowledge or on arbitrary assumption, but it is always presupposed. The calculation of chances, in a word, must be based on a disjunctive judgment, and the hypothetical assertions, which represent the chances, take place within the bounds of that judgment. But disjunction, as we know (Chap. IV.), implies a categorical foundation. This basis of fact is the condition of our assertions about the chances.

§ 35. Take a simple instance. A die has been thrown without our knowledge, or is now about to be thrown before us. As a previous step to reckoning the chances we must make some categoric statements. We must be able to say,

The die will fall (or has fallen), and will fall beside in a
certain way. It must have one side up, and this, whatever else
it is, will at least be not other than all these six sides. It must
have a quality determined as what is common to the six, and
not determined as what will be none of them. On this categorical foundation all the rest is based, and without it there is
no possibility of advance.

This result has a most important application. There is no
probability before all reality. There is none which does not
stand on a basis of fact assumed or actual, and which is not a
further development of that basis.

§ 36. We have seen the foundation of our disjunctive
judgment. What is it that completes it? It is of course the
setting out of exclusive alternatives. These alternative possibilities are given us in the various hypothetical judgments
which we are able to make as to the number on the face which
we know is lying uppermost, or which will so lie. We have
now a disjunctive judgment, enclosing an exhaustive statement
of exclusive possibilities. But we have not yet got to mathematical probability. To reach this a further step is to be made.
We must take the possibilities all to be equal, or, if they are
not equal, we must make them comparable.

§ 37. The possibilities must all be equally probable. What
does this mean? It means that there is no more to be said
for one than there is for another. The possibilities are
each a hypothetical result from certain conditions; and these
results are equal, when, in the first place, they follow each
from no more than one single set of conditions, and when
in the second place, I attach no more weight to any one
set than I do to the others. When, in short, I have no more
reason for making one hypothetical judgment than I have
for making any other, they are possible alike and equally
probable.

X must be a or b or c. X qualified by certain conditions
would be a, if qualified by other conditions would be b, and so
with c. If in my knowledge I have any ground [35] for taking X
in one set of conditions rather than in another, then a, b, and c
are not equally likely. If such a ground is absent, then they
are equal. Again, if X will give a with a single set of conditions, and b or c with more than one set, the chances are

different in the different cases.[56]   Otherwise they are the same.*

§ 38. If the separate alternatives are not found equal, then we must either give up our attempt to reckon chances, or must find some common unit of value. We must analyze one possibility, and find, perhaps, that its final result is really two; or that, though the final result is one, it will follow from two or three sets of conditions, and hence can stand for two or three units. In these cases there were two hypothetical judgments which we joined in one. Again, if we can not divide the greater, we may join the smaller. By considering two or more alternatives as one, we raise the whole to a unit of higher value.

§ 39. Where we have a disjunction the alternatives of which are equally likely, or are reduced to alternatives which are equally likely, we can state the chances. Since we have the same ground to think every possibility true, the probability of each is just the same quantity. In our knowledge they divide the actual fact between them equally. The reality then we represent as unity, and each alternative possibility we represent by a fraction, of which the denominator is the number of equal alternatives, and the numerator is one. Against our belief in the general fact we have nothing to set. Against any one of its developments we have to set the whole of the others.

§ 40. Take the instance of the die. We know it will fall in a certain way. So much is categorical, and we have now to determine the further possibilities. What are the conditions from which in each case our hypothetical results proceed? They are first the general character of the fall, those positive and negative general conditions from which comes a fall with one of the six faces up, and no more than one. Do these furnish a ground for making one fall more likely than others? Clearly they do not.

The general conditions, which we have considered so far, are known to exist. The fact must take place in such a way that these conditions will be realized. But, beside this known

---

* Wolff has expressed the principle very well, " Probabilior est propositio, si subjecto predicatum tribuitur ob plura requisita ad veritatem, quam si tribuitur ob pauciora."

element, there are a number of circumstances about which we are in doubt. The particular throw must be the result of one particular position of the die, the contraction of particular muscles in the thrower, and the character of the surface which receives the fall. The number of different sets of conditions which would lead to the result, is very great, and in part perhaps unknown.[37] Still this makes no difference. They are all at least known or assumed to be compatible with the reality, and they lead indifferently to any *one* of the six results. With respect to each face we have exactly as much reason to think it uppermost, as we have to think any other face uppermost. The chances are equal; and since they are six, and since they divide the sphere of a single unity, they are each one-sixth. We have a certain reason to expect one face, say for instance four, but we have the same reason five times over *not* to look for four.

§ 41. Now suppose one face loaded. The final possibilities are still six in number, but their value is not equal. There are more sets of conditions, which would lead to the loaded face being downwards, than sets which would bring the opposite face into the same position. I have thus more reason to look for one than I have to expect the rest. My task is now to get a fresh unit by breaking up some or all of the possibilities. If I succeed in this, the whole will again be divided into fractions expressing the respective chances, but these fractions will be unequal. The units of reason to look for each face will be more in one case and less in another.

§ 42. The above is, I think, the entire foundation of the doctrine of chances. It is perfectly simple and entirely rational. It need not appeal as a warrant for its existence to those splendid successes which make it indispensable. Rightly understood its principles by themselves are abundantly clear and beyond all controversy.

We have no cause and no right to follow the theory even into its first and most simple applications, but we can not pass over an important point. Where we can not determine numerically the conditions of different possibilities in a way that is direct, we can proceed indirectly. For example, in the case of a loaded die, I may have no *data* for calculating the chances, since I may not have accurate knowledge of the conditions. But I can go to the result in another way. I can throw the die a number of times, and, setting down the numbers for every face, can then in view of an unknown throw state the fractions in accordance with the relations of these numbers. But this inverse process implies no appeal to a different principle.

Let us perceive its nature. I assume that I have no reason whatever to think the unknown throw, which I wish to determine, different from the rest. I therefore take it as simply the same. But I can not take it as the same as any *one*,[38] for then it must be different from others. It is therefore the same in its general character, with possible alternatives which fall within the *data* supplied by the actual series. It remains to reduce these possibilities to fractions.

We are obliged to reason from effect to cause. If a known cause A would produce a given effect, and if we have no reason whatever to believe in any other cause,[39] we assume we can go from the effect to A. The effect we are considering is a certain series, and the question is, Do we know the one cause which would produce that series?

I hardly think we do. However long and however regular the series may be, we can never say that there is one and but one disposition of elements, which leads and must lead to the series we have seen. And if we could say this, and assume beside that the unknown throw will follow from this determinate cause, then there would no longer be any *probability* in the case. The whole thing would be understood and certain. But we obviously do *not* know this one special cause which would produce our series. We can determine no more than its *general* character. It must be such a cause as would give a series possessing certain numerical relations. And we assume that an arrangement of which we can say, " It is the real possibility, with respect to any throw, of chances disposed in those numerical relations," is such a cause. It is therefore probable that the series is the effect of this cause. And since (by another assumption) we have no reason to believe in any other cause, it is certain that the series has resulted from this cause. And since again we assume that the unknown throw has a general character the same as that possessed by the series, we proceed without any further hesitation to reckon its chances directly.

§ 43. We may notice in passing that, if we had to suppose that the series might arise from some other cause, beside the one we have already mentioned, a further complication would be at once introduced.[40] But this we need not consider; for the most simple case of inverse or inductive probable reasoning proceeds as above, and is sufficient to show the principle employed. And we may notice again that there are assumptions involved, which we shall have to discuss in a following section. We may here remark that, if we are not satisfied with a probable conclusion, if we go on to assert that the series has actually been produced by a cause of a certain character, which will operate again in the unknown throw, our assumption is doubtful, if it is not false. But, to resume, however this point may be decided hereafter, the nature of our reasoning on chances is the same in inductive as it is in deductive probability. The chances of the new throw represent the proportion of our grounds for belief. The fact that these grounds have been supplied by a series, and the reduction of that series to its actual or probable cause, makes no difference to the principle. What grounds have we got for determining the throw that is to take place? Those grounds which as causes have determined the known series. What are those grounds? They are those from which we go to the series in hypothetical judgments. What is the nature of these? We do not know them exactly, but, so far as known, we can arrange them as units, and groups of units, which stand to one another in certain relations. But grounds for belief, which stand to one another in numerical relations, are what we mean by the chances of the throw.

§ 44. From this hurried account of the general nature of what has been called the Logic of Chance, we pass to the removal of erroneous ideas. It is evident, in the first place, that probability does not affirm about the fact as such. The event may be past and absolutely fixed, but our alternatives continue to be truly asserted. But, on the other hand, if the chances are not facts, are they nothing at all but our belief about facts? Is probability simply the quantity of the belief we happen to possess? No, that once more would be incorrect. We need not trouble ourselves to discuss the meaning assignable to "quantity of belief," for the whole idea must be banished at once. The amount of our belief is psychological, the probability of a fact is always logical. No matter what it is we happen to believe in, whether it exist or do not exist, our belief itself is unaffected. But an assertion about chances must be true or false. It depends on fact and refers to that, though it is not true or false of the special fact in question.

§ 45. We have not contradicted ourselves. Probability tells us what we *ought* to believe, what we ought to believe *on certain data*. These data are assertions about reality, and the conclusion as to what we ought to believe results from a comparison of our grounds for belief. Since these grounds are the conditions of hypothetical judgments, the judgments again must be true or false, and they rest upon categorical bases. In these two points, (i) the general ground of the disjunction, and (ii) the special grounds of the alternatives, probability is true or false of reality. We call it "objective."

On the other hand probability is "subjective." If I say "The probability of S — P is $\frac{1}{10}$," this may be true although S — P is impossible. It is true to-day, and to-morrow it is true that the chance is $\frac{1}{12}$, and the next day $\frac{1}{4}$. The belief must change with my varying information, and it is true throughout these variations, and is true though every one of them is an error. How can this be "objective"? It seems to lack the very *differentia* of truth.

The solution is obvious. Within the probability [41] what is true or false is not the premises but the conclusion I draw from them. Given certain assumptions, there is only one way of stating the chances. Given certain grounds for belief or disbelief, there is only one correct inference to the fractional result. This result is neither "subjective" nor "relative," if those phrases mean that it might be different with different men. From certain *data* there is but one conclusion, and, if this is different in different heads, then one or both of these heads is mistaken. Probability is no more "relative" and "subjective" than is any other act of logical inference from hypothetical premises. It is relative to the *data* with which it has to deal, and is not relative in any other sense. It starts with certain assumptions about the nature of the fact, and it tells us what, if we are ready to take these assumptions as true, we ought to believe in consequence. If this is not to be "objective" and necessary, then farewell for ever to both these phrases.

Probability as such is not true of the fact, but it always has a reference to fact. It is concerned with certain special deductions from the basis of propositions which are true or false in fact.[42] It certainly is confined to those deductions. But it possesses, when kept within its own limits, truth absolute and unquestionable and that never can vary.

§ 46. Probability is neither simply "subjective" nor yet simply "objective." This vicious alternative is the first of the errors we have to dismiss. It is allied to another elementary mistake, which must next engage us.

It is mere misunderstanding which supposes that chance involves a series, and that the logic of probability is essentially concerned with statistical frequency. It is mere error which finds the necessary meaning of "The probability of S — P is $\frac{1}{4}$," in "Once in a series of four events S — P will be true." This mistaken theory contains some truth, but has taken one part of the truth for the whole.

§ 47. Is the series real or is it imaginary? Let us first take it as real, as something that exists, has existed, or will exist. Must the judgment "The chance of S — P is $\frac{1}{4}$," refer always and essentially to an actual series? The assertion would be preposterous. The event S — P may be hypothetical. It may have a probability of $\frac{1}{4}$ on the ground of assumptions which we know are not true. Where is then the real series? The event again may be unique. The chance of my dying before I am forty is, say, $\frac{1}{4}$. Does this mean that if I die three times, one case will realize the possibility? The event once more need not be an event. It need be nothing which ever could happen in time, and we should deceive ourselves if we gave it that name. "It is even chances that the soul is nothing but a function of the body": the probability is $\frac{1}{2}$. "It is one to two that God is a person": the probability is $\frac{1}{3}$. "It is one to ninety-nine that the will is free": the probability is $\frac{1}{100}$.*

* Of course I do not mean these fractions as an expression of my opinion.

It may be said, no doubt, that the figures are illusory, and that we can not find any unit of value; but I hardly think this objection can stand. Admit that the case is highly improbable, it still is possible that in the mind of some man the grounds, present for and against such judgments as these, might be reduced to a common denominator. How can we deny it? and, if we do not deny it, what becomes of our series?

§ 48. The series clearly can not be real. Let us take it as imaginary. The question is then, Is such a fictitious imaginary series the proper way in which to represent probability? Can we say, It is my meaning, or the only true way in which to render my meaning? This, I think, would be an absurdity. It will not stand a serious examination.

Probability can indeed be always *represented* by a fictitious series. "It is two to one he is guilty" may be rendered by saying, "Two times out of three a verdict on such evidence as this would be right." Even when the possibility is unique, we yet can abstract from that quality and say, "Men such as I am would die before forty two times out of three." Nay, even when we leave events altogether behind us, we still can keep up this mode of expression by a fictitious series. Imaginary judgments here become the events. "It is even chances the soul is a bodily function" may be translated by "In making such judgments as this a man would be wrong through one half of the series and right through the other half."

But is such a way of putting our meaning the real and essential idea we entertain? When we wish to be correct, are we forced so to speak? It always is possible, but is it always necessary? Is it always even natural? And then there remains a question in reserve, Is it not incorrect?

§ 49. Let us begin with its possibility. Why can we always express the chances by making use of a fictitious series? For this reason. When the grounds from which we reckon are considered as causes, we are accustomed to suppose that their issue in a series of phenomena will exhibit the same numerical proportions that our fractions possess. If so, then on one side the causes (or cause) of the series and, on the other side, the series itself will answer to each other. We say what we have to say of the cause, indifferently, either by stating its effects, or by setting out the reasons it gives us to expect one effect and not another. This is natural enough where the fictitious series is imagined to be real. It is not so natural with unique events, where the series strikes us as specially manufactured to express the chance. It is still less natural where the possibility itself is not an event, and the series is nothing but the series of judgments. But even here it still is possible. Since psychologically the grounds are causes (p. 545), since, in other words, the logical reasons which necessitate the result are what produces the fact of the judgment, I can imagine, if I please, a series of judgments, and say, Since these numerically answer to the reasons I have, therefore such a numerical part will be true. The expression by a series is here quite unnatural, but it still is possible.

§ 50. The issuing of a certain series is only one way of putting probability. It is sometimes a natural way; it is sometimes a not unnatural way; it is sometimes most unnatural. But it is never the right way; it is never more than a manner of statement; it is never the real meaning and intent. Even when I start from an actual series, I must leave it before I can get to probability. I must go to its cause by what is called a method of reduction, by an inductive hypothesis. And I can not simply define this cause as that which either has issued, or will issue, in a certain series. I can not do the first, for that would be certainty and not probability. And I can not do the second without an assumption which I am unable to justify.

It is obvious, in the first place, that to take a series, and to say "The cause which has produced this series—has produced this series" is merely frivolous. On the other hand, if I add "will produce this very same series on *other* occasions," that is not frivolous, but is either irrelevant or else unjustifiable. If it means "In another case where the conditions are not discrepant, the same cause will be followed by the same effect," that assertion is true but is quite irrelevant, because merely hypothetical. For in an actual fresh case I do not know the fresh conditions, and, if I did, I do not know what the old cause specially is. I do not know the actual cause (or causes) of the former series. I do not know that these are present again in the unknown case. I do not know what conditions the fresh case brings; and, if I did, I might be unable to deduce the result from the complication of elements. In short I can not go from a given series to an unknown series or an unknown case. To reason directly is of course impossible, and I can not reason indirectly through the cause, because I do not know the actual cause in one case or the other. Its general character, to a certain limit, I do know in one case, and assume in the other, but this general character does not imply a series, and the individual cause itself I do not know and so can not use.

The upshot of this is that within probability you really have not got the effects on one side and the cause on the other. If then you give as the essence of probability the production of a series with certain marks, you go beyond what your *data* will warrant. For your actual series has now [43] ceased to be taken as a series of events produced in time. It has degenerated into a set of conflicting reasons, possibilities as to an event of a certain sort, which in default of detailed information I use in order to determine my judgment. My probabilities do not represent a series as such. I now have nothing whatever but conflicting grounds for belief and expectation, grounds for belief as to any fresh case or number of cases that have the *general character* of my series. And these fractional reasons, which are all I can work with, are the same in any one new instance as in any number of new instances. Thus the supposed *differentia* of an imagined series, in the first place, would add nothing to the probability which already exists apart from the idea of any series. But, in the second place, if it does add, and if it goes on to say that the series *must* have a character answering to the expectation, then it adds what is *false*.

§ 51. And with this we come to an obstinate illusion. There is a common idea that, if you know the chances of any set of events, you really know the character of the actual events which are to take place. It is supposed that the series will correspond to the fractions. For instance, if we take the case of a die, the chance of any one face is ⅙, and from this we argue, "In a series of throws each face will be seen in one-sixth of the run." But we have no right to any such assertion. Not knowing the cause, knowing only a part while part is hidden, we can say no more than that our information leads us to expect a certain result. It is monstrous to argue that therefore that certain result *must* happen. It is false reasoning *a priori,* and *a posteriori* the facts confute it. It is not found in experiment that actual runs do always, or often,[44] correspond *exactly* to the fractions of the chances. That correspondence is after all the most probable event, but to make it more is a fundamental error.

§ 52. I shall return to the truth contained in this error, but at present we must try to get rid, if we can, of the error itself. We may expect an objection. "Experiment," it will be said, "does not disprove the assertion that is made. That assertion is not that in a *finite* series the numbers will come right. They will come right only if we go on long enough, and in the long run." But what is this "long run"? It is an ambiguity or else a fiction. Does it mean a finite time? Then the assertion is *false.* Does it mean a time which has no end, an infinite time? Then the assertion is *nonsense.* An infinite series is of course not possible. It is self-contradictory; it could not be real. And to say that something will certainly happen under impossible conditions, is far removed from asserting its reality. The affirmation that an event may be assumed to take place in an infinite series, and not outside it, would, in the mouth of any one who knew what he meant, be a suggestion that the event may not take place at all.[45]

§ 53. I hope I need not protest that I am hardly so foolish as to attempt to offer an ignorant objection to the use of infinities and infinitesimals within the sphere of mathematics.[46] I would rather say nothing at all on this matter than appear as presuming to doubt the validity of processes employed by the greatest men in the exactest of sciences. But I shall not so be misunderstood. An objection to the use within certain sciences of certain ideas must be taken within the limits of those sciences. But the use of these ideas outside their science carries with it no authority, and, so long as the general meaning is understood, may be criticized by men who are ignorant of the science in which the ideas give brilliant results. It is so with infinity. Outside mathematics an infinite number is an idea that attempts to solder elements which are absolutely discrepant. It could not exist until the world, as known in our experience, was utterly shattered and transmuted from

the roots. I could not find an illustration I would sooner
use to express impossibility. And it is this idea which, outside mathematics, is presented to us in the error we are
combating. Mr. Venn, for whose powers I feel great respect,
and from whose *Logic of Chance* we all can learn, holds that
in the long run every chance will be realized. This "long
run," he tells us, is an infinite series (p. 146), and (unless I
very much misunderstand him) he goes on to call it a "physical fact" (p. 163). His book is much injured by this terrible
piece of bad metaphysics. He has translated a mathematical
idea into a world where it becomes an absurdity.

§ 54. We must everywhere protest against the introduction
of such fictions into logic, and protest especially where the
ideas are not offered in the shape of fictions. The formula
of the "long run" must be banished from logic, and must
carry with it a kindred illusion in the imbecile phrase, "if
you go on long enough." "The event," we are told, "will
answer to the chances." But it does not answer. "Oh, it
will, if you only will go on long enough. You toss a coin
and, the chances being equal, if you only go on long enough,
the number of heads and tails will be the same." But this is
ridiculous. If I toss the coin until the numbers are equal, of
course they will be equal. If I toss it once more then, by the
hypothesis, they become *unequal*. I might just as well say,
"If I only go on long enough the events will certainly *not*
answer to the chances." [47] Your formula is false or else tautologous. If it means "Suppose the numbers are equal, and suppose I then stop, the numbers will be equal," that is surely
tautologous. But if it means the numbers will turn out equal
in an infinite series, then that is false, for such a series is impossible.*

§ 55. But let us turn from the error and see the truth
which lies hid beneath it. It is false that the chances must
be realized in a series. It is however true that they most
probably will be, and true again that this probability is increased, the greater the length we give to our series. What

---

* Cf. Lotze, *Logik,* 437. I may remark that if the formula meant,
"The series is sure to cross and re-cross the point of equality," then,
in the first place it would be *false,* since there is no *certainty;* and, in
the second place, such an oscillation is not *equality.*

reason have we for holding these two beliefs? (i) Why do
we think that the series will probably answer to the fractions?
(ii) Why do we think that in a longer series the correspondence
is more likely?

(i) Probability, we have seen, is not essentially concerned
with any series. It is based upon grounds which, even if we
consider them as real, may not be causal in the sense of pro-
ductive of events in time. They may be *causæ cognoscendi*
and not *essendi*.[48] It is when our grounds are grounds for
belief as to the nature of an agency, which is to produce events
in time, that we are able to consider them as causal elements.
And this is the case we have to suppose.

We know that a series is to be thrown with a single die.
Let us first take one throw. That will have a cause, and the
cause is only partially known. We know that it is complex
and consists of many elements. Of these elements, so far as
they are distinctly known, five parts are hostile to any single
face and but one part favourable. The unknown residue, so
far as it determines the case, is quite unknown; and, though
it is not indifferent and though it can not be so, yet within
our knowledge we must take it as indifferent. In the cause
of the single throw there are therefore, beside the unknown
factors, one sixth part of the agencies favourable to each face.

Now take the whole series. That series, before I throw it,
is as certain and fixed as though I had thrown it already.
But here again I do not know the causes. About one part I
know nothing in detail, and so I must take it as being indifferent, although I am sure it is not so in reality. Of the
rest of the agencies, which I suppose, one sixth is favourable
to each face, and five sixths hostile. What conclusion can I
draw as to the nature of the series? Will one agency produce that result which we suppose it would produce, did the
others not intervene? Will in each case of the series the supposed majority of agents prevail? We have no means of
knowing. The series, absolutely fixed, is fixed by what we
do not comprehend. We must take the possibilities, and
the possibility for which there is most ground is the likeliest.
There is less ground to think that in a series of six throws
one face will be absent, and one twice present, than that
all should show once.[49] In the latter case we do but make

ignorance a ground for complete indifference. In the former
case we give a preference without any kind of warrant. It is
not that each face has any sort of *claim* to come uppermost
once. It is that no face has more claim than another to show
itself twice. This is why we think the most likely series, or
the least unlikely, will be that which corresponds to our
fractions.

§ 56. (ii) But why, it may be asked, does the length of
the series increase this probability? Does the greater length
add any new ground to those we have for believing in the
correspondence of the events with the chances? No, it does
not add any. Does it decrease any ground we had before for
thinking the opposite? Yes, it does do that; and it does it, I
think, in the following way. The unknown residuum in the
cause of each throw was assumed to be indifferent. But it was
not at all assumed to be passive. It supplies the determining
element in the cause. It decides for one face, though we do
not know for which face it decides. Now how does it decide? Does it act regularly and in strict rotation, or is it irregular? That we do not know; but, taking the possibilities,
we believe that those in favour of irregularity are more than
those in favour of rotation. It is therefore most probable that
our series will turn out to be irregular. But, since we know no
reason to prefer any one face, we can not say that any proportion other than strict equality is the most probable. How
are these assertions to be reconciled? Very easily in this
way. Owing to the assumed *indifference* of the causal residue
the faces will probably appear in their right numbers; but,
because of its *irregularity*, their appearance will probably be
irregular, and irregular to an extent to which we can assign
no limit. To combine these attributes it is necessary to suppose that the whole series will be most probably regular, but
will contain periodic irregularities. The greater the irregularity becomes, the less grows the chance of a final regularity, unless the series is proportionately lengthened. Therefore, since we can fix no limit to the irregular sequence of the
faces, we conclude that, the longer the series becomes, the
greater becomes the probability of a regular result. And this
is a rational, and necessary conclusion from our imperfect
data.

§ 57. It is true that, if you make a series longer, you de-crease the chance of irregularity. It is true that, if *per impossibile* the series were so long that, in comparison with its length, every possible abnormal run was a period which other periods might easily balance in the completed cycle—if, I say, *per impossibile* this phantom could be real, it is true that the above chance of irregularity would vanish. If we as-sume that what we do know gives us reason to believe in a series correspondent to our fractions; if we next assume, by virtue of a fiction, that the unknown residue gives no reason to believe in an unbalanced irregularity, then *on these assump-tions* we may go to a conclusion, and we have no ground to disbelieve the statement that the series will exhibit the relations of the chances. But the first assumption is based on ignorance, and the second is based on a known impossibility.[50] If we mean to speak about a series of events that could ever happen, we can say but this. It is certain there will be a series, each throw of which will give a single face. It is possible that in a series of *any* length but one single face should appear throughout. No arrangement is impossible. It is most prob-able that the events will answer to the fractions, but against that probability there still remains another consideration, the chance arising from the possible irregularity of one part of the causal elements. This fraction is diminished by each increase of the series, but it does not disappear and *it can not disappear*.

§ 58. We do *not* know that in the long run the events will correspond to the probabilities. We do *not* know that, if we go on long enough, every chance will be realized. It is mere superstition which leads us to believe in the reality of the fiction which gives birth to these chimæras. When I see the demonstrations, offered to gamblers against a bank, which prove to them that in the long run they can not but lose, I say to myself, On which side do I see the darker illusion? And I answer, On both sides the illusion is *the same*. For what is the root of the gambler's "system"? Is it not his belief that independent events are affected by each other? But this belief is a strict deduction from the premises offered him. If he really *must* lose, if there really is a cycle in which the chances *must* all be realized, then, let him observe the begin-ning of the cycle, and mark the irregularities, and he surely *must* win. Since to equalize the numbers the end of the cycle must balance the beginning, he can speculate on that balance and his " system " is right. " Oh, but it is wrong, for the series is not finite. It is only after an infinite duration of play that the balance is struck. It is absurd to say he can be sure of winning." But is it not then equally absurd to say that he is sure to lose? If you mean he must have lost by the end of his life, you have just admitted your assertion to be false. If you mean *he* must have lost when he has got to the end of infinite time, confess that your meaning is something like nonsense, and that the gambler is right in imagining that you, as a rational man, must mean something else. The truth is that your common assumption is false. There is no *must* about it. The chances consist of grounds for belief in the nature of a series no event of which is known. And all they tell us is this : that we have more reason to expect one thing than we have to expect another, and that the increased length of the series proportionately decreases a reason for doubt, which never quite vanishes.

§ 59.⁵¹ I must not be suspected of a desire to intrude into mathematics if, in this connection, I venture to remark on a well-known paradox. I am to toss a coin, and to go on tossing so long as I throw heads and nothing but heads. I am to receive £2 if I throw head once ; if I throw head twice I am to win £4 ; for three successive heads I get £8, and so on accordingly. The series is supposed to have no limit except the appearance of a tail. And the question arises, how much am I to pay for the privilege of one single trial? The answer given is, An infinite sum ; for it is possible I may throw an infinite series of nothing but heads (vid. De Morgan, *Probabilities,* p. 99). The reasoning on which this conclusion seems to rest is exceedingly simple, and I need hardly say that I do not doubt its perfect validity within mathematics. And I think I see that no *other* answer can possibly be given. Unless an arbitrary limit is fixed, I may be allowed to say in all humility that I think I understand that, if this possibility has any value at all, then the worth of my chance is either incalculable or else is infinite. If this answer is given me by a special science, I dutifully receive it as true—within that science.

But if I am told that in actual fact the result is true, I

must be allowed to protest. I must be permitted to remark that the reasoning is absurd and the result is nonsense. I do not mean merely that it is absurd if we take it as a *practical* precept, because a man can not live for ever, and all the money in the world is finite. I mean that it is a *theoretical* absurdity. It is not true ideally any more than really. Since an infinite sum is an impossibility, the infinite series can not possibly be thrown. There is no chance whatever. There is no fraction at all. It is nothing I could win. It is nothing I can expect. It is nothing for which I can reasonably pay. The result is a deduction from premises known to be false and impossible.

It is idle to answer that the problem is "stated in the ideal form" (Venn, *ibid.* p. 137). There is a difference surely between ideals which as such do not exist, because they are abstractions, and ideals which are downright self-contradictions. It is one thing to say, "There is a connection between abstract elements, so that when one of these is found as a real quality we shall have the other," and another thing to continue this assertion, when we know that the first of these elements is self-contradictory and could not possibly be any quality of reality. In this latter case what is true of fact can not be the consequence of an impossibility, but only the basis of the hypothetical judgment. Neither antecedent nor consequent is taken as real or even as possible. But in a common abstract judgment the antecedent is taken as at least a possible quality of the world.[52] Mr. Venn perhaps would question this difference between an abstraction and an impossibility, and would perhaps assert that an infinite series is really possible. In any case I must be allowed to protest against the invasion of logical reason by mathematical fictions. If an infinite series is thought possible, we should be told how it can be possible. If it is not thought possible, it should not be offered us as if it were.

§ 60. There are other points in the theory of chances which have logical interest, but we have no space to discuss them here. We have said enough to make clear the relation in which that theory stands to our general principles. We have to avoid the fiction of the infinite long run, and the vicious alternative of "objective" and "subjective," and the

false assumption that the essence of chance involves a series
of events in time. If we keep clear of these pitfalls, the truth
is by no means difficult to reach, and we hope above to have
stated it clearly in its general form.*

§ 61. There is an aspect of modality we have neglected
to notice. The omission was intentional, and the mention of
this aspect has been reserved for the present place. There is
an old doctrine which connects universality with necessity,
and that doctrine is true. The necessary we saw was the
ideal consequent, and such a consequent can not come except
from an ideal antecedent. You never can say " B follows
from A," " is because of A," " must be, given A," unless A is
present in a determinate form. A must be a content without
any mixture of mere sensuous conditions.[53] It must be
ideal, abstract, and so universal. If the ancient doctrine on its
logical side may suffer some loss, since necessity becomes for
logic hypothetical, yet it stands all the firmer. The " because "
can not couple anything but universals.

§ 62. We may notice an error which creeps in with this
truth.[54] The antecedent in necessity must be universal, but it
need not be *more* universal than the consequent. Where we
say " because " we do not always appeal to anything more
abstractly general than that which follows from our reason.
" A must be equal to B, because C is equal to both B and A,"
" A must be removed by one foot from C, since B, which
touches both in a certain manner, is one foot long." The
consequence is not less general than the antecedent, and we
deceive ourselves in thinking it always must be so.

No doubt in the cases where you say " because " you may
find what we call the principle of the sequence, and that of
course must be more abstract than the actual consequent.
But the principle is not the antecedent itself. It is the base
of the general connection, not the sufficient reason of the
particular consequent. There is no more need for the consequent to be more concrete than the antecedent, than there is
for the effect to be more special than the cause. These ideas
are nothing but kindred illusions (Book III. Chap. II.).

* The books from which on this subject I have learnt most are
Lotze, *Logik;* Sigwart, *Logik;* Wundt, *Logik;* Jevons, *Principles of
Science;* Venn, *Logic of Chance;* De Morgan, *Probabilities.*

§ 63. We shall have to return hereafter to this point, but have been right to anticipate here the conclusion. We have indeed begun some time back to anticipate the conclusions we have to reach in the following Books, since already unaware we have entered their territory. Silently before in the second Chapter, and now almost explicitly we have made the transition from judgment to inference. In both the latter kinds of modality we reason openly. The possible is that which we argue would follow from certain premises, part of which are taken as true. The necessary is that which we infer must follow, if its grounds are premised. It was in this sense that possibility was one kind of necessity. In both alike we deal with conclusions, reasoned results from given *data*. In logic we find that a necessary truth is really an inference, and an inference is nothing but a necessary truth. This is the secret which we hardly have kept, and with the discovery of which we may pass at once to our Second Book.

ADDITIONAL NOTES

[1] " This doctrine . . . falsehood." This statement needs correction. It is true that there are no degrees of the fact of logical assertion (cf. Chap. I, § 15 (*d*)). It is true that you can not alter the logical mode of asserting S — P without altering S — P itself. On the other hand it is not true that you can abstract the assertion from the asserted content. See Bosanquet, *Logic,* I, 363 foll. On the doctrine of degrees of truth I may refer the reader to my *Appearance* and *Essays.*

[2] " The reference or the denial itself," i.e. taken in abstraction as a mental fact.

[3] " The possible . . . whatever." This sentence must be corrected. It is better, once more here, to substitute " conditional " for " hypothetical." Further, both " conditional " and " categorical " should be taken as falling under " necessary." The merely categorical is the lowest form of necessary (Chap. II, §§ 75 foll.) On the whole subject see Bosanquet, *Logic* (*loc. cit.*), and *K & R,* pp. 114 foll.

[4] " Where necessity is internal &c." So far as the totality is a system which *is* because of its internal necessity, and is viewed in that character, the above statement will not hold.

[5] " Because." On " because " see T. E. II.

[6] " We must admit—fact." This, I think, is wrong. Logic, I agree, should abstain from dealing with the ultimate problem. But on the other hand logic most certainly should not admit and assume that its " because " is not real. To regard logical implication as merely

"ideal" is an error. See T. E. I. And we must remember that "fact," like "existence," is ambiguous. See on Chap. II, §§ 2 and 4.

⁷ "When it ceases to be *merely* necessary." "Merely" here seems misleading. The "necessity" itself is in any case not hypothetical. Cf. § 12.

⁸ On the difference between "if" and "because" see T. E. II. This § 10 is largely erroneous. It wrongly identifies "reality" and "fact," and it wrongly assumes the existence of judgments which really are not mediated. See ibid.

⁹ "The argument from principle." This surely is vicious. There are no "mere ideas" (see on Chap. I, § 10). Logic *must* assume that the ideal is real somehow and somewhere. The idea that did not qualify Reality would certainly fail to be an idea.

As to the "argument from usage" I agree that "must" can be used to weaken an assertion. But this is where we have an implication that our "because" is only partial and is so defective. In an immediate certainty (e.g.) we are sure that we are right somehow though the "how" is not specified. At times, again, we specify the "how" in order to throw doubt on it. We mean that we have *this* reason, and no more than this. Cf. Bosanquet, *Logic* I, 379, and *K & R*, pp. 122 foll. As to the "ultimate premises" which are known immediately, such things I consider to be illusions.

¹⁰ For "conditions" see on § 24.

¹¹ "Assumed to be compatible." These words (Cf. §§ 13, 14, and 21) were overlooked by some critics, who in consequence objected to my account on the ground that I had overlooked the possibility of incompatible conditions. But on the contrary my account assumes, not only that I have all the conditions, one part of which is taken as actual, but also that the rest are, in my knowledge, *not* incompatible. This point, however, should have been brought out more clearly, as it was later in *Appearance*, Index, s. v. *Possible*.

¹² "Taken to exist" should be "taken to be actual."

¹³ "Our basis of fact &c." But we must remember that, for an idea to be an idea at all, it can not, so far, be unmeaning. We have therefore with every idea an assertion that it possesses, so far, the character of Reality, and further is real somehow. No possibility can rest fundamentally on mere privation. The assumption that, beyond the above, an idea is possible *further,* may, however, in a sense, be so grounded. Cf. on Chap. III, § 9. What is certainly wrong is to use "possible," where we are simply ignorant as to impossibility absolute or relative. See *Appearance*, Chaps. XXIV and XXVII. For the meaning of "possible" cf. T. E. XI and the Index of the present volume.

¹⁴ "We have no reason &c." This must be corrected. For in the first place (i) if the idea has a meaning it, so far, is real. And (ii), if there are any facts which suggest a further reality, we have in these surely an additional ground. The "most unfavourable view," to be rational, would have, I think, to rest on the positive knowledge that

body and mind are in themselves, directly or indirectly, inseparable. The following words, "are idle frivolities . . . men," are almost certainly a quotation, and are so marked. But I can not recall the source.

[15] "For . . . supposed." This statement goes too far. The correct account of "hypothetical possibility" is, I think, as follows. If you take the actual (or fully grounded), to which the possible is anywhere opposed, and degrade this actual to possible—your first possibility becomes then possible at a further remove. Or (it is the same thing) take a possibility as actual—and then, in consequence, (on and against this) an even less grounded possibility may be doubly or possibly possible. Cf. T. E. XI.

[16] For this question see Note 6.

[17] "May claim no existence . . . possibility." But, since it must be thinkable, it must also to a certain point be real and possible. See preceding Notes.

[18] "Complete revolution," which revolution I consider necessary.

[19] By "men" I meant here "finite beings." And the same remark applies lower down to "human." In §§ 18 foll. we should bear in mind the following. The ordinary abstract judgment does not deal ostensibly with possibles, since it assumes a world in which these are actual. And it is better not to call it "hypothetical," since the attitude of supposal is not there. We need not, again, take the supposed as possible, though clearly, if in no sense it were so logically for us, we could not in fact suppose it.

The possible, as the partly grounded, is negative of a limited known reality, in the sense that not all of the possible is there. A part falls beyond and is actual only in another world. Thus the possible belongs to both of these worlds at once. But it is not a member of the first limited world, because it is only that in part and also is more. And hence alternative possibilities (r^1, r^2, r^3) are all possible, though they can not all at once simply qualify our limited reality. Thus the possible and the actual may or may not exclude one another. The assertion, e.g. that the actual Universe is not possible is ambiguous. And it is false if it means to go beyond the denial of mere possibility, and to suggest that the "more" must, in every sense and everywhere, exclude the "less." Cf. T. E. XI.

I shall return (§ 28) to the dangerous error which takes "possible" as the contradictory of "impossible." Cf. ibid.

[20] Sections 20 foll. need correction throughout, but I need not repeat everywhere in detail what has now been laid down in general.

[21] "Less actuality than . . . the necessary." But obviously, if and so far as the "necessary" is taken as the "fully grounded," this is the case.

[22] "Privative judgment." This must be corrected. See above on §§ 13, 14. "Bare possibility" is that which is general as against that which is possible here or there. Or it is that which possesses no more than the least amount of the character required for possibility.

23 On "real possibility," and on the "potential" see *Appearance* and *Essays* (the Indexes), and cf. the Index of this work.

24 On Ground and Conditions cf. T. E. II. This section (24) is in part wrong because it once more ignores the various orders of reality (see Chap. II, Note 3). The conditions are the diverse elements of a grounded whole, and therefore are, in some sense and somewhere, actually real. Where in a limited "actual" you have a part of the above totality taken as there present—this limited reality is the "real possibility" of the rest, though the rest is not actually there present, or at least is not taken as being so. In what follows, on "the cause," I had in mind, I presume, the cause taken as mere existing fact. But some correction is required here. See Bosanquet *K & R*, pp. 20-1.

25 "Permanent Possibilities." Cf. *Appearance,* pp. 124-5.

26 I was not denying here that the Hedonistic End can be formulated correctly. I was merely giving another instance where the use of the same delusive phrase takes the place of thought.

27 "The assertion &c.," that is, "apart from designation." See the Index, s. v. *Designation.*

28 "These predicates—reflection." But see Note 6. Further, with regard to the statement, "And to a knowledge . . . possible," we must ask, How far and in what sense would perfect knowledge contemplate unreality at all? It would do so, I presume, only so far as it remained discursive knowledge, and then only so far as the unreality is relative.

In the next paragraph for "directly vanishes" "simply and directly" would, I think, be better.

29 "On the Impossible see *Appearance* (Index), and T. E. VII. The impossible must of course have enough meaning to be what might perhaps be called "possibly possible."

30 "The real does not . . . incompatible." Under "incompatible" here will fall the case of the absence of some predicate. In the next sentence the words "Because . . . else is" go, I think, certainly beyond the first appearance of necessary impossibility. All that, so far, is present there, seems to be re-assertion with an exclusion on the ground of a "must."

31 On Privation cf. Note 13. And see T. E. VII and VIII and *Appearance* (Index). The main point here is this—that a mere absence or exclusion is nothing at all. "Possible" and "impossible" are hence not mere contradictories. If the impossible is not possible enough to have a meaning, it is logically nought. Total absence of compatibility with the Real means sheer nothingness. The real question is as to *further* compatibility, and whether we have positive reason, and if so, how much, to assume that, if there were "incompatibility," that would appear. In other words a mere failure to exclude is logically nothing, and so again is all *mere* exclusion whether of what has sense or is senseless.

The doctrine of §§ 28-9 is, I think, right in the main though some correction is needed. For "pass unabridged" (§ 28) see Note 11. For the rest, no suggestion, if it is a logical suggestion, can be meaningless and elicit no answer at all from Reality. Whether an utterly meaningless suggestion is possible as a psychological fact it would be idle here to ask. In logic the suggested must have a meaning, and must to some extent be real, and the question will be as to its *further* reality. Here, if we have but one possibility, that is real. If, on the other hand, we have counter-possibilities, the question will be as to the value to be attached to each of these upon positive grounds.

Apart from this, the doctrine of § 29 seems correct. We have a vicious identification of the real, as it is, with the real as we find it now mentally present; and we have a vicious conclusion that, if there were incompatibility, I should know of it. The *reductio ad absurdum* seems also correct. If anything is possible, then, if there is no counter-possibility, it is necessary and real.

[32] "The universal . . . nothing." "Nothing" here should be "nothing special." And, in the next sentence, "The universal triangle" should be qualified by "thus held in abstraction." Cf. Chap. III, § 10.

[33] On the doctrine of § 31 see above, Note 31. The statement "then, I admit . . . judgment" is, we have seen, incorrect, unless we understand what follows to deny the privative character of the foundation.

[34] On Probability cf. Bosanquet, *Logic,* Chap. VIII. 2.

[35] Instead of "any ground"—"any *further* ground" would be more accurate.

[36] The reason of course is that in the latter case b (for instance) becomes a common heading of b^1 b^2 &c.

[37] I think that "perhaps" should here be omitted.

[38] "The same as any *one*"—would better have been "the same as any *particular one*."

[39] "Cause" is taken here not as pure cause (where there is reciprocity between cause and effect), but in that looser sense which admits "plurality of causes." See T. E. X and Index s. v. *Cause.*

[40] The "other cause" might, e.g. be loaded dice or some art in the thrower. The question thus raised is answered by considering the comparative probability of each "cause"; and no new principle is involved here.

[41] In "Within the probability" "within" is to be emphasized.

[42] In "true or false in fact" we must here, once more, give a wide sense to "fact" (see Chap. II, Note 3). What in probability is "subjective" is in short merely the amount of my ignorance and knowledge.

[43] The word "now" should be omitted, as it might be wrongly taken in reference to "go beyond."

[44] The words "or often" can not, I think, stand. For, even if they were true, they would be superfluous.

[45] By "be a suggestion" what I meant was "be *at least* a suggestion."

[46] Cf. § 59. I should also have said that I do not pretend to know the sense in which within mathematics the word "infinite" is taken. But, so far as I have been able to understand the meanings in which, outside mathematics, some mathematicians wish to use the term—I am clear that these are self-contradictory.

With regard to "an infinite number," see Bosanquet, *Logic*, II, pp. 161 foll. He points out that it involves the fallacy of counting where you have nothing in particular to count, where, that is, you count in abstraction from any presupposed whole. This objection is in principle the same as that usually urged, which insists on the necessary external determination, and consequent internal incompleteness, of any mere counted sum. If you are led in principle beyond any whole which you take, that is really the same thing as counting without any whole.

If I may be permitted a word of criticism on the later work of Prof. Royce, I would add that whether by the study of mathematics he really was carried over to a better world of ideas—I am quite unable to judge. But the passage by that Lethe, where he crossed, led him (so far as I see), here and elsewhere, simply to forget that way of understanding (good or bad) which he once shared with those who still are able to remember what they learnt.

[47] By aiming at an unnecessary *reductio ad absurdum,* and also perhaps by a misunderstanding of Lotze, I was led here to injure a good case by a superfluous and serious blunder. This was noticed by Dr. Bosanquet, *K & R,* pp. 108 foll., and *Logic,* I, 108 foll. If the series is broken off at such a point that it can not exactly coincide with the ratio, to take this as being in any sense a *deviation* is plainly wrong. See Bosanquet, *Logic* I, 350.

[48] *Essendi* should have been *fiendi.*

[49] The statement here seems at least wanting in clearness. It would be better after "all should show once" to proceed as follows. "It is not that each face has a claim to show itself once, or that no face has a claim to appear twice. It is that there is less ground for the presence than for the absence of deviation from the ratio. This is why we think &c."

[50] The words "But the first assumption . . . impossibility" need some correction. They should, I think, have been "But the first assumption is based on partial ignorance, and the second, as to the unknown residue, is not true. We have *some* reason here to expect irregularity, and we find nothing here about a balance."

[51] On § 59 cf. the Note on § 53.

[52] The sentences "But . . . the world," and the two preceding sentences are partly incorrect (see on § 17). But, since the question here is as to existence in fact, the conclusion remains unaffected.

[53] "Without any mixture of" should be "freed, so far, from." And, in the next sentence, for "so universal," it would be better to write "in this sense universal." I should have added here that

necessity has no meaning outside a whole which is a concrete universal. Lower down "hypothetical" should, once more, be "conditional."

[54] I am unable to remember against what doctrine or writer I was arguing here, and I can not even say that the error noticed exists outside of some misapprehension of my own. See Bosanquet, *K & R,* pp. 209 foll.

BOOK II—INFERENCE

At the end of our First Book we made a transition to the subject of our Second. Modality took us from judgment to reasoning. An inference is either a result or a process. If we take it as a result, we saw that it is the apprehension of a necessary truth. If we take it as a process, it is simply the operation which leads to that result. A truth judged true because of something else, and the going to a truth from the ground of a judgment or supposition [1] are what we mean by conclusion and reasoning. And this starting-place being reached, our right course may seem plain. We should first make quite clear the general character of inference, and should exemplify this by the necessary detail. And then we might proceed at our ease to remove the erroneous doctrines which cumber the ground.

There is an objection to this way of dealing with the subject. The reader would find his difficulties increased. I do not indeed know, after my first Book, if at this stage I have any actual reader; but I am sure, if I have one, that he is not eager to make a great effort. We have perhaps nothing in front of us so hard to cross as what we have passed over, and yet we shall find there are obstacles enough. It is better to make a gradual advance. Instead of going at once from the facts to the truth, and from that to the removal of erroneous theories, I shall aim at reaching an easy vantage-ground, from which we may disperse the mass of mistakes which bar our progress and harass each movement. This will be the object we shall try to gain first. Secure in our rear, we may then proceed upon the final position.

We must therefore in the first of the two following Books be content with a truth which is only partial. We must assume that in every valid inference no less than three terms are given to the reasoner. We shall hereafter see that this assumption is not tenable, but it will serve as a basis from which to operate. It may be a high thing to have no order of convenience, to follow the development of the subject matter, and to let the reader follow if he can. But it is an end more possible, and perhaps not much lower, to help the reader by any means whatever to a better understanding.

The arrangement of this Book as well as its basis must be considered arbitrary. I shall begin by setting down some characteristics of inference which perhaps are likely to be accepted by all. And to these I shall add a few examples of actual reasoning. I shall then proceed to deal with some mistakes, confining myself in the main to the syllogism. In the next place I will point out that inference consists in an ideal construction. And fourthly I will state some principles of synthesis by which we operate to effect that construction. One essential factor in valid inference will then be indicated, and will be seen to rest on a serious assumption; and we shall further show that in every inference at least one premise must be universal. Having reached this point we shall conclude our First Part, and take a fresh departure; and throughout the rest of this Second Book we shall be engaged in the work of clearing the ground. We shall have to criticize in general the alleged Association of Ideas, and especially the Association of Similars. We shall briefly dispose of the supposed way of arguing from particulars to particulars; and shall show by an examination of J. S. Mill's Canons that his Inductive Logic is theoretically invalid. After this, having declined to enter on a discussion of Mr. Spencer's doctrine, we shall end with a review of Professor Jevons' theory of Equational Logic. The position we shall have reached, and the negative results we shall have been forced to gain, will have served to prepare us for a completer view.

ADDITIONAL NOTE

1 "Judgment or supposition." Cf. p. 245, footnote. But to take "supposition" as excluding "judgment" is wrong. There are no "mere ideas." See on p. 4.

PART I

THE GENERAL NATURE OF INFERENCE

CHAPTER I

SOME CHARACTERISTICS OF REASONING

§ 1. When we first consider the subject of reasoning we seem to have nothing but a conflict of opinion. But a second glance reveals some agreement. There are three characteristic features of inference as to which in our hearts we are really at one. I do not mean that we should not deny them if our theories required it, but we should do so unwillingly and with a sense of compulsion. The first of these is a negative mark. There is a difference between reasoning and mere observation; if a truth is inferred it is not simply seen, and a conclusion is never a mere perception. The latter may seem to be given to us bodily, but the former involves some other element. It may indeed be thrust upon us, we may be compelled and constrained to make it, but we can not passively take it in. The fancies we cherish in respect of perception desert us as soon as we come to inference. The external fact or the reflection it throws off can violently break into and enter our minds, or the reality can stamp our yielding substance with its image and superscription. But we can hardly apply these ideas to a conclusion, for we feel that in this there is something that repels them. An inference can not wholly come in from without or be passively received. It is not mere vision, it is more than observation.

§ 2. There is another mark which a conclusion possesses. It is not a mere fragment or isolated unit; it does not exist in and by itself, but is the result of a process. It rests upon a basis, and that basis is something we already know.* In inference we advance from truth possessed to a further truth;

* For the sake of clearness I here ignore the hypothetical character of inference.

and the conclusion would never be reached at all if it were not for knowledge already attained. It is therefore dependent and in a sense adjectival.

§ 3. But there is another attribute which a conclusion has got. It must convey some piece of information, and must tell us something else than the truths it depends upon. We have no inference at all, we have simply a frivolous show and pretence, if taking something we already know we assert the whole or part of this once more, and then say, " I have reasoned and got to a conclusion." An inference must be more than a vain repetition, and its result is no echo of senseless iteration. It is not mere observation yet it gives us something new. Though not self-existent it is more than a shadow. To those who delight in discrepant metaphors we may bring conviction when we so express ourselves: The truth which is seen in the mirror of inference has not wandered in through the window-pane of sense, nor yet is it merely a reflection cast by an article of furniture already in the mind.

§ 4. Except in the interest of a preconceived theory, I think that these statements, at least so far, will not be denied. But I can hardly hope that the examples of reasoning I am about to produce will all escape unchallenged. Yet I shall not defend them, for I do not know how. They are palpable inferences, and the fact that they are so is much stronger than any theory of logic.

(i) A is to the right of B, B is to the right of C, therefore A is to the right of C. (ii) A is due north of B, B due west of C, therefore A is north-west of C. (iii) A is equal to (greater or less than) B, B is equal to (greater or less than) C, therefore &c. (iv) A is in tune with B, and B with C, therefore A with C. (v) A is prior to (after, simultaneous with) B, B to C, therefore A to C. (vi) Heat lengthens the pendulum, what lengthens the pendulum, makes it go slower, therefore heat makes it go slower. (vii) Charles I. was a king; he was beheaded, and so a king may be beheaded. (viii) Man is mortal, John is man, therefore John is mortal. We shall go from these facts to ask how far certain theories square with them.

CHAPTER II

SOME ERRONEOUS VIEWS

§ 1. The task before us in the present chapter is the removal of certain mistaken ideas. And the first to go must be the major premise. We saw, at the end of the foregoing Book, that the necessary truth need be no more particular than the truth it depends on, and that logical necessity does not always come from the application of universals [1] to something *less* universal. But if so, there need not be always a major; and the examples we have given put this beyond doubt.

In (viii) our old friend is still to be found, but in (vi) and in (vii) you will hardly be able to distinguish him from the minor, and in all the rest he has totally vanished. You may say that in (iii) we really argue from " Things equal to the same are equal to each other," and I do not doubt you will find believers. But if such reasoning is reasoning *from* an axiom, how did people reason before axioms were invented? And if without axioms it is impossible to infer, I wonder where all the axioms can have come from (cf. Book II. Part II. Chap. I.). But if we take an example like number (i), will any one show me the major there? " A body is to the right of that which that, which it is to the right of, is to the right of." I know this major, because I have just manufactured it; but you who believe in major premises and who scores of times must have made the inference, confess that you never saw this premise before.

We must either admit that a major is not necessary, or else we must say that my examples are not inferences because they have no major. In either case an effete superstition will be doomed.

Begotten by an old metaphysical blunder, nourished by a senseless choice of examples, fostered by the stupid conservatism of logicians, and protected by the impotence of younger rivals, this chimæra has had a good deal more than its day. Really dead long since I can hardly believe that it stands out for more than decent burial. And decent burial has not yet been offered it. Its ghost may lie quiet when it sees that the truth, which lent it life, can flourish alone (cf. Book III.).

§ 2. The major premise, we have seen, is a delusion, and this augurs ill we may think for the syllogism. Our suspicion is well founded, for the syllogism itself, like the major premise, is a mere superstition. It is possible, no doubt, as in our seventh example, to have a syllogism which has either no major premise, or at all events no minor. And it is unquestionably true that in many arguments a major premise is actually used. Nor will I deny that some three fourths of our valid arguments can be got within the forms of *Barbara Celarent*. But yet after all the syllogism is a chimæra, for it professes to be the model of reasoning, and there are reasonings which can not by any fair means be conformed to its pattern. In whatever sense you interpret it, it turns out insufficient; and in certain cases it will turn out worse. Let us examine the principles of reasoning it lays down.

§ 3. If we take first the axiom of inclusion in extension as it finds expression in the maxim *De omni* &c., we are forced to say that this principle is unsound. It sins against the third characteristic of inference (Chap. I. § 3), for it does not really give us any new information. And, as has been long ago remarked, it embodies a *petitio;* for if, asserting the premise "All men are mortal," I understand by the subject each single man, then I either am aware that John is mortal, or if not my major must be withdrawn. The major premise has asserted something of each member of a collection, and the minor and conclusion do but feebly re-echo one part of this statement. But that is no inference.

We might try to understand the assertion differently. We might say that what "All men" really means is the collection or class and not each one member. But, if so, we fall blindly into a second pitfall. John's personality perhaps has no unity, but he can hardly be called a collection of *men,* and our syllogism now fails through *quaternio terminorum*. It perhaps fails too through falsity of the major.[2]

The *dictum de omni* thus turns out vicious. But if it were

sound it would not be sufficient, for it does not cover all valid reasonings.

§ 4. There is another mode of interpreting the major. " All men are mortal" may be said to assert the identity of the subjects in "men" and "some mortals;" and "John is man and therefore mortal" assures us that the subject, which we distinguish as John, is identical with a member of the class of men and also of mortals. But we know already how this is to be read.[3] The identity of the subject is another way of affirming the conjunction of diverse attributes. The fact we have got is either the co-existence in one single subject of the attribute mortal with the rest of John's attributes, or else the possession by a single thing of the several names "John," "man," and "mortal" (cf. Book I. Chaps. I. and VI.). And interpreted in this way, though the inference is valid, it will not fall under the *dictum de omni*.

§ 5. We may illustrate the above from complete induction. I may show that all planets move in an ellipse by counting and observing each single planet. But in what sense am I then said to perform an inference? I say *"therefore* all planets move in an ellipse," but I know already that every single planet does so move. If there were any planet which I could not so qualify I could not go on to *therefore* all planets. Does the "therefore" simply reiterate the "because"? Then there is clearly no inference. Does the conclusion assert that the collection, or class, itself moves through space in an elliptical manner? If this were true the premises would not prove it. But perhaps it means that, if anything is a known planet, it must have a course which will be found elliptical. We are free to forget that the individuals we know do move in ellipses. We have firmly established a connection of attributes, so that hereafter, given any single individual which we barely perceive to be a known planet, we can go at once from the base of that attribute to elliptical movement. But the conclusion here does not rest on enumeration complete or otherwise; it proceeds from and rests upon a distinguished connection of attributes (Book I. Chap. VI. and Bk. II. II. Chap. III. § 3).

We may sum up the matter thus. If you say "Each individual has a certain attribute and *therefore* each has it," that is absurd. If you say "therefore the collection has it," that is invalid. If you say "Anything belonging to the collection has it and therefore this has it," then that is valid, but the "anything belonging" stands for an attribute. Complete induction shares the fortunes of the syllogism.

§ 6. The principle of inclusion within class extension is not merely insufficient, but unless we interpret it as a connection of attributes it is intrinsically vicious. Let us see if we can find any other view which will come to the rescue and will save the syllogism. "What stands," says Kant, "under the condition of a rule stands under the rule." It is thus he interprets "*nota notæ est nota rei ipsius.*" If you have an universal connection of two attributes, then, given one in a subject, you must also have the other.

It is evident that this principle of reasoning is valid, but it will not cover the whole of the ground; for, confined to the category of subject and attribute, it fails wherever you pass beyond. The subject no doubt is in some way qualified by whatever can be asserted about any of its attributes, but it is idle to expect a result from this where we are not concerned with subject and attributes. "A is prior to B and B to C, and therefore A is prior to C," but what here am I to call the "condition of the rule" or the "*nota*" or "attribute"? I can not take B as the attribute of A, and if I look for that attribute in "prior to B," I fall at once into *quaternio terminorum,* since the second premise has got B simply.

And even when we keep to subjects and qualities, there are inferences which the principle will not justify. The syllogistic third figure can hardly be supposed to exemplify the axiom which Kant has adopted. Not only is the category of subject and attribute (as commonly applied) unable to cover the whole field of reasoning, but within that category it is a further mistake to insist on the necessity of a major premise.

§ 7. It is evident that the syllogism can not be saved or can only be saved in such a way as to be syllogism no longer. The one chance there is of preserving the syllogism is for us to take our stand upon the third figure. "The attributes of one subject are interrelated" will then become the axiom of inference. We have seen (§ 4) that all syllogisms in exten-

sion can be interpreted according to this axiom, since the
identity of the subject was the other side of that relation of
attributes which we wished to assert. And it is evident again
that all relations of attributes can be regarded as based in a
subject. We shall see hereafter (Part II. Chap. IV) that Substitution of Similars can be taken as syllogism within the third
figure; and I will go yet further. There is and there can be
no inference whatever which may not be reduced under the
head of the axiom, since everything which in any way is conjoined can be taken as related within some subject (Book III.
Chap. VI. §§ 33, 34).[4]

We may see hereafter how this reduction is effected. For
our present purpose it is enough to remark that in many cases
it can not be performed without processes which would hor-
rify the conservative logician, and which gain no end worth the
violence they use. Unless "subject and attribute" are used
in a way which is quite unknown to the traditional logic, the
axiom fails of universal validity, for it does not apply to any
of those relations which two or more subjects bear to each
other. "Two pianos are in tune with one fork and therefore
the one is in tune with the other." But in this instance, unless
the terms are manipulated freely, you will not show one subject with its attributes.

§ 8. It is obvious, if we fairly consider the examples which
have been adduced at the end of Chapter I., that the syllogism,
if it keep its traditional form, is in great part impotent. And
I confess I do not know what policy will seem good to the
friends of the syllogism. They may boldly accept the violent
alternative of excluding all examples which they can not deal
with. But I think we may say that such a course as this
would be nothing short of a confession of bankruptcy. If a
savage may know the road that will take him from A to B,
and the road that will take him from B to C, and yet may not
know, and may be unable to find out, the way he should go
from A to C (cf. Spencer, *Sociology,* I. 91), I do not see how
it can be denied that he is ignorant because he is incapable of
an operation.[5] And if that operation is *not* an inference, I can
not see why anything else should *be* inference. The plain and
palpable facts of the case will, I think, be too hard for the
friends of the syllogism. And if they embrace another alterna-

tive, and find their amusement in the manufacture of majors, which would never have been seen if the arguments had not come first, then I think once more that the end must be near. So barren a shift will be the dying effort of a hard-run and well-nigh spent chimæra.

But there is, as we saw, another alternative; it may perhaps be thought possible to save the syllogism by first reforming it. Throw the major premise overboard, and call anything a syllogism which can be brought into the form of elements related within one whole. But if the friends of the syllogism resolve on this policy, I think they are friends it might pray to be saved from. It is better to bury a delusion and forget it than to insult its memory by retaining the name when the thing has perished. And it is better to profess that delusion openly than ostensibly to abandon all but the name, and then covertly to re-instate the errors it once stood for. When a mistake has lasted some two thousand years I am ready to believe that it must contain truth, but I must believe too that the time is come when that truth should be able to stand by itself. We can not for ever with eyes fast closed swallow down the mass of orthodox rubbish in which that truth has wrapped itself up. And if the time has not come for extracting the kernel, the time has come for rejecting the shell.

§ 9. But if the principle of the syllogism is not the axiom of reasoning, can we find any other which will stand the test? We shall see hereafter that the logic of "Induction" is no more satisfactory. We shall allude to the doctrine of Mr. Spencer, and review the theory of Substitution which has found an advocate in Professor Jevons. For the present it will suffice to mention a principle adduced by Mr. Spencer, and which has succeeded in gaining the authority of Wundt. "Things related to the same are related to each other" is the axiom, we are told, of all valid reasoning. "Where judgments are placed in relation to one another by means of conceptions they possess in common, the other conceptions, which the judgments possess but do not possess in common, must stand themselves too in relation to one another, and that relation is expressed in a new judgment."—(Wundt, *Logik*, I. 282.)

We may confine ourselves to the simpler formula.

" Related to the same are related to each other " is wide enough to cover the examples we have given. We shall certainly hereafter have occasion to question if it is wide enough to cover all possible examples (Book III. Part I. Chap. I.). But though I may object to it hereafter as being too narrow, I must object to it here because it is too wide. It is a principle of falsehood as well as of truth; " A runs faster than B and B keeps a dog (C)," " A is heavier than B and B precedes C," " A is worth more than B and B is on the table (C)," or " A is like B and B is like C." You may doubtless extract some kind of inference out of these premises, but you can hardly go from them to any definite and immediate relation between A and C.[6]

§ 10. It is true no doubt that, if A and C are both related to a common term B, we know that some relation must exist between them, since both must be elements in one world of knowledge. But unfortunately we knew thus much before, and independent of the relation of both in particular to B.[7]

And again in defence of the axiom it may be said, In " A is like B and B is like C " the terms are *not* related to a common third term. B resembles A perhaps in one point and resembles C in another different one, and so it is with the other examples. It is not in so far as B keeps a dog that A outstrips him, it is not the B which has a place in time which is heavier than A, B is on the table in one capacity and is worth more than A in an other and different one. Thus the terms related are not related to the *same,* and, if they were, they would be related to each other.

The defence I have invented points towards the truth, and yet it is vitiated by a fatal mistake. It is true to say that in every relation there must always be an underlying identity; that relations, such as those of space and time, presuppose a common character in the things they conjoin. And it is therefore true that, if a third term C stands first in spatial relation with A and again in temporal relation with B, its character in those two relations is different. Hence, if two relations are of different classes, the term common to each will so far not be the same.

But this line of argument, if we follow it out, will make an end of all kinds of relation (cf. Chap. VI. § 6). To say that,

when A is related to B, it is related so far as B is nought else
but its relation to A, is quite suicidal. And, if we will not say
that, and if already B is something different from its relation
to A, on what ground can we refuse it a right to another
relation with C, when at all events it has one point in which
it differs from A? Let us try to see clearly; the terms of
a relation must always be more than the relation between
them, and, if it were not so, the relation would vanish. "A
is equal to B," but if B were mere quantitative identity with
A, we should have no equality; there would be nothing but A.
"A is the same as B or different in quality," but if A and B
were not both different and the same, then the terms and the
relation would all disappear together. "A is north of B or
prior to C;" but if A, B, and C were no *more* than mere
naked positions in space or time, they would not be even that,
and their relations would sink to utter nothingness. There
always must enter into the relation something more than the
actual relation itself. And this being admitted, if you deny
that the B, which for instance is spatially related to C, is the
same as the B which has a relation in time with A, you must
be taken to assert that in the relation A — B the character of
B is perfectly simple, and that B is nothing but that which
constitutes its relation in time. But, if so, it is nothing which
can be related, and the axiom can find no possible application.

The mistakes, which arise from a too wide axiom, may
indicate the truth that related to the same are *not* related to
each other unless they are related *under certain conditions.*
We shall return to this point in Chapter IV., and the following
Chapter will endeavour to convey some general idea of the
nature of inference.

ADDITIONAL NOTES

[1] "*Given* universals" would be better here than "universals."

[2] On the "Collective Judgment" and on "Class" see the Index.
The "falsity of the major" refers to the ambiguity involved in the
above ideas. On Complete Induction and Counting see Bk. II. II.
III. § 3.

[3] "But we know . . . read." It would be better to say "But we

know already how this identity of diverse subjects is here to be read."
See on Bk. I. VI. § 11.

4 See § 1 of the next Chapter.

5 "If a savage &c." The case, as stated, is so extreme as to be
perhaps abnormal, but as an illustration it may stand.

6 "Definite and immediate" should be "fresh and special." See
again as in Note 4.

7 After "in particular to B" add as follows. "Further, when
we have got to know that A and B, B and C, are related in a particular whole which is before us—this mere knowledge, that A and
C are both together as members of that whole, will not be the conclusion that we seek. We presumably are looking for some further
and special relation between A and C, other than their mere co-pres-
ence within one subject."

CHAPTER III

§ 1. Every inference combines two elements; it is in the first place a process, and in the second place a result. The process is an operation of synthesis; it takes its *data* and by ideal construction combines them into a whole.* The result is the perception of a new relation within that unity. We start with certain relations of elements; by virtue of the sameness of two or more of these elements we unite their relations in one single construction, and in that we perceive a fresh relation of these elements. What is given to us is terms conjoined; we operate on these conjunctions and put them together into a whole; [2] and the conclusion is the perception of two terms in relation, which were not related before the operation. Thus the process is a construction and the result an intuition, while the union of both is logical demonstration.

§ 2. Demonstration in logic is not totally different from demonstration elsewhere; proof is only *one* kind of demonstration. Logicians however seem generally not to be aware of this fact. When the mathematician " demonstrates " a conclusion the logician feels uneasy, though he can not deny that the conclusion is proved. But uneasiness becomes protest and open renunciation when he attends at the " demonstrations " of the anatomist. He shudders internally at the blasphemous assertion that " this which I hold in my hand " is " demonstrated." But his trials are not over; the illiterate lecturer on cookery overwhelms him by publicly announcing the " demonstration " of an omelette to the eyes of females.

But I think the logician has no real cause of quarrel even with the cook. For demonstration is merely pointing out or showing; [3] and if the conclusion of an inference is seen and thus may be shown, so also may a nerve or again an omelette.

* As we remarked before, the statements in this Book are subject to correction by the Book that follows.

It is useless to deny this, and the task of the logician is to distinguish inference from other kinds of demonstration.

§ 3. When in ordinary fact some result can be seen and is pointed out, perhaps no one would wish to call this " demonstration." It is mere perceiving or observation. It is called demonstration when, to see the result, it is necessary for us first to manipulate the facts; when you show within and by virtue of a *preparation* you are said to demonstrate. But if the preparation experiments outwardly, if it alters and arranges the external facts, then the demonstration is not an *inference*. It is inference where the preparation is *ideal,* where the rearrangement which displays the unknown fact is an operation in our heads. To see and, if it pleases us, also to show a new relation of elements in a logical construction,[4] is demonstration in the sense of reasoning.

§ 4. In what does this mental preparation consist? We have seen in our account of the synthetic judgment its general character. It demands in the first place certain *data;*[5] it must have two or more connections of elements, as $A - B$ $B - C$ $C - D$; and these are the premises. It is necessary again that these premises should be judgments actual or suggested,[6] and what they assert or suppose must consist in logical connections of content. For if the *data* consisted of unrefined sensuous material, or were mere imaginations, the result would be sensuous or merely imaginary; it would be a psychological effect and not a logical consequence. The premises are thus so far two or more judgments, and the operation on these *data* will consist in joining them into a whole. We must fasten them together, so that they cease to be several and are one construction, one individual whole. Thus instead of $A - B$ $B - C$ we must have $A - B - C$.

Now if this were done arbitrarily it would not be done logically, and we should have no reason to think the result true. If we took $A - B$ and $C - D$ and joined them together as $A - B - C - D$, our procedure would be as futile as if in anatomy we showed connections by manufacturing them, or as if in order to clear a preparation, we employed some agent which radically changed it. In relation to fact our results in this case would be invalid.*

* All this is subject to correction by Book III.[7]

We can not logically join our premises into a whole unless they offer us points of connection. But if the terms between which the relations subsist are all of them different,[8] we are perfectly helpless, for we can not make an arch without a key-stone. Hence, if we are to construct, we must have an identity of the terminal points. Thus, in A — B B — C, B is the same and we connect A — B — C; in A — B — C and C — D, C is the same and we connect A — B — C — D. The operation consists in the extension and enlargement of one *datum* by others, by means of the identity of common links. And because these links of union were given us, therefore we assume that our construction is true; although we have made it, yet it answers to facts.

Having thus turned our premises into one whole, we proceed to our conclusion by mere inspection.* If A — B — C — D is true of reality, then in that we can see A — C or A — D, or again B — D, relations which previously we did not know. Then, leaving out of view those parts of our construction in which we are not interested, we extract the conclusion we desire to assert. We first do a certain work on our *data;* and this work is the construction. We then by inspection discover and select a new relation, and this intuition is the conclusion.[10]

§ 5. I will illustrate the above by several examples. Take three pictures on a wall A, B, and C; if I see them all at once as A — B — C there seems so far no inference,[11] for my mere analytic judgment will give me A — C (Book I. Chap. II.). But suppose I see first A — B, and then afterwards B — C, no mere analysis will give me A — C. I must first put them together as A — B — C, and this is the construction of a synthetic judgment. I then perceive A — C, and this is the conclusion, which is inferred not because it is seen in fact, but seen in my head.

Let us take an instance from geographical position. A is ten miles north of B, B is ten miles east of C, D is ten miles north of C; what is the relation of A to D? If I draw the figure on a piece of paper that relation is not inferred;[12] but if I draw the lines in my head, in that case I reason. In

---

* I omit to consider here the selective action. That is not of the essence of all inference.[9] Vid. Book III. Part I. Chap. I.

either case we employ " demonstration," but only in the latter
do we demonstrate logically.

" A = B and B = C therefore A = C." In this argument
there is no demonstration to sense, for the showing is ideal.
The terms are put together through the sameness of B, and
are combined into a whole united by the relation of quantitative identity. The whole is a series united by that character, and here is the construction. We then inspecting the
series find a new relation A — C, and here is the conclusion.

Take an example we have given in Chapter I.; if three
strings A, B, and C are struck together and we hear that they
all produce the same note, we hardly *infer*[13] that they are in
tune with one another. But first strike A and B, and then
strike B and C; on this, if A and B have no difference in note,
and B and C have no difference in note, I proceed to construct
the ideal group of ABC united throughout by sameness of
note. This is a mental synthesis; and a mere analytical perception then adds that A and C are in tune with one another.

We may see this again in an ordinary syllogism. We
must not state it so as to beg the question, or to have no common term, but may state it thus, " Man is mortal and Cæsar
is man and therefore Cæsar is mortal." There is first a
construction as Cæsar-man-mortal, and then by inspection we
get Cæsar-mortal.

§ 6. It is useless to attempt to lay down rules for either
part of this process. It is the man who perceives the points
of union within his premises—who can put (as the saying is)
two and two together—who is able to reason. And so long
as he secures the unity of his construction he has reasoned
rightly. In the next Chapter we shall see that no models for
construction can possibly be invented. And for the process
of inspection one wants a good eye; for there are no rules
which can tell you what to perceive.

We must free ourselves from these superstitions, if we can,
and there are others beside which have oppressed us too long.
It is ridiculous for instance to think about the order of our
premises. The construction when made need have no order
in time, and the order of its making may be left entirely to
private convenience or else to chance.

And there is another superstition we may here dispose

of.[14] The number of terms is not limited to three. In the geographical example of the previous section we certainly do not argue thus $\begin{smallmatrix}&|A\\C—&|B\end{smallmatrix}\ \therefore C\diagup^{A}$, and $\diagup\begin{smallmatrix}A&D|\\&C\end{smallmatrix}\diagup\begin{smallmatrix}A&D—A\\\therefore\end{smallmatrix}$, but we first complete our construction $\begin{smallmatrix}D|&&|A\\C&&B\end{smallmatrix}$, and then go to D——A. It is true no doubt that in making a construction we are forced to establish one link at a time; but it is wholly false that we are compelled to conclude before we take in another premise. Logic sets no limit to the number of premises which may precede the conclusion, and it is the weakness of our heads which narrows our constructions and narrows them sometimes to the prejudice of our inference. There is no branch of science where constructive power is wholly uncalled for, and certainly some where it is of the first importance. And perhaps we may say without exaggeration that a man, who can not use more than three terms in reasoning, is unlikely to do much in any subject. But, however that may be, the limit is psychological and is not logical.

ADDITIONAL NOTES

[1] This chapter must be taken as no more than a provisional clearing of the ground. Not only is the warning in the footnote to § 1 to be borne in mind, but, in addition, the chapter contains serious errors the correction of which can only be indicated in passing.

[2] " Into a whole " should be " into a connected whole," and (in the next line) " not related " should be " not so related."

[3] " Demonstration is merely pointing out." This is a grave mistake, and the term is, I think, nowhere so used in practice. It everywhere and always means showing the necessary and ideal connection and sequence. Whether and how far you have before you external fact and its alteration, or deal merely with what is " in your head," is utterly irrelevant. The " demonstration " in every case has to bring out—not the fact—but the ideal bond and process. Cf. on Bk. III. I. II. § 5, and T. E. I.

[4] " In a logical construction " should be " in and as the result of &c."

[5] On " data " and " premisses " see Index, s. v. Premisses, and cf. Bosanquet, Logic, II, pp. 12 and 203.

6 The words "actual or suggested" should be omitted. See the first Note on Book II. And (at the end of this paragraph) it would be better to insert "new" before "individual," in the words "one individual whole."

7 "All this" should have been "Much of this."

8 "Different" should have been "merely different."

9 The "selective action" is really quite essential. See the Index s. v. *Selection*. What I meant here was merely that "elimination" is not always necessary. You do not always in the conclusion omit part of the construction. See Bk. III. I. I. § 2.

10 "This intuition is the conclusion." Certainly not so, unless the new relation appears in it as "following." The "conclusion" means seeing as part of the whole and because of the whole. See Note 4.

11 "So far no inference"—except so far as the analytic judgment itself involves inference. See Index, *s. v. Analysis*.

12 "If I draw the figure &c." This and what follows is seriously wrong. See Note 3.

13 "We hardly *infer,* etc." Yes, but how far the "*we hear*" is already itself inferential, still remains a question. See Note 11.

14 "And there is another &c." On this see Bosanquet, *K & R,* p. 307, and *Logic,* II, pp. 12 foll. My statement here was wrong in forgetting that the necessary establishment by synthetic construction of each link, one at a time, itself is inference. On the other side I was right in insisting that in the final conclusion there is an inference from the whole construction without regard to the number of terms contained in that. Cf. Bk. III. I. II. § 5.

CHAPTER IV

THE PRINCIPLES OF REASONING [1]

§ 1. We have seen in outline the main character of inference and we naturally recur to a former question, Is there any axiom or principle of reasoning? The result of our enquiry in the Second Chapter was that we could find nothing quite satisfactory. The syllogistic maxims were all too narrow, and the axiom that " Things which are related to the same are related to each other," we found on the other hand was much too wide. It may serve us however as a point of departure. When properly restricted it will express the truth, so far as is required by the present Book.[2]

I will repeat the result we arrived at before. The principle that elements which stand in relation to a common point are themselves related, is not the actual principle that operates in any given special inference.[3] In its abstract form it is useless for the purpose of getting a conclusion. It assures us, before any construction is made, that anything which we have as an element of knowledge stands in *some* relation with every other element. But it will not enable us to go beyond this, and by combining our premises to get a definite relation. If A is prior to B in time, and B is west of C in space, then on the strength of B we can put these together, but we can not by means of our combination get a definite relation of A to C. We knew long ago that A and C co-existed as members within the universe of knowledge, and we desire to learn now not that general connection, but some special attitude of A to C. But in order to get this, and to be able so to speak to draw a new line from A to C, it is necessary first to connect A and C in a special manner. They must be interrelated not generally and in the universe at large, but in some special world. If one is merely in time and the other merely in space, they have so far not got any binding centre. To be specially related they must be related to the same, and under conditions which secure an unity of construction.

If what operates in inference is the principle of the individuality of synthesis, the axiom of that operation must not be taken too widely, and at the cost of clumsiness we must state it in two pieces. " Where elements A and C are related homogeneously to a common B, A and C are related within the same genus. Or where one relation only (either A — B or B — C) is within the category of subject and attribute, there is a valid conclusion within the category of either A — B or B — C." To express the same otherwise, " There is no conclusion where the relations are heterogeneous unless one of the two joins an attribute to a subject. In the latter case an inference is possible even outside the category of subject and attribute."

§ 2. We found first in our examination of the syllogism that there were inferences which fell outside its single category of subject and attribute. We found again that if we kept outside *all* special categories, mere interrelation was much too vague to form a bond. The conclusion, which in the next place naturally offers itself, is that inference must take place within several special categories (such as time, space, subject and attribute, &c.), but must always be confined in each case to one category. To get a relation of time in the conclusion you would have to keep in your premises to time-relations, and the same thing again with other kinds of relation. And, if this were true, the axiom would run, " Things related to the same within one kind will be interrelated within that kind."

But there are inferences which will not submit to this principle. " Gold is heavier than lead and lead is a metal," " A runs faster than B and B is twice as tall," " A is stronger than B and B is full grown," " A is equal to B in weight and B is moved with such or such velocity " are premises which certainly will yield conclusions, and yet their relations are heterogeneous. And this shows that we may cross from category to category. On the other hand we are unable to do this unless there exists a special condition; one relation must be that of attribute to subject. From " A is equal to B and B has such velocity " we have seen you can not get to the conclusion " A has such velocity." You can not do so till you predicate of A that point in B which brought it into relation with the other element (C). And from "A is equal to B and B is in my pocket" you can not infer that A is in my pocket, since the spatial relation which is affirmed of B is not true of B as equal to A. You can not argue to a relation of A to my pocket, but your conclusion must be "A is equal to something which is in my pocket." We have still the old relation of A to B, but qualified by the addition of an adjective of B. And it is true, I think, in all possible cases that the relation between a subject and attribute is the only one which, if used with another category, is able to give us a new relation.*

The remarks we let fall in a previous chapter (II. § 7) may have prepared the reader for our result. The categories do not stand on one and the same footing.[5] It is possible after all to express unconditionally the principle of inference, and it is possible to do this within the one category of subject and attribute (p. 296). But we are not yet arrived at the stage where this is possible, and must content ourselves here with the formula that ended the foregoing section, "Related to the same within the same kind are interrelated within that kind," with a further axiom of possible inference where one relation is that of subject to attribute.

§ 3. Our main principle, it is obvious, will have as many forms as there happen to be categories or kinds of relation. It is not the business of this work to elaborate any theory as to how these kinds are connected or are subordinated. It is again not our purpose to draw out and defend a complete enumeration or scheme of such classes. But in order to make clear the general result, I will state and illustrate four or five main principles which operate in inference. We may call them the principles (i) of the synthesis of subject and attribute, (ii) of identity, (iii) of degree, (iv) of space, and (v) of time.

I. *Principle of synthesis of subject and attribute.*

---

* Other examples are "A has a voice (B), that voice overpowers Z's voice (C), therefore A overpowers C." "A has a voice (B) which is in tune with C, therefore A has something in tune with C." In the first of these the relation of the conclusion is hardly between a subject and attribute.[4] A by virtue of its attribute, which attribute acquired a momentary independence, has got a new relation to another subject.

(*a*) The attributes of one subject are interrelated.

(*β*) Where two subjects have the same or a different attribute they are alike or different.

(*γ*) (i) Where the attribute is not taken as distinct from every subject, what is asserted of the attribute is asserted of its subject. (ii) Where the subject is not taken as distinct from every attribute, what is affirmed of the subject is affirmed of any attribute considered as its attribute.

Examples. (*a*) This man is a logician, this man is a fool, therefore a logician may be * (under some conditions is) a fool.

(*β*) This dog is white, this horse is white (or brown), this dog and this horse are alike (or different).

(*γ*) (i) This figure is a triangle, a triangle has the angles equal to two right angles, this figure has the angles equal to two right angles. (ii) Gold is heavier than lead; lead is a metal. Therefore lead-metal (or some metal) is lighter than gold, or metal may be lighter than gold.

I may remark on (*γ*) that, if we were to say "What is true of the attribute is true of the subject, and what is true of the subject is true of the attribute," we should fall into an error. The subject *qua* subject and the attribute *qua* attribute have each predicates which can not be applied to the other. Thus "Iron is heavy, heavy is a quality" is no ground for the assertion "Iron is a quality," nor from "Iron is heavy, iron is a substance," can you go to the conclusion "Heavy may be a substance" (*cf.* Book I. Chap. III. § 10). If on the other hand we laid down as a condition of the inference that this attribute and this subject must be taken together, we should then have become circular.[6]

II. *Synthesis of Identity.*

Where one term has one and the same point in common with two or more terms, there these others have the same point in common.

Examples. "Coin A has the same inscription as coin B, and coin B as coin C, therefore A as C;" "Instrument A is in tune with my tuning-fork (B), and so too are instruments C and D, therefore they are all in tune with one another;"

---

* *May be* because, the subject being undefined, the conditions are partly unknown. Vid. Book I. Chap. VII. § 26.

" If A is the brother of B, and B of C, and C is the sister of D, then A is the brother of D."

III. *Synthesis of Degree.*

When one term does, by virtue of one and the same point in it, stand in a relation of degree with two or more other terms, then these others also are related in degree.

Examples. " A is hotter than B and B than C, therefore A than C; " " Colour A is brighter than B and B than C, therefore A than C; " " Sound A is lower in tone than B and B than C, therefore A than C." I will not enquire here whether " A = B and B = C, therefore A = C," falls under this head or under the previous head of the synthesis of identity.

IV. and V. *Synthesis of Time and Space.*[7]

Where one and the same term stands to two or more other terms in any relation of time or space, there we must have a relation of time or space between these others.

Examples. " A is north of B and B west of C, therefore C south-east of A; " " A is a day before B, B contemporary with C, therefore C a day after A."

This list, as we have said, does not pretend to be complete, and it would not be possible for us here to discuss the questions which any such pretence would at once give rise to. Take for instance the synthesis of cause and effect. Does this fall entirely under the head of time? Does it fall under the head of subject and attribute? Does it fall under both or again under neither? The answers to these questions would be hard to get, and, if we got them, they would be of no use to us here. They would not much serve to confirm the result we already have reached; they would possibly supply one more illustration, where I hope enough have already been given.

§ 4. But there is another question which can not be passed by. We have called these syntheses Principles of inference, and have ejected the syllogism to enthrone them in its stead. But how are we to understand the title they lay claim to? We know what the syllogism tried to accomplish, for it professed to control from a central office every possible event in all parts of its kingdom. It issued some two dozen forms of reasoning, to which all inference was expected to conform. Thus you had always some model with relations ready drawn between all the terms both in premises and con-

clusion, and no liberty was left you save to fill up the blanks
with terms of your own. The moods and figures were a bed
of Procrustes into which all arguments had somehow to be
. forced, and they were therefore not merely principles of reasoning, but actual canons and tests of inference. Within
this pale you were secure of salvation, and on the outside it
was heresy to doubt you were lost. Such was the claim
which the syllogism put forth, and enforced as long as it had
any strength.

Like some other chimæras that have had their day, the
syllogism is effete and its realm is masterless; and the question
for us who aspire to the inheritance is to know in what character we mean to succeed. Do we wish to substitute one des-
potism for another? Are our principles of inference to be
tests and canons? Most assuredly not; for if the thing were
desirable, and I am much too staunch a Protestant to desire
it, it is at all events thoroughly impossible.

§ 5. Our principles give us under each head of inference
the general and abstract form of the operation. They do not
profess in all cases to give us the individual operation itself
which is necessary. It is not merely that the terms are left
blank, for the special relations of the premises and conclusion
are also left blank. The kind of construction is indicated
generally, and the kind of conclusion you will find within it;
but the actual construction, and the actual new relation to
which that will give rise, are left entirely to private judgment.[8]

From such premises as " A to the right of B and B to the
right of C," there is and there can be no form of reasoning
which will give you the conclusion. It is true that the axiom
goes so far as to assure you that A and C must be related in
space, for [9] you do not know that unless you know that the
two space-relations belong to one world. And you do not
know this unless you are sure that they have a common
meeting-point in space (Book I. Chap. II. § 21). But the
axiom will not tell you anything beyond. It will neither give
you the definite relation, nor even assure you that you will be
able to attain to any such relation. A is greater than B, and
C is greater than B, therefore (if the point in B is the same)
A and C must certainly be related in degree; but you do not
know how. B is south of both A and C, therefore A and C are

related in space; but you have no means of getting to know their particular relation. For the individual construction can not here be drawn, and it is that alone which can supply the conclusion.

Where the inference is valid, the special operation by which it is performed falls outside the axiom, and it is impossible therefore that the axiom can supply any test of validity. Where the inference is invalid, what makes it invalid may fall without the axiom, and the axiom is therefore no test of invalidity. If I like to argue that, because A and C are both greater than B, they are equal to one another, the principle has nothing to say against it. If I choose to go from " B is south of both A and C " to, " therefore A and C lie east and west," again the principle is perfectly satisfied. It can no more tell me that here I am wrong than that I am right if I say, " A is due north-west of C, because B is five miles south of A and again the same distance west of C." The general form is valid in either case, but the actual operation, whether erroneous or correct, is in either case beyond the scope of the principle. It is not a matter for superior direction; it is a matter for private inspiration and insight.

§ 6. It is impossible that there should be fixed models for reasoning; you can not draw out exhaustive *schemata* of valid inference. There are principles which are tests of the general possibility of making a construction: but of the actual construction there can be no canons. The attempt to manufacture them would lead to the search for a completed infinity; for the number of special relations has no end, and the possible connections in time, space, and degree are indefinite and inexhaustible. To find the canons of valid inference you must first make a list of valid inferences. You will manufacture a major premise for each, and that major premise derived from each operation will appear as its canon. Your success, if you succeeded, would be the capture of a phantasm, but in the endlessness of the field you would be for ever eluded. No canon will fix for us the pale of orthodoxy, until that day comes when the nature of things will change itself to gratify our stubborn illusions.

§ 7. The popular belief in logic endows it with ability to test all reasonings offered it. In a given case of given premises the logician is thought to be a spiritual Director who, if he can not supply, at least tests right and wrong. Thus, if logic is no art which provides us with arguments, yet, once give it the premises, and it is both the art of extracting conclusions and of assaying all those which amateurs have extracted without its authority. But, understood in this sense, logic has no existence, for there is and there can be no art of reasoning. Logic has to lay down a general theory of reasoning, which is true in general and in the abstract. But when it goes beyond that, it ceases to be a science, it ceases to be logic, and it becomes, what too much of it has already become, an effete chimæra which cries out for burial.

§ 8. It should not lie alone. There is another false science more unlovely in life and more unpleasant in decay, from which I myself should be loath to divide it.[10] Just as Logic has been perverted into the art of reasoning, so Ethics has been perverted into the art of morality. They are twin delusions we shall consign, if we are wise, to a common grave.

But I would not grudge Casuistry a Christian burial. I should be glad to see it dead and done with on any terms; and then, if all the truth must be spoken, in its later years it has suffered much wrong. That it became odious beyond parallel and in parts most filthy, is not to be denied; but it ill becomes the parents of a monster, who have begotten it and nourished it, to cry out when it follows the laws of its nature. And, if I am to say what I think, I must express my conviction that it is not only the Catholic priest, but it also is our Utilitarian moralist, who embraces the delusion which has borne such a progeny. If you believe, as our Utilitarian believes, that the philosopher should know the reason why each action is to be judged moral or immoral; if you believe that he at least should guide his action reflectively by an ethical code, which provides an universal rule and canon for every possible case, and should enlighten his more uninitiated fellows, then it seems to me you have wedded the mistake from which this offensive offspring has issued. It may be true that the office of professional confessor has made necessary a completer codification of offences, and has joined doctrinal vagaries to ethical blunders. We may allow that it was the lust for spiritual tyranny which choked the last whisper of the unsanctified conscience. It may be true that, in his effort theoretically to exhaust the possibilities of human depravity, the celibate priest dwelt with curious refinement on the morbid subject of sexual transgression. But unless his principle is wholly unsound I confess that I can hardly find fault with his practice; for if there is to be an art and a code of morality, I do not see how we can narrow its scope beforehand. The field is not limited by our dislikes, and whoever works at the disgusting parts, is surely deserving not of blame but of gratitude. Hence if the Utilitarian has declined to follow the priest, he has also declined to follow his own principles; he has stopped short not from logical reasons but from psychological causes.

§ 9. It is natural to think that logic has to tell us how we are to reason from special premises; and it is natural to think that ethics must inform us how we are to act in particular cases. Our uncritical logic and our uncritical ethics naturally assume these doctrines as self-evident. But the mistake, if natural, is in both cases palpable. Unless you artificially limit the facts, then models of reasoning can not be procured, since you would need in the end an infinitude of schemes to parallel the infinitude of possible relations. And a code of morality is no less impossible. To anticipate the conclusion in each special case you would have to anticipate all possible cases; for the particular condition which makes *this* conduct right here and wrong elsewhere, will fall outside the abstractions of the code. You are thus committed to a dilemma: at a certain point you must cease to profess to go right by rule, or else, anticipating all possible combinations of circumstances, you must succeed in manufacturing countless major premises. The second alternative is in the first place illusory, since the principle is really got *from* the intuition, and in the next place it is impossible, since the number of principles will be limitless and endless. But if you accept the first alternative, and admit that only in certain cases it is possible to deduce the conclusion from a principle, you have given up the hope of your " practical reason," and denied the axiom from which you set out.

The syllogistic logic possesses one merit. If its basis is mistaken and its conclusion false, at least it has not stopped short of its goal. In *Barbara Celarent* its code is perfected, and it has carried out the purpose with which it began. We can not say so much of the Casuistry of Hedonism. The confident dogmatism of its setting-out has been lost in vagueness and in hesitation. It flies to ambiguities it does not venture to analyze, and sighs faintly to a Deity which it dares not invoke. But if the principle of our most fashionable Ethics is true, then an art of Casuistry and a Science of Sin are the goal of that Ethics, and the non-recognition of this evident result, if creditable to the heart, does no honour to the head. If the popular moralist will not declare for a thorough-going Casuistry, if he retires in confusion from the breath of its impurity, he should at least take courage to put away the principles which have given it life. We may apply to him as he stands a saying of Strauss, " He partly does not know what he wants, and partly does not want what he knows." *

§ 10. If we return to the subject of the syllogistic logic, we may see on the one hand that its moods and figures will not take in any one of our syntheses except the synthesis of subject and attribute. The fifth, the fourth, the third, and the second, refuse to enter the traditional limits. On the other hand the first of our syntheses covers every argument of the syllogistic logic. An inspection of the figures would at once assure us that with positive reasoning this assertion holds good, and we must now proceed to test our conclusion by applying it to the subject of negative inference.

* Compare on the subject of Casuistry my pamphlet, *Mr. Sidgwick's Hedonism*, § 8, and *Ethical Studies*, pp. 142, 174, foll. (Ed. II. pp. 157, 193, foll.).

ADDITIONAL NOTES

¹ There is a main point in this Chapter where, if not correction, at least some explanation seems necessary. All inference depends on the unbroken individuality of a single subject; and in this sense all inference may be said to fall under the category of subject and attribute (Bk. II. I. VI. § 13). But, so understood, this category must not be taken as merely one among others. It is pre-supposed throughout as the condition of the rest, which, as against it, will be subordinate and special. On the other hand there are inferences which are made simply under and by the use of the above category in an individual case. This will be true, for instance, of the entire syllogistic logic. Hence to say that on my view logic is confined to the sphere of subject and attribute, or substantive and adjective, would be true or false

according to the sense given to such a statement. Everything, I agree, must with me fall under this main principle, and I know of no other main principle which to myself is intelligible. But to add that on my view the other special categories are not necessary, and that the conclusions got under these categories could, so far as correct, be got without them, would, I submit, be untrue. And I am bound to claim whatever merit is due to me for having insisted on the opposite. But this double sense in which, in this Chapter and elsewhere, the category of subject and attribute may be said at once to preside and yet to be co-ordinate, is, I admit, misleading. And this double sense, if borne in mind throughout these pages, tends, I think, to make part of the detail superfluous.

The reader should further keep in view the following distinctions. We have, first, the knowledge that everything falls within and qualifies one individual Universe. We next, in any particular case, have to do also with some subordinate individual whole. Now, so far as this whole is not taken as known immediately, all the elements within it must be somehow interrelated. They all are at least related among themselves as common adjectives. Further, having distinguished the adjectives within the whole, you can go on to qualify this whole by what beyond it is true of any of these adjectives—so long, that is, as you do not, by a further abstraction, set free and substantiate this adjective. And so again, subject to the same condition, you can infer similarity (§ 3).

But the knowledge you so far possess does not enable you to draw conclusions under the more special categories—such as Space or Time or Degree. These have powers and rights of their own, though, while acting by and under these, you can, at the same time and concurrently, make use in addition of your power under the more general category of subject and attribute. But, so long as we remain clear in principle, the effort to distinguish in detail the precise limits as to where, in this or that case, the above concurrent use comes in, seems really superfluous.

² "So far as is required &c." Cf. Bk. II. I. II. § 9.

³ "Is not the actual &c." "Is not *by itself* the actual &c.," would have been better. And (lower down) "anything which we shall have" is better, I think, than "anything which we have." Again lower down, for "get a definite relation" substitute (in the *first* sentence) "a more definite relation," and (in the *second* sentence) substitute "a new direct relation." And (still lower down) after "not that general connection" add "nor even anything that follows from the mere co-inherence of A, B, and C in a new apprehended whole."

⁴ The statement "in the first of these &c.," seems clearly wrong. And, otherwise, the conclusion would become illegitimate.

⁵ "The categories . . . footing." See § 1. And cf. the Index.

⁶ To "We should then have become circular" add "or should have failed altogether." So far, that is, as you take this attribute and

this subject as *immediately* one, you remain within one individual whole of immediate qualification.

[7] Here Nos. IV and V must be corrected by the insertion of "within one world of time or space" after "Where one and the same term." We can not assume the spatial or temporal unity of all spaces or times. (See *Appearance,* the Index.) Whether a similar correction should be made in No. III will depend on the sense which there is given to "by virtue of one and the same point."

The real question everywhere is whether the consequence is the self-development of that which we take as the subject, or whether, by the intrusion of something foreign, the identity of the subject is broken. When we are asked by a writer in *Mind* (I regret to have lost the reference), whether in "A cheats B, B cheats C, and therefore A cheats C," we have a valid inference—the answer is easy. We have here a good inference if we take the action of A on B as itself developing itself, without loss of identity, through B into action on C. On the other hand the inference is vitiated, so far as we suppose a foreign condition to be necessary, such as to destroy the process when viewed as the self-development of A's action.

In connection with the Synthesis of Degree I may remark that, though I failed in this volume to notice what is called the argument *a fortiori,* I should at once have placed it under the above head. The argument obviously depends on the comparative amount of ground.

[8] "Private judgment" should be "individual judgment"; and a similar correction should be made in the last words of this section.

[9] "For you do not know, etc." The "for" seems here to involve some confusion. When (see Note 7) the axiom has been corrected, it would be better to substitute for "the two space-relations belong to one world" the words "the premises fall under the axiom."

[10] It would, I think, have been better if this attack upon Casuistry and Hedonism had been shortened, if not omitted.

CHAPTER V

NEGATIVE REASONING [1]

§ 1. The general nature of negative reasoning does not vitally differ from that of positive. We have, given us in the premises, two or more relations presenting us with certain identical points, and on the basis of these points we combine the relations into an individual whole. We then by inspection find a new relation within that whole. The conclusion may connect two terms directly, as in $A - B - C$ ∴ $A - C$, or it may connect them indirectly, as $A - B - C$ ∴ $A - (B)C$, or $A(B) - C$.[2] The new line that is drawn may fall clear of the middle-point of the construction, or may pass through it on the line of the old relations. Negative reasoning and positive have all these qualities in common. It is true that in a negative inference the line that connects the terms of one relation is a line of denial; one part of the figure, which ideally we construct, consists of a repulsion; and the fresh connection we draw from that construction is a connection by exclusion. But these differences are varieties within the same main principle.

§ 2. It might seem as if nothing remained for us to do but to state and illustrate those negative formulæ which correspond to the axioms of affirmative reasoning. And to this we shall at once proceed to address ourselves; but it is right to premise that there are further difficulties which lie in wait for us at the end of this section.

In negative reasoning we may so state the principle,[3] " If B is related within one genus positively to A and negatively to C, then A and C are negatively related within that genus. And if the affirmative and negative relations $(A - B, B - C)$ are heterogeneous, yet, if one is in the category of subject and attribute, there is a negative inference within one or both of the two categories which have appeared in the premises." Unless $A - B$ $B - C$ are within the same genus, or unless one is a relation of subject and attribute, there is no connection at all.

I. *Synthesis of subject and attribute.*

(*a*) Where the attribute is not taken as distinct from every subject, what is denied of the attribute is denied of the subject, and where the attribute is denied the subject is denied.

(*b*) Where the subject is not taken as distinct from every attribute, what is denied of the subject is denied of its attributes, and where the subject is denied then, in that sense, the attribute is denied.

(*c*) Where two subjects have the same or a different attribute, they are so far not different or not the same.

Examples: (*a*) " A triangle has not got two right angles; this is a triangle, and has therefore not two right angles." " A rectangular triangle is not equilateral; this figure is equilateral, and therefore can not be a rectangular triangle." (*b*) " Man is not a quadruped, man is a mammal, therefore a mammal may be (the human mammal is) not a quadruped; and a quadruped is not a mammal in every sense of that adjective." (*c*) " My horse is vertebrate, this animal is a worm, and therefore is not the same as my horse."

II. The Synthesis of Identity must become a Synthesis of Identity and Difference, " Where two terms have the same point in common, and one of them by virtue of this point is different from a third, there the other and the third differ in this same point."

Example: " A piano (A) is in tune with B, which is not in tune with C, and therefore A and C are not in tune with each other."

In the Synthesis of Degree, of Space, and of Time, we have no occasion to alter the formulæ. We may give as examples,

III. A is as heavy as B, B is not lighter than C, therefore A is not lighter than C.

IV. A is not before B in time, B is contemporary with C, therefore A is not before C.

V. A is due east of B, C is not north of B, therefore C is not north of A.

§ 3. We seem to have performed our task successfully, but must deal with a further complication. We may be taken to have sinned against two prominent rules of the traditional logic, since on the principles we have given you may get a conclusion from two negative premises, and that conclusion may at least in part be affirmative. Yet I can not reject these traditional rules as errors, and if they have committed oversights is a question which turns on their interpretation. Without doubt if you interpret negative premises strictly, that is, take them in the shape of bare denials, then the rule which forbids an inference is valid. And the second rule, which confines the conclusion to a mere denial, is without doubt valid unless you break through another syllogistic precept. If you insist on eliding the middle term, then not only must the result be partly negative, but it really is limited to a judgment which denies. And thus, if in their statement the rules turn out to have gone too far, they at all events have been based on a solid foundation.

It is not hard to understand this; from two bare denials there can come no conclusion, because there can not be any construction. Why no construction? Because there is either no common point, or, if there is a common point, because you do not know the position of the other terms. Let us take the last first; in negative reasoning we may represent the denials by lines of exclusion; but, if we interpret the premises strictly, we find ourselves unable to give these lines any definite position. A is not C nor B, but the exclusion of C and the exclusion of B, though we represent them truly by lines of rejection, fall we know not where. The excluded has got no determinate position, and therefore no known relation to other elements.

And this is not all, for if we wish to see the real state of the case, we must go back to our doctrine of the negative judgment (Bk. I. Chap. III.). A mere denial does not in any way give existence or position to the thing it denies.[4] Thus in " A is not B " we assert the simple rejection of B by an unstated quality belonging to A, and in respect of B we know nothing at all but its banishment from our universe. But it is obvious that, when a term is so banished, we know about it nothing definite save its rejection by A. No matter then how many negative premises we may have, since by adding to the number of our banished terms we do not get any nearer a conclusion. The exiles do not move in any real world at all, and to unite them by a line of connection is impossible.

Thus even if two denials have a common subject, we can

not go from those denials to a further relation.* And we are stopped elsewhere by another obstacle, for we have not got the common centre required for a construction. In " A is not B and B is not C," we have in the one case the exclusion *of* B, and in the other case the exclusion *by* B; we have first absence and then presence. And again, if we give our premises another form and say " B is not A and B is not C," we can not go to a relation between A and C, since (apart from other reasons) the quality of B may be quite different in each denial. Perhaps from " C is not A and B is not A " we might be tempted to argue to a positive relation of partial identity between C and B. But here again our centre would be wanting, for we do not know if the quality which ensures the rejection is not wholly different in each of these cases. And thus our premises may furnish a ground for suspicion, but they no more give us proof than would such positive premises as " A is like B and C," or " A is like B, and B is like C." In short given two denials there is either no common point, or else the two relations which start from that centre terminate in nothing which can be related.

The rule which forbids all the premises to deny is thus shown to have a solid foundation; and we may say the same of the rule which prohibits a positive conclusion. For since the predicate denied is completely expelled from the world of the subject, we are left with no relation beside the repulsion. It is clear then that you can not have a positive connection either between the predicate and that which exists in friendship with the subject, or between the subject and what shares the fortunes of the predicate. In " A — B B — C," if one relation is negative, we can not in any way draw a line A — C which falls outside B. For A and C will be separated in two different worlds, and if one is in any way to come in contact with the other, the line of connection must pass through B. But on one side of B is a mere rejection, and it is therefore evident that a positive line can not be drawn beyond the centre, and that the new relation must add to the rejection which already exists in B. It is indeed not true that this

---

* In " A is not B and not C, therefore B and C are so far alike " the premises are positive. B and C are both discrepant in quality with A, or have the psychical fact of rejection in common.

extension is a *mere* denial, and again it is not true that the conclusion must be *wholly* negative; but for all that the second traditional rule has, like the first, a rational foundation.

§ 4. But though both the precepts stand on a solid basis, the meaning of the first calls for some restriction, and the second is not true without an exception. Two denials should not give a conclusion at all, and yet you can not say that of two premises which deny. In his *Principles of Science,* p. 63, Prof. Jevons has called attention to the subject;

> "Whatever is not metallic is not capable of powerful magnetic influence, (1)
> Carbon is not metallic, (2)
> Therefore, carbon is not capable of powerful magnetic influence (3)."

This argument no doubt has *quaternio terminorum* and is vicious technically, but the fact remains that from two denials you somehow *have* proved a further denial. " A is not B, what is not B is not C, therefore A is not C." The premises are surely negative to start with, and it appears pedantic either to urge on one side that " A is not-B " is simply positive, or on the other that B and not-B afford no junction. If from negative premises I can get my conclusion, it seems idle to object that I have first transformed one premise; for that objection does not show that the premises are not negative, and it does not show that I have failed to get my conclusion.

And if we leave the limits of the syllogistic logic examples come to us from every side; " A degree A can not be less than B, B is not less than C, therefore C can not be greater than A, or A must be equal to or greater than C; " " Event A is not before B, C is not after B, therefore A is not before C, or C is simultaneous with A or before it; " " C is not north of B, B is not north of A, therefore A is not south of C, or A is due east, or west, or on the north side of C." It is bootless here to fall doggedly back on the technical rules of mood and figure, since, if we keep to these, we can not even prove the positive conclusions from the positive premises. If " A to right of B " is a positive relation of A to B which can not be reduced to predicate and copula, why should we not have in " A not to right of B " a negative relation which is also irreducible? The traditional logic may object to the latter, but it has put itself out of court by first objecting to the former; and, if it is quite wrong in one case, it may be quite wrong in another.

§ 5. In this case it is not wrong, for it happens to be right. The restricted portion of the field it occupies happens here to be the limit of the subject. For denial as such can not fall outside the single category in which the syllogism is shut up.

A denial as such, we have seen long ago, is merely the exclusion of an ideal suggestion, and hence no negative relation between positive existences can ever be expressed by a mere denial. But then on the other hand a *bare* denial can never be found, for, when A excludes some relation to B which is offered in idea, there must always be a ground for that rejection. The base of the rejection must be a positive quality, unspecified but necessary; and hence, wherever we have negative judgment, we have in addition some positive assertion, which may not be explicit but which must be there. And this, as we saw, is such a fount of ambiguity that in denials we seldom know all we are saying (p. 125).

We may verify this in the examples we have used. In the first we assume that A has degree, and upon that basis of positive assertion we proceed, by exclusion of the alternatives denied, to a positive result. In the second the argument really starts from " A is an event with a position in the series after or simultaneous with B." In the third we assume that A falls in space and in a relation to B marked out by exclusion. In all these if we kept to mere denial we could not prove anything, since we may deny " less than B," or " prior to B," or " north of B," of what has no degree and no time and no position. Such a course might be unusual but is legitimate and recognized, because the denial as such covers all possibilities.

§ 6. If we take as our rule that from negative premises you can not argue, then, stated so, that rule is incorrect; and it is false even to say that denials give no inference, since every denial has a positive side. That positive side is latent and may escape us; in " 7 is not less than $5 + 1$, $5 + 1$ is not less than 4, and therefore 7 is not less than 4," we do not *say* that 7 is a number at all and must stand in some numerical relation with $5 + 1$. And thus in assuming it we have passed beyond the denial, though not beyond what the denial implies. It is necessary therefore in expressing our rule to make a distinction. You can not argue, we must say, from two denials, so long as you keep to bare denial. If you treat the assertion which those denials imply, then you are not keeping to the side of denial. And, if we formulate it so, the rule will hold good.

Denial implies removal or exclusion, and from exclusions or removals you can get a conclusion. "Removal of A is removal of B, removal of B is removal of C," gives "Removal of A is removal of C;" and "Absence of A is absence of B, absence of B is absence of C," proves that absence of A is absence of C. But here our real premises are "*What* removes A removes B," and "*That which* is without A is also without B." You can hardly say that these premises are quite positive, but they contain much more than a bare denial. Thus negation must always remain ambiguous (Book I. Chap. III.), for "No A is B," may merely banish B, while again it may assert "The absence of A is the presence of B." "If A is there then B will not be there," and "Since A is not there B must be there" are both expressed by this doubtful formula. But if we confine negation to mere denial it is the exclusion of an idea by an unspecified quality, and if we confine the denial to its negative side it is the mere exclusion of a suggested idea. It is upon this last understanding that the traditional rule is actually valid.

It would not be valid if negation were assertion. If in "A is not B" the exclusion of B were a condition necessary to the existence of A, then B must be banished if A is to be there, and if B is not there B can not be banished. And from negative premises, if so interpreted, it no doubt might be possible to get some conclusion. But this interpretation we long ago saw was erroneous. The denial excludes an ideal suggestion, and the fact which lies at the base of the exclusion need be no relation of A to B, but on the other hand a quality of A or again of some more ultimate reality. But this quality is latent and wholly unspecified.

§ 7. We have seen that, upon a strict interpretation of negative premises, the first of the rules we mentioned is valid.

What then is to become of our principles of synthesis, since they collide with the rule and can not be true? But I think it is better to leave them standing, for they are valid if the sense of negative premises is not confined to what they deny.

Otherwise of course they must be corrected. It is impossible to have any negative inference which will fall wholly within the categories of identity, or time, or space, or again degree. One premise at least must confine itself to the relation of subject and attribute.

This is very obvious. One premise must deny, and no denial as such can be referred to any category beyond the relation of attribute to subject. The denial is the exclusion of an ideal suggestion, and a relation of time, or space, or degree falls within this suggestion which the subject repels. It is clear then that the denial of a connection, say of space, is not a connection in the category of space. The subject excludes, it is true, by a quality, but you do not know what that quality is. And since you do not know what quality repels, the repulsion and the quality which forms its basis can not pass beyond the sphere of simple attribution. Thus " A is not north of B," if restricted to denial, means " A repels the suggestion A to north of B; " and we can not possibly take this as anything more than an adjective of A.

If we refer to the examples we gave in illustration (§ 2), we must so interpret the negative premises. " B is not in tune with C" means " B excludes the attribute of being in tune with C," and " B is not lighter than C" means " B excludes a certain relation of degree to C." But of course B might repel these relations with C although it possessed no note at all, and although it had no degree of any kind; and in the same way the denial that B is in such a position may be true though B has no place whatever. If one of the premises be confined to denial that premise is shut up within the category of subject and attribute.

But having so restricted the character of our premises it is natural to expect a restricted result. Our rule will now be, " In all negative inferences the conclusion is confined within the relation of subject and attribute, *unless that conclusion can in any way be affirmative.*"

§ 8. But can the conclusion be anything but negative?

This is the question we have next to discuss. The rule forbade an affirmative result, and we saw that this rule was based upon truth. For since in A — B B — C one relation is negative, A — C can not be joined by a line of connection which passes anywhere except through B. And, since part of this line must consist of an exclusion, we saw that A — C must have a negative character (§ 3).

The result is unshaken, but it omits a possibility. The conclusion need not take the form of A — C, since the result which we get from the union of our premises, may be found in the whole ideal construction. The syllogistic practice is to elide the middle; but if we do not choose to perform this elision, who on the one hand can order us to do so? And on the other hand who can deny that the result which we obtain is a real inference? " A takes precedence of (is lighter than, sits on the right of) B, B is not younger than C, therefore A takes precedence of (is lighter than, sits on the right of) a person (B) not younger than C." There is here no direct conclusion A — C, and there is again no inference within one category, and at the same time one premise seems to be used as mere denial. On the other hand I see no reasonable ground on which we can deny that we have got a conclusion. Yet this conclusion is neither a mere denial, nor does it fall within the category of subject and attribute.

We may go beyond this. In the syllogism itself, if we decline to elide the middle term B, we may have an inference the conclusion of which is more than a denial. Take an instance in *Celarent,* " A lung-breathing animal (B) is not a fish (C). All Cetacea (A) breathe by means of lungs (B)." From this the regular conclusion is " A is not C." But " All Cetacea have a quality, viz., breathing through lungs, which excludes the assertion that any are fish," will surely come without flaw from the premises. It certainly is more than a bare denial, and it is no mere repetition of the premises. And to say, If A does not exclude C after the middle has been elided, there shall be no inference and there can be no conclusion, seems purely arbitrary. Nor indeed do I see how this insistence on elision, if we pressed it to its consequences, would prove compatible with the general validity of the third figure.

§ 9. The result we are left with may thus be stated. From

two denials there is no conclusion. If one premise denies and keeps to denial, then one premise at least is limited to the *genus* of subject and attribute. If the middle term B falls out of the conclusion, if A and C are connected through B, but not by means of an intermediate B, then the conclusion denies and falls also within the above-named *genus*. But if B is kept standing, the conclusion may at least in part be positive, and is not confined to a single category.

The general formula for negative reasoning, if we confine ourselves to the side of bare denial, may be stated as follows: [5] If B repels a content C, and is in relation with a third term A, then A and C will either be related directly by way of denial or else will be elements in a whole A — B — C, of which at least one member will be confined to the *genus* of subject and attribute. And I think with this we may take leave of a subject which has proved perhaps more troublesome than interesting.

ADDITIONAL NOTES

[1] The statement that all reasoning, negative as well as positive, depends on an ideal whole, and that this whole can be called a construction, is so far correct. But otherwise this section, and much of what follows, is unsatisfactory. Every negation (see on Bk. I. Chap. III.) implies a disjunction. And only because, and so far as, negative reasoning is based on and further develops a disjunctive totality and system—does it possess a real value. For an admirable exposition of this view the reader is referred to Bosanquet's *Logic*.

If we keep to mere denial, what is denied will certainly fall somewhere else in the Universe, since no mere ideas are possible. But, because the variety of special worlds within the Universe is indefinite, and because the merely denied is not, so far, located, you can base no special connection on the fact of mere simple denial. If negation is to be fruitful, it must (to repeat this) stand upon and move within a scheme of specialized alternatives, related to each other at once as positive and negative.

Hence it is scarcely worth while for me to attempt to correct this chapter in detail. I will, however, touch on a certain number of points.

[2] The usual demand for the elision of the middle term seems not defensible, and any rule that the conclusion must *merely* deny should therefore be modified. See § 8. But the rule which condemns

two negative premisses, in the sense of two denials, must stand. For what is denied may fall in worlds not so connected as to make a construction possible. Hence, unless by going beyond mere denial one premiss becomes positive, no conclusion can be reached. In §4 after *quaternio terminorum*" we should add " or else one positive premiss."

³ If you keep to mere denial, as distinct from exclusion, repulsion or absence, all that is implied is an unspecified whole (x) containing two diversities (A and B). These must be positive, but, so far as you merely deny one of the other, you attend simply to their difference. Further, by identifying one of them (A) with C, you can deny the other (B) of C. But neither here nor elsewhere is there any inference through mere denial beyond the category of subject and attribute. As soon as you have assumed worlds containing arrangements and relations other than those of identity and difference, you have gone beyond mere negation in the sense of denial.

Hence the "general formula" (§9) can not stand, and should perhaps be read thus—"If you deny of B a content C, C can also be denied of that which is identical with B, and can further be related indirectly by denial with that which is related positively to B." But, though in the latter case the "conclusion" need not be "confined to a single category," the inference, and what actually is concluded, never goes beyond the category of subject and attribute. Statements to the contrary (§§ 2, 8, and 9) are erroneous.

⁴ In the way of minor corrections I may here note that we should insert "definite" before "existence or position"; and (at the end of the paragraph) should read "move in any *one* real world at all." And, generally, I would remind the reader that such terms as "removal," "exclusion," "repulsion," and even "absence," all are affirmative in the sense of at least containing a positive aspect. And this aspect goes beyond what is contained in negation, if and so far as we take that as mere denial.

⁵ For "the general formula" see Note 3.

CHAPTER VI

TWO CONDITIONS OF INFERENCE

§ 1. We may briefly recapitulate the result we have reached. An inference is always an ideal construction resulting in the perception of a new connection. So far as this perception of the conclusion is concerned, there is no possibility of laying down rules, and the syllogistic logic teaches a superstition. That logic again has failed to include all the principles of synthesis which operate in construction, and it is falsely confined to a single category. It is wrong again as to the number of the premises; and, in insisting on the necessity of a major premise, it is clinging blindly to exploded metaphysics in direct defiance of the most palpable facts. And it makes a further mistake as to the necessity of elision.

It might seem that having thus rejected the syllogism we must throw in our lot with its hereditary enemies. But yet, if the friends of the syllogism will allow it, we would rather take a place on their side. Our differences are trivial compared with our agreements, and as against the enemy our cause is the same, for we have in common these two beliefs: (i) It is impossible to reason except upon the basis of identity, (ii) It is impossible to reason unless at least one premise is universal. It will be time to say *vicerunt empirici* when these positions have both been forced.

§ 2. (i) I will begin with the necessity of an identical point. We know that an inference is an ideal construction, and the reality of this construction depends on its unity; if the construction is not individual it is merely fictitious. But how can any construction have unity unless it is united by a common point? And how can any point be common, unless in both the premises it is one and the same?

It is obvious that suppose the problem before us is to find the relation of S to P by means of their common relation to M, and if, by the hypothesis, S — M and M — P must be given separately, an advance is impossible, unless in both premises

M is the same. Given S — M¹ & M² — P you can make no construction, for you have no bridge to carry you over from M¹ to M². The back of your inference now is broken and the extremities no longer belong to any individual principle. Unless M in both cases is absolutely the same you can not interrelate S and P.

If we are willing to give up the superstition of the copula and to admit a diversity of relations in judgment, we may say that in inference every pair of premises has one term the same, and that, if it is not the same, there can be no inference.

§ 3. It is obvious, if we dismiss our hardened prejudices and consider the question fairly by itself, that you can not argue on the strength of mere *likeness*.[1] Whatever else may be right this at all events must be wrong; "A is similar to B, and B to C, and therefore A is like C," is a vicious inference, one that need not always be mistaken in fact, but that always must be a logical error. In practice I think we should all admit this. An inference based on nothing but likeness is utterly invalid; it is certainly ambiguous and probably false.

Likeness and sameness should never be confused, for the former refers properly to a general impression. Similarity is a perceived relation between two terms which implies and rests upon a partial identity. If we say that A and B are alike, we must be taken to assert that they have something the same. But we do not specify this point of sameness, and the moment we do that we have gone beyond mere similarity. If A and B for instance both have lungs or gills they are so far the same, and, on the strength of and because of this partial identity, they may present themselves to us as generally similar. But now add to these the further statement " B and C are alike." If we reduce the likeness here to partial identity we *may* find that the common point is here once again the possession of lungs or gills, and on the strength of this we may go on to argue that A and C (the extremes) are alike. But what actually interrelates A and C is not general similarity at all. If all you knew was that B was like C, the point of identity would be quite unspecified, and the fact might be, not that both had lungs or gills, but that each had one eye or the freedom of the will. In this case though each pair has its own internal likeness, you could not infer the similarity of A to C.

And if in answer I am told that this is irrelevant, and that it does not apply where the likeness is exact, I can only reply that I am waiting, and have been waiting for years, to be told what is meant by an " exact likeness." " A and B are not the same, but they are exactly alike, and therefore whatever is true of B must be true of A." But what can this mean? In the case of some twins it might be right to punish one for the other, and we should no longer care to identify criminals. If a picture is " exactly like " a person, then if one is not dead the other will be alive. If a cast is " exactly like " an original I suppose the same thing will be in two places at once; and it is no mere metaphor if in certain cases the father is said to survive in his children, though the children might then cease to survive the father. But it is idle to pursue these frivolous consequences; the meaning which " exactly like " carries to my mind is nothing whatever but " partially the same " or " identical in some point or points." Likeness is always a perceived relation based upon a partial identity. In mere general similarity the identity will be indefinite; where the likeness is more special it must at least be partly defined, and where the similarity is called " exact " I understand that there is a definite point or points, in respect of which the sameness is complete. And if likeness did *not* imply identity all inference based upon it would be vicious. In practice every one would allow it to be vicious, nor do I understand how in theory it is possible to take it as having any other character.

I am most anxious to enter into (if I can), and to discuss the meaning our " advanced thinkers " may have attached to " likeness " or " similarity." But I am forced to say again in this place what I had to say elsewhere some years ago.* While our " advanced thinkers " merely sing the old song which they have learnt and which their fathers have taught them, they can hardly expect to have its meaning discussed, nor can they complain if they are treated as having no real meaning.

§ 4. A construction of given premises is not possible unless each pair of premises has a common point. And this

* *Ethical Studies*, p. 151 (Ed. II. p. 167).

common point must be an identical term. Thus in " A — B
B — C therefore A — B — C," the B in each premise must not
be merely alike, but must be absolutely the same. But here,
after having avoided one error, we are threatened by another
and opposite mistake. For if it is wrong to say that B is not
the same, it is equally wrong to deny that it is different.

This may look mysterious but is really quite simple. If
B in both premises were so far the same that no difference of
any kind belonged to it, then it is obvious at once that both
premises must be identical, or else that their differences do
not concern B. But in each of these cases the inference disappears. If the premises are the same their repetition is
meaningless, and if the differences they contain are indifferent
to B it is clear that no construction can be made, since, if B
is the centre, it carries no *radii* and has no circumference. An
identity which is not a synthesis of differences is plainly inert
and utterly useless.

B is the same amid difference, and though different is the
same, for it is an ideal content, the product of abstraction,
appearing in and differenced by two several contexts. So far
as it is the one content B, so far it is absolutely and entirely
the same; so far as it is a member of diverse connections, so
far it carries with it a difference. And the process of inference
depends entirely on this double aspect; for it is because B is
different and yet the same, that its differences are able to be
interrelated. If it were not different it would have nothing
to connect, and if it were not the same there could be no
connection. Inference rests upon the assumption that, if the
ideal content is the same, then its differences will be the *radii*
of one centre. In other words if B is the same, what is true
of it in one context is true of it in another.

§ 5. We have returned to what we called the Principle of
Identity (Book I. Chap. V.). We might call it again the
Axiom of the Identity of Indiscernibles, and we can put the
thing in more simple language if we say that inference rests
on the principle that what *seems* the same *is* the same,[2] and
can not be made different by any diversity, and that so long as
an ideal content is identical no change of context can destroy
its unity. The assumption in this principle may be decried as
monstrous, and I do not deny that perhaps it is false. In a

metaphysical work this question would press on us, but in logic we are not obliged to discuss it (Book III. Part II. Chap. IV.). The axiom may be monstrous or again it may be true, but at least one thing is beyond all doubt, that it is the indispensable basis of reasoning. It may be false metaphysically, but there is no single inference you possibly can make but assumes its validity at every step.

§ 6. It is easy to misunderstand it, and it is sure to be misunderstood. I shall be told that spaces and times are indiscernible and yet are not identical. But this objection rests on a complete mistake. As spaces or times of a certain character A and B surely *are* identical; as different elements within the same series A and B are surely *not* indiscernible. It is one superstition to think you have relations whose terminal points are nothing beyond the relation.* It is another superstition to fancy relations as an arbitrary network stuck on from the outside by destiny or chance, and making no reasonable difference to anything. And the root of both superstitions is the same. It is the refusal to recognize that

---

* I am prepared to go a good deal beyond this.[3] If occasion offered I should be ready to argue that you can not have a relation between points that are not different in quality. Not only, for instance, must spaces related be more than a mere relation in space, but they must also have a difference in quality. It is not possible to contemplate points in relation unless you distinguish them by a qualitative reference to the right or left or upper or lower sides of your body, and the different sensations which are at the root of these divisions, or again unless, by a qualitative mark such as A or B, you choose to make one different from the other. It may be objected that in certain cases the difference of quality is only one aspect of the whole relation. This view at least recognizes the existence of the difference, and I will not here discuss it. The ultimate connection of quality and relation is a most difficult problem. But it is clear that taken in their phenomenal appearance the one can not be reduced to the other. Is this double aspect true of the reality? Has that, as we are forced in the end to apprehend it, a single nature which combines two sides, and is so the root of the double appearance? Can we suppose that qualities are generated by the strife of some counterpart of what appears to us as relations? Or is it true that supersensible qualities are the reality which *we* perceive as phenomenal relations? Or is the question unanswerable? If it is, we at least must not do violence to the given on the strength of a theory which we can not defend (cf. Book I. Chap. II. § 65 foll.).

the content of the given has always two sides,[4] sensible qualities and relations, and that one side can never, except by an
artifice, be separate from or merged in the other. I do not
say that these two elements are metaphysically irreducible;
I do say that, taking them each as it stands, you must treat
them each as a character of the given. It is a dire illusion
to take the content of the given as either qualities without
relation or relations without qualities, or to treat the one
side as external to the other. Both are given together and
given within the content. It was shown above (Bk. I. Chap.
II. § 21) that space and time-relations are no *principium in-
dividuationis;* for they fall within the *what,* and do not make
the *this.*

And another result was brought out in that Chapter. Unless judgments of sense make a false assertion they affirm
or deny connections of content, and they do not affirm anything else whatever. It is absurd to object that if Cæsar is
the same, he is in Gaul and in Italy, two places at once, or
that if he is thirty he is also twenty-nine. The " at once "
and the "also " conceal the old error. Of course it is not true
that the identical Cæsar *under the same conditions*[5] can be
differently related to Italy in space or to his own birth in
time; but then surely the conditions vary indefinitely. The
mere lumping together unspecified conditions under the head
" is now " does not show that the conditions are indiscernible,
and that striking the differences out of the account we are
forced to predicate contradictions of Cæsar. What is true of
Cæsar in a certain context is true of the same Cæsar in any
other context. But this does not mean that one context *is*
the other or is to be confused with the other. It means that
Cæsar has two different contexts, and that the truth of one
can be no reason whatever for the falsehood of the other. If
we fancy this is so we have given to one or to both assertions
a meaning which is *false,* and we must be sent back once
more to study the discussions of Book I. Chapter II.

§ 7. And there is another misunderstanding against which
we must guard. That what is true of B here is true of B
everywhere, means that, wherever B happens to be, you can
say of it always what you have said of it once. This B you
assert of is the self-same B that appears in the differences, but

it is not the B just *as it appears* in those differences.   In
A — B, B — C, the B is identical, and A and C are connected
by that identity.   But A and C are not themselves identical,
and you can not predicate B — C of A — B.   The B, of which
what has once been said holds good for ever, is not the B
which is one thing with A or one thing with C.   It is the abstraction,[6] the idealized content B, which is different from its
contexts and yet connected with them, and, on the strength of
its oneness connects them together.   The identity is always a
synthesis of differences which themselves are not identical the
one with the other, and apart from these differences the
identity disappears into blank indiscriminateness.

I will try to illustrate the whole question briefly.   We
have a shed in the corner of a field, and, that shed being burnt,
another is set up not distinguishable in itself from the first.
Let the first be B — A and the second B — C; in what sense
is it true that what holds of B once will hold of it always?
The objection is obvious, In the shed B — A an event D happened, but can we say that the event took place in B — C?
And if we can not say that, and if B is not distinguishable, how
are we going to defend our axiom?

We are in no kind of perplexity.   The content B is obviously not the individual shed.   The two sheds are made
individual by their places in the series, and those places fall
outside the abstraction B.   What is true of B is universal
propositions and is nothing besides.   The event D can not
be asserted truly until it becomes a hypothetical statement
(Book I. Chap. II.).

But the objection will be pressed, " The sheds and their
environment are a certain content, and that content is the
same.   If, on the strength of this content, we said of the shed
B — A 'D happened here yesterday,' why can we not also
upon this ground now say of the shed B — C ' D happened here
last year '?   The content is what we go from, and we have
that in both cases."   I reply, By all means: the content is
the same.   Let us try to carry out the process you recom-
mend.   We can not of course connect D with B — C unless
we establish a chain of relations through the identity of their
end-points (*ibid.*).   You can not go *direct* from the content B
to the temporal event D, for that, as we have seen, is not

predicated categorically (*ibid.*).[7] You must start from the content as given in one time. Well, starting from B — A you got a chain of events which took you back to D. But, if you start from B — C, you have a chain of events which takes you back first to the origin of B — C, when B did not exist, and then again through the destruction of B — A, to the time when B once more existed and was connected with D. Your process informs you that D the event will *not* fall within the identity of the ideal content B — C. That content has been qualified by a limitation in time, and qualified again by a definition of its component elements, which excludes their identity with the elements of B — A. If you deny that these qualifications are objects of knowledge, *then* I admit D *is* true of B — C, and why in the world should we *not* think it true? But if you admit that these qualifications are distinctions, then the content of the sheds is *not* indiscernible, and therefore by your admission is not identical.[8]

This, I think, is a sufficient answer to the objection, but it omits to take notice of several difficulties. There are questions which no doubt might occasion us trouble, but they do not seem to concern us here. We have been forced to notice a metaphysical problem which, at least in this work, we can not deal with, and hence objections which we can not here attempt to answer may be directed against us. But at least on one side I think we are safe; we need fear no collision with the Philosophy of Experience, for that philosophy does not know the ground it stands on. Since Hume's bold speculations on the subject of identity were suppressed by himself, the English school has repeated a lesson by rote and flaunted a blind ancestral prejudice.

§ 8. The importance of the subject may excuse a repetition. That what is the same ideally is really the same is without any doubt an enormous assumption, and I do not say that this assumption is true. What I do say is (*a*) that all inference presupposes it, and (*b*) that the objection to it rests on nothing but metaphysics.

(*a*) If we only will look at the palpable facts, we must admit that logic stands or falls with this axiom. Wherever we join one premise with another we must do so by means of an identical point, which, given as it is in diverse presentations, is held to be the same because it has the same content, and which, so far as it is not ideally discernible, is taken as one. Failing this identity the construction falls apart. I confess I do not know how to make this any clearer. I can only say to any one who doubts it, Show me an inference where this does not hold good, and I will show you a vicious inference, and you yourself shall admit that it is vicious.

(b) It sounds terrible to say that Identity is an ideal synthesis of differences, and that this identity is real fact. The words are strange to the common mind, but it has always tacitly accepted their meaning. We believe that a body has changed its place, but at the end of the movement the change that is past is no fact of sense. We abstract the body from its present position and, treating this abstraction as a continuous identity, we predicate of it the changing differences. But do we doubt that motion is a real fact? And if we are told, It is the material atoms which are the same throughout; then why I would ask do we take them for the same, despite their differences of time and space, except because their ideal content is the same? The identity of indiscernibles may be true or false, but not only is it impossible to reason without it, but it is the abstract formula for our common-sense belief.

The authority of common sense is no authority for me, but the result we have reached may bring out one fact. The objection, raised by the Philosophy of Experience against a real identity, does not rest on any difficulty felt by common sense, and it is not an objection it would ever think of raising. It is a metaphysical objection, and it rests entirely on a metaphysical doctrine. It is because the Philosophy of Experience is sure that there is no reality except exclusive particulars, that it is horror-struck at the thought of a real universal. And because its belief is not proved nor thought to need proof, nor in any way discussed, because it is a mere inherited preconception which has got to think itself a real fact, it is scarcely so much to be called a doctrine as an orthodox dogma and traditional superstition.

And, as it must happen with all orthodox dogmas, its votaries do not take their professions in earnest. If an universal content may ever be real, on what ground can they deny the identity of thoughts because one is yesterday and the other to-day? But if such ideal sameness is *not* real, then how can any process or change or continuity be anything but illusion? If a thing *is* not now the same that it *was,* if it is only alike, then it can not have changed. And if it *is* the same, on what ground do we make that assertion except on the ground of identity of content? It is frivolous [9] to say that identity may be real, where existence is continuous and is not broken in the series of time, but is not real anywhere else. For if you allow that any lapse or change is a fact, you have admitted the reality of an element not confined to this or that particular, and you have admitted it on the ground of the identity of indiscernibles. You have already thrown your principle overboard, and if it is false in one place it may be false in another. Or to put the same thing in another form, if you are afraid to break with common sense in one point, what makes you so very bold in another? If I am to answer the question for you, I am forced to say that you have partly no head and partly no heart. You do not see the consequences deducible from your doctrine, and when a consequence begins to look like a *reductio ad absurdum,* you refuse to follow it. And this is what we call or used to call " advanced thinking." [10]

§ 9. It is against such opponents that the syllogism is right. The doctrine of copula and terms which it cherishes is indefensible, but it is right in demanding an identity in reasoning. The middle is an identity which connects the differences, and, being such an identity, the middle is an universal. In this point again the syllogism is right. For though the major premise is a superstition, one premise at least must be universal or else there can be no inference at all. We have here again a condition necessary to reasoning.

§ 10. (ii) We saw in the second chapter of Book I., and later on again in Chapter VI. § 39, that in the end no judgment is really particular.[11] They are all universal. And we might content ourselves here with recalling the result we there have reached, but, perhaps at the risk of superfluity, we may add some further remarks on the subject. If one of the premises were not universal, how could they both have a common identity? The term B must be shared by both the premises. It is a single content in two different contexts. But, since thus it is universal, at least one premise must have the same character.

This simple consideration is, I think, sufficient for any one who has put himself at the right point of view. But notwithstanding all our previous discussions, there no doubt will be readers still unwilling or unable to follow us in this argument. " In ' A precedes B and B precedes C ' can B," we shall hear, " be really universal? Nay even in the syllogism, if we take the third figure, is the middle term really an universal? It is so technically because it is distributed, or understood in its full extension, but these technical distinctions have long ago been thrown overboard, and with them has gone the universality of singulars." I will briefly reply to the above objection.

§ 11. An universal judgment is one that holds of any subject which is a synthesis of differences. It is a proposition the truth of which is not confined to any single this. The subject extends beyond the judgment, and, where the subject goes, the judgment is true. In this sense we have seen that all judgments are universal. But we are limited here to a simpler issue, for we have to show, given a valid inference, that at least one premise is universal. It is quite enough, as we have just remarked, to consider the identity of the middle term: but a more detailed exposition may perhaps be welcome.

There are certain cases which call for no discussion. Where the middle term is an abstract attribute, and this forms the subject of one of the premises, there one premise must be allowed to be universal.*

The difficulty which is felt arises from those cases where the middle term is a singular, or where it is not the ostensible subject of either premise. Take for instance " A is to right of B, and B of C, and therefore A of C," or "A and C have the note B in common, and therefore C is in tune with A, and both related by the identity of B." How in such inferences as these can we show that one premise must be universal?

---

* In order to bring arguments into this form we may freely convert any negative judgments. Thus in the second figure we may convert, as required, negative premises or conclusions. The case of *Baroco* presents no difficulty.[12]

§ 12. Unless our previous discussions have led us quite wrong, such a question as this can be readily answered. " B is to right of C " is an universal judgment because B is an identity which has the differences of its spatial relations to A and C.¹³ It transcends the context B — C and is therefore universal. Or, from another point of view, the relation B — C is true of a subject which extends itself beyond those limits, and is the identical subject of which the relation A — B is also true. If you take the relations as qualifying B, then B is the universal which exhibits these differences. Or again if you go somewhat further back, then the unity of the common space is the genuine subject of which these relations are diverse attributes. We can always find an identical subject although that subject need not be apparent. In " Cæsar is angry and Cæsar is silent, and therefore silence may accompany anger," it is the grammatical subject which supplies the universal within whose identity the synthesis holds good. But where from " A has a certain note B and C has also the self-same note," we infer a relation between A and C, it is doubtful where the actual subject lies. If we are willing to accept the grammatical subject, then in " C has the note B," C is our universal. For C is disturbed from its original context and expanded ideally so as to form a whole with A. And, if it were not universal, it could not be treated as a subject waiting to receive a predicate beyond its original given existence.* This would be the right interpretation if A and C are to be considered as subjects. But it is better here, I think, to take the middle as the actual subject of both the premises. B is the universal of which we predicate the difference B — A and the difference B — C, and it is the bond of identity which interrelates the whole.

§ 13. We shall see hereafter that every inference may be taken as holding within the identity of one subject (Book III. Part I. Chap. VI. § 34), and if we take this view it is obvious that the subject of both premises is universal. For the present it may prove sufficient to remember that, inference being an ideal construction and involving therefore an ideal centre, one premise must be taken as true beyond the limits of a par-

* Of course if you suppose the relation A — C to be a perception got simply from the given, then there is no inference and *cadit quæstio*.

ticular subject. If we keep hold of this reflection we shall not be shaken by any puzzles which are laid before us. In the previous Book I have endeavoured to anticipate and to cut the root of those difficulties which are the most likely to be raised, and it is to the discussion of that Book that I must refer back the reader who is still inclined to hesitate.

In the ensuing Part of the present Book we shall criticize some inadequate views of inference, and shall begin with that belief which is most opposed to the doctrines set forth in the present Chapter.

ADDITIONAL NOTES

¹ On Similarity, Likeness, and Identity, see the Indexes, to this volume and to *Appearance* and *Essays*.

² "What seems the same is the same." It should be "is *so far* the same." Error as to the exact point of sameness remains possible. And after "diversity" should perhaps have come "further" or "added". What must be rejected everywhere is the idea of a similarity which does not imply sameness. The "Axiom"—so far as it is an axiom—holds obviously also in Metaphysics. On the ultimate difficulty as to Identity, see *Essays*, Index.

³ These points have been taken up by me in later works. There is here a partial failure to realize the true conclusion that, just as terms and relations are neither present at the beginning of knowledge, so both alike are subordinated and transformed in the ultimate end. Terms and relations are (as is seen in this volume) alike abstractions, and (we must add) are, each alike, unreal as such.

⁴ "The content of the given has always two sides." We must remember here that, if so, Immediate Experience or Feeling must not be called "given." See Bk. III. I. Chap. VII, and *Appearance* and *Essays*.

With regard (three lines below) to "metaphysically irreducible," we can not possibly (I should say) "reduce" these "elements." But we can know that in the ultimate whole they lose their characters, as such, and so far as irreducible.

⁵ "Under the same conditions." What is true of B once is true of B always under the same conditions. And, if you object that the different conditions must both be true of B, that must be admitted. It points to the conclusion that, while *mere* B — A and *mere* B — C are in the end abstractions and *neither* in the end true, both are still true relatively. We have to assume a concrete whole containing still further conditions such as to modify these terms and to unite them in something higher. But in this whole, we must remember, conditions and terms cease in the end, as such, to exist.

⁶ " It is the abstraction." It would be better to say " the universal," because the identity may perhaps be that of an organic individual whole, and, so far, not " abstract."

⁷ " Is not predicated categorically." " Unconditionally " would be better.

⁸ " Is not identical." And even in the case of a single shed, where it remains throughout one and the same, it still is qualified by its temporal diversity, so as to be *also* so far different, and, so far again, *not* indiscernible.

⁹ " It is frivolous to say, etc." " Frivolous " may perhaps in some cases go too far, but " irrational " would, I think, hold everywhere. If you keep to change as perceived, then within that perception you have identity in diversity, and you have ideality, though so far you do not abstract it. Either that, or your perception is not the perception of change.

On the relation of Continuity to Identity, see further *Appearance,* the Index and the Note on p. 616.

¹⁰ " Advanced thinking." The above tirade, if unnecessary, was in 1883, I still think, wholly justifiable.

¹¹ " No judgment is really particular." We may put it thus, that all judgments are of content, and that no content sticks in the mere " this." See *Appearance,* Index. And further, on Designation, see *Essays,* Index. The lesser conclusion as to one premiss is, however, sufficient here. Cf. Bosanquet, *Logic,* II, pp. 203-4.

¹² This footnote might without loss have been omitted.

¹³ " Because B is an identity, etc." " Because, in making the inference, B is used as an identity, etc.," would have been better. And so below, in " For C is disturbed, etc.," we should perhaps insert after C the words " in the inference."

BOOK II.—PART II

CHAPTER I

THE THEORY OF ASSOCIATION OF IDEAS [1]

§ 1. The end we had before us in the first part of this Book was to give a general account of inference. The account was in a certain sense provisional, since the examples it dealt with did not pretend to illustrate every kind of inference. But within those limits the result we arrived at seemed irrefragably true. The end we have before us in this Second Part, is the criticism and refutation of certain theories which are out of harmony with the conclusion we have reached.

The title of this chapter calls for explanation. " The Association of Ideas," it may be objected, " is not so much a theory as a fact; a fact which on the one hand is quite indisputable, and which on the other hand can be discrepant with no theory except a theory which runs counter to fact." But the objection would rest on an entire misunderstanding. The psychological fact of " Association " is of course unquestionable. The account of that fact which is given by the orthodox English philosophy, is in my judgment not only questionable but false. And, beside being false, it is incompatible with any tolerably accurate theory of reasoning. For the universality and identity, which we saw were necessary for every inference, do not exist in the theory of " Experience." We are offered in their stead a fictitious substitute, which does not exist and therefore can not work, and which would not work even if it existed.

§ 2. " Inseparable Association," and the " Chemistry of Ideas," are phrases which are only too familiar to most of us. They recall a controversy which has served in some measure to obscure the questions it professed to elucidate. But the more refined developements of the Association doctrine do

299

not immediately concern us here.* For they have no direct
bearing on the theory of inference; and it is solely as it
touches the subject of reasoning that we have here to do with
Association. We may confine our attention to the common
doctrine, as exemplified in the ordinary working of the Laws
of Resemblance and Contiguity.

§ 3. The "association of ideas" is a phrase which may be
taken to express a well-known psychological fact. And if
taken so, it is nothing but a title. The fact, which it stands
for, is a familiar experience, and the meaning of the title is
not proposed as an accurate theory of that fact. It is a name
which must not be pressed into a doctrine.

But, as understood by the Philosophy of Experience, the
"association of ideas" has long ceased to be a way of marking
a thing which we all admit has real existence. It has become
the battle-cry of a school, and a metaphysical doctrine and
theory of things. It contains a belief as to the nature of the
mind, or at least as to the mode in which the mind works,
which is irreconcileable with the views we have already
adopted. Hence if "association" is to stand for a mere
psychological fact, then of course, like every one else, I believe
in it; and I propose to give here the explanation of that fact.
But, if "association" means that view of the fact which has
been embraced by a certain school, then I do not believe in it;
and I propose to show that in this latter sense "association"
has no real existence. It has not only been extended to take
in phenomena which can not properly come within its limits,
but within any limits, however narrow, it is a false view of
things.

§ 4. The word Association, I suppose, implies properly
some kind of *voluntary* union. That signification of course
disappears, but it leaves a shade of meaning behind. For
things are not associated by their own necessity, and by virtue
of some internal connection. Such a group as the family, and
even the state, can hardly be called associations in any strict
sense. Association implies chance, that is, it depends on
circumstances external to that which is conjoined. And so,
when we use the term, we must be taken to suggest that, if
A and B had not been associated, they would nevertheless

* We shall append some remarks at the end of this chapter.

have been A and B. For the conditions, which happened to
bring them together, do not follow in fact, nor are deducible
in idea, from the existence or character of mere A and B.
We may perhaps explain by a reference to the hypothetical
judgment. In such a judgment, if the condition is known,[2]
you assert not a conjunction but always a connection. But
in a categorical judgment of perception, and that means in a
hypothetical judgment where the condition is unknown, you
assert a conjunction and not a connection. The former word
corresponds to Association. The conjunction with B is predicated of A on the strength of a condition, that does not
come into the subject, but is imported by the force of such
circumstances as, in their relation to A, are chance.

Association thus comes to mean chance-conjunction, and
in our mental history we find of course very often that ideas
are conjoined by the merest accident. If you take these
ideas and consider them by themselves, you can find no connection and no reason for their union. Mere circumstances,
which, so far as the ideas are concerned, might never have
existed, did bring them together. And a union caused by
such chance-conjunction is the common meaning of Mental
Association. In this sense of the term it answers to that
which, I suppose, we all admit to be fact; but it conveys no
theory of any kind whatever. It makes no assertion as to the
nature of ideas, and it makes no assertion as to the laws of
their reproduction. It calls attention to one fact among others.
It does not profess to reduce well-nigh everything in the mind
but sensations, impressions, or feelings, to this single fact.

§ 5. The school of Experience, in its more consistent development, has turned the metaphorical expression of one
fact into a theory which may be said to cover all. It has a
doctrine as to the ultimate constituents of mind. They are
particular feelings and particular ideas, in either case repellent
units. And they have absolutely no internal bond of connection. There is no ground common to the different units,
which could serve as a real basis for their union. Universality and identity are derided as fictions. In the procession
of these units we may separate two trains, the train of sensations and the train of ideas; but these all are separate
individual realities. " All our distinct perceptions are distinct

existences, and the mind never perceives any real connection among distinct existences " (Hume). The philosophy of Experience is psychological Atomism.

There is nothing which the atoms possess in common, and there could be no " real connection " between them. They are conjoined by the agency of chance or fate. That impressions should come to us in a certain arrangement, and should in some cases precede feebler counterparts of themselves—this springs from the unknown necessity of a nature, which we can not say is the nature of the units. And the secondary conjunction of impressions with ideas and of ideas with one another, what is this but the accident of Association, whose laws are nothing but general expressions for certain recurring kinds of irrational combination? Destiny and chance are two names of one lord that sways the procession of fleeting units. In their short-lived occupation of that void which is the soul, they are combined by the accident of presentation or by the fate of association. And the " final inexplicability " of J. S. Mill may recall an echo of the " free will " of Epikurus.

§ 6. Having thus anticipated by a sweeping theory the nature of everything that is to be experienced, the school for the future, so long as it keeps true to the metaphysical doctrine on which it stands, may call itself the Philosophy of Experience. And it is also analytical [3]; for does it not assume that every complex phenomenon of the mind is resolvable into the units which its theory has established? Its first principles no doubt are never analyzed; but analysis, it is obvious, must be broken off somewhere. If the " analytical school " is content to stop, then the limit of human thinking has been reached. If the Philosophy of Experience is content with the result, then surely the product of analysis must be fact. Analysis in the future will consist in the attempt to reconstruct synthetically the phenomena of the mind from elements gained in accordance with first principles, and according to the Laws which first principles have established (cf. Book III. Part I. Chap. VI. § 10). It is hardly necessary that in every case the existence of each element should be verified *a posteriori*. If, for the explanation of visual extension, it were first necessary to verify in actual observation the fact of colour-sensations devoid of all extension, it is possible that the analysis could not be performed. And, since that analysis has been firmly established, it is clear that its basis can not be unreal. If we confine ourselves to the limits and the method of the school of Experience, we may be sure of one thing; if we are true to Experience we must be true to fact.

§ 7. We can appreciate now the nature of the claim which is laid to the titles of " experience " and " analysis." But we must hasten to examine the character of those Laws which rule the void and which move ideas. They answer, in the psychical empty space, to what is called " cohesion " or " attraction " in the external void (Hume, *Treatise,* I. 1. 4). The two main principles are the law of Contiguity, and the law of Similarity or Agreement.

I. " Actions, Sensations, and States of Feeling, occurring together or in close succession, tend to grow together, or cohere, in such a way that, when any one of them is afterwards presented to the mind, the others are apt to be brought up in idea." Bain, *Senses,* p. 327.

II. " *Present* Actions, Sensations, Thoughts, or Emotions tend to revive their LIKE among *previous* Impressions, or States." *Ibid.* p. 457.

Or, to put the same thing in the opposite order, " Of these laws the first is, that similar ideas tend to excite one another. The second is, that when two impressions have been frequently experienced (or even thought of) either simultaneously or in immediate succession, then whenever one of these impressions, or the idea of it, recurs, it tends to excite the idea of the other." J. S. Mill, *Logic,* II. p. 440, Ed. IX.

A briefer, and on the whole more accurate expression, would perhaps be this; Mental units which have co-existed cohere, and mental units which are like recall one another—at least in image.

§ 8. In saying that I entirely and utterly reject each one of these statements, I may be taken to deny the existence of fact. But (to repeat once more a distinction I have drawn) what I find it impossible to make myself believe is *not* the fact which these formulæ may be taken as loosely indicating. It is on the contrary their theory of that fact which I can not swallow. And I have no insurmountable objection to the *use* of such statements; but I can not for one moment allow that they are *true*.

I shall give hereafter in greater detail those reasons which lead me to believe that these laws are nothing but fictions. But the main ground of objection may be stated at once. The ideas which are recalled according to these laws are particular existences. Individual atoms are the units of association. And I should maintain, on the contrary, that in all reproduction what operates everywhere is a common identity. No particular ideas are ever associated or ever could be. What is associated is and must be always universal.

It will be found, I think, the most convenient course, if I first give some account of the way in which I conceive association is effected, and then attempt to show that the method, commonly accepted as fact, is wholly fictitious.

§ 9. In the previous Book (p. 34, foll.) I have to some extent anticipated this discussion, and, trusting that the result to which we there came may be recalled by the reader, I may perhaps be here allowed to be brief. I have no hope of persuading the orthodox believer, and others may be willing to help in working out the sketch of a doctrine.

The main Law of Reproduction may be laid down thus; Any part of a single state of mind tends, if reproduced, to re-instate the remainder; or Any element tends to reproduce those elements with which it has formed one state of mind. This may be called the law of Redintegration. For we may take this name from Sir W. Hamilton (*Reid,* p. 897), having found nothing else that we could well take.

There are several points in the formula which call for explanation. We might ask, in the first place, What is a single state of mind? Does it exclude succession? It certainly does not do so. It may be further defined as any psychical complex which is present together, presence signifying presentation, a certain direct relation to the mind which does not imply succession in time. As I have endeavoured (p. 53) to throw some light on the meaning of this term, I must be excused from a further discussion of it here.

In the second place the "parts" of this present state need not be either perceptions or ideas. For the formula includes

every possible kind of mental element; and this is the reason
why we can not accept the principle as we find it laid down
by Wolff and others. I will not here ask, if in the end it
is not possible that association is confined to intellectual or
perceptive elements (vid. Book III. I. Chap. III. §§ 20–22).
It is better for ordinary purposes to suppose that it also applies to desires and feelings. But subject to this correction
we may adopt, if we please, Wolff's statement of the law.

" Si quæ simul percepimus et unius perceptio denuo pro-
ducatur, sive sensuum sive imaginationis vi; imaginatio producit et perceptionem alterius—seu quod perinde est—perceptio præterita integra recurrit, cujus præsens continet
partem " (*Psych. Emp.* § 104).

Maas, following Wolff, has thus formulated the principle.
" Given an idea or perception, then all those ideas, which belong with it to one total perceptive state, may immediately
associate themselves with it, and no other ideas can do so."
Or " Every idea, or perception, recalls to the mind its total
perceptive context " (*Versuch,* Verb. Ausg. 1797, § 13).

This law of Redintegration, we must bear in mind, does
not exclude any succession of events which comes as a whole
before the mind; and it is not to be confined to perceptions
and ideas.

§ 10. The law of redintegration is a very different thing
from the law of contiguity, as that is understood by the school
of Experience. Superficially alike, they are separated by the
chasm that divides irreconcileable views of the world. For
contiguity is cohesion between psychical units, and its elements
are particular existing phenomena. What it couples is the
actual individual impression or image, as such. It is not association between universals. But Redintegration is not anything *else*. For it never re-instates the particular fact. It
can not deal with anything that could be a phenomenon, or
could ever exist. It does not couple psychical units, but is
entirely confined to what is universal.

We should find it hard to overstate the enormous diver-
gence of these two interpretations of the fact of association.
Contiguity asserts a conjunction between existences. Redintegration asserts a connection between universals, which as
such do not exist. What operates in the first is an external

relation *between* individuals. What works in the second is an
ideal identity *within* the individuals. The first deals with the
that, and the second with the *what.* The first unites facts, and
the second mere content.

According to the view which to me seems the truth, to
talk of an association between psychical particulars is to utter
mere nonsense. These particulars in the first place have got
no permanence; their life endures for a fleeting moment. In
the second place they can never have more than one life;
when they are dead they are done with.[4] There is no Hades
where they wait in disconsolate exile, till Association announces resurrection and recall. When the fact is bodily
buried in the past, no miracle opens the mouth of the grave
and calls up to the light a perished reality, unchanged by the
processes that rule in nature. These touching beliefs of a
pious legend may babble in the tradition of a senile psychology,
or contort themselves in the metaphysics of some frantic
dogma, but philosophy must register them and sigh and
pass on.

There is nothing we know which can warrant the belief
that a particular fact can survive its moment, or that, when it
is past, it can ever live again. We know it is true in our actual
experience that reproduction presents us with particular
images; but to assert that these *are* the perished originals is
to demand a miracle to support our false beliefs. We have
absolutely no kind of warrant in experience for our assurance,
that what comes into the mind by Association is the particular
as we had it. For the particular fact is made particular by
an elaborate context and a detailed content. And this is *not*
the context or content which comes back. What is recalled
has not only got different relations; itself is different. It has
lost some features, and some clothing of its qualities, and it
has acquired some new ones. If then there is a resurrection
assuredly what rises must be the ghost and not the individual.
And if the ghost is not content with its spiritual body, it must
come with some members which are not its own. In the hurry
of the moment, we have reason to suspect, that the bodies of
the dead may be used as common stock.

But if we are willing to throw over our orthodox creed, we
may escape with less demand on our faith. The doctrine of

Redintegration does not ask us to subscribe to the belief that what is past exists over again. It offers a simpler explanation of the facts. Given any presentation X, which has a content such as . . . *a b c d e* . . ., it asserts that the oneness of this presentation is in a certain sense a connection of its content. The *fact* of the presentation absolutely disappears. What is left behind is a mental result,[5] into the ultimate metaphysical nature of which we do not here enquire. But this result is not a phenomenon, not a particular image or relation of such images. It is an alteration of the mind, which shows itself to us as a tendency to pass from content to content. It is a connection, not between this *a* and this *b,* or this *c* and this *d,* but between the universals *a* and *b,* or *c* and *d.* It is a quality of the mind which manifests itself in the fact that, if we have one part of the content which appeared in X, then—although everything which particularized that content in X, and gave it existence, has disappeared—this bare universal *a, b, c,* or *d,* when given with a different set of particulars, may re-instate by its ideal identity any other of the universals, *a, b, c,* or *d.* It will recall it certainly in a particular clothing, but this clothing will be determined by present mental circumstances, and will not be the clothing of its past existence. And this particular clothing, again and in the second place, is not the bond which *works* in the reproduction. What works is the connection between the universals, and the basis of that working is the ideal identity of some element in what is present and in what is past.

§ 11. I have illustrated my meaning already by anticipation (p. 35), and shall illustrate it hereafter. At present I must hasten to meet an objection. I maintain that all association is between universals, and that no other association exists. Every kind of reproduction, in my judgment, takes place by virtue of identity *plus* the connection of universals. "And do you really," there may here come a protest, "do you really believe this holds good with emotions? If castor-oil has made me sick once, so that I can not see it or even think of it without uneasiness, is this too a connection between universals?" I reply without hesitation that I believe it is so; and that I must believe this or else accept a miracle, a miracle moreover which is not in harmony with the facts it is invoked to explain. *You* believe then, I feel inclined to reply, that the actual feelings, which accompanied your vomiting, have risen from the dead in a paler form once more to trouble you. I could not credit that even if it answered to the facts. And it does not answer, since the new feeling is clearly different from the old one. The old feeling was the event it was, by its presence in a certain series of events. It had a number of accompaniments, conditions, and circumstances, which belonged to it as this feeling. The psychological environment was in great part different. Nay, if we could observe it, we should probably find that its actual internal content has varied. We should see degrees or shades of quality, which in the two cases would probably not be the same. Your miraculous supposition is therefore not even a fiction which will work.

And if you say that, by the sameness of the feeling, you mean a feeling which is the same in kind, and for all practical purposes one with the other, this is exactly the thesis which I wish to establish, and which you have objected to. The feelings of sickness are the same in the main, that is, they have an identical content, which is the same although the contexts are different. But, if so, is it not, I would ask, admitted that what is reproduced is not the particular but is the universal? The first conjunction of castor-oil and sickness has no longer the smallest existence as fact. But it gave rise to a connection of elements in the mind, which elements are an idealized part of the content of this perished fact. The new presentation of castor-oil is a fact which is certainly not the old fact; yet it has a content which is partly the same. The presence of this identical universal supplies the antecedent to the hypothetical connection of elements in the mind, and this then passes from hypothesis into actual fact. In other words the ideal identity of this castor-oil with that castor-oil recovers ideally, and in an universal form, another element of the original context, And, so far as mere reproduction goes, nothing but the universal could ever be called up. It is the *fresh presentation* which adds detail to the reproduced element. This new perception re-particularizes the universal, and does so in a way which will not be the old way, and in many cases will be strikingly different. But such re-particularization (if the term may be allowed) is *not* association, and is *not* reproduction. For though the new particular feeling of sickness is no doubt the *result* of reproduction, yet *it* never was associated, and *it* can not have been reproduced, since it exists now for the first time. You may say that by a miracle the old feeling of sickness without detriment to its sameness has been changed *en route;* but this very change and this very difference is the denial of your doctrine, unless your doctrine too is from time to time changed by a parallel miracle.

I do not say that we should be right to reduce all reproduction to *logical* redintegration.[6] That is a point on which I shall touch hereafter (Book III. I. Chap. III. § 20). It does not concern us here. For it is not necessary to believe that the " idea " of a feeling is a *logical* idea, and that it is a conscious or even an unconscious symbol. What must however be believed is that it is an universal. And this need give rise to not the smallest psychological difficulty. Whatever differences may separate the various kinds of psychical phenomena, they are all alike in one point. They all have content [7] as well as existence. They are not confined to the " that," but each has a " what," since there is a complex quality and relations of quality.* And, this being so, we have all that is required for the formation of universals. For an identity of content in different contexts is and must be an universal, whether we are dealing with perceptions or feelings or volitions.

§ 12. To suppose the presence and the operation of universals in all reproduction, introduces a unity into our view of the soul. It enables us to interpret all stages of mind as the growth of one principle. We can thus accept without abridgment the very highest phenomena, and we can show their root in the lowest and rudest beginnings of the soul. We may say that experience will begin when a present perception has one part of its content identical with a past, and when this common universal re-instates another part of the original context. But that past element most certainly does not reappear in its particular form. It too is universal, and it is the connection of these universals which operates in the mind. Hence the content of the perception, which is now

* Quality at this stage covers quantity.

present, is extended by means of this ideal synthesis, and, itself individual, individualizes the result. This true account is in harmony with fact. But, on the other hand, to suppose that one or more particular feelings or images are magically recalled and adhere to the perception, is directly contrary to the plain facts of observation. For these separate particulars are palpably absent; and in order to explain their obvious absence it is necessary to invoke a Law of Obliviscence, by which their details may again be shorn off. But this Law of Obliviscence has no title to exist in the shape which is given to it, except that it is demanded by an erroneous theory (vid. inf. § 25). A miracle is first invoked to explain the facts, and then a fiction introduced to square the facts to the miracle.

But the unviolated facts support redintegration by identity. In a rudimentary soul a present sensation has *its* content increased by internal extension. There are not several facts before the mind, but there is a single fact whose content, after enlargement, consists in part of an unconscious inference. The sensation is extended by an ideal supplement, and this supplement, through union with the individual sensation, becomes for the mind individual fact. On this view there is no psychical phenomenon which intervenes between the sensation and the resulting perception. We have not to postulate the irrelevant and conflicting detail of particular images, and have no need to rid ourselves of this palpable fiction by any arbitrary Law. Or again, if the result of the new sensation be desire or action, our theory still maintains its superiority. Let us however try to exhibit this in detail.

What is the fact to be explained? It is, I think, this. A sensation Ab has once led to an action Cd; and now a sensation Eb (the same with A in respect of b) is presented. Eb is then followed by an action Fd, which in respect of d is identical with Cd. Such is the fact, and we have two competing explanations. On the first and incorrect interpretation Eb calls up a particular image of Ab. The latter is associated with the particular idea of an action Cd, and Cd produces Fd. The transition is thus, $Eb - Ab - Cd - Fd$; and this transition is discrete from atom to atom. This is the first interpretation. On the other, Eb directly redintegrates d, and Ebd directly produces $EbdF$. The transition may be stated as $Eb - d - F$;

but, since *b* and *d* are universals and are not psychical phenomena, the actual transition is unbroken from E to F. Now
which of these explanations accords best with fact? The fact
is that the supposed intermediate units, A*b* and C*d,* can not be
verified in observation. Their presence is deduced *a priori,*
and is not pointed out *a posteriori.* We are then asked to
believe that their presence exists though we can not see it;
for it is hidden by the Laws of Obliviscence. But this mysterious agency has itself been manufactured *a priori.* It again
can not be verified in actual experience. Hence we have first
a principle which produces something other than our fact,
and then an arbitrary invention to patch up this mistake.
Such is the first interpretation; and let us look at the second.
On that, I will not say that nothing is asserted either more
or less than what can be observed, but I will say this. Not
only is one principle used throughout, and that one sufficient
to explain the facts, but there is no result, and not the fraction
of a phenomenon, postulated by this principle, but what can be
shown *a posteriori.* And, even apart from all question of truth
and falsehood, a theory which demands two compensating
hypotheses, must surely be rejected in favour of a theory,
which works as well with one single hypothesis.

§ 13. But I shall be told, " This statement of the case is
absurd. In the first place, and apart from truth and falsehood,
the theory you advocate does not cover the facts. It fails
to explain the suggestion of similars. Again and in the second
place, the hypothesis you adopt is demonstrably false. And a
single hypothesis is not admissible if it is insufficient, if it is
not true, and if a true explanation is within our reach. I
answer, In the first place, as I shall soon point out, the
reduction of suggestion to redintegration is an accomplished
fact. And in the second place the falsity of redintegration
can not be shown; but on the other hand what can be demonstrated is, that *your* hypothesis is false. For (i) there is no
such thing as Association by Contiguity; (ii) there is no such
thing as Association by Similarity. I will try to make both of
these last points quite plain, and will then return to defend
the true explanation.

§ 14. (i) Let us begin with Contiguity. What is the true
view? The true doctrine is that, when elements have co-

existed, they tend to be connected. What does this mean? It means that if (say) in a perception A the elements β and γ are conjoined, the mind gets a tendency to join one to the other whenever either reappears. But what are β and γ ? They are universals. They have been detached from their original environment, and to some extent stripped of their particular qualities. They are not individual images. Thus if I have seen a black man stabbed with a sword in a certain street at a certain time and under certain conditions, what is left in the mind is not a connection between these special sensations, or between special images which are their feebler counterparts. I might shudder when I saw a white cow threatened with a butcher's knife at another time and place and under different conditions. For what is associated is not the images, it is always universals or types, which as such have no real existence, even in the mind. This is the true view. We will pass to the consideration of the erroneous doctrine.

There is not much doubt, I think, as to what that doctrine really is. But its adherents allow themselves a looseness of statement which is sometimes excessive; and we hardly know the point at which their mythology becomes conscious. We are at times led to think that past perceptions continue to exist, and on occasion rise to be seen of men. For observe the definition.

"Actions, Sensations, and States of Feeling, occurring together or in close succession, tend to grow together, or co-here, in such a way that, when any one of them is afterwards presented to the mind, the others are apt to be brought up in idea." "When two impressions have been frequently experienced (or even thought of) either simultaneously or in immediate succession, then whenever one of these impressions, or the idea of it, recurs, it tends to excite the idea of the other."

A definition is not the place where one looks for fancy, but for actual belief. But consider these phrases, "*when any one of them is afterwards presented,*" "*whenever one of these impressions recurs.*" Are they feasible unless the writer believes in the coarsest form of subterranean existence and of the Resurrection of the Body? But neither of the writers professes to hold that belief. They both repudiate it. And yet that does not prevent both of them from speaking as if they accepted it in full, and at least one of them from reasoning on the assumption of its truth.*

§ 15. This point perhaps may be dismissed as a mere question of statement; for there is no doubt that our authors would stoutly deny that the past impression is recalled to life. " Whenever one of these impressions, or the idea of it, recurs " are words that must be used in a popular sense. Then what is the exact sense? Are we to amend the formula by writing simply, " whenever the idea of one of these impressions recurs "?

Even so we are still in the land of mythology. The " ideas " that are meant are particular existences. The fleeting impressions in their passage through the void throw off feebler counterparts, shed pale doubles of themselves. And the idea, like the impression, is a particular unit; it is no universal but an actual phenomenon. It certainly is called " the idea *of* the impression," but this phrase does not mean that the two have any substantial identity. It means that one follows the other in time, and in fainter traces shows a similar detail. But if this is what is meant, it is not what is said.

" Whenever," we are told, *" the idea of it recurs."* But the idea, like the impression, exists only for a moment. Then how can it " recur " unless it is the same; and how can it be the same unless it has remained? We may figure to ourselves the faithful ghost, haunting the place where the body is not, and called up to the light by the spell of Association. But we surely must know that these pious legends are not literally true. For the image, like the sensation, endures but for a moment. And if the impression does not " recur," then the idea does not " recur "; since in this respect there is no difference between them.

It is mere mythology to talk of the copy, which the impression has sloughed off, persisting in the world and preserving its identity through the flux of change. The word *recurs* must be struck out of the formula. There are a train of images, there is not one image. And with this fable must depart another loose phrase. We have no right to call a broken procession of several images, *" the idea* of an impression."

*I refer to J. S. Mill. See his *Hamilton,* Chap. XI. and Appendix.

We must call them " different ideas of the impression." And here, I think, we are approaching danger. For we naturally consider that, in a case of association, there is some one connection throughout all the instances. We can hardly help believing, and talking as if we believed, that when (as we should like to say) something " recurs," then something else " recurs " also. But we must strip off this illusion, or wear it only when we come before the public. There is *nothing* that recurs. The original impression is one mental unit, the first idea is another, the second idea is a third passing atom, and so on for ever. There is no real bond which unites them together. There is no common internal identity, which is the same in all and recurs amid change. If we call them " the ideas of one impression," even this is mere fable. We have a *likeness* no doubt, in all these cases. A hundred images, or more it may be, with all their differences and all their particularity, are yet each of them particular in such a way that they are all like each other, and all like the impression. This is startling, I admit, but even this does not warrant us in considering any one to be the *same* as the other, and united by holding the one substance of their prototype. If we desire a legend which perhaps may be harmless, we may call them all " ideas *of* the impression " in the sense that, like Abraham, the impression while it lived had them all in its loins. For no vehicle conveys the eternal verities half so well as does the labyrinth of a fantastic genealogy, with its one-sided begettings and abnormal parturition.

§ 16. " Whenever one of these impressions, or the idea of it, recurs, it tends to excite the idea of the other." This is what we started from. What are we left with? " Impressions " is gone: " recurs " is gone: " idea *of* it " is gone. It seems that we must thus amend our formula, " Whenever an idea like one of these impressions occurs, it tends to excite the idea of the other." This surely will stand: this at last must be true. Unfortunately not so; for it still says too much and must be further cut down; and yet already it has begun to say too little, and will now no longer cover the facts. But I will at present keep to the too much. The phrase " to excite *the* idea *of* the other " must at once be corrected. It should run " to excite *an* idea *like* the other." And we must further amend the beginning of our formula. For "when two impressions have been frequently experienced" is quite mythological. *If* two impressions *were* "frequently experienced," they would be *two* no longer. The phrase is nonsensical, unless several experiences are one experience: and that we know is not true. We must alter this also, and in our final correction the law must be stated.

"When we have experienced (or even thought of) several pairs of impressions (simultaneous or successive), which pairs of impressions are like one another; then whenever an idea occurs which is like all the impressions on one side of these pairs, it tends to excite an idea which is like all the impressions on the other side."

This I believe to be the meaning of Association by Contiguity. And at this point perhaps it may occur to us to ask, what is it that is contiguous, and what is it that is associated? The impressions are not *associated;* I presume that is obvious. They are conjoined in presentation, just like anything else we perceive together is conjoined. It is the ideas which are associated, since one, as we see, can bring up another. But then in what sense are the ideas *contiguous?* They are now successive, or simultaneous, *because of* the contiguity. Contiguity conjoins them, and it would be nonsense to say that they become conjoined because already they *are* contiguous. For if they *are* contiguous, then both must be there, and how can one call in the other? And if they are *not* contiguous, then it is not *their* contiguity which brings them together. This consideration seems to me quite palpable; but the result is fatal to the Law of Contiguity.

The law operates by means of and through contiguity, and therefore presupposes it. But there is no contiguity save that of the impressions. It must be then the contiguity of the impressions which works. Because they *were* together once, the ideas *come* together now. But, if so, what becomes of the association? For the impressions are not associated, and the association is, if anywhere, between a present and an absent idea. What is associated was therefore not contiguous, and what was contiguous is now not associated. Association and contiguity fall hopelessly asunder; and hence let our law be never so real, it can not be the Law of Association by Contiguity. In short, the whole thing comes to this. If impressions *have been* contiguous, then ideas which are like them now tend to excite one another. And for myself, I can not see how in any intelligible sense this is the *association* of ideas.

§ 17. And now (to come to the other side of the failure) if we state the law in this corrected form, it will not cover the facts of the case. For commonly an *impression* is what is first given, and then this *impression* calls up an *idea*. Thus if one fire has already been felt to be hot, then, if another fire is *seen,* the *idea* heat comes. Thus an idea is excited by what is not an idea, and by what never has been contiguous to anything. We must once more and finally thus amend our formula, " If any mental units have been contiguous, then any others which resemble them may excite one another." There is not left here a vestige of *association.* And the union of the elements somehow takes place by virtue of the past contiguity of something else.

§ 18. Association by contiguity may be taken as exploded. But the philosophy of Experience is, to some extent at least, prepared for this result. It will admit so much, that *mere* contiguity will not work by itself. And it proposes to support it by another agent. There is no such thing, it is ready to allow, as association by *bare* contiguity. All reproduction in a certain sense depends on similarity.

" There never could have been association by contiguity without a previous association by resemblance. Why does a sensation received this instant remind me of sensations which I formerly had (as we commonly say), along with it? I never had them along with this very sensation. I never had this sensation until now, and can never have it again. I had the former sensations in conjunction not with it, but with a sensation exactly like it. And my present sensation could not remind me of those former sensations unlike itself, unless by first reminding me of the sensation like itself, which really did co-exist with them. There is thus a law of association anterior to, and presupposed by, the law of contiguity: namely, that a sensation tends to recall what is called the idea of itself, that is, the remembrance of a sensation like itself, if such has previously been experienced." " There is, therefore, a suggestion by resemblance—a calling up of the idea of a past sensation by a present sensation like it—which not only does not depend on association by contiguity, but is itself the foundation which association by contiguity requires for its support." J. S. Mill, *on James Mill,* I. 112, 113.

"There can be no contiguity without similarity, and no similarity without contiguity. When, looking at a river, we pronounce its name, we are properly said to exemplify contiguity; the river and the name by frequent association are so united that each recalls the other. But mark the steps of the recall. What is strictly present to our view is the impression made by the river while we gaze on it. It is necessary that this impression should, by virtue of similarity or identity, re-instate the previous impression of the river, to which the previous impression of the name was contiguous. If one could suppose failure in the re-instatement of the former idea of the river, under the new presentation, there would be no opportunity given to the contiguous bond to come into operation." Bain, *ibid.* p. 121.

Let us try to understand this amended doctrine. In the first place we must remember that, when *identity* is spoken of, it is not really *meant.* What *is* meant is more or less of similarity. And this point must not be lost sight of.

In the second place I must be allowed to complain of a serious inaccuracy in the extract I have quoted from Professor Bain. It surely is nonsense to talk of "re-instating the previous impression," and I must add that in this context the nonsense seems inexcusable. And again in the first of the extracts there is ambiguity. The "remembrance of a sensation," we must clearly understand, does not revive the sensation itself, and does not establish any actual relation with that mental unit which no longer exists. If this is not so, and if a psychical phenomenon can maintain or recover its existence and identity through the flux of events, then the whole theory from which the school of Association starts has been tacitly thrown over.

But, if an impression when past is done with, if it is really non-existent, then not only can it not be re-instated bodily, but *itself* can not even be re-instated in idea. The fact which is covered by the delusive phrase " idea of it," is merely the fact that a sensation came first, and then subsequently there came a paler counterpart. And, when we once discern this fact through the mist of ambiguous and misleading formulæ, there is an end to the theory which hides or obscures it.

What *was* contiguous is now non-existent, and what is " re-instated " has *never* been contiguous. Let us look at the facts. A sensation A excites by similarity an image *b,* and, on this, contiguity has to do all the rest. But has *b* ever been contiguous to anything? In the case before us there are two possibilities. The fact from which we start is this—we *have had* an impression B along with an impression C, and we *have* an impression A. Now what are the two possibilities? In the first place it is possible that *we never have had a feeble image resembling* B. And this is more than possible, for in an early mind it is also probable. But in this case, when A excites an image *b,* there is absolutely no contiguity of anything with anything. Not one of the supposed elements in our reproduction has ever been contiguous with any other; and, this being so, reproduction will not take place. This first possibility appears to me to have been overlooked. Let us now pass to the second. We here have had the contiguous impressions B — C. These we suppose to have been followed by one or more pale pairs of images $b^1 - c^1$, $b^2 - c^2$, $b^3 - c^3$. These are all like each other, but they all are realities each of which is not the same as any other. We now experience a sensation A. This also is *like* the previous sensation we have called B, and is *like* the images b^1, b^2, b^3. But every one of these, I must beg the reader to remember, is by this time absolutely non-existent. What then is to happen when A is presented? It calls up by similarity an image b^4. But this is not what we want. For we want an image $b^4 - c^4$; and *contiguity* is invoked to present us with c^4. But is invoked in vain. For as yet c^4 has never existed, and *ex hypothesi* it is to be *made* to exist by means of contiguity. On the other hand b^4 has never been contiguous to anything at all. We have reached once again the old result. There is no association by contiguity. What is called up by association has never been contiguous; and what has been contiguous can not be called up. The contiguity which now operates is a *past* contiguity, which is not recalled and can not be recalled, but which, according to the pious legend, is somehow passed on like original sin.

But if this is so, then Association by Contiguity is exploded finally. No exciting of similars will save it from annihilation. For the similars excited have not been contiguous, and what was really contiguous can not be excited. If present sensations are qualified by images in the way described, still on that (false) hypothesis there is no reproduction by *association*. There can be no association where the elements are not co-existing associates. But if they do already co-exist and thus *are* associated, then how in the name of all that is miraculous can one bring about the co-existence of the other, and by means of their co-existence?

§ 19. If the school of Experience is in earnest with its principles there can be no such thing as Association. But is it in earnest? Notwithstanding all its public protestations may it not secretly look for the Resurrection of the Body? Does not the charm of Similarity shake the realm of Hades, and conjure from its grave the reluctant past? Is anything too hard for Association? Its spell has prevailed over the mind of its votaries, and, though their lips may deny, yet Association itself has helped their unbelief by its own divine power. They *do* believe in the miracle of resurrection. But they believe blindly and unconsciously, compelled by the strength of a tacit conjunction of meaning with phrase.

We saw that, by the admission of its advanced disciples, association depends upon similarity. If there is no reproduction by Similarity, it is admitted that there is no Association at all. I shall now press this consequence. If you do not believe in this kind of Association, you believe in none. But if you do believe in it you believe in a miracle which upsets all law. And furthermore there is no evidence *a posteriori* to confirm this miracle. In plain words Association by Similarity is a downright fiction. It is not called for by the facts; and it involves besides metaphysical assumptions which I confess stagger me, and which I think may somewhat surprise others. I shall show the reader how the school of Experience has swallowed the most outrageous metaphysical doctrines, and that he must follow their example or leave their company.

§ 20. (ii) Association by similarity, if it is anything at all, is a means of exciting ideas that are not present. If it will not give us what at present, and apart from its agency, we are without, then it surely is a self-condemned *fiasco,* that is not worth discussing. We may perhaps agree that an agency which recalls and yet recalls not anything but what is already on the spot, is something like a piece of nonsense. And I propose to show that Association by Similarity *is* this piece of nonsense.

Similarity is a relation. But it is a relation which, strictly speaking, does not exist unless both terms are before the mind. Things may perhaps be the *same* in certain points although no one sees them; but they can not properly *resemble* one another, unless they convey the impression of resemblance; and they can not convey it unless they are both before the mind. This is not merely an assertion I have chosen to make.[8] Let us see what is told us by J. S. Mill.

" Any objects, whether physical or mental, are related, or are in a relation, to one another, in virtue of any complex state of consciousness into which they both enter " (*on James Mill,* II. 10).

" Likeness and unlikeness are themselves only a matter of feeling: and that when we have two feelings, the feeling of their likeness or unlikeness is inextricably interwoven with the fact of having the feelings. One of the conditions, under which we have feelings, is that they are like and unlike: and in the case of simple feelings, we can not separate the likeness or unlikeness from the feelings themselves. It is by no means certain, however, that when we have two feelings in immediate succession, the feeling of their likeness is not a third feeling which follows instead of being involved in the two " (*ibid.* p. 18).

" I have two sensations; we will suppose them to be simple ones; two sensations of white, or one sensation of white and another of black. I call the first two sensations *like;* the last two *unlike.* What is the fact or phenomenon constituting the *fundamentum* of this relation? The two sensations first, and then what we call a feeling of resemblance, or of want of resemblance. Let us confine ourselves to the former case. Resemblance is evidently a feeling; a state of the consciousness of the observer " (*Logic,* I. 75).

Is not this quite plain? Does it leave any doubt? Is it not clear that two mental elements are not like, unless I have them before me at once or in immediate succession? But, if so, what meaning can we attach to the calling up of an idea by similarity? If the relation does not exist until the idea is called up, how can the idea be called up by the relation? Is it not, the moment we look below the surface, mere verbiage and nonsense?

§ 21. In the first place what is called up is absolutely non-existent. We are told, not once but again and again, that a feeling gone is gone for ever. And the same thing holds of particular images. If these exist, then the past exists, and the procession in the mind is not real but illusory. Are we to believe this, and believe it in the teeth of our asseverations? But if we can not believe it, and if the past does not exist, then we must believe in a relation between the existent and the non-existent; and believe that the whole (relation and relateds) is one state of our minds. If, on the other hand, the past can exist, this miracle will not save us from annihilation. In the relation of similarity both terms must be present, and the fact that one *calls up* the other by this relation, postulates that one of the terms must be absent. It is therefore both present and absent at once. On either hypothesis we are landed in contradictions; and I have redeemed the promise I gave to the reader. An idea is absent and at the same time present. It is not there and so is brought in by a relation, which relation is nothing if the idea is not there. And a union, which is impossible out of the mind, persists between the existent and what is wholly non-existent. Could anything be more insane than this wild metaphysic?

§ 22. But I shall be told " You are deceiving us; it is incredible, it is impossible that our sober countrymen can have been so imposed upon." I answer, That question is easily settled. It is admitted that by " association " they must mean something, and what *else* do they mean?

The Experience Philosophy has to meet two objections. It has to explain how the non-existent can be related to the existent. And when it has done that, it must explain how the absent can be recalled by the present, when similarity implies common presence and reproduction excludes it. Suppose that the former difficulty has been slurred over by some metaphysical formula of "the potential and the actual," or some distinction between *my* mind and *other* minds, yet the second remains. Suppose that your past series somehow exists, yet how, I ask, are you going to get at it? Mere partial identity of the present and the past would not be what you want, since this would not be an actual relation *in your mind*.

This is what Maas meant by the following objection. "The mere similarity of two ideas (or sensations) can not possibly be a cause of their association. For similarity is an objective relation of the ideas themselves; while association is a subjective connection in the imagination. But the latter does not follow from the former, nor tend to follow from it" (*Versuch,* p. 55). By "similarity" Maas of course here meant "partial identity," and his argument is quite simple. The question is, Why does *my* mind go from one element to another? If you say, it goes because the elements *seem like to it*—that supposes both to be there. But if you say, it goes because they *are like apart from it*—then it goes by a miracle, for it is influenced by something which to it is nothing. Sir W. Hamilton (*Reid,* p. 914) has replied to this argument by a criticism which shows that he did not understand it.

The Experience Philosophy may have a reply to these objections, but I confess I can not anticipate its answer. Perhaps it may fall back on a simpler view. It may say, after Wundt (*Phys. Psych.* 788), "every perception or idea tends to call into consciousness another like itself." As to the *truth* of this expression I shall have something to say afterwards. But at present I say this. Whatever else it is, it is giving up Association and throwing it overboard. For it is the mere statement of a phenomenon; and it is *not* an explanation. The entirest belief in the truth of this formula is compatible with the entirest disbelief in the doctrine of Association. We might explain the alleged fact that, given any one element, another like it may come up, by a theory of the spontaneous fission or gemmation of ideas; and this in my opinion would be a theory which, by the side of Association, is sober and rational. We might explain it again by a physiological disposition to a certain cerebral function, which (given the stimulus of a new perception or idea) passes into fact. And against this explanation I will not say one word. I will insist only on this, that *it is not a psychological explanation at all*, and that in the hands of those who know their own business it is not offered as such. If this is the only possible explanation, then a psychological explanation is relinquished as impossible, and the Laws of Association as commonly given will not explain anything. Thus the Philosophy of Experience must take its choice. It must either rehabilitate its barbarous mythology, or admit that, though the fact of reproduction is known, it has no psychological explanation to offer, and is confessedly bankrupt. It has rested its all on reproduction by similarity, and we have shown that this is an impossibility.

§ 23. But our proof no doubt will not cause much disquiet. I shall be told "You can not demonstrate away the facts." And I will therefore proceed to my second contention. The explanation offered is not only impossible, but it is also uncalled for. There is no evidence for it *a posteriori*. The facts of reproduction are much better explained on another theory. We have seen this already in our first Book, but I will exhibit it once more.

Let us take a fairly simple instance of reproduction. A young child, or one of the lower animals, is given on Monday a round piece of sugar, eats it and finds it sweet. On Tuesday it sees a square piece of sugar, and proceeds to eat it. In this we have of course volitional phenomena as well as intellectual, but perhaps we may simplify the case so as to make it serve.

Now on the Association theory how is the fact interpreted? I suppose in some way like this. The presentation to the eye of Tuesday's piece calls up by *similarity* the idea of Monday's piece. That is a feeble counterpart of the original sensation, and it calls up by *contiguity* feeble counterparts of Monday's felt movements and Monday's following sweet taste. The fact which ensues is hence the mental presence of Tuesday's perceived square piece, felt to be like another paler imagined round piece, with which latter a whole set of other images come in. Now the conclusion, at which we have to arrive, is the qualification of Tuesday's piece by these images which are attendant on the idea of Monday's piece; and at first sight there seems no way to this result. For the conclusion is not merely a vicious inference, but it does not even look like a probable mistake. Tuesday's sensation and Monday's image are not only separate facts which, because alike, are therefore *not* the same; but they differ perceptibly both in quality and environment. What is to lead the mind to take one for the other?

Sudden at this crisis, and in pity at distress, there leaves the heaven with rapid wing a goddess Primitive Credulity.[9] Breathing in the ear of the bewildered infant she whispers, The thing which has happened once will happen once more. Sugar was sweet, and sugar will be sweet. And Primitive Credulity is accepted forthwith as the mistress of our life. She leads our steps on the path of experience, until her fallacies, which can not always be pleasant, at length become suspect. We wake up indignant at the kindly fraud by which the goddess so long has deceived us. So she shakes her wings, and flying to the stars, where there are no philosophers, leaves us here to the guidance of—I can not think what.

The school has not yet accepted this legend, and I narrate it partly because I am not sure that it is not relevant, but mainly because it has always seemed to me perhaps the most striking of all those creations which we owe to the imagination of Professor Bain (*Emots.* p. 511 and foll.).

§ 24. The less poetical but not less fabulous view would appear to be this. Given a perception A together with an image *b,* which resembles it and has a train of attendant images *c, d,* and *e*—the problem is how to transfer to A the content of *e.* And what accomplishes the feat is the Law of Obliviscence. This powerful agent obscures everything in the train between A and *e;* and it also obscures any part of *e* which is not suitable to A. The residue of *e* then adheres to A; that is, I think, the two run into one. And so we get the conclusion "This piece of sugar is sweet," by a process which logically may seem rather vicious, but which appears none the less to be the essence of reasoning.*

---

* In the lowest stages of mind this theoretical conclusion of course would not appear. There would be action or attempt without anything like a judgment. The principle however would be exactly the same; and when the theoretical conclusion comes, it must come in this way.

I can not say if this statement of the Association doctrine is fair, but I hope it may be so. Let us see what objection we can find to its process.

The main objection is that there is a great deal too much of it. It is much too elaborate for simple phenomena. It first introduces a complication which does not exist; and then, having invented this complication, it removes it by a process which is not real.

It is obviously no fact which we can discover by observation, that when Tuesday's sugar is presented to sense, a similar piece or similar pieces come up, in their particularity and with all their differences, before the mind. No one gets such a fact from observation. It is in short a theoretical fiction. I do admit that afterwards, when memory is developing, there is something which can give ground for a mistake of this kind. But then of course reproduction must come before memory, and in the present case we are not concerned with the latter (cf. p. 36). The *fact* before the mind is that *this* sugar suggests both sweetness and eating without any images of any other pieces of sugar at all. In the first Book I enlarged on this point by anticipation, and, I confess, it seems to me quite plain.

§ 25. But I shall be told, that although we can not be aware of them, these images exist, and they are removed or adapted by the Laws of Obliviscence. But this process strikes me as another fiction, piled up to support the first fiction against the pressure of experience. I will quote a passage from J. S. Mill.

" The reader . . . is now . . . familiar with the . . . fact, . . . that when, through the frequent repetition of a series of sensations, the corresponding train of ideas rushes through the mind with extreme rapidity, some of the links are apt to disappear from consciousness as completely as if they had never formed part of the series. It has been a subject of dispute among philosophers which of three things takes place in this case. Do the lost ideas pass through the mind without consciousness? Do they pass consciously through the mind and are they then instantly forgotten? Or do they never come into the mind at all, being, as it were, overleaped and pressed

out by the rush of the subsequent ideas?" (*on James Mill,*
I. 106).

The question opened in the above quotation may be stated
thus: Given an indirect connection of ideas in the mind, to
find the way in which it becomes direct. I do not wish here
to enter into this general question. But I must point out that
Mr. Mill has raised it in a form which precludes any satisfactory solution. For the ideas connected are not really a
mere series of particular images, and the fact has thus been
perverted beforehand. And if we suppose that, in some exceptional case, we have got a mere train of individual images,
then not one of the "three things" could possibly be operative. For so long as the ideas remained these mere images,
no connection at all would be established between them. We
may be sure that, whatever in the end may be the detail of
the psychological process, one side of it would consist in turning these images into universals. And for this reason the
Laws of Obliviscence, as we have them stated by Mr. Mill,
are fictitious processes. Even if you start with a complication and a train of ideas, yet they can not deal with it.

But the point on which I desire to insist, is that in an
elementary case of reproduction, such as we are now considering, the complication presupposed by these Laws has no
existence at all. The *data* from which they start are pure
inventions, and it is hence an impossibility that any one of the
suggested "three things" should happen. The fact which
Obliviscence postulates is this: A is the sugar calling up by
similarity an image of sugar *b;* and *b* calls up by contiguity
an image of movement *c;* and *c* calls up an image *d* of a
particular sweet taste. But this fact does not exist, and the
alleged process stands therefore on unreality.

There is in the first place no reason to suppose that this
train of ideas, which is presumed to rush through the mind, is
a counterpart of the original perception and action. What
ground can we have for an assumption that the particular
images, *b, c,* and *d,* are like in all their detail to any train of
impressions we ever have had? Admit the train, what reason
have you to affirm that there is anything more than a *general*
likeness? What ground have you for the assertion that, if
you could look into the past, you would see a train of impres-

sions B, C, and D, of which these present images are *copies?* Why must *d* be an "exact likeness" of the particular pleasant eating D? These dogmas seem to me to be nothing but postulates. The fact, so far as I observe it, shows me that, without respect for the past, such images vary freely within a certain limit, and that this limit is fixed by the universal connection which appears in all of them. But, if so, then what is associated is not particular images. The universal which has been deposited is the active principle, and the particular images as such are quite inert.

And in the second place the alleged process imports another gross fiction into the *data*. It tells us that similarity calls up an image *b,* which is a copy of Monday's piece of sugar. We have just seen that, if present, the image need be no copy: and now we go further. For in our elementary case the image *b* has no existence. I repeat once more that it is a pure invention, necessary for the theory but absent from the fact. When Tuesday's piece of sugar is present, the attributes of whiteness and crystalline appearance reproduce the ideas of movement and sweet taste, without any such link as another and different piece of sugar. It is not merely that we can not find such an image *now*. We never could have found it. It never has been there. And we need not ask at length if the Laws of Obliviscence could serve to obscure it, unless some evidence is produced to show that it is more than a mere chimæra.

And, as we have seen, it is a chimæra that will not work. For when you have got your image of Monday's sugar, you are left precisely where you were before. You have got an element which has just been born, and which therefore can never have been contiguous to anything in its life. And if you say "But it resembles what *was* contiguous;" then this is not only to desert your principles, but it also tends to expose you to ridicule. If you want what *is* the former piece of sugar, you can not get it. But if you want what is *like* the former piece, then you have it already *in the present perception.*

Your fictions do not help you, and why should you cherish them? Why invent the existence of similar images which lure the unwary to vicious inferences? Why suppose that "trains of ideas," of which the mind knows nothing, float across it in procession, and then go on to manufacture a Law of Obliviscence which ties a bandage over its eyes? Because, if you do not, you are forced to admit that the mind does not go always from particulars to particulars, that indeed it never can go from particulars direct to particulars, that in short the Experience psychology is exploded.

§ 26. Let us give once more the natural interpretation of the simple fact. The natural view is that Monday's experience remains in the mind, not in the shape of particular images, but as a connection between elements of content. This is a result which in its metaphysical nature we can not here characterize,[10] but, in its appearance to us, it is easy to describe. It is a tendency to pass from one universal to another, whenever the first of these is presented in an actual perception or image. In the instance we are examining, the shape, the size, the person giving, the where, the when, and the how have all gone. Nothing is left but a tendency to pass from element to element, from whiteness and crystalline appearance and hardness to eating and sweetness.

Monday's experience, let us say, has established the connection "white-eaten-sweet." On Tuesday "white" is given, and so we have "this-white." We advance by means of an elementary synthesis to "this-white-eaten-sweet," and, ignoring that part which does not interest us, we get "this-eaten-sweet," or, elliptically, "this-sweet." I grant you the "sweet" is now fully particular, but its particularity has had nothing to do with its recall. On the contrary its detail depends upon the context which has recalled it. And there is no particular image of "white" at all; for the universal "white" is what has worked, and that of course was given in the present perception.

Where is Similarity here? It does not exist. Similarity implies the feeling of diversity, and here the difference of particulars never comes before the mind; it is in no sense present.

Let us give up Similarity + Contiguity + Obliviscence or Primitive Credulity. Let us postulate Identity + Contiguity, and then all is easy. But there are two things we must remember. The contiguity is a connection of universals, and is therefore not the contiguity of the Association school. And the identity is not present to the mind. The mind, if you keep to simple cases, knows nothing of any difference. It goes straight from what is given to an additional fact.

§ 27. Let us state our view as a working hypothesis, something that need not be true or even possible. Let it be granted there is a mind X with certain functions; let it be granted that X may be stimulated to perform again any function which it ever has performed; let it be granted that in every function there is a connection of elements, as a–b; let it be granted that presence of a tends to excite X to perform again the function which contains a–b; then let a be given in a fresh context, as Ca. On this X is stimulated to go on to b thus, Ca–b; and the product Cab now comes before the mind—which is the fact to be explained. If this explanation is false, admit at least that it is simple.

We are asked to believe it is more in accordance with "experience" to say, Similarity is a *tertium quid* ensuing only on the presence of a pair of elements, *and*, when but one is present, Similarity brings the other. It is "science" when we asseverate that mental phenomena are realities which can exist only while they are perceived, and then speak of "recalling" them, as if they were ambassadors on foreign employment, or "calling them up" as though they were servants in the kitchen, and as if "relations" were wires that rang the bell, or were fishing-lines baited with similarity to draw up from non-existence the ghosts of the past. It is "positive knowledge" to make that come before the mind which does not come before the mind, and then to remove it by a fictitious expedient. Yes, sooner than run the risk of believing in metaphysics, there is no superstition so gross, no mythology so preposterous that we ought not to believe in it, and believe anything sooner than cease to believe in it.

§ 28. But what is it that forces us to these desperate shifts? Not the facts themselves, for we violate them. It is simply the shrinking, as we think, from metaphysics. And this, after all, *is* nothing but metaphysics. It is our unreasoning fidelity to a metaphysical dogma which has driven us to adopt these embarrassing results. For why is it we are so sure that identity is impossible, and that a synthesis of uni-

versals is a "survival" of superstitions, which in the nine-
teenth century are out of date? It is because we are sure
that there can be no reality but particular existences, and no
mental connection but a relation of these units; and that
hence identity is not possible. But this is of course a metaphysical view, and, what is more, it is nothing but a dogma.
The Philosophers of Experience have, so far as I know, never
offered any proof of it; they have heard it from their fathers,
and their fathers had heard it. It is held true because of
the continuity of tradition in a Church, which must have truth,
since it has never failed to preserve its continuity. Has the
school ever tried to support it by any mere rational considerations?

So far as I know, it has been assumed that, if you are not
able to swallow down this dogma, you are forced to accept
an intolerable alternative. You are given a choice between
naked universals, existing as such, and bare particulars. You
can not stomach the first, and so you take the last. But why
should you take either? Why not adopt the view that the
real is the concrete individual, and that the bare particular
and abstract universal are distinctions within it, which, apart
from it, are only two forms of one fiction? You say, This is
unintelligible. But perhaps you never heard of it, or heard
of it too late, when you were already compromised, and had
no inclination to begin life again. Let it then be unintelligible; but permit me to add that the view you have adopted
calls for something stronger, to back it against facts, than an
a priori deduction from a metaphysical alternative.

§ 29. We have shown so far that, in the extension of our
experience, there is a synthetic construction by virtue of
identity, and that association by similarity has no part in it.
We have shown that the test which we bring to inferences, in
order to examine their validity, is also the principle which
operates in all extension of experience. On our view the
origin of the fact is explained, and its existence is at the
same time justified. But, on the fashionable theory of Association, early inferences are made by what afterwards we find
to be the essence of *bad* reasoning. And, to explain the origin
of this unjustifiable fact, open fictions have had to be invented.

But not only is Association by Similarity a fictitious account of the reasoning process. It is a fiction altogether; there is no evidence for it at all. And it is to the final proof of this point that we must now address ourselves.

Our previous objections have raised at least a presumption against the alleged phenomenon. Let us now ask, Is there any evidence of any kind which tends to confirm it? I know of none whatever.

We are told (J. S. Mill, *Hamilton*, p. 315, note) that the elementary case of the suggestion of similars will not come under the head of redintegration. But the answer to this is very simple. Reproduction by mere similarity is a fact which, *if real,* would certainly stand by itself. Who doubts it? But then the existence of this fact is just what we deny. The general fact that ideas and perceptions give rise to others which are like them, is of course admitted. But this not only *can be* reduced to redintegration, but long ago it *has been* so reduced. I will exhibit this in a concrete instance.

§ 30. I am walking on the shore in England and see a promontory A, and then suddenly I have the idea of another promontory B which is in Wales, and I say How like is A to B. This is the fact which is to be explained. The false theory tells us to explain the fact by postulating a direct connection between A and the idea of B, for it says The suggestion is perfectly simple. But in the first place the postulate demands an absurdity, and in the second place the suggestion is certainly not simple. If instead of asserting we are willing to analyze, we soon find the true explanation of the fact.

The content of A, *like the content of every other perception,* is complex, and has several elements. Let us say that it has an element of *form* which is p. Now let us look at B, the idea which is to come up. That also possesses a complex content, and we find in it the same element p, in connection with others, q, r, s, t. These are the conditions, and let us see what follows.

In the first place A is presented, and so presents p, which by redintegration stimulates the mind X to produce qr. What happens then?

Several things *may* happen, and it is exceedingly difficult to work out the minute psychological conditions which settle the result. But this is a question with which we are not here concerned. One result would be the identification of *qr* with A*p*. A would then be qualified as A*pqr,* and this would be an unconscious inference. In the present case we are to suppose that this can not happen; for we suppose that *q, r* (say a certain colour and a certain size) are discrepant with A. What then may we expect? We might expect that *qr* would be simply dropped. It might not catch the attention, and the mind might be arrested by a new sensation. We might expect again that, if *qr* is not dropped, it might be used as a means for a wandering course through a train of ideas, foreign to both A and B, and which might take us anywhere. But we are to assume that none of these possibilities become real; and that instead the idea B rises in the mind. How do we explain this?

Very simply. B (we remember) had a content *pqrst,* and now we have A which has brought in *p,* and so introduced *qr.* But *qr* will not coalesce with A. Let them then instead go on to complete the synthesis *pqrst,* a synthesis which by its discrepancy with A is freed from union with it. But an independent *pqrst* is B, and may be recognized as B. And now, B being there along with A, the perception of its resemblance calls for no special explanation. This account of the matter appears to me simple and natural and true.

§ 31. It may be objected, in the first place, that, if the sensation is simple, this theory will not work. I admit it, and I should be sorry if in such a case it *did* work. I would rather that any theory, which I adopt, did *not* explain impossibilities. And that any actual presentation should be simple is quite impossible. Even if it had no internal characters, yet it must be qualified by the relations of its environment. And this complexity would be quite enough for the purpose. For the identity of the simple internal character, over against the difference of two sets of external relations, would give rise to redintegration and to the perception of the resemblance. I think a sober antagonist will hardly deny this. And if it should be denied, then I am inclined to reply with a *reductio ad absurdum.* If the suggestion is quite simple, perhaps there is *no* difference between the similars, or perhaps they are *quite* different. But on either alternative they can not be

similar; and again, if neither alternative is true, then the suggestion is now admitted *not* to be simple, because the elements
have a complex content.

I can think of another case where mistake is possible, and
where suggestion might seem to dispense with redintegration.
If an idea before the mind is unsteady and wavering, it tends
to pass into something different. This difference may be
recognized, and may appear as an idea, which is not the first
idea, and yet is seen to resemble it. But the unsteadiness
will in no case be reproduction by similarity. If the new
idea, which is similar to the other, is produced by a change
in the actual impressions, then this of course is not reproduction at all. But if the alteration takes place apart from the
stimulus of a fresh sensation, it will still be a case of redintegration. For that will be the principle which determines the
direction of the idea's unsteadiness.

We must pass next to an objection which I feel bound to
notice, though I confess I am not able to understand it. We
are told that the form, say of a triangle, is not one single
feature among others, which therefore could call up the other
features; and that yet a triangle may call up another which
is similar in nothing but form (J. S. Mill, *on James Mill,* I.
113). But *why* the form of a figure is not to be a " feature "
of it we are not told, and I at least can not imagine. I was
glad to find when, after forgetting this passage, I came on it
again, that accidentally (§ 30) I had chosen to work out an
instance where the form is the base of the redintegration.
And I will say no more.

And there is another misunderstanding which we may
remove in conclusion. After pointing out that " in the very
heart of Similarity is an indispensable bond of Contiguity;
showing that it is not possible for either process to be accomplished in separation from the other," Professor Bain, if
I understand him rightly, goes on to argue that, notwithstanding this, at least a partial reproduction by pure Similarity
does actually take place.

" It might, therefore, be supposed that Similarity is, after
all, but a mode of Contiguity, namely, the contiguity or association of the different features or parts of a complex whole.
The inference is too hasty. Because contiguity is a part of

the fact of the restoration of similars, it is not the entire fact. There is a distinct and characteristic step preceding the play of this mutual coherence of the parts of the thing to be recovered. The striking into the former track of the agreeing part of the new and the old, is a mental movement by itself, which the other follows, but does not do away with. The effect above described, as the consciousness of agreement or identity, the flash of a felt similarity, is real and distinct. We are conscious of it by itself; there are occasions where we have it without the other, that is to say, without the full re-instatement of the former object in its entireness. We are often aware of an identity without being able to say what is the thing identified; as when a portrait gives us the impression that we have seen the original, without enabling us to say who the original is. We have been affected by the stroke of identity or similarity; but the restoration fails from the feebleness of the contiguous adherence of the parts of the object identified. There is thus a genuine effect of the nature of pure similarity, or resemblance, and a mode of consciousness accompanying that effect; but there is not the full energy of reproduction without a concurring bond of pure contiguity. A portrait may fail to give us the consciousness of having ever seen the original. On the supposition that we have seen the original, this would be a failure of pure similarity " (Bain on *James Mill*, I. 122–3).

Before I criticize this passage, let me show how easily the fact which it mentions comes under our theory. When the promontory A by means of *p* calls up *q, r,* these are not referred to A. And, unless the synthesis *p, q, r, s, t* is completed, they can not re-instate B. The uneasiness of partial but incomplete recognition is caused by the presence of connected elements, such as *p, q, r, s,* which, by actual incompleteness and by vague suggestion of completeness, give us the feeling that at every moment another object is coming. But, although the whole *pqrs* keeps calling in other elements such as *u, x, y, w,* yet none of these makes up a totality we are able to subsume under any head which we know. Should, however, *t* be called in, then B comes at once. In this case we have the feeling of discovery, while in the former case we have the feeling of search. And all is consistent.

In Professor Bain's account we have no consistency.[11] His view, as I understand it, is that though, for the full reproduction of B, contiguity is required, yet partial reproduction takes place without it. In other words, the stroke of similarity affects us enough for us to strike into a former track, but the adhesion of the contiguous bond is too feeble to drag on the mutual play of the parts. The hammer of similarity comes down, but the flash of agreement is a flash in the pan, which fails to explode the barrel of contiguity. But in this place again, I think truth has been sacrificed to imagination.

If anything is brought up which suggests agreement, then this must involve what is called contiguity. For apart from such contiguity there would be nothing to recognize. This is readily shown. In the first place let the similarity "amount to identity": let the differences, which went along with and qualified B, be none of them called up. Then what is there? Why *nothing* but one part of the content of A, say *p*. And *p* agrees with nothing; for what can it agree with? There *is* nothing save *itself*. But in the second place, if the differences which qualified B and made it B, are called up, then obviously we have contiguity at once; for *p* by contiguity has re-instated *pqrst*. "Oh but," I may hear, "we do *not* go on to *t*, and so we never do get so far as B. We go only as far as *pqrs*, so that we are not able to recognize the result. It would be contiguity if we went from *p* to *t* : but if we stop at *s*, it is not contiguity at all.

But this would surely be no less feeble than arbitrary. If the whole of the differences between a portrait and the idea of the original can not be given by contiguity, why then should any of them? Why not *all* be given by similarity? And if *any* are given by contiguity, why should not *all* be given, for all of them are demonstrably "contiguous"? In other words, if similarity will not bring up all the differences, why should it bring up any? Why should not all be left to contiguity?

Because as before we do not start from the fact, but start from a vicious theory of that fact. In the perception A*p* the *p* is not really a particular image; and if you said *q*, *r*, *s*, *t* were associated with this mere adjective *p*, you would have deserted your vicious theory. You try to save it by inventing a fictitious substantival image *p*, which then can be brought in by similarity. But the result is a system of compromise and oscillation. You will not boldly say that A brings up all of B by similarity, and your theory forbids you to say it does so by contiguity. To satisfy both the fact and your theory you say, One arbitrary part is done by one agency, and the rest by the other. And you satisfy neither your theory nor the fact. For what is actually contiguous is not like, and what is supposed like could never have been contiguous. The particular image, which on your theory is called up, has never been contiguous to anything whatever. And the actual element, which does re-instate *qrst* by contiguity, is not anything we can call *like* A at all. It is an universal which is part of A's content. Into this confusion we are led by forcing on the facts our bad metaphysics; and the confusion at once gives place to order when we recognize that Association by Similarity has no existence.

§ 32. We have seen that reproduction of a similar idea comes under the general head of Redintegration. And if the English votary of Association, instead of declaiming against the blindness of Germans, had been willing to learn from them, he might long ago have amended his theory.

" *Si quod nunc percipitur specie vel genere idem est cum eo, quod alias una cum aliis perceptum fuerat, imaginatio etiam horum perceptionem producere debet.* Quæ enim specie vel genere eadem sunt, ea sibi mutuo similia sunt, quatenus ad eandem speciem, vel ad idem genus referuntur (§ 233, 234, *Ontol.*), consequenter quædam in iisdem eadem sunt (§ 195, *Ontol.*). Quare si nunc percipimus A specie vel genere idem cum B, quod alias cum C perceperamus; quædam omnino percipimus, quæ antea simul cum aliis in B percepimus. Quamobrem cum perceptio ceterorum, quæ ipsi B inerant et in A minime deprehenduntur, vi imaginationis una produci debeant (§ 104); imaginatio quoque producit perceptionem ipsius B. . . .

" Idem confirmatur a posteriori. Ponamus enim nos in convivio simul vidisse hospites et vitra vino plena. Quodsi domi die sequente oculos in vitra convertis, quibus vinum infundi solet; extemplo tibi occurrit phantasma hospitum ac vitrorum vino plenorum rerumque ceterarum in convivio præsentium. Vitra, quæ domi conspicis, specie saltem eadem sunt cum vitris, quæ videras in convivio." * Let us hear now what Maas has to say. I translate from the second edition of his *Versuch über die Einbildungskraft,* 1797.

" The first of these rules we have mentioned is the so-called Law of Similarity: All ideas which are like are associated.† I am aware that many psychologists give this law a place co-ordinate with the law of partial perception " [redintegration] " and consider it independent. But on this view the former stands too high, and the latter too low. Similar ideas can not be associated unless, and so far as, either they or their marks form part of one total perceptive state. But this holds good without exception. Two ideas, *a* and *b,* are like one another in so far as they have a common mark β. Suppose now that it is a fact that *b* has associated itself with *a.*" [The explanation of this fact is that] " *b* contains the marks β, δ, ε, and *a* the marks β, α, γ." [On the presentation of *b*] " the marks α, γ associate themselves with the β," [which appears in *b,* and $\beta\alpha\gamma$ is then recognized as *a.*] " The association which takes place is thus between connected ideas, which are parts of one perceptive state." s. 55.‡

I admit that the passage is so brief and cramped that I have been obliged to interpolate a commentary. But there

---

* These quotations are from § 105 of Wolff's *Psych. Emp. Ed. Nova,* 1738. First published in 1732.

† "Ideas" here includes perceptions.

‡ " Die erste von den eben erwähnten Regeln ist das sogenannte Gesetz der Aenlichkeit: alle ähnlichen Vorstellungen associiren sich. Es ist mir nicht unbekannt, dass diese Regel von vielen Psychologen dem Gesetze der Partialvorstellungen koordinirt, und für ein, von diesem unabhängiges Gesetz gehalten wird. Allein das heisst dem erstern einen zu hohen, dem andern einen zu niedrigen Rang anweisen. Aehnliche Vorstellungen können sich nur in sofern associiren, als sie, oder ihre Merkmale, zu einer Totalvorstellung gehören, welches aber bei ihnen ohne Ausnahme der Fall ist. Zwei Vorstellungen *a* und *b* sind einander ähnlich, sofern beide das gemeinschaftliche Merkmal β haben. Wenn also *b,* der die Merkmale $\beta, \delta, \varepsilon$ zukommen, sich mit *a* worin die Merkmale β, α, γ angetroffen werden, vergesellschaftet; so associiren sich α, γ mit β, sind also zusammengehörige Partialvorstellungen."

are other passages, which I need not quote, which would settle
the meaning even if it were doubtful.

From these extracts it will be plain that the school of
Association have had something to learn which they never
have learnt.*

§ 33. There is a possible objection we may here anticipate.
" Admitted," it may be said, " that your theory explains the
suggestion of similars, yet it does so indirectly. *We* explain
it directly and by a simple law. And the simpler explanation
is surely the better one." Anything more unscientific than
such an objection I can hardly conceive. It proposes to give
a simple explanation of a complex case; in other words, to
decline analysis, and to reassert the fact as a principle. And
it proposes in consequence (as we have shown at length) to
treat the simple as a complication of the complex. But the
price you pay for turning a derivative law into an ultimate
principle is somewhat ruinous. You have to import into the
simplest processes a mass of detail which is demonstrably not
there. And this is surely a procedure which science will not
justify.

And if I am told, " At all events the process of suggestion,
as you describe it, is much too complex for a primitive mind,"
that objection once more only serves to strengthen me. For
the process *does not exist* in a primitive mind. Similarity is a
somewhat late perception, and hence can not appear at an
early stage. For a rude understanding, if things are not the
same, they are simply different. To see, or to feel, that two
things are not the same and yet are alike, are diverse and yet
in part identical, is a feat impossible for a low intelligence.
It demands an advance in reflection and distinction which no
sane psychology can place at the beginning of mental evolution. No doubt you may say that from the very first mental

---

* Sir W. Hamilton not only refers to the true account of Association by Similarity, but even criticizes it. Unfortunately he had not
the least idea of its meaning. He tells us first that we are to discount
" Wolff who cannot *properly* be adduced." I have no notion what
" properly " stands for here, and perhaps Sir W. Hamilton did not
really know what Wolff says. He then proposes an emendation in
the passage from Maas, which reduces it to nonsense, and his criticism
shows that he had no idea of the real meaning of either Wolff or his
followers (vid. *Reid*, 913-14).

elements *are* alike, although the mind does not *perceive* it.
But in saying this you open a question not welcome I should
judge to the disciples of Experience. For if states of mind
can *be* alike, and yet not like to the mind, what is such similarity but the identity of elements within these states? The
distinction on the one hand between what *is* or *was in* the
mind, and, on the other hand, that which is *felt by* the mind
or is now *before it,* is, if admitted, quite fatal to the orthodox
English creed. We should have an attempt to purchase consistency by suicide.

If the school of Association desired to be consistent, it
might find perhaps in the " mechanism of ideas," apart from
consciousness, a way of propping its tottering beliefs. But
that mechanism implies metaphysical doctrines as to the unity
of the soul and the permanence of ideas, which in themselves
would be somewhat difficult to maintain, and which would
give the lie to our most cherished prejudices.

But if consistency can be reached by no way but suicide,
something after all may be said for the admission of the
doctrine we have adopted—that all association is between universals, and that all consists in redintegration by identity.

§ 34. The answer no doubt will be the old " *Non possumus.*
No two states of mind can have anything in common; for, if
so, they would be the same, and that is impossible." On this
rock of obstinate metaphysical prejudice our explanations are
broken. It would be useless to point out, as we have already
pointed out, to the disciple of Experience that his own theory
has been wrecked on this same iron dogma. He would say,
I suppose, " Let the facts go unexplained, let miracles be
invoked and fictions multiplied, let analysis be neglected and
experience contemned—only do not ask me to be false to my
principles, do not ask me to defile the grave of my fathers.
An advanced thinker once, an advanced thinker always." And
I could not answer or reproach. I respect a fidelity which I
can not imitate.

But to those whose honour is not yet pledged I may perhaps in conclusion be permitted to address myself. Do you
wish, I should like to ask in the first place, to speculate on
first principles, or are you content to engage yourself on
special subject matter? In the first case I would beg you

seriously to examine the question for yourself, and not to take any assertion on trust. I can not venture to anticipate the result you will then reach (if indeed you reach any), but I feel sure that any conclusion you do come to, will not be quite the same with the orthodox doctrine as handed down in England. And to those who are not prepared for metaphysical enquiry, who feel no call towards thankless hours of fruitless labour, who do not care to risk a waste of their lives on what the world for the most part regards as lunacy, and they themselves but half believe in—to all such I would offer a humble suggestion. Is it not possible to study the facts of psychology, without encumbering oneself with beliefs or disbeliefs as to the ultimate nature of the mind and its contents? You can not have metaphysical disbeliefs without corresponding beliefs; and, if you shrink from becoming a professional metaphysician, these beliefs must be dogmas. Would it not be better to study the facts, and to let metaphysics altogether alone?

If this can be done in the other sciences, it surely can be done in psychology too. In the other sciences we know how it is done. The so-called principles which explain the facts are working hypotheses, which are true because they work, and so far as they work, but which need not be considered as a categorical account of the nature of things. The physicist, for example, is not obliged to believe that atoms or ether do really exist in a shape which exactly corresponds to his ideas. If these ideas give a rational unity to the knowledge which exists, and lead to fresh discoveries, the most exacting demand upon the most exact of sciences is fully satisfied. The ideas are verified, and the ideas are true, for they hold good of the facts to which they are applied. And to suppose that the metaphysician should come in, and offer to interfere with the proceedings of the physicist or to criticize his conclusions, is in my judgment to take a most wrong view of metaphysics. It is the same with psychology. There is no reason why in this science we should not *use* doctrines which, if you take them as actual statements of fact, are quite preposterous. For the psychologist, as such, is not interested in knowing if his principles are true when taken categorically. If they are useful ways of explaining phenomena, if they bring unity into the subject and enable us to deal with the fresh facts which arise, that is really all that, as psychologists, we can be concerned with. Our principles are nothing but working hypotheses: we do not know and we do not care if they turn out to be fictions, when examined critically.

That is the way in which psychology surely might be studied. And if we studied it in this way we should escape some controversies. I, for instance, should lose all right and all desire to criticize the " Laws of Association " on the ground of their untruth, if they only ceased to proclaim themselves as statements as to the real movement of the mind. Within the same field of empirical psychology I should offer what I think is a more convenient hypothesis, and any objection to that which rested on metaphysics would be at once ruled out of court. We might perhaps thus advance the study of the subject in a way which now seems quite impossible. And if we did not make much advance in knowledge, we should save ourselves at least a good deal of bitterness.

§ 35. The suggestion is offered in great humility, since the obstacles it must meet with are overpowering. The first obstacle is the prejudice of a bad tradition. It is supposed that the psychologist must be a philosopher. He is used to think himself so, and he is not likely to accept a lower place. And this objection is in fact, I fear, unanswerable. I would give him the name of philosopher for his asking, but I could not admit him as a student of first principles. And the second obstacle is like the first. We get into what, I suppose, deserves the name of an antinomy. The psychologist is to confine himself within certain limits; he is not to cross over into metaphysics. But unfortunately if he is not a metaphysician he will not know what those limits are. And it is the same to some extent with all the sciences. The physicist, for instance, is constantly tempted to think that his ruling ideas are ultimate facts. And this temptation is fatal to the mere specialist. It is only, on the one hand, a general culture and largeness of mind, or else some education in metaphysics, which saves him from this error. And it is much worse in psychology.[12] The subject brings with it a special temptation; and, if all the truth must be told, the same great minds that devote themselves to physics, to chemistry, or to biology, do not take up psychology. And then again the psychologist is probably a dabbler in metaphysics. A little metaphysics is not enough to show that his so-called principles are fictions. And our leading English psychologists perhaps only know a very little metaphysics. And, having a limited acquaintance with the subject, they persuade themselves, and (what is worse) one persuades the other, that they have completely mastered it. It is to be feared that this evil must to some extent continue.

And there is a final obstacle. The student of metaphysics may form an opinion as to the real nature of psychical phenomena. And knowing, as he thinks, the truth about these facts, he will be led to insist on a psychological interpretation which is strictly true. He will interfere with the empirical psychologist, and will himself contribute, by what he thinks good metaphysics, to the begetting of bad metaphysics in opposition. This is certainly an error, but it is an error, I fear, which will never quite vanish. When a man has once seen that every single science except metaphysics makes use of fictions, he is apt to conclude that the next step is for him to remove these fictions and to substitute the truth. But, if he looked closer, he would see that human beings can not get on without mythology.[13] In science, in politics, in art, and religion it will always be found, and can never be driven out. And, if we confine our attention to science, we must say that there is only one science which can have no hypotheses, and which is forbidden to employ any fiction or mythology, and that this science with some reason is suspected of non-existence.

§ 36. We have approached a large subject which we can not deal with, and which might well occasion misgiving and doubt. We need give way to neither in our rejection of the principles of the school of Association. We reject them in the name alike of metaphysics, of psychology, and of logic. In behalf of metaphysics we protest against the basis of dogmatic Atomism, and we protest against the superstructure of a barbarous mythology. It is not true that mental phenomena are mere particulars. It is not true that ghosts of impressions leave their graves. It is ridiculous to couple the existent and non-existent, or the present and the absent, by a relation which implies the presence of both. In defence of psychology we protest against an hypothesis which has to postulate phenomena which are clearly absent, and then to postulate their removal by a process which is not present. When a single hypothesis explains the facts, it is surely unscientific to employ a complication which works no better. And, in behalf of logic, we must protest once more. The essence of inference can hardly be a principle which later we recognize as a principle of error; and which, if the theory of Association were true, we should hardly get to perceive was false. It is an ill omen for Logic if it fails to show that what in the highest stage is accepted as a canon, was active from the first development of the soul as the guide of its conduct and ruler of its life.

NOTE TO CHAPTER I

§ 1. Though I have no space, and perhaps no strict right, to deal with the subject here, I must yield to the temptation of making some very brief remarks on the doctrines noticed in § 2 of this chapter. These go by the names of Indissoluble Association and the Chemistry of Ideas.

The first of these doctrines is supposed to have a very great metaphysical importance. Mere chance conjunction, if often repeated, will beget, we are told, an union of ideas which is irresistible. This shows that what seems to be a necessary connection may be no more than an accidental adherence. From this we conclude that a necessary connection is no canon of truth. And this proves that our trust must be placed elsewhere. The Logic of Experience tells us, of course, what it is we are to trust to.

For myself, in the first place, I never could get any information from that Logic which seemed intelligible, and so I will confine myself to the former part of the preceding statement.

§ 2. The first fault I have to find is that it does not go far enough. We need not have a *repeated* conjunction. One single instance is enough to give rise to a necessary connection. For, as we should say, what is once true is true always.

§ 3. I have to complain, in the second place, that all kinds of combination are called *association*. But association surely implies that the elements which are joined might not have been joined. And this should be proved, or at all events made probable, before co-existence is assumed to be mere association.

§ 4. It may be replied, "Even if the things are connected, yet, as we perceive them, their union *for us* must be chance conjunction, and therefore association." But this again should in no case be asserted without some ground. It is not always self-evident that the mind *could* have had one element without the other. And where you fail to show that this is the case, you cannot talk of association.

§ 5. I shall be answered, "What we prove is that in certain cases mere chance association has produced necessary connection; and we argue from this that it may be fairly suspected of doing so in all. The possibility is proved and the possibility is enough." I can not enter here into the merits of this argument which I shall hereafter show is logically vicious (vid. Bk. III. II. Chap. III. § 22)[14]; but suppose that for the present we admit it. What conclusion follows? That we are fallible men? We knew that before. That we are to trust to anything else? Then what else? Admit for argument's sake the possibility that *all* our beliefs are baseless, what then? Why nothing. If we mean to go on living and thinking, we dismiss this possibility as *idle*. Suppose we all are victimized by chance conjunction, are we not *right* to be so victimized?

§ 6. Association implies *other* conditions. It implies contingent circumstances. When a chance conjunction is taken by an error for a necessary connection, the mistake really consists in defective analysis. The remedy is found in the progress of analysis, assisted probably by fresh fact. Where this remedy is impracticable, no remedy can be applied. For no other is possible.

§ 7. Apart from mental chemistry, which we shall consider presently, a connection of ideas could not continue to be necessary when it demonstrably has arisen from association. And this is quite obvious. For the connection of ideas supposes a content which is ideally inseparable, and the knowledge of the association involves this ideal separation. The experience which shows the fact of the association, is at the same time the analysis which loosens its bond.

§ 8. This however is a minor point. To the objection that *possibly* all truth may be nothing but chance association, we reply (as above) that, supposing this for argument's sake to be true, we can not trouble ourselves with idle possibilities. But if you wish to go beyond this idle possibility, you must show cases where unreasoning chance conjunction has produced false belief *without confusion*. You must show, that is, that the belief in the connection was *wholly* false; that it was not a true belief in a real fact made false simply by a confusion between the relevant and irrelevant elements in the connection. But this, I think, has never been shown.

§ 9. If association rests on conjunction in perception, then that is a valid ground for belief. It is deceptive merely so far as it is unanalyzed, and confuses the irrelevant with the relevant. Otherwise it is a *proof* of necessary connection. But then this latter is not *mere* association. For it is not every conjunction in presentation which can be called an association, but only those conjunctions which result from chance. And chance disappears before analysis.

§ 10. I will now turn to the doctrine of mental chemistry. Elements by virtue of repeated chance conjunction are said to cohere in such a way that they form a third product which has the qualities of neither. But this in the first place would not be *association,* since that term implies that the individuals continue. In a chemical union [15] the molecules of the substances cease to be molecules of either substance. It is therefore nonsense to say that they are *associated*.

§ 11. This of course may be said to be a question of words. But the fact of such union in the case of ideas has, at least in my knowledge, never yet been shown. It can not be called impossible, nor should I at least have said that it was even improbable, but I have never seen any certain instance of it.

§ 12. In the case of *emotions* this "chemical union" does seem to take place. But even here there might be doubt if the emotion should properly be considered as an "union." It might rather be a new reaction on a fresh compound material.[16] But, however that be, it is true that the emotional product often can not be analyzed.[17] It can only be reconstructed perhaps in part hypothetically. And again if we take intellectual *functions,* there is no doubt that in the process of mental development "faculties" are produced which are different in kind from what went before.[18] But then again these functions are hardly unions of ideas. When you strictly keep to mental *objects*, I think you must say that no instance of what looks like chemical combination has yet been found.

§ 13. It is of course mere waste of time to bring forward as evidence cases where the *fact* of the association is not admitted. It is for example a mere circle to instance the idea of visual extension, since visual sensations *without* extension are the merest hypothesis. Not only can this alleged fact not be observed, but there are very strong reasons for rejecting it wholly.* It is not less idle to bring forward a product, such as the sensation of white, and then roundly assert that it is the fusion of different sensations. Perhaps it is, but you would have to show the existence of these sensations in the particular case, and give some reason for your belief that *they* were transformed. It is finally ridiculous to adduce, as a chemical product, an idea which can be separated at once and with ease into its component parts. J. S. Mill when hard pressed seems to play as his trump card the idea of *infinity* (*Hamilton*, Note to Chapter XV.). But infinity, as he understands it, hardly calls for analysis. Of itself it falls apart into its elements, for it is a mere *mechanical* union.

The conclusion must be that the chemistry of ideas is no more than a hypothesis. I do not think in any case it would be the right way to state the fact. But the fact itself has not been clearly shown to exist.[19] In the second place, were we convinced that mere chance conjunction was able to lead to it, then nothing would follow except what we know, viz. that there is some general antecedent probability that any conviction is false. This result makes no difference either to theory or to practice.

* Vid. Stumpf, *Raumvorstellung.*

ADDITIONAL NOTES

[1] The length of this Chapter was, I think, justified by the general state of psychology in England in 1883. The reader is asked to bear in mind that perhaps the greater part of it was written at a particular time, and for a special purpose, and hence should now be superfluous. This remark does not, however, apply to the doctrine that Association holds only between universals. This doctrine, as I have long ago mentioned (in *Mind* N. S., No. 20, p. 472, and, I think, elsewhere)— I owe to Hegel (*Encyk.* §§ 452 foll.). For my indebtedness to him in psychology otherwise see on Bk. III. I. VII. I may add here that, so far as I remember, in 1883 I had not yet made the acquaintance of Herbart, with Drobisch and Volkmann, or even of Waitz or of Lotze's *Medicinische Psychologie*. I had, however, read most of Steinthal's *Sprachwissenschaft,* I.

[2] "If the condition is known." It would be better to say "is taken to fall within the subject," and for "where the condition is unknown" to write "where you can not specify the condition."

[3] "Analytical." Cf. Bk. III. I. VI. § 10.

[4] "When they are dead, etc." I should certainly have used other language here with reference to "survival," if I had been better acquainted with the excellent work done in psychology by Herbartian writers. The doctrine that every mental state still survives and is active below the conscious level, was, and is, as a working hypothesis, not to be treated with contempt.

[5] "What is left behind is a mental result." Cf. § 26. We have here the problem of Dispositions. This, I should say, is in the end insoluble, if you ask for anything beyond an empirical Law or Laws. Cf. *Mind* (O. S.), No. 47, p. 363, No. 13 (N. S.), p. 25, and No. 33, p. 9.

[6] "Logical." Cf. Bk. III. I. III. §§ 20 and 23. Association becomes logical by its use for, and subordination to, a logical end; where, that is, it is controlled, for the purpose of truth, by the identity and individuality of an object. Cf. *Mind* (O. S.), No. 47, pp. 381-2, and *Essays*, pp. 362 foll.

[7] "They all have content." Cf. §§ 30 and 31. The point here is that you do not anywhere have a psychical fact which is purely simple and in this sense unique. Everything given, we must remember, is always in some sense itself qualified by its context. See T. E. V.

[8] "This is not merely an assertion I have chosen to make." Prof. Sully on the other hand, in *The Human Mind*, I, 331 (1892), says (I understand) that it is so. While directing the reader to this criticism I may add that I neither saw nor see any need to reply to it. The reader who can not deal with it for himself will, I think, have read this Chapter in vain.

[9] "Primitive Credulity." Cf. Bk. III. I. VI. § 32, and *Essays*, p. 377.

[10] "This is a result." See Note 5.

[11] "In Professor Bain's account, etc." Though the temptation was irresistible, I am sorry that I treated Bain, here and elsewhere, with so little respect. Let me say now that, so far as I know, he was the only writer of his time and school who made an original contribution to psychology. Though one may find him at times to be absurd, one seldom finds that he has not at least made an instructive effort to see the facts for himself.

[12] "And it is much worse in psychology." The reader here must not forget that I was pointing to psychology as it was in England, still at least in the main, in 1883. To use such language now would be absurd and even monstrous.

[13] "Mythology." Cf. my *Appearance* and *Essays*, and, in particular on psychology, see *Mind*, Vol. IX, N. S., No. 33. It is hardly necessary, I hope, for me to inform the reader that this view of truth, as being more or less mythological everywhere outside metaphysics, came to me from Plato and again still more from Hegel.

[14] Cf. here *Appearance*, p. 620.

[15] "Chemical union." I am of course here not endorsing but merely adopting the view offered me as to the real nature of chemical union.

This, I presume, might be the place to discuss the doctrine of *Fusion*—whether of one sensation with another or with ideas and Dispositions—or again of these two last, each with themselves or with one another. But I can not venture upon such a difficult subject here.

[16] "It might rather . . . material." This seems certainly the better view. No psychical state, as a unity, can be wholly resolved into the mere compounding of units—even "chemically."

[17] "Often can not be analyzed." The meaning here is that there are some emotions, to "analyze" which, except quite inadequately, you must have recourse to what you believe is their origin.

[18] "Functions" and "faculties." This statement of course will apply to much of what are called "instincts."

[19] "But the fact itself . . . exist." By "the fact itself" I mean the appearance of a complex psychical state, in which the elements, as such, have become indistinguishable, and which can nevertheless be taken as the mere product of their union. There are but few psychologists, I should think, who would now accept such a fact. However that may be, we can and must, I should say, maintain that new products have been developed, but certainly not by chemical union of ideas. Every new mental product is rather a fresh reaction from the individual totality; and, to explain, we must seek to find the Laws by which Dispositions are formed, and by which the result of former experience meets and more or less transforms the incoming stimulus.

CHAPTER II

§ 1. At the point which we have reached a discussion of this subject may seem inexcusable. If we have shown that no association is possible except between universals, and that in the very lowest stages of mind universals are used, we may fairly be reproached by the reader who is anxious to learn something new, if we linger over errors the root of which has long since been torn up. For supposing that the results we have attained to are sound, the question is settled. To reason directly from particulars to particulars is wholly impossible. It must be at most a desire of the mind which this world can not gratify, a postulate *a priori* given by an intuition, that disappears before analysis and is rejected by experience.

§ 2. But since it is possible that the reader of this Chapter has not accepted the conclusions we obtained, since it is not unlikely that he has passed them over, let us try once again if we can not do something to turn the light into this refuge of darkness. We must not expect to persuade the disciple of the Experience Philosophy. It is not for anything we are likely to offer, that he will desert the fashionable and easy creed in which he has been reared. But at least we shall have tried not to leave him an excuse. He must not say that we have been afraid to look his idol in the face.

There is however one thing we will not do for his sake. We decline to supply a direct examination of the well-known chapter in J. S. Mill's *Logic*. It would require much more space to set out the ambiguities inherent in that chapter,[2] than we can give to the discussion of the question itself; a discussion to which, I may remind the reader, I consider that at this stage he has no right.

§ 3. Why should we not reason from mere particulars? Do our reasonings never rest upon fact? And what are facts if they are not particulars? Either then we never, starting from fact, conclude to fact, or else we infer particulars from particulars. This result may so be deduced from first principles. And common experience supports the result. From cases we have known we go to fresh cases without an appeal to any general principle. We have seen something happen and, given a new instance, we argue at once that it will happen again. But we have no reason other than this fact to give for our conclusion. We thus in the second place have proved our thesis *a posteriori*, as before we proved it *a priori*. And now we add an indirect proof. If for reasoning were wanted major premises, then the lower animals could not reason. But they do reason, and therefore the thesis is proved.

§ 4. How shall we escape from this array of proofs? Are they not unanswerable? To me they seem unanswerable, and I have not the smallest wish to escape them. I admit them and embrace them; but I ask a question, *What is it that they prove?*

They prove first that, when we go from experience of facts, this experience is the foundation of our inference. They prove again that we do not always go from an explicit major premise, and that therefore another way of reasoning is possible. And in defence of these results I am as zealous as any of my readers can be. If he likes to say beside that a syllogism in extension is a *petitio principii* and no argument at all, he will urge what long ago I have endorsed. But let us come to the conclusion. If you mean to argue to no more than this, that experience of particulars is a basis of inference, and that no explicit major is required, I am ready to support you. But if you mean to conclude, *Therefore* we reason from particulars as such direct to particulars, I object at once. The conclusion does not follow from the premises, and it also is wholly contrary to experience.

§ 5. We have in fact to do here with a common-place logical blunder. The thesis *to be* proved is that an inference is made direct from particulars, as such, to other particulars. The conclusion which *is* proved is that from experience of particulars we somehow get a particular conclusion. Not to see the enormous difference of these assertions is to fall into a gross *ignoratio elenchi*. To prove the thesis in dispute it is necessary to assume that *either* we go direct from particulars to particulars, *or else* advance through an explicit syllogism (perhaps even an explicit syllogism in extension). No sort of evidence is offered to show that this alternative exhausts the possibilities; and it disappears the moment we confront it with facts.

§ 6. In reply to the assertion that we are able to argue from particulars to particulars, I would ask in the first place what particulars are meant. Am I to understand that the past experiences in their particularity are the premises used in this supposed inference? If I am told this is so, of course I reply that we have here a mere psychological fiction. Particular images of past occurrences, which retain the special marks of the originals, are not available. The doctrine that each perished perception leaves an unblurred unabridged counterpart of itself, is a preposterous invention (cf. pp. 35-7, and Book II. II. Chap. I.).

§ 7. It is again a mere error which sees in the lowest form of inference the presence of one or more images of the past, together with a fact which they are used to qualify. When a present perception is modified by the suggestions of past experience, these suggestions do not come from particular images of perished events. This theory is a second pure invention (cf. *ibid.*).

§ 8. In the third place when, at a higher stage of development, the past event is as such called to mind, and when we do argue from a particular image, yet even then we do not argue from its particularity, from its psychological environment and temporary colouring. We argue from the content, the idea which can exist in different times and under diverse psychological conditions. And once more, and in the fourth place, this idea itself need not be used as a whole, but we may argue from one part of it.

§ 9. A child has come to know that, when the dog is pleased, he wags his tail. On this he argues that, when the cat wags its tail, it must be pleased. What is it he proceeds from? The error we are considering actually supposes that one or more images of foregone occasions, presenting the dog pleased and with his tail in motion, come before the mind, and that, on this, the perception of the cat now moving its tail directly gives rise to the conclusion, The cat is pleased. But the

question arises, How is it that one attribute is taken from the
dog-images and given to the cat, without the rest going with
it? Does not this use of one part of the dog-images, and the
neglect of the rest, show that something happens to the images
in question, and that, however it has come about, the inference
is *not* drawn from the whole of any one of them? Suppose
again that they differ among themselves, do we argue direct
from the whole of all of them? But if not, from what else?

§ 10. The facts, I should have thought, would have left
little doubt that the result of experience is a connection of
attributes, where the differences of their particular subjects are
blurred—a confused universal, which may appear to the mind
in a particular imagery, but is used without any regard to
that. I confess I should have thought that it was very clear
that, in the special cases where we argue from recollection, we
use the past event as a type or instance. And since both this
past event and the present perception come to us as instances,
we neglect some of the differences that exist between them.
We do not know the principle, but we feel " it is the same
thing " in both cases. But, if so, the premise from which the
conclusion directly comes, is not the particular. It is an
universal extract, what we call a " general impression."

§ 11. Reasoning from a particular to a particular is obviously an argument from analogy. In this we all know that
we do not use the whole of that particular from which we
argue. It was an inference by analogy which deceived the
child (§ 9). He took from the dog a relation of qualities and
transferred it to the cat. What he argued from was this
general relation, and it was a false analogy, just because it was
a bad generalization. Again, why do we object to false
analogies? Is it not because in them we treat some fact as
another instance of a rule, when there is no common rule and
the facts are not instances? And is not this a hint that in
true analogy we use a principle though we can not state it?

§ 12. This leads us to put another question. Suppose that
per impossibile we did have before our minds a number of
particular images, and did argue from them directly; would
not this inference be a very bad one? If I say " A, B, and C
are *a,* and there is *no difference* between D and A, B, and C,
therefore D is *a* "—is not this a circle—a frivolous *petitio?*

Again if I say " A, B, and C are *a,* and D is *different* from
A, B, and C, *therefore* D is *a* "—is not this a bad argument,
so glaringly bad that no child and no beast could be got to
use it?

But if we amend this semblance of reasoning, and bring it
to the form of a real inference—if we say " A, B, and C are *a,*
and therefore D, *which resembles them,* is *a,*" we are no longer
arguing from mere particulars. We are arguing from the
resemblance, from a point or points which D has in common
with A, B, and C. It is *not* because A, B, and C are *a,* but it is
because in them some element β is *a,* and because again we
find β in D, that we argue " *therefore* D is *a.*" For whenever
we reason from resemblance we reason from identity, from
that which is the same in several particulars and is itself not a
particular. And is it not obvious that, in arguing from particular cases, we leave out some of the differences, and that
we could not argue if we did not leave them out? Is it not
then palpable that, when the differences are disregarded, the
residue is an universal? Is it not once more clear that, in
vicious inferences by analogy, the fault can be found in a
wrong generalization?

§ 13. I will conclude with an appeal to common experience.
We all know very well that in our daily life we reason habitu-
ally from the results of past experience, although we may
be wholly unable to give one single particular fact in support
of our conclusion. We know again that there are persons,
whose memory is so good that they recall past details in a
way which to us is quite impossible, and who yet can not
draw the conclusions which we draw, since they have never
gone beyond the reproduction of these details. It is not the
collection of particular facts, it is the general impression one
gets from these facts which is really the *sine qua non* of
reasoning ; and it is that from which we really go to our result.

If you begin the discussion of a question, such as this, with
a vicious disjunction, you can not go right. As a preliminary
to discussion you have excluded the truth. From the alternative—either an explicit syllogism or an inference from particulars to particulars—you can hardly fail to get a false result.
You may infer—The syllogism in extension is no argument,
and *therefore* we go from particulars to particulars. You may

infer—It is not possible to argue from particulars, and *there-fore* we reason always in syllogisms, explicit and (if you like) also extensional. But to me it is nothing which conclusion you adopt. For both are errors, and both at bottom *are one and the same error.* They are twin branches from one root of inveterate prejudice and false assumption.

§ 14. The present chapter has been so short that I take this opportunity to deliver my mind from a weight that oppresses it. I intend to be guilty of what some readers may think an unpardonable omission. It is true that I do not undertake to criticize every theory from which I dissent; but there is one of those theories which I propose to pass over, that may seem to call for recognition and enquiry. Mr. Spencer, in his *Psychology,* has developed a view of the nature of inference, which, despite its ingenuity, despite its perception of some of those truths which the syllogism has forgotten, I am obliged to consider fundamentally mistaken. It has always seemed to me so arbitrary and so forced, so far away in the end from the real facts, that I can not believe a discussion of it here would tend to throw any light on the problems of logic.[3]

More than once, I admit, Mr. Spencer's position in English philosophy induced me to think that I had no right to omit all notice of his peculiar views. The sacrifice of space, the chance that I had failed to follow the process which had brought him his results, did not weigh against the danger that I might have seemed to avoid confronting my own doctrines with those of an established master in the subject. But there came to my mind another consideration, which decided the result and fixed my purpose to omit the examination. The late Mr. Mill and Professor Bain have both written systematic treatises on logic. They have entertained a view of Mr. Spencer's powers and philosophical performances which is not mine. Mr. Mill especially has expressed his conviction in such terms, that beside it those praises, I should otherwise have felt were due to Mr. Spencer, would sound like detraction. Both must have been aware that Mr. Spencer has more than once published what appears to be a novel theory of reasoning. And yet neither (so far as I know) has examined the most peculiar and salient assertions of that theory.

And I thought that I might venture on a humble imitation
of their common silence. Did they fail to follow Mr.
Spencer's demonstrations, did they even think them an unprofitable subject, in either case I claim the protection of their authority.
But, if neither is the truth and they considered Mr. Spencer
to be of one mind with themselves, and to say the same thing
in a different form, then once again they unite in excusing me.
I surely am not wrong if I too omit all criticism, or at least
delay it till I have seen some cause to think that it is wanted.

ADDITIONAL NOTES

[1] On the argument from particulars, beside the references given,
cf. also Bk. III. I. VII. § 8 and III. II. I. § 5.

[2] "The ambiguities inherent in that chapter." These are such that
apparently (given sufficient good will) the chapter can mean that we
never do or can argue directly from particulars (see *Appearance*,
p. 596, note). With regard to J. S. Mill the questions to be answered,
if any one thinks them worth answering, are these. (i) Had J. S.
Mill *any* new view to offer? (ii) If so, what was it? (iii) What is
the view logically required by his general position? But I must be
forgiven if I go on to add "Let the dead bury their dead."

[3] With regard to Mr. Spencer's view I would suggest, as a possibility, that it never was taken from the facts, but was a development
of or from something about Comparison which he found in Hamilton.
Reading so few books, Mr. Spencer was naturally more at the mercy
of those that he did read.

CHAPTER III

THE INDUCTIVE METHODS OF PROOF

§ 1. We have seen that in reality there is no such thing as an inference from the particular to a fresh particular. In this chapter we approach a cognate superstition. In England, at least if we go with the fashion,[1] we all have to believe in an Inductive Logic, which, starting from particular given facts, goes on to prove universal truths. Its processes, exact as the strictest syllogism, surrender themselves to the direction of Canons, reputed no less severe than *Barbara* and believed with reason to be far more fertile. I am afraid I may lose the reader's sympathy when I advise him to doubt the union of these qualities.

§ 2. To question the existence or deny the efficacy of those methods of reasoning (whatever they may be), by which modern science has made its conquests, would of course be absurd. To succeed on a great scale is to prove one's title. And it is not within the scope of this work to investigate either the nature of the processes which science employs, or the amount of evidence which it accepts as proof. What I wish to assert is that, starting from particular perceptions of sense, there is no way of going to universal truths by a process of demonstration perfectly exact, and in all its steps theoretically accurate. The induction of logicians, so far as it professes to make that attempt, I shall try to show will not stand criticism.

§ 3. We need not discuss at any great length the Method which is called Complete Induction.[2] To examine a number of individuals and to say of *all* what you say of *each,* is in the first place no inference to an *universal* truth. A collective term, if taken collectively, is no more universal than if taken distributively (p. 82) ; and the inference, if admitted, does not reach the conclusion which we have in view. But in the second place, the inference itself is inadmissible. In other words, if you start from *each* and end with *each,* there is no process; but if you predicate of the collection what is true of each member, there is palpable error. The Induction by way of Complete Enumeration must be rejected as either tautologous or false (cf. Book II. I. Chap. II. § 5).

Or again if we take the Induction in another sense, it changes its character. If first by counting you arrive at *all,* and then from *all* pass on to *any,* that is not a process which need be false or need merely repeat the fact it began with; but then it is not based simply upon the particular *data.* If a flock of sheep have all had medicine, I know that, within the given enclosure, any sheep has been dosed, and I connect the attributes without thinking of the individuals. The conclusion is valid and is really universal; but it implies a process which goes beyond counting. " This sheep and that sheep and the others are dosed; " that is the first premise; but a second is wanted. We may write it " This sheep and that sheep and the others are every sheep that is within this fold," or again " The fold does not contain any sheep but these which we have counted." It is on the strength of this premise that we go on to conclude, " If any sheep is now within the fold he must have been dosed." We seem to argue from "all" to "any," but the " all " has ceased to be the *mere* collection.

We have first the assurance that the whole field has been surveyed, and that we have not neglected any relevant matter. Counting is the way in which we attempt to obtain this assurance. But the enumeration, if it is to be complete, must be qualified by the privative judgment, Nothing in this fold can have been uncounted. The collection is thus identified with every possible sheep that comes under the condition of being in the fold. This is one side of our process. The other side consists in an act of abstraction, and in the selective perception of one connection of attributes throughout our whole subject matter. Then, given an individual possessing the condition of belonging to our fold, we pass at once to the other connected attribute.

Now the procedure by which we get this general connection is in a sense "inductive"; and assuredly once more it has employed counting. But then the counting *by itself* is not the induction, and is not by itself a generalization. The discriminative analysis, that goes with the counting, is the real agent which procures the universal, and which contains the " induction " (cf. Book III.). It is this which generalizes from the facts. But it does not go beyond one single case,[3] since its validity depends on the privative judgment by which any folded sheep must be one case with the sheep observed.

To repeat, if you confine yourself to mere counting, you get no general result. If you attempt to advance from the basis of mere counting your ground is unsafe. If you proceed from a *complete* Enumeration, then the warrant of completeness falls outside the counting. What generalizes is the selective perception which isolates and secures the connection of adjectives. But the conclusion depends on the guarantee of completeness. It is valid because the connection is found in a whole, which is warranted to anticipate every possible case of a certain kind.

§ 4. But induction by way of Enumeration is not the method we are asked to believe in.* In the treatise which, partly from merits of its own and partly also from other causes, has threatened to fasten itself on us as a text book, we find the so-called Canons of Induction, collected and developed from other writers, and formulated with a show of rigorous accuracy. It is the illusory nature of these self-styled proofs that I wish to point out in the present chapter. We must not be afraid of the shadow of authority. The balance of authority among modern logicians is, I think, against the claim of the inductive proofs, and is not on their side. And perhaps already, from experience we have had, we may be prepared to find that Mr. Mill may at times be mistaken.

§ 5. We must remember above all things throughout this discussion that the question is *not,* Can discoveries be made by the use of the Methods? They may be as efficacious in actual practice as is asserted by some, or as practically inadequate and unsuited for work as is affirmed by others. That is not the issue which we have before us. The question we have to answer here is, Are they valid ways of proof, by which we can go from facts to universals?

For that is the claim which the Canons set up. " The

---

* The reader of Mill's *Logic* will remember, on the other hand, that with him the whole inductive process is taken to stand or fall with a proof by way of *incomplete* Enumeration.

business of Inductive Logic is to provide rules and models (such as the Syllogism and its rules are for ratiocination) to which if inductive arguments conform, those arguments are conclusive, and not otherwise. This is what the Four Methods profess to be " (J. S. Mill, *Logic,* Bk. III. ix. § 6). " In saying that no discoveries were ever made by the Four Methods, he affirms that none were ever made by observation and experiment; for assuredly if any were, it was by processes reducible to one or other of those methods " (*ibid.*). " But induction is not a mere mode of investigation." " Induction is proof; it is inferring something unobserved from something observed; it requires, therefore, an appropriate test of proof; and to provide that test is the special purpose of inductive logic " (*Logic,* III. ii. § 5). We can have now no doubt about the nature of this claim; and this claim it is that we are going to discuss.

§ 6. I shall endeavour to show three things: first that the Four Inductive Methods can not be used if we start with mere facts, that the Canons presuppose universal truths as the material upon which the work is to be done; and that therefore, if valid, the Methods are not *inductive* at all, in the sense of generalizing from particulars. In the next place I shall briefly exhibit the real nature of the reasoning used in the above Four Methods, and shall point out that its essence is not thus inductive. And finally I shall show that not one of the Canons is a test of proof, and that by every one you can bring out what is false. None of these three positions depends on the others. If the Canons are invalid, if their essence is not inductive, or if they can not be applied to individual facts—if, in short, any one of these contentions is established, the inductive logic is certainly refuted. And I hope to establish firmly all three.

§ 7. (I.) In the first place there is no doubt at all that the basis, from which we are to start in induction, consists primarily of particular given facts. I need cite no passages to establish this point. We naturally expect then to see on the one side the material as yet untouched by the Methods, and on the other the operation of these agents on the crude subject matter with which they must begin. This natural expectation is doomed to disappointment.

(*a*) A suspicion of the shock which we are destined to

receive may have come from the effrontery of the Method called " Residues." This estimable exemplar of " our great mental operation " comes up to us placarded as one of " the means which mankind possess for exploring the laws of nature by specific observation and experience," and then openly avows that it depends entirely on " previous inductions." Unless supplied beforehand, that is, with one or more ready-made universal propositions, it candidly declines to work at all. We enquire of " Residues " where we are then to begin, and it says, " I do not know; you had better ask ' Difference.' " We anxiously turn to consider " Difference," and are staggered at once by the distressing extent of the family likeness. A chilling idea now steals into the mind; but we have gone too far to retreat at once, so, resolutely turning our back upon " Residues," we begin our examination.

(b) We look at the samples of the work produced, and we find the same thing turning up everywhere. The material supplied to be dealt with by the Methods is never facts but is always universals. Sometimes an open and professed generalization is used as a starting point. But, where this is not done, the material is never a particular fact. It has always been subjected to such previous operation that it is able at once to be taken and used as a " case " or " instance." But this means that already it is an abstract statement, ideal and not real, capable of repetition with other environment, and without doubt universal. Take the very first instance: " Let the antecedent A be the contact of an alkaline substance and an oil. This combination being tried under several varieties of circumstances, resembling each other in nothing else, the results agree in the production of a greasy and detersive or saponaceous substance " (*Logic*, III. viii. § 1). And this is the *raw material* which is supplied. Before I begin my induction I am to know already that, under certain sets of definite conditions exactly known, certain results have followed. But, if I know this, I also know that these results will *always* follow given the conditions. Every one of the instances is already an universal proposition; and it is not a particular fact or phenomenon at all.*

§ 8. It seems at first a strange obliquity of instinct to

* Cf. Whewell, *Philosophy of Discovery*, p. 263.

choose illustrations which *can not* illustrate.* But on turning
to examine the Canons themselves, our surprise gives place to
another feeling. The illustrations have been selected, not
according to choice, but from hard necessity. For the Canons
are such that *ex hypothesi* they can not possibly work upon
any material but universal propositions.

FIRST CANON.

*If two or more instances of the phenomenon under investi-
gation have only one circumstance in common, the circumstance in which alone all the instances agree, is the cause (or
effect) of the given phenomenon.*

SECOND CANON.

*If an instance in which the phenomenon under investiga-
tion occurs, and an instance in which it does not occur, have
every circumstance in common save one, that one occurring
only in the former; the circumstance in which alone the two
instances differ, is the effect, or the cause, or an indispensable
part of the cause, of the phenomenon.*

THIRD CANON.

*If two or more instances in which the phenomenon occurs
have only one circumstance in common, while two or more
instances in which it does not occur have nothing in common
save the absence of that circumstance; the circumstance in
which alone the two sets of instances differ, is the effect, or
the cause, or an indispensable part of the cause, of the phenomenon.*

FOURTH CANON.

*Subduct from any phenomenon such part as is known by
previous inductions to be the effect of certain antecedents, and
the residue of the phenomenon is the effect of the remaining
antecedents.*

FIFTH CANON.

*Whatever phenomenon varies in any manner whenever
another phenomenon varies in some particular manner, is
either a cause or an effect of that phenomenon, or is connected*

* There is an exception which I will deal with in § 9

with it through some fact of causation. (Mill, *Logic,* III.
viii.)

Consider the phrases "*only one circumstance in common,*"
"*every circumstance in common but one,*" "*nothing in common save the absence of that circumstance.*" Only think for a
moment and realize what they mean, and then take on the
other hand a given fact of perception. The fact is *made* a
particular fact by the presence of that, the absence of which is
postulated beforehand by these formulas. A universal judgment is *made* universal by just those attributes which are
pronounced indispensable in the material for these Methods.
The moment you have reduced your particular fact to a perfectly definite set of elements, existing in relations which are
accurately known, there you have left the fact behind you.
You have already a judgment universal in the same sense in
which the result of your "induction" is universal. Let us
take once again the very first instance. The universal which
you come to is "that the combination of an oil and an alkali
causes the production of soap." The universals which you
start with are that an oil and an alkali, if combined under conditions *bc* and *de,* in each case produce soap. But how can you
deny that these latter are universals? No doubt they are
impure; but the result of the "induction" is surely not quite
pure. And is an impure universal no universal at all? If
you assert this, you deny the efficacy of your "induction."
If you will not assert it, then you admit that your "inductions" are not inductive, since the base they start from is
not individual facts. If we regard the formulas for a little
steadily, we must surely see that an "instance" which is
capable of being so formulated, has had already done upon it
that work which we heard the Methods, *and the Methods
alone,* were capable of performing. And, if so, these Methods
must retire from the field or withdraw their claims. Something like a farce has been played before us, whether we
consider the airs and pretences of the Canons, or remember
the promises and the boasts of their patron.

§ 9. But I may be reminded of and in fairness I must quote
an instance, selected by the author himself, to show that his
Methods can deal with common material. And the instance

has the greater relevancy here, since he devised it expressly to meet the objection that the conditions of his formulas could not be found in facts.

"If it had been my object to justify the processes themselves as means of investigation, there would have been no need to look far off, or make use of recondite or complicated instances. As a specimen of a truth ascertained by the Method of Agreement, I might have chosen the proposition ' Dogs bark.' This dog, and that dog, and the other dog, answer to ABC, ADE, AFG. The circumstance of being a dog, answers to A. Barking answers to a. As a truth made known by the Method of Difference, ' Fire burns ' might have sufficed. Before I touch the fire I am not burnt; this is BC; I touch it, and am burnt; this is ABC, aBC." (*Logic,* III. ix. 6.)

The Canons we think are not hard to content if this will satisfy them. But surely their author had forgotten them for the moment. By seeing three barking dogs I perceive that they " *have only one circumstance in common.*" By standing in front of a burning fireplace, and then touching the fire and being burnt, I am to know that the two facts " *have every circumstance in common but one.*" Is not this preposterous? Surely it is clear in the first case that Mr. Mill's way of arguing might prove just as well that all dogs have the mange, and in the second that every fireplace blisters. And these conclusions hardly seem to be sound.*

If we have succeeded so far in establishing this point, then the Methods of induction are placed in this dilemma. Because they *presuppose* universal truths, therefore they are not the only way of proving them. But if they are the only way of proving them, then every universal truth is unproved.

§ 10. (II.) The second assertion I have now to make good, is that the process of the Methods is not *inductive*. I do not mean merely that, as we have seen, they can not be applied except to universals. I mean in addition that it is not at all

---

* As a test of the writer's accuracy in small points, we may notice that in the second example there is a mistake in the working of the Method. The right conclusion is " Touching burns "; for the fire is not the differential condition. It was there before I touched it, and if it was not there, then we have *two* differences and another kind of mistake.

of the essence of their process to bring out a conclusion more
general than the premises. The process is one of elimination
(cf. Book III. p. 412). By removing one part of an ideal construction you establish the remainder. And hence the result
will be more abstract than the whole original *datum,* but it
need not be more abstract than some of the premises; on the
contrary it may be less so.[4] If five plums, two apples, and ten
nuts balance the scales against three pears, two peaches, and
six grapes, when I know that the nuts weigh the same as the
grapes, and the apples as the peaches, I infer that the plums
and the pears are equal by an ideal process of removing the
rest. But if this is "induction," then "$x + 5 - 3 = a + 4$
$- 2$, and therefore $x = a$," and again "A is either b or c, A
is not c, and therefore it is b," will also be inductions. And
if everything is induction which is not syllogism, then certainly these inferences are all inductive. But such an assumption would surely be quite erroneous. It finds its parallel in
the counterpart mistake, that, because the Inductive Methods
are not really "inductive," therefore they are syllogistic.

The Methods are all of them Methods of Residues or
Methods of Difference, and they all go to their conclusion in
the self-same way. They fix a relation between certain wholes,
and then, by the removal of parts of each, establish this
relation between the remaining elements. In the Methods of
Agreement and Concomitant Variations the principle is the
same as it is in the rest. In the former the *data* are ABC —
def, AGH — *dij,* AKL — *dmn.* It is then assumed that the *d*
in *def, dij,* and *dmn,* can not be produced by a different cause;
and hence, since BC, GH, KL are different, they do not
produce *d*. A is the residue or difference, and therefore A is
the cause. The process we shall see is vicious, but, such as it
is, it is elimination. In Concomitant Variations we seem to
have $A^1BC — d^1ef$; and then, when A^1 becomes A^2, we have
$A^2BC — d^2ef$. From this whole take away $^1BC — {}^1ef$, $^2BC —$
^2ef and the conclusion is $A — d$. The principle involved is the
same throughout, and the apparent failure to see this, and the
setting down of two or three co-ordinate axioms for the
different Methods, is another sign that the writer had never got
really inside his subject. The different Methods are different
applications of one single process, and since the premises

eliminated may be just as abstract as the conclusion left behind, this process can hardly be called "inductive."

§ 11. Having seen first of all that the Canons will not work unless applied to universals; having seen, in the second place, that within these limits their procedure is not essentially one of generalization, we come now to the third of our objections. The Methods are vicious and the Canons are false.

(III.) I do not mean to say that, for all the purposes of discovery, the flaws in the Methods amount to serious mistakes. Such a contention would lie beyond the scope of my volume. It is certain, however, that independent logicians, such as Dr. Whewell and Professor Jevons in our own country, and Professors Lotze and Sigwart in Germany, have taken a view of the process of scientific discovery which is not favourable to the claims of the Four Methods. But whatever may be the usefulness of these Methods, the point here at issue is their validity as *proofs*.

What I wish to show is that they will not prove anything beyond this or that individual case. They pass to their more general conclusion by illegitimate assumptions.

§ 12. I think the reader will agree that, if a method will prove a false conclusion from premises which are true, then that method must be logically vicious, and its Canon, which serves as a test, must be false. Now it is stated by Mr. Mill himself that the Method of Agreement will prove false conclusions (*Logic*, Chap. X.). The Method is "uncertain" and has an "imperfection." But it still continues to figure as a proof, and the Canon is left standing in its naked falsity. We also have "axioms" implied in this Method, which can hardly be true if the Method is false, and which yet are left exposed to the daylight. We are told (Chap. X. § 1) that in chapters preceding false assumptions have been made, and yet the chapters with all their contents are recommended to us still as a sort of Gospel. And here I must frankly confess myself at a loss. Can the writer really have known that all his Canons were false statements? Whether he did or did not, I will not here enquire, for the discussion would not be likely to profit us. It will be perhaps convenient for the sake of argument to assume that he did not know the full vice of all his Methods.

The Method of Agreement starts from the premises ABC — *def*,* AGH — *dij*, AKL — *dmn:* and its conclusion is that A is the cause of *d*. The principle it goes on is (as we saw before) that whatever is different in the different cases can be eliminated. And this principle is false, since a consequence, such as *d*, need not always follow from the same antecedent.[5] The generalization is therefore vicious, and the Canon which regulates it is false. The axioms also, given in § 2 of the same eighth chapter, are no less false. To make them true you must qualify them by adding " in this one case." But that means you must destroy their generalizing power.

§ 13. The Method of Difference is no less vicious.† From the premises ABC — *def*, BC — *ef*, it goes to the conclusion that A is the cause or an indispensable part of the cause of *d*. But this conclusion is fatally unsound. A may be here a single factor in the production of *d*, the presence of which is quite accidental. The rule may be for *d* to be produced entirely without A, and for A to be present without producing *d*. The foundation of the Method ‡ " that whatever can not be eliminated, is connected with the phenomenon by a law " is quite false, unless we add to it *" in this one case,"* and thereby make it ineffectual for the purpose of generalizing.

The Method of Joint Agreement and Difference is essentially the same, and presents the same flaw. Its premises consist of ABC — *def*, AGH — *dij*, AKL — *dmn*, BC — *ef*, GH — *ij*, KL — *mn*. It infers from these the conclusion A — *d*. The mistake is the same as that which vitiated Difference. The right conclusion is that, *in these three cases*, A has gone to produce *d*.

In the Method of Residues the process is the same, and is bad for the same reason. From ABC — *def*, B — *f*, C — *e*, the Method goes on at once to A — *d*. But it could do so legitimately, only if it excluded the possibility of B or C, or

---

* I have *of course* altered Mill's lettering. If his letters *mean* anything, they involve a flagrant *petitio;* and if they do not, their suggestion must tend to confuse us.

† For further explanation see Bk. III. II. Chap. III. §§ 11 foll.

‡ There is no material difference between this and what is wrongly given, in the same § 3, as different, and as the ground of the Method of Agreement; for you have postulated a connection in your premises. I have given above the real ground of the Method of Agreement.

both, having influenced, and been influenced by, A. Otherwise the conclusion like all the rest is vicious, and its Canon is false, unless qualified by the words "*in this one case.*"

We come in the end to Concomitant Variations, and the principle of this has, I think, not been formulated with the desirable exactness. In the first place the words *whenever* in the Canon itself and *invariably* in the Axiom assigned to it are both ambiguous. If they mean that the groups of elements are causally connected, then this must rest upon a previous Method, and not upon mere facts. And in the second place, if we consider the process as a conclusion from these idealized premises, still it is impossible even then to demonstrate a result which will hold beyond this or that case (or cases). The premises appear to be $A^1BC - d^1ef$, $A^2BC - d^2ef$, $A^3BC - d^3ef$, and the conclusion arrived at seems to be $A - d$. We have apparently to eliminate *everything* but $A - d$, which is hence left as proved. But since once again the factors are not isolated, we have the old mistake of Difference once more. The real conclusion is "*In this one case (or set of cases*) without A no *d.*" Because the modification of A has altered the result, therefore A is relevant to *d* in *this* alteration, or series of alterations. I may add that no amount of instances and of "approximation" will suffice to *demonstrate logically.*

Should however finally the premises not have been so idealized as to be reducible to the formula we have given—if we really have nothing whatever to start with but a certain number of observed concomitances—then there literally is no conclusion at all, for the co-existence always *may* be mere chance coincidence. And, according as we understand the Canon and the Axiom, we must pronounce them to be either insufficient or false.

§ 14. I have shown that, if used in order to generalize beyond this or that individual instance as prepared for treatment, the Methods are vicious, and their Canons false. Their eliminative process will only show that the whole antecedent has been concerned in producing the whole consequent (cf. Book III.). The attempt to go further and, by isolating the factors, to transcend the limits of the premises supplied, we have seen has broken down at all points.[6]

In the premises $ABC - def$, $BC - ef$, you are supposed to

know that *def* is connected with ABC, and *ef* with BC: what you do *not* yet know is if, in ABC, A is really a factor. For it might be irrelevant, and BC without it might produce *def*. But now, having BC — *ef,* and resting on the assumption which we call the Principle of Identity (Book I. Chap. V.), you are sure that, if BC — *ef* is once true, it will be true for ever. And you proceed from this to argue that BC — *def* must be false. For to produce *def* B must have been altered: and since in ABC — *def* the result is produced with no possible alteration except mere A, A there must be relevant to the presence of *def.* Hence A *in this case* (of ABC — *def*) must be, directly or indirectly, relevant to *d.* But you must not go further, and try in any way to specify the connection. For you can not do that without closing possibilities, and assuming something not given in your premises.*

And we must not forget that even this conclusion depends on our having assumed in the premises that, in ABC — *def, d* is not irrelevant. Unless we are perfectly sure beforehand that the whole *def* has been produced by ABC, we can not advance one single step. This shows once more how absurd it is to imagine that the Methods can be applied to particular facts. They depend entirely on such an artificial preparation of the material supplied, as has already reduced it to the form of an universal. It would be waste of time to dwell further on the detail of the Four (or Five) Methods, since the process in all is the same at bottom.†

§ 15. We have seen that the Methods are not " inductive," since they will not generalize beyond the given instance. They fail again of being " inductive," since they can not be applied to simple facts. They will not work unless they are supplied with universals. They presuppose in short as their own condition the result they profess alone to produce. Once more, the essence of their procedure is as much deductive as it is " inductive." The conclusion in some cases has less generality than some of the premises.

On any one of these grounds (and I hope on all of them)

---

* I should like here, and on the whole subject, to refer to Lotze's *Logik,* II. VII.

† I must refer to the following Book for an account of inference by way of Elimination.

we may set down the Inductive Logic as a *fiasco*. And, if I am told that these flaws, or most of them, are already admitted by Inductive Logicians, I will not retract the word I have used. But to satisfy the objector I will give way so far as to write for *fiasco, confessed fiasco.*

§ 16. If it really is the case that the Methods are not sound; if it really is the case that the Canons are not true; if it really is the case that "induction" is *not proof,* and that he has all along known this, and been well aware of it—in that case I would suggest to the Inductive Logician that he has provoked a possible harsh remark. And however mistaken that harsh judgment might be, yet I can not help thinking that it would be better if *he* were to tell the public, what they certainly do not know, and the opposite of which his too large professions have led them to believe. But if, as I suppose, the Inductive Logician himself makes the mistake which his public has accepted—if, that is, while admitting that, like all things human, his Methods have "imperfections," he has no idea that, taken as proofs, they are radically vicious —in that case I will end by expressing the hope of a final agreement.[7] By abridging claims that will not stand criticism, and by reforming the root and principle of his fabric, he will bring no ruin to the bulk of his edifice. Even if we confined ourselves to Mr. Mill's Logic, we should find that, when his so-called Four Inductive Methods were wholly removed, and his inference from mere particulars banished as a misunderstanding, the more valuable and even the larger part of his discussions on Science would remain untouched.

ADDITIONAL NOTES

[1] "If we go with the fashion." I have to remind the reader once more that this refers to the year 1883.

[2] This account of Complete Enumeration and the Collective Judgment is very seriously wrong. Indeed what is said in this volume about the Collective Judgment (see Index) needs correction perhaps throughout. For a true account of the matter I must refer the reader to Bosanquet, *K & R*, pp. 76 foll., and *Logic*, I, 152 foll. The main point is this, that all counting presupposes and depends on a qualitative Whole, and that the Collective Judgment asserts a generic

connection within its group. Hence no mere particulars can be counted. I regret the superficiality of my treatment in this work.

[3] " One single case." If this means " One single sheep," it is obviously wrong; and it is still wrong even if it means " each single sheep." What is true is that the group is taken as a region within which a universal connection holds throughout. Hence, and hence alone, we can use such expressions as " any " and " one case with."

A minor point is that for " any folded sheep " we should read " any sheep folded *here.*" This difference points to the weakness of the Collective Judgment. But on the whole subject see Bosanquet, *Logic,* I, 152 foll.

[4] " On the contrary it may be less so." What I meant here is this, that the residue *may* be less abstract than something which has been removed, or which has at least been used in the removal. But the point (however defensible) might have been omitted as superfluous.

[5] " Need not always follow from the same antecedent." This statement would, of course, be false if the sequence were pure and so " reciprocal." But here you can not assume that your premises are pure, since you are not taken to know *what* your " one circumstance " really is. On the Method of Difference cf. Bk. III. II. III. § 13.

[6] " At all points," i.e. if induction is taken as proof.

[7] There is no positive doctrine as to " Induction " set out in this work, nor had I any independent view on the subject. In the main I should have accepted, and should still accept, the view advocated by Jevons, with its two main features of Hypothesis and Verification.

CHAPTER IV

JEVONS' EQUATIONAL LOGIC [1]

§ 1. It is pleasant, after leaving the delusions of one's youth, to find oneself in contact with something like fact. The Equational Logic has proved by its results that it has a hold on the world of reality. What works must at least be partially right. And this new theory of logic does work. One may see that its method remains inapplicable to part of its subject. One may question its convenience in certain cases, and even doubt its formula in all. But one must believe so much as this. At the lowest estimate the new system will prove whatever the syllogism is able to prove. In some points it certainly is a far more rigid test of true reasoning. It deals very easily with many of the problems which accommodate themselves to numerical reasoning. And it maintains, on the ground both of reason and experience, that, in comparison with the syllogism, it is both easier to learn and harder to forget.

In writing this chapter on equational logic, as it appears in the theory of Professor Jevons, I wish I could do two things I can not do. I wish I could give an account of the doctrine intelligible to those who have no acquaintance with it. And I wish I could form something like an estimate of its educational value and practical powers. But both want of space and want of experience compel me to a narrower and less grateful task. The object of this chapter is to ask if that account of the reasoning process which has been offered us is strictly accurate, whether as a theory it is free from mistakes. An answer in the negative will be given to this question.

§ 2. We may divide the enquiry into three main parts. In the first (A) we shall ask if propositions are identities: in the second (B) if direct reasoning consists in substitution. In the third (C) we shall discuss the Indirect Method, and with it the claims of the Logical Machine. It may prove convenient to state beforehand the main results which we expect to reach. We shall show in the first place (A) that, though every propo-

370

sition does and must assert identity, yet that is not the *object* of all propositions. Our second conclusion (B) will be that substitution is not the real essence of reasoning, and that certain inferences will not by fair means come under this head. We shall show again that, although most arguments can be exhibited in the form of equations, yet the formula of inference which our author has given is not correct. In the third place (C) we shall argue that the Indirect Method, though perfectly valid, does not proceed by substitution: and finally we shall give our reasons for contesting a part of the claims put forth by the Machine. The reader is supposed to have made some acquaintance with the early part of *The Principles of Science*.

§ 3. (A) In asking if propositions are equations, we must remember that the sign = does *not* mean *equal* (cf. p. 23). It denotes sameness or identity. So that the word "equation," which we have chosen to start with, may at once be dismissed. The question is, Do judgments consist in the assertion of identity? This point has already come before us, and great part of what follows is repetition.

1. If we dismiss all theories and look simply at the facts, then to ask that question is to answer it in the negative. How can it be said that in "Cæsar is sick," or "This pond is frozen," or "Mammals are warm-blooded," we really mean to assert self-sameness? To say that, in making such statements as these, our real object is the denial of difference—that we wish to say, Although Cæsar is sick he still is Cæsar—is palpably absurd. We do not wish, premising the difference, to insist on the identity. The difference itself is the information which we wish to convey.

2. If all propositions asserted mere identity, then every proposition would have to be false. If $A = B$ and $B = BC$, and we go from this to the conclusion $A = C$, then either B makes a difference to A or it makes no difference. In the one case the proposition becomes quite false, and in the other it disappears, since $B = o$. How can it be true that ABC is the same as A? Is BC nothing, then nothing is asserted. Is BC a difference, then how are they the same?

Partial identities are thus all false; but simple identities will fare no better. If " = " is taken to stand for "is the same as," then "$A = B$" can not possibly be true. If there is

no difference, then nothing is said; if anything is said, then
sameness is denied.

3. It is obvious, if we are to keep to identity, that subject and predicate must be wholly the same. $AB = AB$,
$ABC = ABC$. But even here it is doubtful if we can stay.
For even when we reach a tautologous statement we have still
a difference in the position of the terms (cf. Book I. Chap. V.).
If we wish to be consistent even that must go. We must
take one side of our former reduplication; we must say, for
instance, AB or ABC. In that, having given up our search
for identity, we suddenly find the whole content of our assertion. Assume AB, then A is B. Assume ABC, then A is C.
In our seeking to get an equational truth, we got all the differences together on each side. But the synthesis of these
differents was just what we really wanted to assert. Strike
out one side, and strike out the " $=$," and we have the content
of the whole judgment.*

Assertion is not confined to the affirmation of sameness,
and identity and equality are but one kind of predicate. If
we use the language of the traditional logic, then in " $S = P$ "
the " $=$ " has nothing to do with the copula: it falls entirely
within the predicate, and " $A = AB$ " is " $A-=AB$." If
we wish to say that A is equal to or the same as B, the natural
mode is, I think, to say that A and B are the same or equal.
If we will not do that, and so openly admit the existence of
difference, we must come in the end to " $A = B$," on the left
hand side, is just the same as " $A = B$," on the right hand
side. And since the sides are different even that is not true.

§ 4. The foregoing section merely asserts that a difference
is affirmed by every proposition. Judgment can not be reduced
to one-sided identification. In the attempt to reduce it we
found that we got the whole matter of the judgment on each
side of the copula. Thus in " sodium $=$ sodium metal conducting electricity " the judgment falls on the right hand side.
The assertion consists in the synthesis with sodium of the
being a metal and conducting electricity; and, when we know
that, the " sodium " and the " $=$," of the subject and copula,
are false or meaningless. You say that it makes no difference

---

* We are not dealing here with "simple identities." For them
see § 6.

to sodium that it is a metal and conducts electricity. That surely is a rather odd method of saying that there is no difference whatever to make, and a still more eccentric method of implying that this makes all the difference to sodium.

§ 5. No proposition asserts *mere* identity, but without the statement or implication of identity no judgment can be made. The solution of this puzzle, which the end of the foregoing section hints at, is that sameness and difference imply one another, and are different sides of the self-same fact. Mere identity or difference is therefore unmeaning. And hence, although it is false that in judging we always mean to identify the subject and predicate, yet in every judgment an identity can be found. For where sameness is asserted difference is presupposed. Where difference is asserted there is a basis of sameness which underlies it. And it follows as a consequence that, if you do not mind your implications being put on a level with your meanings, you can show every judgment in the form of difference united by identity.

§ 6. For in every judgment the differences joined may be taken as the qualities of a single subject [2] (cf. p. 27, and p. 180). In "sodium = sodium metal" we assert that within the subject called sodium the attributes sodium and metal are conjoined; and if you please you may express this by saying, that, under the differences sodium and metal, there is yet no change from one subject to another. Again, in "Equilateral triangle = equiangular triangle" what I mean to say is that, despite these differences, you still have one and the same triangle, or again that, if one of these qualities exists, you will have the other in the self-same subject. Take again "The Pole Star = the slowest-moving star:" this means either that one star possesses these two differences, or that, in spite of these differences, the star is the same. In every case we have identity and diversity, and, though we accentuate one or the other, yet in every case both must co-exist.

I will illustrate the foregoing by other instances. Take "These fifteen statements are every one perjuries." The identical subject is here either each statement or the quality of perjury which appears in each. There are hence four meanings. In the first I assert that in every statement perjury must be added to its other qualities. In the second

I deny that, though the statements are false,[3] we have any right to abolish the perjury by making thirty statements out of fifteen. In the third I complain that a single crime has occurred with fifteen different sets of details. In the fourth I refuse to admit the diversity of the fifteen qualifications as any proof that the crime is not the same.

Or take the instance of equality or sameness itself. When I say that A and B are equal, I assert that in the differents A and B their quantity x is for all that the same. If I say " A and B are precisely the same," I must first take A and B as differenced by place or time or some other particular, and then against that assert their identity. The equality in one case and the sameness in the other may be treated as the subject in which A and B co-exist as attributes.

If the doctrine already put forward is true, there can be no such things as "simple identities." " Equiangular triangle = equilateral triangle " is false if it denies the difference of quality, or is false if it ignores the distinction of subjects. The identity it asserts must exist under differences. Thus among triangles the subject of equilateral is one and the same with the subject of equiangular. The natural way to state the fact is to say, The different subjects are the same, or The diverse qualities imply one another.

§ 7. The result of our enquiry as to propositions is not of good augury for the doctrine of Substitution. True we find that all subjects assert an identity, but then they no less assert a difference. Our sign " = " has turned out quite inapplicable. If S and P are made quite identical, the judgment disappears or falls only on one side. If again S and P are allowed to be different, the sign of identity asserts a falsehood. This so far is ominous. It is ominous again that every identity can be shown as the connection of attributes within a subject. And there is another omen we have not yet noticed. All judgments, we long ago have found, can be understood as assertions of identity. But the class of relations in time and space, it appears, are not amenable to the Method of Substitution, or at least in public decline to appear so (cf. Book I. p. 22). I can not but think that with such auspices against it any cause must be lost.

§ 8. (B) We come now to the second branch of our sub-

ject. Does the process of reasoning consist in substitution?
The foregoing has shown that this is not possible.

(1) The terms which we substitute must be the same: but
if the same then you can not substitute. If your process does
not give you a difference, it is no process. If it gives you a
difference you have broken the identity. Thus if reasoning
consists in substitution, its essence lies in the substitution of
differents.

Let us take as an example, "A is equal to B, and B to C,
and therefore A to C." It is impossible here by substitution
of identicals to come to any conclusion whatever. For what
is there identical? A is not the same as B, nor B as C, nor is
"equal to B" the same as A. The identity really lies in the
quantity of A, B, and C. The quantity of A and B is the
same, and so is that of C and B. The quantity therefore of
A and C is the same. But you can not show this by substitution. For in the *quantity* of each there is *no difference*.
The terms are x A, x B, x C. Now if you substitute x A for
x B, you substitute things which are not the same. But if you
substitute mere x, you do nothing at all, for already you have
the term x B. A is equal to B, but it is not the same. The
quantity is the same, but it is one and not two.

The real process of the reasoning consists in connecting
the differences A and C on the basis of their common identity
x. It may also be stated as a substitution. Take x with any
one of the differences, and substitute x with any other difference. The differences then found co-existing in x will be the
conclusion which we require. But this substitution is a replacement by *differents*.

§ 9. (2) Substitution, so far as it works at all, is an
indirect method of synthesizing differences. The rule is to
substitute the "expression" for the term. But the "expression" is the judgment about the term. The rule then says
"Substitute the judgment for the term." In other words,
a term will not do; you must have a premise, and that means
a judgment. You must leave your identity and get to differences.

In "sodium is metal and conducts electricity" (§ 4),
sodium-metal takes the place of sodium, and metal gives way
to metal-conductor, and we say this makes no difference to

sodium, or sodium is the same with all this difference. But the real subject, which remains the same, is something which underlies these differences; and the real process is the addition of difference which developes the connection of attributes in this subject. It is entirely to mistake our object in view if, while we try to get the synthesis of diverse attributes, we talk as if all we wanted was to keep the identity of the subject. It is simply to stand the process on its head, if we make every step by uniting differences, and then speak as if throughout we had done nothing but remove them.

"Substitute for the terms their expressions," that is in other words *combine the premises*. It is an artificial way of performing the old task. For reasons which I can not here enter into, the artifice in some cases is very useful. But it is simply the syllogism turned upside down, and it is confined to the same insufficient limits.

§ 10. (3) The method of Substitution has set itself free from some of the superstitions of the traditional logic. For certain purposes it is far more useful. Everything again that can be proved by syllogism can also be proved by its modern rival. But on the other hand Substitution will prove nothing that can not be shown by syllogism. The limit of both is precisely the same. They are confined to the relation of subject and attribute and the connection of attributes within a subject; and beyond that category neither will work (cf. Bk. II. Part I. Chap. II. § 6).

To prove syllogistically that, because A and C are both equal to B, they are equal to one another, is quite impossible.* But it is just as impossible to prove the conclusion by substitution. The premises you have got are A = A equal to B, B = B equal to C; and the *quaternio terminorum* can only be avoided by taking the premises in a sense which is false.

It is needless to repeat against the equational logic the

---

* "Quantity of A is the same as quantity of B, quantity of B is the same as quantity of C, and therefore quantity of A is quantity of C" will not do at all. If the quantity is taken in abstraction then it certainly is the same, but you can not show from that that A, B, and C are related as equals or related in any way. But if you take the quantity in its relations to A and B and C, in that case you have *quaternio terminorum*, or otherwise the premises become false. The relation of equality never could be got out in the conclusion.

objections we have urged against the syllogism. If a logic
will not deal with the syntheses of degree, of space, and of
time; if even, as we shall see, its own Indirect Method falls
outside its boundaries, then that logic does not give the true
method of reasoning. It is not made too narrow because it
requires an identity underlying the terms of its premises. It
is made too narrow because in its conclusions it is confined to
the category of subject and attribute. In a remarkable passage (*Principles,* Ed. II. p. 22) I understand Professor Jevons
to admit these limitations. His logic, so far as it exists at
present, appears to be confined to " simple relations." " A
simple logical relation is that which exists between properties
and circumstances of the same object or class." But, if that
is so, then the theory of reasoning will cover only one portion
of the facts.

§ 11. (4) We have seen that, within the syllogistic limits,
equational logic will work very well; and we also have seen
the nature of its process. However right it is to insist that in
reasoning identity is necessary, yet exactly the same must be
said of difference. And I can not think that, in laying down
his principle of inference and in reducing it to a formula,
Professor Jevons has avoided serious mistakes.

" So far as there exists sameness, identity or likeness, what
is true of one thing will be true of the other." " In whatever
relation a thing stands to a second thing, in the same relation
it stands to the like or equivalent of that second thing " (pp.
9, 17).

Now if the " likeness " in these formulas means absence of
difference, we see at once that they are tautologous or false.
For so far as *mere* identity exists, what is true of any one
thing must for that very reason be false of another. If, in the
case of A, B, and C, the judgment A—C is true of A so far as
A is simply the same as B, then it either is not true of A at
all, or else the differences have all disappeared, and the judgment becomes $x = x$. So again, if A is related to B, it is
related to that which is the same as B. But " the same as B "
will be simply B, and we have not advanced one single step.

§ 12. But if the formulas have another meaning, then what
shall we say that their meaning is? They certainly can not
mean that mere likeness will do. A need not be like C because

both are like B. And it is obvious that if B and C are "equivalent," A need not stand in one relation to both. Two coins are equivalent and one is in my pocket, but neither logic nor fact makes me master of the other. It is clear that this can not be our author's meaning.

The equivalence or likeness, to be that which is meant, must exist to a sufficient extent or degree. But what is the degree which is sufficient? "The general test of equality is substitution" (*Principles*, p. 19). But here again our question is not answered. It would never do to say, you may substitute when you have a sufficient degree of likeness, and that degree again consists in your ability to make a substitution. And this is not what is meant. What I think is meant is that a certain amount of likeness will give conclusions, and that, when you can substitute, you may know it is there. But I do not think that Professor Jevons has anywhere told us in what that degree itself consists.

§ 13. Still I think he has given us the materials for an answer. The question we have before us is this: Given a term B in relation with C; or otherwise, Given C as what is true of B, then what amount of sameness between A and B will warrant us in writing A for B? The first answer to be given is that no amount is wanted. There is not the very smallest need for A and B to be like or equivalent. But the second answer to be given is this: the sameness required is the sameness of the one subject. If A and B are both qualities of X, or again if B is a quality of A, then A and C will be interrelated. The quality of the subject is the middle term, whose predicates in some way qualify the subject. Or the identity of the subject [4] is the middle term and, so far as this identity extends, the attributes must all be related and conjoined.

We have finished our examination of the theory of propositions, and also of reasoning by substitution. We come now to a third and most important point, the question of the Indirect Method and the Logical Machine. I will anticipate briefly the result we shall reach. (*a*) The essence of the Indirect Method is a process which can not possibly be reduced to substitution. (*b*) In part of that process substitution may be used, but another form of reasoning is just as applicable.

(c) The Machine will not really give complete conclusions.
(d) It is improperly limited to one kind of reasoning.

§ 14. (C) (a) The Indirect Method is a process of exclusion. In using it you must first find all the possibilities, and then by removal of the rest you leave only one. In other words, you have a disjunction, and remove all alternatives except a single remainder. *Because* the subject, if taken as real, must be taken as fully determined and particularized, *therefore* the remaining possibility is real (cf. Book I. Chap. IV.). A is *b, c,* or *d,* it is not *b* or *c,* it *therefore* is *d.* This is the essence of the Indirect Method, and we already have to some extent made its acquaintance.

§ 15. We know that this process falls outside syllogism. And from that we might argue at this stage of our enquiry that it can not be reduced to substitution. But if it can not be reduced to substitution, Professor Jevons' best work contradicts his theory. Let us see how he tries to avoid this consequence.

"The general rule is that from the denial of any of the alternatives the affirmation of the remainder can be inferred. Now this result clearly follows from our process of substitution; for if we have the proposition—

$$A = B \cdot | \cdot C \cdot | \cdot D,$$

and we insert this expression for A on one side of the self-evident identity

$$Ab = Ab,$$

we obtain $$Ab = ABb \cdot | \cdot AbC \cdot | \cdot AbD;$$

and, as the first of the three alternatives is self-contradictory, we strike it out according to the law of contradiction; there remains

$$Ab = AbC \cdot | \cdot AbD.$$

Thus our system fully includes and explains that mood of the Disjunctive Syllogism technically called the *modus tollendo ponens*" (*Principles,* p. 77).*

But this, I think, will not stand a moment's examination.

* I may remind the reader that $\cdot | \cdot$ here means "or," and *b* means "Not-B." I do not use these signs in the text.

In the first place the operation of striking out one part and asserting the rest *is the essence of the method,* and yet it is not even in appearance reduced to substitution. In the second place in this example the reasoning by substitution is perfectly useless. It does not bring you one step on your way towards the conclusion.

I will take a perfectly simple instance. "A is b or c," and "A is not b." These are the premises, and from these I should say that you go directly to the conclusion "A is c." Professor Jevons, if I understand him rightly, contends that you go through a process of substitution. $A = b$ or c, $A = $ not-b. Insert the expression for A, "A is b or c," on one side of A not-b = A not-b. Then A not-b, = A not-b and b or A not-b and c. But A not-b and $b = o$, therefore A not-b $= o$ or not-b and c.

But surely, if words have any meaning, when I know that A is b or c, and that A is not b, I do know at once that b must be removed. And, on my removing b by an ideal experiment, c by itself is what I have left. If I please I may write this "c or o." But I really can not perceive what advantage I get by turning in a circle to come back to my starting-place. A is b or c, and it is not b. If possible however let A be b. But, if it is b, it will be b and not-b. That is impossible, and therefore follows—what? Why simply that A is not b. I have used the premise to prove *itself.* And, if in answer I am told that this is not so, for I have enriched what was given me by the alternative "or o," then it seems to me that I may fairly reply, If you do not know, given *only* b and c, that when b is gone, c is what is left behind; then how on earth can you tell that, given "c or o," when o is gone, c is all that is left? I confess to me one is no clearer than the other.

§ 16. What I think has occasioned this complete mistake is an erroneous idea as to indirect reasoning. For that we must have a disjunction to start with, and by removing one member we prove the other. And we *generally* have to use direct reasoning downwards. We assume as one of our premises that alternative which we want in the end to get rid of, and on this assumption we bring out a conclusion which contradicts something contained in the premises. This is the usual course, but it is not more than *usual*. Direct reasoning downwards is not *always* wanted. For when the premises themselves give the removal of one alternative, what more *can* we prove by such direct reasoning? We have in our hands not only the disjunction, but *also* the exclusion of one alternative. Where direct reasoning is required it is simply preliminary to the final operation, and is wanted merely to prepare the subject; and when the premises give the subject ready prepared, what is there which we possibly can have to wait for?

And I think this mistake is connected with another. I suspect that an error as to the Laws of Contradiction and Excluded Middle has helped to lead our author into this pitfall. But when we know that the Law of Excluded Middle [5] is one case of disjunction, and in no sense the basis of it (Book I. p. 151), we see at once that no mystical force arises from the proof of a self-contradiction. If we get to that by turning in a circle, the end will hardly justify the means. It has no power to absolve our consciences from the ordinary sin of logical fallacy.

I must not be considered as wanting in respect, if I illustrate what I mean by another instance. Suppose that my premise is " A is *b*." Will any one deny that to prove from this that " A is *b* " is a frivolous circle? But it is easily done. For, if possible, suppose that A is not *b;* then A will be both *b* and not-*b*: or insert, on one side of the self-evident identity A not-*b* = A not-*b*, the expression for A. Then A not-*b* = A not-*b* and *b*. As one side of our equation is now self-contradictory, we strike it out according to the law of contradiction, and then there remains A not-*b* = o, or A is *b*. I must be allowed to state my conviction that this circle is the same as what we had above. In both cases alike the premise has been used to bring out nothing whatever but that which it gave.

The Indirect Method, we so far have seen, can not be reduced to a process of substitution.

§ 17. (*b*) If we consider that Method as employed by Professor Jevons, it does make use of the equational form, but there is no real necessity for its so doing. This process consists of the following four steps.

" 1. By the Law of Duality develope the utmost number of

alternatives which may exist in the description of the required class or term as regards the terms involved in the premises.

2. For each term in these alternatives substitute its description as given in the premises.

3. Strike out every alternative which is then found to break the Law of Contradiction.

4. The remaining terms may be equated to the term in question as the desired description " (*Principles,* pp. 89-90).

The one part of this process which employs substitution, we see, is the second. But it is performed just as well by the ordinary method. All the possible combinations of the terms are given us, and our object is merely by means of the premises to remove those combinations which the premises contradict. In what shape then ought we to have our premises? Surely one would say in the shape of combinations. It is just such combinations that the ordinary process would give us directly, and we get them by substitution in a roundabout way. For the " description " of the term is, as we saw, the judgment we make about the term. Hence this part of the method, as employed by Professor Jevons, is valid just so far as it can be stated syllogistically. For the premises are combinations of attributes. They are related, as Professor Jevons says, " just as the qualities of the same object " (*ibid.* p. 114) ; and if they were anything else, his method could not deal with them. We can combine them directly, if we please: and it is simply our choice, and perhaps sometimes our convenience, if we combine them from behind through their common subject.

Thus we *may* use substitution to prepare for our conclusion. But we can not use it to draw that conclusion. Its operation ends with the second step.

§ 18. We see, from examining the method itself, that it deals with syntheses or combinations, and does not deal at all with equations. And the method, as practically worked with the machine, confirms the truth of the view which we have taken. Professor Jevons himself with the greatest candour has called attention to this consideration.

" It is no doubt a remarkable fact that a simple identity can not be impressed upon the machine except in the form of two partial identities, and this may be thought by some logicians to militate against the equational mode of representing propositions" (*Principles,* 112).

It would be to me even more than remarkable if the machine *could* work with simple identities. But the fact, which Professor Jevons rightly finds remarkable, has I think a still more remarkable counterpart. The conclusions of the machine, if I understand them properly, contradict one another when read as equations in the sense of assertions of simple identity. $A - B - C$ is consistent with Not-$A - B - C$;[6] but how can we reconcile $A = C$ with $C = $ Not-A?

§ 19. (*c*) We come now to the subject of the Logical Machine, and we have to enquire what work it performs. Of the mechanism employed I have no knowledge. I am so incompetent to say anything about it, that I can not have the pleasure of congratulating Professor Jevons on what I must believe is no small achievement. But what the machine does perform is this. All the possible combinations of the terms are worked out, and are lying ready drawn up in the machine. The operator puts in at one end his premises, each in the shape of a combination. The combinations of these premises remove, each one, all the possibilitites with which it is irreconcileable. And what comes out, so to speak, at the other end of the machine is all the residue of possible combinations which have not been so excluded by the premises. It is easy to exaggerate the powers of the machine. But I think it is impossible to deny that it executes such work, as must otherwise be done by a process of thinking. For myself I do not hesitate to say that it performs mechanically an operation which, if performed ideally, would be an inference. And in this sense I think Professor Jevons is justified in his claim to have made a reasoning machine.[7] Apart from the practical utility of the instrument, which in certain cases may be considerable, we must admit that, from a merely theoretical point of view, it is a most interesting and instructive phenomenon. If Professor Jevons had made no other contributions to logic, we might yet be sure that his name would go down with the history of the science.

But to say on the other hand that the machine will execute the whole process our minds perform in the inference—that the raw material goes in at one side, and the finished conclusion comes out at the other, would be travelling far beyond the fact. Before the premises can be worked on the instrument, they have of course to be reduced and formulated, so as to take the shape of combinations of letters. But this is not the most important point. The result that comes out and is presented by the machine, is not really the conclusion. The process is not finished when the machinery stops; and the rest is left to be done by the mind. What is called "*reading*" the conclusion is to some extent *making* it.

§ 20. I will explain what I mean. In the machine is drawn up a complete disjunction of the possible arrangements of those terms which we employ. Before we begin to work the problem the machine thus supplies us with *one* of our premises. It states *all* possibilities, and this is its strength. But it states *mere* possibilities, and this is its weakness. We begin our operation, and insert the combinations which are given us by our *data*. These combinations are the *rest* of the premises. The machine, as it receives each combination, removes from the list of all the possibilities those which are inconsistent with this *datum*. Then the remainder of the possible combinations are exposed. But they still remain *bare* possibilities, and are never stated as actual facts.

The process may be taken as having five parts. 1. The complete disjunctive statement of possible combinations. This is given ready-made by the machine. 2. The reduction of the premises to the shape of combinations. This is done entirely by the operator. 3. The discovery of those alternatives which are inconsistent with the combinations of the premises. This step is performed entirely by the machine. 4. The removal of those alternatives. This step again is performed by the machine, and it is the first part of that final inference which gives the conclusion. 5. The assertion that what is left is true, and that, if but one possibility remains, that is fact. This is absolutely necessary to complete the inference, and *this is done entirely by the operator*.

The final step may seem to some persons a final superfluity. But on that view of the nature of reasoning by way of the exclusion of alternatives which has seemed to me true, it is integral and essential. Yet it can not be said to be performed by the instrument.

§ 21. I wish to stand on this statement of the case. But

it is possible to use also an *argumentum ad hominem*. If the too undiscriminating friends of the machine assert that its result is a categorical statement, they can hardly fail to compromise it deeply. They will make it an instrument for the production of falsehoods. Let us take one result that is given by the machine (*Principles*, 109).

A — B — C.   Not A — B — C.
Not A — not B — C.   Not A — not B — not C.

Now, there being here but *one* possibility, if A is assumed, we are *practically* safe in contending that the machine categorically asserts this one possibility. But, suppose we take the same line throughout, we plunge at once into a sea of nonsense. Contradictory possibilities can co-exist as long as they remain mere possibilities, but the moment you affirm them as actual fact, they exclude one another. And, if so, either the machine brings out false conclusions, or *all* must be read as mere possibilities. You have no warrant from the machine for the assertion A *is* C. A *may be* C; and because it may be, and because there is nothing else that it may be, and because you know that it must be something to C one way or the other, *you* therefore *infer* that A *is* C, a conclusion not given to you by the machine.

§ 22. (*d*) The machine performs more than we have a right to ask, and it is a pity to credit it with fictitious powers. We have seen that it does not bring out a conclusion. But it is limited beside in another respect. Although it does not work by substitution, yet its range is limited to that kind of inference which is possible in equational logic or in syllogism. It can not deal with any other combinations than those which represent the co-existence of qualities within a subject. And this is a very serious defect; for it means that the machine refuses to touch more than a part of the subject.

This is not the fault of the Indirect Method itself. Apart from restrictions artificially imposed on it, that is applicable everywhere and to all kinds of matter. If my premises are " A is to the right of B, and B of C," I may go directly from these to my conclusion; but, if I choose, I may use the indirect method. The possibilities of A with respect to C are

either absence of any spatial relation, or A to the right of C, or
to the left of C, or *neither* and above it, or below it, &c. But
the premise " A to the right of B," will exclude (as we should
see by an ideal construction) every alternative we can find
other than A to the right of C. For, if we assumed any one of
the others, we should bring out a result incompatible with our
premise. The remaining possibility is therefore fact. This is
perfectly familiar and common-place reasoning, and a system,
in which it can find no place, must assuredly be called at least
incomplete.

§ 23. The result of our perhaps too brief examination may
be stated as follows:—

1. The Indirect Method has absolutely no vital connection
with the Substitution of Similars.

2. That Method itself is flawless and complete, but as used
by Professor Jevons it is improperly limited.

3. The machine which works within these limits will not
actually give a categorical conclusion.

4. These unfortunate limits are also those of equational
reasoning.

5. They coincide exactly with the boundary of the syllogism, and a large part of reasoning falls entirely without them.

6. The method of Substitution is syllogism upside down,
and its principle has not been accurately formulated by Professor Jevons.

I must leave this subject with an expression of regret. I
am sorry to have had no more space available; and I am
sorry to have dwelt almost wholly on those points in which I
am unable to follow the author. It would have been more
pleasant, if it had been possible, to have called attention to
the various merits of his logical work. But still, even if my
praises could do him any service, fortunately he does not
stand in need of them. I may end this chapter by expressing
my belief, that no living Englishman [8] has done one half the
service to logic that Professor Jevons has done. No living
writer, to the best of my knowledge, now Professor Lotze is
dead, has done more. Personally to myself, and so far as my
own studies are concerned, Professor Jevons' book has been
of very great use; and I could not truly say that of any other
English Logic. It is not inability to accept conclusions which

prevents one learning. And there can not be any one who has left unread the *Principles of Science,* who has not something to learn from it.*

* Since this chapter was written Professor Jevons' lamented death has taken place, and has deprived me of any opportunity I might otherwise have had of learning from him in what points I have failed to understand his doctrines. I have thought it best to leave the chapter as it stood.

But there is another point on which the reader may look for some explanation. He may ask why I have failed to examine one of those views of Equational Logic which treat the subject mathematically. And I am compelled to throw the burden of the answer on those who had charge of my education, and who failed to give me the requisite instruction. It would have been otherwise a pleasure to have seen how the defects of the Equational theory appeared in a mathematical form. For, at the risk of seeming no less prejudiced than ignorant, I am forced to state the matter so. If I knew perhaps what Mathematics were, I should see how there is nothing special or limited about them, and how they are the soul of logic in general and (for all I know) of metaphysics too. Meanwhile I may suggest to the mathematical logician that, so long as he fails to treat (for example) such simple arguments as " A before B, and B with C, therefore A before C," he has no strict right to demand a hearing. Logic is not logic at all if its theory is based on a previous mutilation of the facts of the subject. It may do something which perhaps is very much better, but it does not give *any* account (adequate or inadequate) of reasoning in general. And at the risk of exhibiting prejudice once more, I may say that this consideration seems to me to be vital.[9]

ADDITIONAL NOTES

[1] On the subject of this Chapter see the Notes on Book I, Chap. VI, and also T. E. III.

[2] " Single subject," " self-same subject." Cf. Bk. I. VI. § 11 and T. E. III.

[3] " Though the statements are false." These words would, I think, have been better omitted. The " four meanings " are as follows. (i) Every statement contains a diversity, but (ii) its diversity does not make it *two,* so that by dividing it you can get rid of the connected unity which makes its character—here of wilful falsity. And the essence of its character, while (iv) remaining throughout one and the same, is yet (iii) affected by, and made more intense by the number of its instances.

[4] " The identity of the subject." See Note 2.

⁵ " Excluded Middle." See Bk. I. V, Note 12.

⁶ " A — B — C is consistent, etc." It would be better before " is " to insert "(as commonly understood)"; for, if A is taken as pure, i. e. as unconditional, the above statement would be incorrect. Cf. § 21, and see the Note on Bk. II. II. III. § 12.

⁷ " A reasoning machine." Dr. Bosanquet (K & R, pp. 327 foll., and Logic, II, 150) has called attention to the point that all instruments of measurement and observation have a right to be called " reasoning machines."

⁸ " No living Englishman." This was of course published in 1883, and I think that it was true. My eulogy may perhaps on the whole be exaggerated, and that question I leave to others to decide. What I wrote remains as the expression of the gratitude I felt towards one whose book had helped me greatly in my logical struggles.

⁹ The second paragraph of this foot-note would have been better omitted. When writing it I did not know of the existence of a mathematical logic which was not equational. But even now I am in effect perhaps in no better case.

Whether a student of logic, who is incapable of learning mathematics and has therefore to leave out of his theory a recognized part of the facts, should never have written on logic at all, or should later at least suppress all that he once wrote—I will not offer to discuss. And what should be his attitude towards a claim to base the principles of logic on mathematics, I once more hardly know. If a person like myself ventures to point out that something of what is thus offered seems to himself to be untenable and irrational —he can be met with the reply that, if he understood mathematics, he would forthwith think otherwise. And what his answer to this should be, I confess I can not say.

I am of course unable to accept a claim made on behalf of mathematics to have rationally solved logical and metaphysical problems in a way unintelligible except to the mathematician. And there is one thing only which would incline me to accept such a claim. It would have to be made by a man, who can meet on their own ground the non-mathematical logicians and metaphysicians—can show that he understands and enters into their views and their puzzles—and can inspire the belief that he himself is somehow able better, even outside mathematics, to deal rationally with ultimate problems. But my whole acquaintance with this subject is unfortunately too limited even to justify perhaps what now I have ventured to set down.